D1539026

BARRON'S
BUSINESS
REVIEW
SERIES

Marketing

Second Edition

By
Richard L. Sandhusen

BARRON'S EDUCATIONAL SERIES, INC.

All inquiries should be addressed to:
Barron's Educational Series, Inc.
250 Wireless Boulevard
Hauppauge, New York 11788

International Standard Book No. 0-8120-1548-7

Library of Congress Card Catalog No. 92-38978

Library of Congress Cataloging-in-Publication Data

Sandhusen, Richard.
    Marketing / by Richard L. Sandhusen. — 2nd ed.
        p.   cm. — (Barron's business review series)
    Includes bibliographical references and index.
    ISBN 0-8120-1548-7
    1. Marketing. I. Title. II. Series.
HF5415.S272 1993
658.8—dc20

                                                    92-38978
                                                    CIP

PRINTED IN THE UNITED STATES OF AMERICA

  56   800   987654

CONTENTS

PREFACE

This book is designed for students in introductory marketing courses, and for business people who need a concise, clear, comprehensive understanding of marketing problems, practices, and applications.

In content, style, and structure, this book was written to embody four characteristics calculated to create a stimulating learning environment in which modern marketing concepts can be understood and applied.

1. *It is comprehensive:* A content analysis of leading marketing texts confirms that there is little in these texts that won't be found in this book. Beyond this core content, this book expands in a number of areas not emphasized in many texts, but of considerable importance in light of contemporary marketing theory and practice. Thus, special emphasis is placed on strategic options the marketing manager faces in creating marketing plans, modern tools and techniques for segmenting markets and forecasting sales, and the integrated complex of systems used to plan, implement, and control marketing programs in both domestic and international markets.

2. *It is concise:* Format, style, and structure combine to create an extremely efficient vehicle for quickly and clearly conveying information. As to format, each chapter focuses on a single case situation, specifically designed to illustrate the nature of marketing concepts, and how these concepts are applied in actual situations. As to writing style, this book is written in a tight, active journalistic style, not the passive, labored academese characterizing many textbooks. As to structure, chapter content is sequenced in terms of the logic of the marketing process, eliminating the need for unnecessary repetition. Here is how the stages of the marketing process are sequenced in this book:

    *   The first three chapters lay a foundation for what is to come by defining basic marketing concepts (chapter one), examining the role of the marketing manager in planning and implementing marketing strategies (chapter two), and surveying environmental constraints which must be considered by the marketing manager in bringing together marketing mix offerings and target markets (chapter three).
    *   The next three chapters focus on integrated company systems through which marketing plans and programs are carried out, including systems for organizing, planning, and controlling marketing efforts (chapter 4), and the marketing information system, with its marketing research input, that underpins the entire marketing management process (chapters 5 and 6).
    *   The next five chapters look out into the marketplace, defining the nature and scope of consumer markets (chapter 7), processes whereby con-

sumers arrive at buying decisions (chapter 8), and characteristics and buying decision processes of organizational markets (chapter 9). Chapter ten focuses on approaches and techniques for segmenting consumer and organizational markets and positioning products to advantage in these markets. Chapter 11 examines approaches and techniques for forecasting market and sales potential in these markets.

- The next eight chapters examine the four components of the marketing mix which marketing managers combine to attract target market members, including the product element (chapters 12 and 13), the place element (chapters 14 and 15), the price element (chapters 16 and 17), and the promotion element (chapters 18 and 19). Chapter 20 integrates concepts from other chapters in offering an approach for understanding and entering the global marketplace.

3. *It is interesting and involving:* As you read each chapter from the perspective of a marketing manager of an illustrative case company, you move away from a role as passive observer to one as an active participant in the marketing process, anticipating problems the marketing manager will encounter and second guessing decisions he or she makes. In effect, you learn by doing—the most effective way to learn—in an interesting, challenging environment. This involvement carries over into the end-of-chapter exercises, which continue to challenge your understanding and ability to apply marketing concepts with thought-provoking questions and a diversity of real-world case problems.

4. *It is current:* Although footnote references are kept to a minimum, most of them are recent, reflecting the contemporary orientation of text content.

ACKNOWLEDGMENTS

If this text succeeds in its goal of presenting comprehensive marketing information in an efficient, effective, *usable* manner, much credit belongs to the reviewers and editors who offered insights and suggested revisions. In particular, I would like to single out Professor Roy Brown, whose academic and practical expertise in the promotion field is strongly reflected in chapters 18 and 19, and Lora Moore, whose editorial judgments are reflected in chapters 14 and 15 on the distribution function.

Richard L. Sandhusen
November, 1992

1
THE MARKETING PROCESS: BASIC CONCEPTS

KEY TERMS

exchange the process by which two or more parties give something of value to one another to satisfy needs and wants

markets sets and/or places of actual or potential buyers in a position to demand products

marketing mix the set of product/place/promotion/price variables the marketing manager attempts to control and orchestrate; also called "the offering"

need a state of felt (mental or physical) deprivation which can be ignored, sublimated or satisfied

products anything capable of satisfying needs, including tangible items, services, and ideas offered for attention, use, or consumption

---

HOW NEEDS TRIGGER EXCHANGES

The following situation provides examples to clarify marketing terms and concepts in this chapter:

> The Islandshares Group: A young professional couple from Atlanta, Georgia—he a lawyer, she an accountant—has just purchased a time-share from the Islandshares Group, a large real estate development firm on Hilton Head Island, South Carolina. The $8,000 purchase price gives the couple title to a one-bedroom condominium apartment during the first week of June each

year. This apartment is fully equipped and located within walking distance of two golf courses, a tennis complex, and a private beach. If the couple desires, they may sublet or sell the unit, or trade it for a time-share for the same, or another, week at another time-share in a worldwide network of resorts.

The following definitions of needs, wants, demands, products, exchange, markets, the marketing mix, and competition lead to definitions of the marketing process in this first chapter section.

Needs are defined as a state of mental or physical felt deprivation. In developed economies, needs are numerous and arise on different levels. In the time-share case, above, possible needs on a number of levels can be recognized: a basic need for shelter; a social need for status that time-share ownership might bestow; individual needs to improve a tennis backswing or a golf swing.

Wants are the forms human needs take as shaped by the individual's culture and personality. Like needs, wants also expand as societies grow and people are exposed to more objects that arouse interest and curiosity. In the time-share case, the Atlanta couple might want a time-share ownership because friends have persuaded them that this is a wonderful way to satisfy a need for self-expression through recreational sports. An important function of marketing is to convert needs to wants by focusing on need-satisfying benefits resulting from products being marketed. In this text, the terms "wants" and "needs" are used interchangeably.

Demands are wants backed by purchasing power. The couple's want for a time-share becomes a demand when they can pay its $8,000 cost. This $8,000, plus all the other money spent for time-shares by other people, represents the total demand for these time-shares. Understanding the nature and extent of demand is an important starting point for developing marketing plans.

Products are broadly defined as anything, tangible or intangible, offered for attention, acquisition, use, or consumption and capable of satisfying wants, including objects, people, places, services, organizations and ideas. Products range from the highly tangible (a ton of coal, a bar of soap) through less tangible services to intangible ideas (Human Rights, Women's Lib). The satisfaction people get from products can be functional (they do what you expect them to do), social (they enhance your prestige), or psychological (they make you feel better) and can derive from any aspect of the product: its size, shape, brand name, warranty, service guarantee, or supplementary use.

Exchange is the process by which two or more parties give something of value to one another to satisfy needs and/or wants. As such, exchange is both the objective and common denominator of all marketing activity, and can take a wide variety of forms: exchange of tuition for an education, votes for promised political action, skills for a job, money for a meal, and so on.

In exchanging $8,000 for a time-share, the Atlanta couple completed a **transaction**, the term used to define the actual trade of values among parties when exchange takes place. We will use *transaction* and *exchange* interchangeably.

The time-share purchase also illustrates the four conditions required for a voluntary exchange to take place:

1. at least two parties, each with something of value to the other party

2. each party capable of communication and delivery

3. each party free to accept or reject the other's offer

4. each party believing it appropriate or desirable to deal with the other

To conclude an exchange, there must be:

1. agreed-upon conditions

2. a time and place of agreement

3. legal authority, such as a law of contracts, to protect the agreement

To illustrate the benefits of the exchange process to individuals and societies, consider some other ways whereby the Atlanta couple might have procured the time-share. Using the "self-sufficiency" approach, they might have taken time off from their jobs to build their own condominium time-share. Or they might conceivably have coerced someone into giving them use of a time-share.

Unlike self-sufficiency, or coercion, exchange encourages people to do what they do best, to specialize. Thus, the Atlanta couple can earn money to purchase the time-share by doing what each of them does best, while the time-share developer can do what he does best. Thus, exchange benefits all parties. And unlike the other approaches, the exchange process, by involving a trade of one thing for another, increases overall wealth, productivity, and quality of life.

One purpose of the marketing process is to create and resolve exchange relationships. The main focus of Islandshares' marketing efforts, for example, would be to create plans and programs to facilitate many exchanges of money and time-shares to the benefit and satisfaction of all parties.

Markets, from the perspective of marketing managers, are sets of actual or potential buyers who have a willingness and the means to purchase and demand products.

The young Atlanta couple, purchasing a time-share unit for personal use, is part of the consumer market, consisting of all individuals and households who buy or acquire goods for their own use or benefit. The Islandshares corporation, purchasing products to build and maintain its time-share units, is part of the organizational market, comprising businesses, industries, governmental units, and large institutions, which buys products for resale, for use in making other products, or for day-to-day operations.

An important job of the marketing manager, selling in consumer markets, is to identify and define groups of people, called **target markets**, who have access to the marketed products, are qualified to purchase them, and exhibit a sufficiently high degree of buying power and interest in the products to justify marketing programs designed to attract them. The young professional couple from Atlanta, along with other young professionals in adjacent states with similar needs and income, is part of such a target market.

The marketing mix is the combination of marketing tools that a marketing manager attempts to control and orchestrate in order to create exchanges with target market members. These tools, often referred to as the **Four P's**, include:

1. the **product** with all its attributes
2. the **place** where this product is made available to market members, including the means by which it arrived there
3. **promotion** programs undertaken to persuade market members to purchase the product
4. the **price** they pay for the product

From the perspective of the customer, the marketing mix is called the offering. In combining marketing mix elements, the marketing manager considers the effect each element has on the other elements. In the time-shares case, for example, a prestige product, in a posh location (place), might dictate a soft-sell promotional campaign and justify a competitively high price.

Competition is defined as all the other ways customers can satisfy wants aside from making an exchange for the offering. For example, the Atlanta couple might decide to purchase a time-share with the same attributes as the one they purchased, but from another developer, in which case it would be direct competition. Or it might be indirect competition, such as membership in a local country club, or graduate courses to improve career prospects, instead of the time-share. Although direct competition is the main concern of marketing managers, they must frequently take indirect competition into account in planning and preparing marketing campaigns.

YOU SHOULD REMEMBER

An important job of the marketing manager is to identify unsatisfied needs in the market place, then develop and carry out marketing plans or programs to satisfy these needs. In so doing, the marketing manager attempts to identify and define worthwhile target markets, and create product/price/place/promotion marketing mix offerings to attract target market members. The ultimate goal of this planning effort is to encourage and facilitate exchanges, involving trading one value for another, from which all parties to the transaction benefit.

HOW MARKETING CLOSES GAPS AND CREATES UTILITIES

To the extent that the activities of the marketing manager succeed in creating beneficial exchanges, these activities also help to

1. close market gaps between sellers and buyers
2. create utilities for sellers and buyers

To illustrate these marketing benefits to individuals, organizations, and entire societies, consider some characteristics of the transaction involving the exchange of $8,000 from the young couple for the Hilton Head time-share. You will see that several gaps were closed.

A **spatial gap** was closed by arranging transportation for the couple to view a number of time-share properties from which the final selection was made.

A **knowledge gap** was closed by providing the couple with information about each potential purchase (price, access to amenities, accommodations, etc.) which clarified some misconceptions and helped them arrive at a purchase decision.

A **value gap** was also closed when the final price was finally agreed upon, which represented a compromise between the developer's and the couple's notions of what the time-share was worth.

A **temporal gap** was closed in that the time-share was made available to the couple when they wanted it.

Finally, an **ownership gap** was closed when the new owners took title to the property.

FOUR UTILITIES

In addition to closing gaps, the marketing process also creates four utilities beneficial to individuals, organizations, and societies. The four utilities are:

1. place
2. time
3. possession
4. form

To illustrate, the time-share was where the Atlanta couple wanted it to be, so place utility was created. The couple also had their time-share when they wanted it, so time utility was created. And when title of this property passed over to them, possession utility was created.

The marketing exchange process can even help create form utility, which is usually thought of as being created by the production process. For example, marketing research feedback to Islandshares management might describe dissatisfactions of time-share owners that would produce changes in the future form of these time-shares.

YOU SHOULD REMEMBER

By making products available at the right time and in the right place, and bringing about beneficial exchanges, the marketing process creates time, place, and ownership utilities. It also closes five gaps between seller and buyer: a value gap between different perceptions of product worth; a knowledge gap between different notions of product attributes and benefits; a spatial gap between location of buyer and seller; a temporal gap between when the product is produced and when it is needed, and an ownership gap between possession by the seller and possession by the buyer.

THE EIGHT BASIC MARKETING FUNCTIONS

Earlier in this chapter, we noted that the major focus of this text would be on the marketing manager's role in identifying and defining target markets, and devising marketing mix offerings to satisfy unmet needs. In carrying out this role, the marketing manager also deals with eight basic marketing functions which are essential and cannot be eliminated; someone must perform them for satisfactory exchanges to take place.

• *EXCHANGE FUNCTIONS*

First, to create these exchanges, a seller needs something of value, so the **buying** function is important: searching for and evaluating products that will prove attractive to prospective customers. Then, to consummate these exchanges, prospective customers must be informed about and persuaded to buy these products, so the **selling** function is important. These two functions—buying and selling—are called *exchange functions*.

• *PHYSICAL DISTRIBUTION FUNCTIONS*

Once products have been purchased for sale or resale, they must be transported from producer to buyer and, perhaps, be maintained in inventory until they are purchased. These two functions—**transportation** and **storage**—are called *physical distribution functions.*

• *FACILITATING FUNCTIONS*

Finally, the marketing manager would deal with four *facilitating functions* in building satisfactory exchanges:

- **Grading**: products for resale are sorted into different quantity and quality categories for more efficient storage and display.

- **Financing**: arrangements are made for the firm to pay suppliers, and customers to pay the firm, for purchased products and services.

- **Risk taking**: the firm assumes a number of risks associated with buying, selling, storing, and financing products, including the risk that people won't buy the products, or won't pay for them, or that these products will be made obsolete by newer products.

- **Developing marketing information**: underlying all the other functions is this extremely important function which helps reduce risk by providing the marketing manager with intelligence required to make better decisions. For example, marketing information helps the marketing manager find buyers, identify buyer needs that the firm is capable of profitably satisfying, create effective marketing mix offerings which satisfy company objectives and customer needs, and monitor the progress and results of marketing plans toward objectives.

YOU SHOULD REMEMBER

In developing marketing plans and programs which relate marketing mix offerings to target market needs, marketing managers deal with eight essential functions which cannot be eliminated: two exchange functions (buying and selling); two physical distribution functions (transportation and storage); and four facilitating functions (grading, financing, risk taking, and developing marketing information).

THE MARKETING PROCESS: NATURE AND IMPORTANCE

This section builds on concepts already defined to clarify the marketing process and to examine why marketing is a worthwhile field of study.

MARKETING DEFINED

A few years ago, the American Marketing Association (AMA) revised its definition of marketing to stress what the marketing process achieves, as well as what it does.

> Marketing is the process of planning the conception, pricing, promotion, and distribution of goods and services to create exchanges that satisfy individual and organizational objectives.

Other definitions view the dynamics of the marketing process on either the *micro* level of the individual company, or the *macro* level of society as a whole. On the micro level, the marketing process is defined as:

> A total system of business activities which directs the flow of goods and services from producer to consumers or users in order to satisfy customers and accomplish company objectives.

From the perspective of this systems definition, marketing is one of three major subsystems in the firm:

- The **accounting-finance** subsystem generates and manages the firm's capital and operating funds.

- The **production** subsystem processes raw materials into goods or services delivered to the marketplace.

- The **marketing** subsystem determines what is to be delivered (the offering), to whom (the target market), and how.

On the macro level, the marketing process is defined as:

> The design of fair and efficient systems to direct an economy's flow of goods and services from producers to consumers and accomplish the objectives of the society.

From the perspective of this definition, the study of marketing focuses on these issues:

- defining a fair system in terms of the equitable distribution of goods and services to all parties involved, including buyers, sellers, and the society at large

- defining an efficient system in terms of the most cost-effective, flexible use of resources to direct the flow of goods and services

- legal and public policy issues involved in maintaining fair, efficient marketing systems

- consumption and use patterns in the four large market aggregates (business, consumer, institutional, government), along with important trends and developments which shape these patterns

WHY STUDY MARKETING?

As a field of study, marketing is important to people, companies, and the society at large:

• *IMPORTANCE TO PEOPLE*

An individual responds to marketing every time he or she buys a product. The fact that this product meets this person's needs, is effectively promoted, and is available at a convenient time and place, attests to the effectiveness of the marketing system. The marketing field also offers career opportunities which are less affected by cyclical and economic fluctuations, and offers better opportunities than many other career paths for growth and advancement based on personal merit. Starting salaries in the marketing field rank high among all occupational fields. In terms of future prospects marketing positions typically offer salaries as high as, or higher than, any other field.

**Table 1-1: Annual Entry- and Senior Level Compensation
Managers in Selected Marketing-Related Fields**

POSITIONS	COMPENSATION RANGE
Advertising	
Copy/art trainee	$ 12,000–30,000+
Account supervisor/group promotion manager	40,000–70,000+
Marketing Research	
Junior analyst	$ 15,000–23,000+
Research director	70,000–100,000+
Product Management	
Marketing analyst	$ 15,000–30,000+
Group product manager	40,000–100,000+
Retailing	
Executive trainee	$ 17,000–25,000+
General merchandise manager	40,000–100,000+
Sales	
Trainee	$ 15,000–30,000+
Manager	31,000–75,000+

Source: Joel Evans and Barry Berman, *Marketing,* Fourth Edition (New York: Macmillan Publishing Company, 1990)

• *IMPORTANCE TO COMPANIES*

As the firm's sole revenue-producing system, marketing generates income which is managed by financial people to generate and maximize profits. By expanding sales and sales revenues, marketing helps to spread fixed costs over more units, thereby enhancing profit return throughout the firm.

• *IMPORTANCE TO SOCIETY*

In free-enterprise, market-driven economies, the marketing process, as the major force in creating mass markets, mass production, and mass distribution, also helps create high levels of business activity, increased investment opportunities, and high employment. These statistics attest to marketing's productive role:

- More than 50 percent of every consumer dollar spent supports such marketing activities as advertising, personal selling, retailing, packaging, and transportation.
- About 45 percent of family expenditures are spent on services (health care, education, recreation, etc.), where emphasis is on marketing, rather than production, activities.
- Twenty-five to 35 percent of employed people in the United States have jobs directly or indirectly related to marketing functions.

Even in highly planned economies, marketing activities assume an important role, as evidenced by the increasing growth of advertising, personal selling, distribution and other marketing activities in ex-Soviet bloc countries. In less-developed Third World countries, marketing institutions represent a dynamic element for breaking poverty cycles.

YOU SHOULD REMEMBER

Defined in terms of what it does, the marketing process creates opportunities for exchange by harmonizing the elements of the marketing mix (product, price, promotion, and place) in a manner that satisfies individual and organizational objectives. The marketing process can be studied on the micro level of the individual firm, with emphasis on the system of activities that bring customers and offerings together, or on the macro level of the entire economy, with emphasis on

1. the nature and scope of macro markets

2. issues of fairness and efficiency in directing the flow of goods and services to these markets

3. legal and public policy issues involved in directing this flow

4. consumption and use patterns in large market aggregates

Whether viewed from a micro or macro perspective, the study of marketing is worthwhile from an individual perspective, the perspective of companies, and the perspective of the entire economy. By helping to identify and create mass markets, mass production, and mass distribution, it also satisfies needs, creates interesting, rewarding jobs, and many opportunities for innovation and profit.

EVOLUTION OF MARKETING PROCESS: SELF-SUFFICIENCY TO CENTRALIZATION

To illustrate the stages of the marketing process, and the philosophies associated with each stage, envision a community consisting of only four families.

EARLY STAGES: SELF-SUFFICIENT, DECENTRALIZED

During the early, self-sufficiency stage of the marketing process—around the Middle Ages—each family provided completely for its own needs, sewing garments, hunting game, making furniture, and so on. Then, during the next decentralized market stage, each family began specializing in an activity at which its members were most proficient: one family made clothing, another built shelters, another provided food, and so on.

Along with these specialized efforts came

1. **division of labor**, as each family member performed activities he or she was best at

2. **standardization**, as each family developed routinized parts and procedures in producing its output

THE CENTRALIZED MARKET STAGE

As productivity became more efficient, so did methods for distributing output. In our four family community, as specialization, standardization, and division of labor took hold, each family could satisfy its needs by purchasing products from each of the other families. This had required a total of twelve separate trips—three by each family—to fulfill the needs of all the families.

Then, as each family became still more efficient and productive, each found that it could provide more of the specialized products it made than was required to satisfy the needs of all four families. To eliminate this surplus, each family set up a booth in a centralized market place to exchange its surplus products for the surplus products of other families in other communities.

During this centralized market stage of the marketing process, each family in the original community had to make only one trip, to a centralized market, to fulfill its needs, enhancing transactional efficiency.

ENTER MONEY AND MIDDLEMEN

Although transactional efficiency was enhanced by these early centralized markets, they still contained inefficiencies. For one thing, while members of each family were tending the family booth, they couldn't be specializing their efforts to produce surplus products to sell. For another, the bartering process of exchanging their surpluses for surplus products produced by other families tended to get cumbersome and complex: just how many chairs are three pigs worth, and who is going to carry them back home?

Both of these problems were solved with the advent of money and middlemen. Money became the common unit of value that replaced all those products families exchanged to meet their needs, further enhancing transactional efficiency.

Middlemen, who specialized in arranging exchanges between buyers and sellers, took over family booths to sell family surpluses, making it possible for these families to spend more time at their specialties.

Then, during the past 300 years, sufficient surpluses accumulated to justify trade beyond local barriers, and large wholesalers came into being.

As surpluses were distributed over greater distances and centralized markets became more complex, they also became more varied. Modern markets can grow around anything of value, including labor, money, real estate, and charities.

Today, in modern, market-driven societies, producers and middlemen are given the role of satisfying customer wants, and customers are free to make their own decisions pertaining to the exchange of values in various markets. Governments, acting for the community at large, make rules to regulate exchange processes, and, in exchange for taxes and votes, provide certain necessary services—such as a standing army—which can't be efficiently provided by the private segment. In general, markets are permitted to grow or decline, according to supply/demand dictates, without unnecessary bureaucratic interference.

A key distinction between market-driven and planned economies is the extent to which central planners attempt to control the flow of goods and services to their ultimate destinations, making consumers' decisions for them in the process.

EVOLUTION OF MARKETING PHILOSOPHIES: PRODUCTION TO SOCIETAL MARKETING

MAJOR MARKETING PHILOSOPHIES

As marketing evolved from its self-sufficient beginnings to today's diverse, dynamic, complex institutions, five distinct marketing philosophies also evolved to meet the needs of parties to the exchange process, including buyers, sellers, and society at large: the production philosophy; the sales philosophy; the marketing department philosophy, the marketing concept philosophy, and the societal marketing philosophy.

• *THE PRODUCTION PHILOSOPHY*

From the decentralized market stage and well into the late 19th century—when the industrial revolution was taking place and most major wholesaler centers were established—emphasis was on producing and distributing products in sufficient quantities to meet the burgeoning demand for them. The prevailing philosophy, "a good product will sell itself," implied a strong emphasis on production, rather than sales, functions.

• *THE SALES PHILOSOPHY*

The production philosophy was replaced by the sales philosophy in the early 1920s, when mass production technology, spawned by the industrial revolution, produced more products than markets could effectively absorb. This product glut, combined with dramatic increases in consumer discretionary income, led to an emphasis on sales forces and advertising campaigns to find new customers and persuade resistant customers to buy. As in the production philosophy era, however, there was rarely a unifying force within the organization to integrate these sales-oriented activities in terms of defining and satisfying customer needs: communication with customers was unilateral, and the sales function was generally subordinate to finance, production, and engineering functions.

• *THE MARKETING DEPARTMENT PHILOSOPHY*

As supplies of products continued to outstrip demand, many firms, in the late 1920s and early 30s, perceived the need for an integrating force which would coordinate the activities of production, research, procurement, and sales in planning sales campaigns. As with the sales philosophy, however, emphasis was still on finding and selling to customers (including wholesalers and retailers), rather than on identifying and satisfying customer needs. Most planning was short-range in nature.

• *THE MARKETING CONCEPT PHILOSOPHY*

By the 1950s, continuing productivity increases, combined with dramatic decreases in income and demand during the depression years of the 1930s, brought about a new, post-war marketing philosophy, guided by customer needs that the firm could profitably satisfy.

Called the **marketing concept**, this modern marketing philosophy differs from its predecessors in a number of significant ways:

- It defines the firm's mission in terms of benefits and satisfactions it offers, rather than in terms of products it makes and sells.
- It emphasizes two-way communication to identify customer needs, then develops and markets products to satisfy these needs; gone is the emphasis on one-way communication to persuade people to buy products already made.

• It emphasizes both long- and short-range planning to achieve profits by meeting customer needs; gone is an exclusive focus on short-range planning to achieve sales volume objectives.

• It emphasizes a total systems integration of all departments to achieve profit goals; gone is the exclusive focus on the efforts of individual departments and sales forces.

In a modern, market-driven firm, this customer-oriented philosophy is implemented by extensive computerization and an organizational structure designed to seek out and profitably serve customer needs. A key component of such organizational structures is the marketing manager in a potent new role: integrating and directing company resources toward satisfying customers.

• *THE SOCIETAL MARKETING PHILOSOPHY*

In recent years, the marketing concept philosophy of working back from defined customer needs to marketing mix offerings calculated to profitably satisfy these needs has come under increasing attack from critics who claim that this "customer knows best" pandering to a broad diversity of needs is inefficient and wasteful.

The societal marketing philosophy, which responds to these attacks, doesn't oppose the free enterprise notion of determining needs of target markets and delivering desired satisfactions more efficiently and effectively than competitors. It does maintain, however, that these satisfactions should be delivered in a way that also enhances the well-being of society. In short, market managers should balance three interests in setting policies and formulating programs: the buyer, the seller, and society at large. Referring to the Islandshares case with which this chapter opened, for example, this philosophy might dictate the demarketing of time-shares and other resort amenities if the ecological balance of Hilton Head Island were threatened by overdevelopment.

CRITICISMS OF MARKETING PHILOSOPHIES

Criticisms of the marketing process—and answers to these criticisms—generally focus on one or another of the philosophies behind the process, and one or more of the three parties—buyers, sellers, and the society at large—involved in marketing exchanges.

Thus, the sales philosophy was criticized for attempting to stimulate rather than satisfy consumer needs using one-way selling messages. This criticism was answered with the marketing concept philosophy, which recognized that it was both easier and more profitable to identify and satisfy existing needs than to try to create these needs.

The marketing concept philosophy, in turn, is criticized for pandering to a diversity of perceived needs, thus creating wasteful, unnecessary product features, and adding to the price paid for products. Answers to these criticisms maintain that the marketing concept philosophy produces a broader range of product choices, and improves product quality by stimulating competition.

Another frequent criticism of the marketing process—that it deceives people and manipulates them into purchasing products they don't really need—is usually answered in two ways. First, deceiving people simply isn't a profitable long-range strategy, and modern marketing is interested in long-range profits. Second, even if a firm were to embark on such a suicidal policy, the various state, federal, and consumer watchdog agencies could make it extremely difficult to implement.

Other fairly common criticisms of modern marketing—that it creates monopolies, or diverts scarce resources into unproductive areas, or is creating a nation of materialistic, "buy now, pay later" debtors—are frequently answered in terms of the precepts of the societal marketing concept, which attempts to offset the bad effects of marketing with socially responsible good effects. This contemporary philosophy, in turn, also receives its share of criticism: Marketing should not get involved in social planning; concern for social welfare in one area leads to social damage in other areas; it's the job of governments to right social wrongs, and so on.

YOU SHOULD REMEMBER

Highlights in the evolution of the marketing process:

1. Specialization and division of labor produce surpluses and lead to decentralized markets and greater transactional efficiency.
2. Money and middlemen lead to centralized markets.
3. Still more surpluses, wholesalers, and the industrial revolution lead to today's international markets.

Marketing philosophies associated with these stages of marketing evolution emphasized, successively:

1. efficient **production** and **distribution** to meet burgeoning demand
2. effective **selling** to push products when supply exceeded demand
3. **marketing departments** to improve selling efficiency by coordinating direct and indirect selling functions (advertising, sales promotion, personal selling, etc.)

With the advent of the **marketing concept,** many traditional notions were replaced. Thus, long- and short-range planning for profits replaced short-range planning for sales volume; two-way communication to determine customer needs and market products replaced one-way communication to sell products; a total systems integration of all company departments to define and satisfy customer needs replaced uncoordinated activities of individual departments; and the marketing function itself achieved parity or preeminence as compared to engineering, production, and finance functions.

Recently, however, the marketing concept has come under increasing criticism: claims are made that it wastes resources and sacrifices production efficiencies by pandering to target markets, while overlooking the needs of less desirable markets. In response to these criticisms, the societal marketing concept attempts to balance the needs of the buyer, the seller, and society at large in exchange processes. The societal marketing concept has also come under criticism for creating dislocations and inefficiencies by confusing social planning with marketing.

KNOW THE CONCEPTS

DO YOU KNOW THE BASICS?

1. From the perspective of the manufacturer of a new bicycle, give examples of the different needs this product might satisfy, and of the different kinds of competitive products a consumer might purchase to satisfy these needs. Why would these considerations be important to a marketing manager?

2. Give examples of products you purchased during the past month that were largely tangible and examples of some that were largely intangible. Why is a product rarely, if ever, *completely* tangible or intangible? What are the implications of this for the marketing manager?

3. Briefly argue either side of these criticisms of marketing:

   • Marketing is/isn't wasteful of resources.

   • Marketing does/doesn't create monopolies.

   • Marketing does/doesn't deceive people.

4. A homeowner buys supplies at a local lumberyard to build a children's playhouse in his back yard. Explain how the marketing process closed four *gaps* and created four *utilities* during this single exchange.

5. Put yourself in the place of the manufacturer of a hammer sold to the homeowner above, and describe how the three subsystems of the firm (production, finance/accounting, and marketing) interacted to create the four utilities.

6. Describe an objective that might have been achieved by you, the seller, and society at large when you bought an article of clothing.

7. Think of the sales presentation given by a salesperson trying to persuade you to buy that article of clothing. How might this presentation differ if it reflected the following philosophies: sales? marketing department? marketing concept? societal marketing concept?

8. Give two reasons why you might be interested in the study of marketing as
   a. an individual looking for that first job after college
   b. the president of the firm that hires you
   c. the president of the country where the firm is located

9. How do automobile lemon laws and laws mandating the use of seat belts address common criticisms of marketing?

TERMS FOR STUDY

buying function	promotion
centralized marketing	risk taking
competition	sales philosophy
consumer markets	segmentation
decentralized markets	self sufficiency
demands	selling function
exchange	societal marketing concept
form utility	spatial gap
markets	standardization
marketing concept	storage function
marketing mix	target markets
needs	time utility
perceptual gap	transaction
place utility	transportation function
possession utility	value gap
price	wants
production philosophy	

PRACTICAL APPLICATION

1 Put yourself in the place of the owner of a Chinese restaurant, and describe how the four elements of the marketing mix might interact in preparing a marketing plan for your restaurant. For example, how would the fact that you have a takeout menu (i.e., the distribution, or place, element) affect the other three marketing mix elements?

2 Assume you are the manager of a branch store in the Computershack chain responsible for profitably marketing a complete line of personal computers computer software, and computer peripherals. Briefly describe how, in a single day, you might involve yourself in all eight marketing functions

3 Now put yourself in the position of a customer, in the market for a personal computer, visiting the Computershack branch mentioned above. How would the following concepts facilitate the exchange process should you decide to purchase one of the models Computershack has on sale: specialization? division of labor? standardization? money? middlemen? centralized markets? segmentation? marketing management?

ANSWERS
KNOW THE BASICS

1 Among the needs the bicycle might satisfy. for exercise, for recreation for socialization, and for status—all of which could conceivably be met by joining a bikers club Other kinds of competitive products to address some or all, of these needs would include other similar bicycles; other different bicycles (for example, a 5-speed instead of a 10-speed); other ways of satisfying a need for socialization, recreation, and exercise, such as joining a health club or buying a time-share, or other ways of enhancing the individual's status, such as joining a prestigious club. From the marketing manager's perspective, it is frequently important to understand all forms of competition for the satisfactions of prospective customers, and to take them into account in developing plans for marketing products.

2 Examples of tangible products, which you perceive and value as physical entities, would include most items purchased in most markets from apples to yo-yos. Intangible products, purchased less frequently, include any means of satisfying a need that can't be perceived and valued as a physical entity. For example, the satisfactions offered by a social club, or a consulting firm, or a political philosophy, or a religious affiliation simply don't lend themselves to precise conceptualization or evaluation, yet can be worth much

more to the individual than any tangible substitute. Products are rarely, if ever, completely tangible, however, because there are almost invariably intangibles associated with them, like the satisfaction an industrial buyer gets from the reputation of the manufacturer, or follow-up service a buyer receives from a vendor selling a tangible product like steel or aluminum. On the other hand, "purchase" of an intangible service usually entails the purchase of tangible products as well, such as the artifacts associated with many religious and social satisfactions.

3. *Marketing is/isn't wasteful:* To the extent that marketing panders to consumer needs that might be considered frivolous or unnecessary, while diverting resources that might help achieve more important social goals, it might be considered wasteful. On the other hand, who is to say that pandering to the needs of enlightened consumers in a market-driven economy isn't the most productive way to allocate resources? And, even if it isn't, the societal marketing concept is designed to address these shortcomings.

    Marketing does/doesn't create monopolies: Using the domestic automobile industry as one of many possible examples, one might argue that intensive marketing efforts over the decades have made entry into this industry exceedingly difficult. One might also argue that other factors, such as the capital-intensive nature of this industry, are the primary causes of this difficulty, or that marketing made it possible for foreign competitors to gain strong market share in this industry.

    Marketing does/doesn't deceive people: Examples of highly publicized marketing deceits abound (bait and switch advertising, mail fraud, etc.), but it can also be argued that deceiving the public is a suicidal long-run policy that reputable firms shun. Even if a firm decided to embark on such a course, a broad diversity of "watchdog" agencies, representing a broad diversity of constituencies (consumers, government, advertisers themselves), make success unlikely.

4. A spatial gap was closed, and place utility created, by making these supplies available where the buyer wanted it, instead of having the buyer travel to the factory to purchase the supplies. By making the supplies available when the buyer wanted them, a temporal gap was closed, and a time utility created. By handling details of the exchange, an ownership gap was created, and a possession utility created. The price the homeowner paid for the supplies represents a compromise between the price he was willing to pay, and the price the manufacturer would have liked to get, so a *value* gap was closed. Later, the form of some of these supplies was changed based on the response of this homeowner and other buyers to their present form.

5. Finance provided the funds for production to manufacture the hammer, for which marketing found customers and arranged exchanges. Some of the profits generated by these marketing efforts then went back into the firm to finance more production.

6. Some possible examples: your need for social approval was facilitated by wearing the garment; the price you paid for the garment contributed to the manufacturer's profit objective; society at large benefited from the taxes paid by the manufacturer on this sale.

7. *Sales philosophy:* an aggressive, one-way, hard-sell presentation extols product benefits without reference to your needs.

   Marketing department philosophy: still a hard-sell, one-way presentation, but now supported by a diversity of supplementary sales aids, including publicity, direct mail, and media advertising designed to persuade the buyer to visit the store.

   Marketing concept philosophy: a soft-sell, two-way presentation which first defines your needs, then tries to find a suit to satisfy these needs.

   Societal marketing philosophy: the salesman points out that the garment can be laundered with biodegradable soap powder in cool water.

8. a. Marketing jobs tend to pay more, and offer more opportunities for advancement, than other jobs.
   b. Marketing is the only function that raises revenues, and has a significant impact on profits—for example, by generating mass-market economies of scale that reduce costs associated with each unit produced.
   c. The health and growth of the economy are largely dependent on macromarketing activities.

9. *Lemon laws* mandate that a manufacturer must make "restitution in kind" if an automobile proves to be a lemon according to various prescribed standards. These laws assume that the marketing process, in certain instances, will attempt to take advantage of consumers, and that these consumers are relatively defenseless in the face of these deceptive, manipulative practices. Seat belt laws mandate that drivers must wear seat belts under penalty of legal prosecution. These laws assume that legislatures, in certain instances, must make decisions for consumers who lack the knowledge or experience to make such decisions for themselves. Both lemon and seat belt laws are criticized in some quarters for recognizing neither the true nature of marketing processes, nor the true ability of people to arrive at their own conclusions.

PRACTICAL APPLICATION

1. The owner might *promote* the fact that the restaurant delivers orders from its takeout menu (*place*), with only a small additional charge (*price*). The owner might also promote the fact that the order is guaranteed to be hot when it arrives (*product*).

2. As manager of the Computershack branch, you or your associates might involve yourselves in the eight marketing functions in these ways: process purchase orders to *buy* products for resale: *grade* and *store* the products when they arrive; *sell* (and pre-sell) these products to customers and, if necessary, arrange for them to be *transported* to their destinations; extend credit to customers (*financing*), and *assume the risk* that customers won't pay. Underlying all these activities, *marketing information* will help you make better decisions to serve your target markets at a profit.

3. The personnel in the Computershack branch specialize in marketing computers, and have divided up the workload so each staff member does what he or she does best (selling, buying, repairing computers, etc.). You are part of a market segment whose wants and needs these specialists are trained to satisfy. They are centrally located so you don't have to travel all the way to the manufacturer's plant to purchase your computers or accessories and, should something go wrong with your computer, standardized parts will make it easier and less expensive to repair.

2
THE MARKETING MANAGEMENT PROCESS

KEY WORDS

marketing management analysis planning, implementation, monitoring, and control of programs designed to create, build, and maintain beneficial exchanges with target buyers to achieve organizational objectives

strategic marketing planning the managerial process of developing and maintaining a strategic fit among the organization's resources and objectives and its changing market opportunities. It relies on developing a clear company mission, supporting objectives and goals, a sound business portfolio, and coordinated functional strategies

This chapter examines activities of the **marketing manager** in developing and maintaining a strategic fit between the organization's goals and resources, and its changing market opportunities.

We will illustrate these activities by showing, step by step, how a marketing strategy was created to address enrollment and growth problems faced by the fictitious Roper College. This strategic plan envisioned the creation of a completely new business and professional education center called the Executive Learning Institute, or ELI.

> **The Executive Learning Institute:** Roper College, a large, private institution offering majors in education, liberal arts, and business administration, had four successive years of falling enrollments brought on by changing demographics (population shifts, defused baby booms, etc.), depleted funding sources, and much keener competition from other state and private colleges for the dwindling pool of high school seniors. Before the problem reached crisis proportions, Roper's administration decided to retain the services of a

consulting firm that specialized in developing academic marketing programs.

Following a series of analyses described in the remainder of this chapter, the consulting team recommended the creation of a new educational institution, called the Executive Learning Institute (ELI), to share the Roper campus.

WHAT DO MARKETING MANAGERS DO?

In devising and implementing strategic plans that relate organizational goals and resources to market opportunities, the marketing manager engages in

1. **analytical** activities that identify and assess threats and opportunities in the marketplace

2. **planning** activities that develop long- and short-term strategies to cultivate attractive marketplace opportunities

3. **implementation** activities that coordinate, motivate and direct people to attain business and marketing objectives

4. **control** and monitoring activities that take appropriate measures when performance falls short of objectives

Anyone in the organization who is involved in marketing analysis, planning, implementation and control activities is a marketing manager. This includes sales managers, product managers, marketing research managers, advertising managers and sales promotion managers. Even salespeople managing their territories qualify as marketing managers, to the extent that they plan, implement, and control sales calls and presentations based on an analysis of the needs of prospective customers.

CREATING AND MAINTAINING DEMAND LEVELS

Although many people in a marketing organization qualify as marketing managers, our focus in this text will be on the person with the title at the top of the marketing department pyramid. In creating and carrying out strategic marketing plans designed to relate marketing mix offerings to target market needs, the marketing manager also creates or maintains various states of demand consistent with the firm's objectives.

EIGHT DEMAND STATES

Kotler[1] identifies eight demand states that marketing managers must, on occasion, recognize and respond to:

- **Negative demand**, where a significant segment of the market dislikes the product, and may pay to avoid it. This was the situation facing the leisure/travel industry in 1990 when a significant number of Americans cancelled trips to Europe and the Middle East following well-publicized terrorist incidents and the Persian Gulf War. Here the marketing manager's task is to define reasons for this demand state, and plan strategies to counteract it, like the Greek government's "Come Home" campaign featuring prominent Americans who planned to visit Greece despite the negative publicity.

- **No demand** where target customers are unmotivated or indifferent to the product, like a Broadway play that opens to lukewarm reviews. The job of the marketing manager, then, is to connect potential product benefits with the needs and interests of prospective customers. For example, the play *The Wiz* surmounted mixed reviews through a promotional campaign that encouraged word of mouth endorsement of values the critics had presumably overlooked.

- **Latent demand** where many prospective customers share a strong desire for a satisfaction that can't be provided by existing products. Hair restoration or painless diets are examples of such satisfactions. Here, the job of the marketing manager is to measure the size of potential demand and develop products to meet it.

- **Falling demand** illustrated by problems facing many colleges as a shortage of high school seniors causes dramatic enrollment declines. Here the job of the marketing manager is to analyze causes and plan marketing strategies to reverse the trend.

- **Irregular demand** where seasonal, daily, or even hourly demand fluctuations cause significant differences in product usage. This problem faces most mass transit systems, with rush hour peak demand occurring only a few hours each day. Here, the marketing manager attempts to alter demand patterns by altering marketing mix variables, like flexible pricing programs or special off-season promotions.

- **Full demand** when the firm has all the business it needs, it becomes the marketing manager's job to monitor changes in customer needs and in the competition to maintain this desirable demand level.

- **Overfull demand** where demand is higher than the organization can or wants to handle. Yellowstone Park, with its annual hordes of campers, is an example of overfull demand, which is discouraged by manipulating

---

1. Philip Kotler, *Principles of Marketing* (Englewood Cliffs, NJ: Prentice-Hall, 1991), pp. 9–10.

marketing mix variables, like higher prices or fewer product features. Using marketing mix variables to decrease demand is called "demarketing."

- **Unwholesome demand** for products like cigarettes and alcohol challenges marketing managers not representing these products to devise marketing mix strategies to persuade people to give them up.

DEMAND MANAGEMENT THROUGH STRATEGIC PLANNING

In a large, modern, consumer-oriented firm, many strategic marketing plans are formulated each year for products in a variety of demand stages—some falling, some full, others irregular, and so on. Each plan tries to maintain a strategic fit between the firm's goals and resources and changing marketing opportunities. Taken together, these plans comprise the firm's **marketing program**, which becomes the responsibility of the entire company.

In developing and carrying out these plans, a distinction is made between strategies and tactics. A marketing **strategy** is a long-range plan describing how a target market and a marketing mix will be brought together; **tactics** are short-range plans designed to help carry out these long-range plans.

Some strategic plans for the Executive Learning Institute (ELI) and tactical plans used to implement these strategies are shown in Figure 2.1. The fact that all the firm's strategic plans are blended into a single organizational marketing program means that each plan must coexist harmoniously with other plans in the program, and be consistent with the firm's overall mission and objectives.

The focus of this chapter will be on considerations and constraints involved in creating marketing plans and programs.

Strategic policies	Tactical decisions
Product: Diversify to attract new "business/professional" segments to ELI programs	Add, change or drop programs as target markets change
Place: Develop ways to deliver ELI programs to off-campus members of target markets	Develop correspondence courses for ELI programs, explore videotape program possibilities
Promotion: Keep promotion attuned to market opportunities and competitive threats	Change advertising to reflect nature and needs of target segments. For example, determine when and where promotion should aim to achieve "awareness," "understanding," and "action," and design campaigns to achieve these objectives.

Figure 2–1. Relation of strategic policies to tactical decisions

YOU SHOULD REMEMBER

Individual strategic marketing plans, formulated by marketing managers to specify how objectives will be achieved by bringing together marketing mixes and target markets, come together in **marketing programs** that become the responsibility of the entire organization. In devising and carrying out these plans, the marketing manager **surveys** the marketplace to identify threats and opportunities; **plans** long-range strategies and short-range supporting tactics to cultivate attractive marketplace opportunities; **implements** plans by coordinating, motivating, and directing people in goal-oriented activities; and **controls** that monitor these activities by taking appropriate measures when performance falls short of goals. All these activities respond to a diversity of demand states, ranging from negative to overfull demand.

GOOD MISSION STATEMENTS LEAD TO GOOD OBJECTIVES AND PLANS

We will begin this discussion of considerations and constraints involved in creating marketing plans and programs with a model of the strategic marketing planning process, shown in Figure 2.2. In the remainder of this chapter, we will refer to the Roper College/ELI case to define each step in this process, and show how each might be applied.

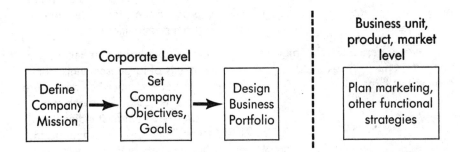

Figure 2–2. Steps in Strategic Planning Process

DEFINING THE FIRM'S MISSION

Properly phrased, a firm's mission statement, describing what it aims to accomplish in the larger environment, serves a number of useful purposes:

1. It helps shape the firm's business and marketing objectives, and the plans devised to achieve these objectives.

2. It gives people a sense of purpose and sets priorities.

3. It provides a benchmark against which to measure performance.

An effective mission statement usually defines the major domains in which the firm operates, products it offers, customer groups it serves, and needs its products satisfy.

In his article "Marketing Myopia"[2], Theodore Levitt proposed that marketing definitions of a business, which emphasize customer benefits, are superior to definitions which focus on product or technological features. Roper College's mission statement, for example, focuses on benefits.

> To help create rewarding, well-rounded careers and lifestyles by encouraging understanding and critical evaluation of a broad diversity of ideas and opinions in a supportive, democratic learning environment.

Note that this mission statement is broad enough to encompass other possibilities (for example, the ELI concept), but not so broad that it becomes a meaningless abstraction ("We aim to provide the best possible education"). Also note that it suggests objectives that will have to be achieved to realize Roper's mission, such as creating a "supportive, democratic learning environment."

Mission statement problems arise when the statement no longer accurately describes the firm's mission or, if it does, does not motivate people to want to achieve this mission. For example, a mission statement for Roper like "To make money by providing an adequate education for average students," while possibly true, doesn't have much motivational punch.

To achieve the proper focus for a firm's mission statement, start with present offerings (Roper started as a small business college), then move to higher levels of abstraction, with each level suggesting new opportunities (as did Roper's original mission statement). Stop just before a level is reached which is beyond the firm's grasp.

---

2. Theodore Levitt, "Marketing Myopia," *Harvard Business Review*, July-August 1960, pp. 45–50.

SETTING ORGANIZATIONAL OBJECTIVES

An effective mission statement leads logically to a hierarchy of business and marketing objectives which must be achieved to achieve the firm's mission. For example, here is how ELI's mission statement helped define its business and marketing objectives:

> **Mission statement:** " . . . to help business executives and professionals become much more efficient and productive by providing the best teachers, courses, and accommodations for learning to apply modern management tools and techniques."
>
> **Business Objectives:** generate profits
> attract top-level instructors
> install unique, state-of-the-art executive education programs and facilities
> construct luxury accommodations and facilities

Note that these business objectives derive logically from the mission statement, and are logically ordered: first, top-level instructors will be required to develop ELI's programs and to determine the facilities needed to conduct these programs. Then, with this understanding of programs and markets for these programs, necessary living and training accommodations can be built.

These business objectives, in turn, point to a logically ordered hierarchy of marketing objectives required to achieve them. Initially, promotion programs will be required to attract educators to plan and develop ELI's programs. Marketing research studies will identify unsatisfied needs in the executive education field which ELI can satisfy, and product, price, place, and promotion mixes to provide these satisfactions. To generate profits from enrollment dollars, the school will have to maintain a level of costs. These marketing objectives, in turn, point to strategies and tactics which will be incorporated into ELI's marketing plan. Promotion programs designed to achieve specific goals, such as improved awareness of ELI's benefits, will have to be planned and executed.

YOU SHOULD REMEMBER

An effective mission statement, which describes the firm's product/market domains in a benefit-oriented manner, provides a sense of purpose and significance and leads logically to productive business and marketing objectives. These objectives, in turn, point to strategic and tactical plans required to achieve them.

SETTING STRATEGIES

Designing strategies for products in the firm's business portfolio involves, first, assessing the firm's present portfolio of products to assure that they are consistent with company strengths and missions and, second, planning growth strategies for products deemed worthwhile.

• *ASSESSING THE PRODUCT PORTFOLIO*

The process of assessing new and existing product opportunities involves systematically measuring these products against criteria which reflect corporate goals and missions. In the **Planning Subsystems** section of Chapter 4, we will examine three ways to systematically conduct assessments of existing and prospective market opportunities. Right now, we will simply note that, as a way to improve Roper's growth and profit prospects, the ELI concept was consistent with both Roper's educational mission and the goals arising from this mission (goodwill, growth, enrollment volume).

• *PLANNING STRATEGY APPROACH*

Product portfolio assessments might point to any one of four broad strategic options, also examined in Chapter 4: a hold strategy, to preserve existing market share; a harvest strategy, to increase the product's cash flow regardless of long-term consequences; a divest strategy, to liquidate the product and use marketing resources elsewhere; or a growth strategy, to increase profits and share of market. Before recommending the ELI option as the strategy for reversing Roper's declining fortunes, the consulting team would have systematically assessed various market growth strategies and the competitive consequences of each.

MARKET GROWTH STRATEGIES

The growth strategy options considered by the consultants were broadly classified as intensive, integrative, and diversified.

INTENSIVE GROWTH STRATEGIES

Intensive growth strategies, which stress a more intensive cultivation of the firm's present markets, are appropriate in situations where existing product/market opportunities have not been fully exploited. The three strategies considered by the consultants in this area included a penetration strategy, a market development strategy, and a product development strategy.

• *PENETRATION STRATEGY*

A **penetration strategy** would focus on more aggressive marketing of existing programs to members of Roper's main high school graduate target market. Typically, penetration strategy brings in revenues and profits by

1. persuading present customers to use more of the product

2. attracting customers from competitors

3. persuading undecided prospects to become customers

The consultants in our case history rejected these penetration strategy options because

1. Most Roper students were already taking a full course load.

2. It would be too expensive to persuade students at other colleges to re-enroll at Roper.

3. Given the fast-depleting pool of high school graduates available and the fierce competition for these graduates, there wasn't a sufficient number of "undecideds" to justify the expense of subjecting them to an all-out promotional campaign.

• *MARKET DEVELOPMENT STRATEGY*

A **market development strategy** focuses on attracting members of new markets. In our case, it would focus on attracting students other than high school graduates to Roper's programs. These additional enrollees might emerge from new geographical segments (foreign students, perhaps), new consumer segments (such as senior citizens), or new institutional segments (for example, hospital personnel who might enroll, en masse, in Roper's hospital administration program). The consultants rejected market development as a strategic option after deciding that none of Roper's programs would be sufficiently attractive to these new market segments.

• *PRODUCT DEVELOPMENT STRATEGY*

A **product development strategy** involves developing new products to attract members of existing markets. In our example new programs to attract Roper's existing high school graduate market would be developed. Here, additional enrollments might emerge from either new programs of interest to present or prospective students, such as career-oriented business courses, or new ways to package and distribute these programs, such as videocassettes to reduce the cost of a college education for high school graduates. Although they later adopted elements of this strategy in their ELI strategy, the consultants rejected it as Roper's major strategic option because they felt it would entail too large an investment for the possible benefits it would produce.

INTEGRATIVE GROWTH STRATEGIES

Integrative growth strategies are generally appropriate in situations where the firm's industry is strong and supportive, and the firm can gain by moving backward, forward, or horizontally.

- **Backward integration** occurs when the firm increases its control over its supply sources, as when a retailer like Genesco or A & P controls its wholesaler supply sources.

- **Forward integration** occurs when the firm increases its control over its distribution system, as when a large oil refinery owns and controls its network of service stations. Some firms, like J. C. Penney, integrate both backward and forward, controlling manufacturing, wholesaling, and retailing functions.

- **Horizontal integration** occurs when the firm increases its control over its competitors.

The consultants agreed that neither forward nor backward integration applied to Roper's situation, but saw some possibilities in horizontal integration. Under this strategy, Roper might attempt to achieve some degree of control over its competitors. With this in mind, the consultants explored the possibility of negotiating a consortium arrangement whereby each of a number of colleges, Roper included, would specialize in a single academic area. In so doing, each college could distinguish itself in a single area that would prove attractive to targeted segments of the high school graduate market. Unfortunately, competitive colleges showed little interest in this arrangement.

DIVERSIFICATION GROWTH STRATEGIES

Diversification growth strategies are appropriate in situations where few opportunities exist for growth in the firm's own field, but many opportunities exist outside this field. Since few growth opportunities existed in Roper's product/market area, the consultant team found this the most attractive of the strategic option areas. They considered three types of diversification strategy: horizontal diversification, conglomerate diversification, and concentric diversification (the strategy that led to ELI).

• *HORIZONTAL DIVERSIFICATION STRATEGIES*

Horizontal diversification strategies entail adding new products to the firm's product line, unrelated to the firm's existing products but designed to appeal to members of the firm's existing target markets. For example, Roper might invest in a first-rate athletic team to enhance its prestige and possibly increase enrollments among high school graduates.

• *CONGLOMERATE DIVERSIFICATION STRATEGIES*

Conglomerate diversification strategies entail marketing new products unrelated to the existing product line. Unlike horizontal diversification strategies designed to attract new members of existing target markets, these strategies are designed to attract new categories of customers. For example, the consultants considered publishing and real estate ventures which might market Roper resources—faculty authors and portions of its large, and largely unused, campus—to members of new target markets. As with horizontal diversification strategies, however, a cost/benefit analysis showed that the potential benefits didn't offset the considerable risks and costs involved.

• *CONCENTRIC DIVERSIFICATION STRATEGIES*

Concentric diversification strategies introduce new products bearing technological or marketing similarities to existing products designed to attract new market segments. Essentially, this was the ELI strategy the consultant team finally recommended, involving professional programs that were generically similar to Roper's undergraduate programs, but designed to attract new market segments vastly larger and more expandible than the shrinking "high school senior" segment.

In its report, the consulting team emphasized that this concentric diversification strategy was totally consistent with criteria for "successful emerging businesses" identified by Michael Porter. [3]

1. **High barriers to entry:** Considering the high initial financial outlay required to create ELI, the specialized academic expertise needed to make it work, and the limited resources, such as "name" professors, available to staff it, it seemed likely that most competitors would find entry difficult. Roper, on the other hand, could take advantage of existing resources, including a beautiful campus and a number of underutilized buildings.

2. **Weak competitors:** Research indicated that few, if any, professional educational institutions in Roper's market offered the combination of values—blue chip educational programs and posh accommodations—which business and professional people desired in a back-to-college institution.

3. **Weak substitutes:** Research also indicated that alternatives to formal, accredited professional programs ELI would offer were generally inadequate to the needs of business and professional people. For example, few in-house educational programs were adequately staffed or accredited.

---

3. Michael E. Porter, *Competitive Advantage* (New York: Free Press, 1985), pp. 4–8 and pp. 234–36.

4. **Weak buyers:** Since this proposed new college would offer business and professional people a unique and needed combination of values, and since enrollment fees would be, largely, a deductible business expense, it did not seem likely that companies sending their people to ELI would cooperate to force price concessions.

5. **Weak suppliers:** In general, the team foresaw few problems in dealing with suppliers of basic services and facilities required by the new college. For example, "name" professors borrowed from other colleges usually had flexible schedules that could accommodate the needs of ELI. In addition, some suppliers, such as prestige motel chains and hotels interested in providing accommodations under an ELI franchise, would be extremely interested in this profit opportunity.

YOU SHOULD REMEMBER

Designing business portfolio strategies involves, first, analyzing new and existing products in terms of their compatibility with organizational missions and objectives, then planning strategies (growth, hold, harvest, divest) appropriate to each product/market situation. Market growth strategies are classified as intensive, integrative, or diversified. **Intensive strategies,** including penetration, market development, and product development strategies, stress more intensive cultivation of existing markets; **integrative strategies,** including backward, forward, and horizontal integration, are appropriate in strong, supportive industries; and **diversification strategies** with changes in both products and markets, are appropriate in situations where few opportunities exist for growth in the firm's own field.

COMPETITIVE STRATEGIES

Competitive strategies focus on relationships and responses among competitors, rather than on threats and opportunities in the marketplace.

However, since competitive strategies result from market-oriented strategies, and present threats and opportunities of their own, they were included in the consultants' search for an overall strategic plan for Roper College.

Specifically, they examined the competitive climate that would result if Roper adopted a concentric diversification strategy. Under this proposed strategy, ELI would compete, aggressively and expensively, for students in the business/professional segment, and Roper College would be better positioned to compete for students in the high school graduate market.

Given this situation, the consultants identified four types of emergent competitive strategies, each representing threats or opportunities; a leader strategy; a challenger strategy; a follower strategy; and a market nicher strategy.

LEADER STRATEGY

A **leader strategy** is employed by firms like Coca Cola and Goodyear, which dominate the market through superior products and/or competitive effectiveness. Leader firms tend to have greater immunity from competitive threats, and hence tend to maintain their leadership positions. For example, when Goodrich competes against leader Goodyear, Goodyear tends to gain much more from Goodrich's marketing efforts than Goodrich from Goodyear's efforts. Also, because it has a larger share of the market, Goodyear benefits more from mass market "economies of scale" in making and marketing its products. However, leader firms do face the threat of being the main target of all their competitors.

In planning ELI's strategy, the consultants recognized the value of achieving a position of leadership in the management education field. Once that position was achieved, they recognized, two strategy options would be available: to increase the overall size of ELI's market by finding new users and uses for ELI programs, and to gain additional market share by investing heavily to attract customers from competitors. The two strategies conflicted: using the first, ELI would cooperate with competitors to increase market size, in the sure knowledge that ELI, the leader, would have the largest slice of this bigger pie. Using the second strategy, ELI would attack competitors head-on, inviting ill will and competitive countermoves.

The consulting team decided that if ELI achieved leader status, it would employ a version of the first, cooperative strategy, which would also incorporate a preemptive defense strategy by launching new programs and products to keep competitors from becoming major threats.

CHALLENGER STRATEGY

Challenger strategies, adopted by runner-up firms, could take three forms:

1. **frontal attacks** by strong challengers on ELI's entire marketing mix—programs, price, distribution, promotion

2. **flank attacks** by weaker challengers, focusing on perceived ELI weaknesses, such as its high tuition rates

3. **bypassing strategies**, competing in areas not covered by ELI, such as educational programs for white collar workers looking to achieve managerial status

FOLLOWER STRATEGIES

Follower strategies would be employed by runner-up firms not interested in challenging ELI directly or indirectly. These firms would try to maintain their market shares and profits by closely following ELI's product, price, place, and promotion policies.

MARKET NICHER STRATEGIES

Market nicher strategies would be adopted by smaller competitors specializing in serving market niches that major competitors overlook or ignore—for example, market segments that ELI finds it cannot serve profitably.

Ideally, the consultants agreed, ELI could grow and prosper best in a competitive climate consisting largely of follower and nicher firms, with a minimum of strong challengers. Its own planned cooperative leader strategy would help bring about this climate.

YOU SHOULD REMEMBER

Competitive strategies, which focus on relationships and responses among competitors, are determined by product/market strategies undertaken by these competitors. A **leader strategy,** assumed by the firm which dominates the market, makes the leader less vulnerable to competitive inroads. This strategy frequently involves cooperation with competitors to increase overall market size, from which the leader will gain the most. Other strategies, including **challenger, follower,** and **market nicher** strategies, create varying degrees of competitive pressures for the leader.

KNOW THE CONCEPTS
DO YOU KNOW THE BASICS?

1. What is the relationship between the marketing management process and the strategic marketing planning process?
2. What are the benefits of strategic marketing planning to companies? to customers?

3. Using a local department store as an example, distinguish between strategic planning, strategies, and marketing programs.

4. Describe how the four marketing management activities might be applied in planning and implementing a job quest strategy for yourself.

5. How might jobs you are seeking exhibit some of the various demand states that marketing managers manage, and how might an understanding of these states affect your job quest strategy?

6. Come up with a mission statement for yourself that might appear on your job resume.

7. Describe the extent to which your career decision to invest in a franchised outlet for one of the large fast food chains meets Porter's criteria for a worthwhile opportunity.

8. Explain how the steps in the strategic marketing planning process are interrelated.

9. What is the relationship between market growth strategies and competitive strategies?

10. Distinguish between intensive, integrative, and diversification strategies. Use the local department store discussed in question 3, above, as an illustrative example.

TERMS FOR STUDY

backward integration
business objectives
business portfolio
challenger strategies
competitive strategies
concentric diversification
domains
falling demand
follower strategies
forward integration
growth strategies
horizontal diversification
horizontal integration
intensive growth
irregular demand
latent demand
leader strategies

market development
market niche
marketing management
marketing myopia
marketing objective
marketing program
mission statement
negative demand
no demand
penetration strategy
planning
product development
strategies
strategic marketing plan
tactics
unwholesome demand

PRACTICAL APPLICATION

1. Write benefit-oriented mission statements which describe the following product/market situations:

   • A large television network, in common with its major competitors, faces problems attracting advertisers to sponsor its programs. Cable TV networks are making competitive inroads, and advertisers are becoming more and more reluctant to meet high sponsorship costs. In a dramatic mission change, the network decides it is no longer in the entertainment business. Its customers will no longer be viewers of its programs (who pay nothing to view these programs), but advertisers, like General Motors and Proctor and Gamble. Its product will no longer be TV shows, but *access to target audiences,* which is also the need satisfied by the network's product. Its competitors will now be *all media,* instead of just other TV networks, and its major strengths, or weaknesses, in fulfilling its new mission will be its ability to compete against other media.

   • A large center-city hotel, facing extreme competitive pressures from other hotel and motel chains, decides to reposition itself. No longer is it in the hotel business; it is now in the business communication business. Now, its main product will be facilities for business meetings, conventions and presentations, with lodging assuming a secondary position. Instead of aiming its marketing mix offering at travelers, this offering will now be directed toward local and national business firms, clubs, and associations. Its main competitors will no longer be other hotels; it will be premier hotels and other institutions and organizations (including the American Management Association, and local colleges) which offer business communication programs.

2. Taking either of the mission statements you wrote for question 1, above, write a hierarchy of business objectives and a hierarchy of marketing objectives that might emerge from this statement.

3. Excerpts from an article in the *New York Times* entitled "Another Coup for the Fighting Gallos":

   > With one-year old Bartles & Jaymes, the Gallo brothers have stormed into first place in the booming wine cooler business, one of the few bright spots in an industry suffering from flat sales. . . . That coup . . . was only the latest of a remarkable string of successes that allowed the E & J Gallo winery to grow from a shed in the Great Depression into the world's largest winery. And the cooler's success has left its stunned competitors gaping in awe. . . . In addition to ranking No. 1 in wine coolers, its E & J Brandy is the best selling brandy in the country. Its Andre champaign,

available for $2 a bottle, is the best-selling sparkling wine. It is also the leading supplier of low-priced flavored wines . . . and inexpensive table wines. . . . Even in premium varietal wines, for which it is not known, Gallo sells more than anyone else. . . .

Key to Bartles & Jaymes's success, . . . indeed, the winery's success, . . . are Ernest and Julio Gallo, who have perfected a system of clever advertising, adroit product positioning and brute-force sales and marketing, backed up by the most vertically integrated and efficient production process in the industry. . . .

Basing your answers on these excerpts,

a. Speculate on how the four steps of the strategic marketing planning process might have been employed to create the Bartles & Jaymes's success story.

b. Identify and describe the following growth strategies implicit in the Gallo success story: penetration; product development; market development.

c. Describe how Gallo might employ the two conflicting leader strategies discussed in this chaper; and how R. Stuart Bewley might employ challenger strategies to compete with Bartles & Jaymes. Bewley is the co-founder and president of California Cooler, "which started the wine cooler craze and until six months ago was the leading seller."

4. First, match up the failed strategy in column two with the strategy category in column one:

Strategy		Failed Strategy
a) growth:	intensive penetration market development product development integrative diversification horizontal conglomerate concentric	Sales of the 1992 Chevrolet Caprice—a full-sized, rear-wheel-drive automobile said to mimic the jelly bean shape of the Ford Taurus—nosedives to the point where General Motors has to close the huge Willow Run plant where the car is made.
		Ross Perot, focusing on his ability to "get this country running again," spends more than $60 million in support of his goal of "taking all 50 states" in the 1992 Presidential election campaign. He ends up taking none.
		In June, 1992, a year late, Sprint introduces its MORE program in response to MCI's hugely successful "Friends and Family" program, which gives 20 percent discounts on telephone calls to designated members of customer calling circles. Despite a large scale promotional campaign featuring Candice Bergen, results are disappointing.

Strategy		Failed Strategy
b) competitive:	leader challenger follower nicher	Carvel ice-cream loses in the courts to California outlets which also want to handle products of other premium ice-cream makers.
		OPEC countries helplessly watch oil prices drop as uncooperative members fail to hold the line.

Now, speculate as to what these failures seem to have in common.

ANSWERS
KNOW THE BASICS

1. The marketing management process encompasses a series of activities, involving analysis, planning, implementation, and control, which combine to create "matches" between an organization's resources and objectives and its changing market opportunities. Strategic marketing planning (SMP) encompasses a series of steps which define how, where and when marketing management activities are applied. These steps include defining the company's mission, setting company objectives, designing the business portfolio, and planning strategies for marketing products or business units comprising the portfolio.

2. Strategic marketing planning (SMP) benefits companies by helping to identify and exploit worthwhile marketing opportunities to achieve worthwhile objectives and make effective use of resources. SMP benefits customers in that the process typically satisfies an unfulfilled market need, or a fulfilled market need more effectively, resulting in better products or product-related attributes (price, distribution, etc.).

3. For a department store, a strategic plan might identify and define worthwhile target markets for the product-price-place-promotion offerings of a given department (housewares, sports equipment, etc.), then devise a plan relating these offerings to identified needs in this target market. A strategy would encompass the annual plan to bring together the offering and the needs, including special seasonal promotions, markdowns, changing merchandise mixes, and so on. The marketing program for the department store would encompass all the plans for all its departments.

4. You might first analyze the situation by listing skills and abilities you could offer a prospective employer, specific fields (accounting, banking, etc.) where these skills might be applied, and specific employers in these fields.

   Then, you might devise a plan for conveying information about your skills and abilities to these prospective employers, including the preparation of a resume and cover letter, and a schedule of mailings and follow-up calls.

Next, you might implement this plan by sending out the letters, making follow-up calls, and going for interviews.

Finally, you might exercise control by modifying your original plan (revise your resume, redirect your mailings) if performance doesn't meet expectations (i.e., if you don't get a job after the first effort).

5. Categorizing jobs in terms of these demand states will help you avoid negative or no demand jobs (as a dishwasher, say), or interesting jobs for which demand is falling (a professor of modern languages, for example), or which have many more applicants than jobs (a Broadway actor or actress). On the other hand, you might create a job for yourself from a latent job opportunity that doesn't presently exist, or get a part-time irregular demand job to complement your regular job. By all means, however, avoid the temptation to apply for that unwholesome job as a part-time safe cracker.

6. Such a statement should be a benefit-oriented exposition covering such domains as products, customer groups covered and customer needs satisfied. Domains in such a statement would be fields in which you are applying for a position; products, the skills you bring to the job; customer groups, prospective employers; and needs, the requirements of unfilled jobs. The following statement by an accounting major would meet these criteria:

> To conduct audits for small business clients of a large public accounting firm which will enhance my employer's profitability by enhancing the profitability of its clients.

7. Depending on the size of the investment required to purchase the franchise, barriers to entry may or may not be high. On all the other counts, however, Porter's criteria seem to indicate a questionable opportunity: competition in the fast food business is strong; substitutes proliferate (eating at home, for example); buyers are strong in the sense that they can force your outlet's price down by using one of these substitutes; and your supplier, the franchiser, holds most of the cards in controlling your supply of the products you will be selling.

8. The mission statement defines the needs of the firm's target markets (domains) and shows how features and benefits of its offerings will satisfy these needs. These definitions, in turn, suggest what objectives the firm can realistically expect to achieve, as well as the product portfolio and other marketing mix elements best calculated to achieve these goals by bringing together offerings and target markets.

9. Market growth strategies, if successful, engender competitive strategies by organizations interested in emulating the innovator's success, or enhancing their own success at the other's expense. These competitive strategies, in turn, encourage counter-competitive strategy initiatives on the part of the innovator firm to maintain its competitive advantage.

10. Intensive growth strategies, including penetration, market development, and product development strategies, would be used by the department store to better exploit existing product/market opportunities. For example, it might attempt deeper penetration of existing target markets with more effective promotions, or attempt to attract more members of these markets with new product lines (product development), or seek new markets for its existing lines (for example, provide transportation to the store for senior citizens). Integrative growth strategies might involve the department store in controlling its supply sources, as Sears does (backward), with other department stores in the community for special promotions (horizontal), or controlling smaller, less centralized retail outlets (forward). Diversification growth strategies would be employed by the department store in the event that opportunities in its present market disappear, perhaps through a change in the composition of the neighborhood. Horizontal diversification would entail the store getting into other businesses (such as banking), unrelated to its existing business, to attract the remaining members of its existing market, while conglomerate diversification would market these new, unrelated businesses on new categories of customers. Concentric diversification would entail the store getting involved in businesses technologically related to its present business, such as a catalog buying service, to attract new categories of customers.

PRACTICAL APPLICATION

1. The following statements were written with these mission statement criteria in mind: Statements should cover such domains as products, customer groups served, and needs satisfied; be benefit oriented; and allow for future growth possibilities.

   - *The television network:* To provide advertisers with the most productive, efficient access to target markets of any medium through a comprehensive, state-of-the-art service involving identification of target markets, matching markets to advertiser offerings, and creating TV programming attuned to the needs of defined markets.

   - *The repositioned hotel:* To make business and professional people more efficient and productive by creating a meetingplace environment hospitable to the generation and dissemination of knowledge and information. This environment will emphasize congenial surroundings and state-of-the-art education and communication capabilities.

2. The hierarchy of business objectives for the television network, as mandated by its mission statement, would entail:

   - establishing strong market and media research capabilities to develop targeted media plans for clients in a broad diversity of markets (not just the consumer market), and

• reorienting TV programming focus toward target, rather than mass, markets. This might involve classifying the network's library of existing programs by individual markets, and developing new programs to appeal to specific markets.

These business objectives would in turn suggest a diversity of marketing objectives, including marketing research to position the new service in the highly competitive TV programming environment and development of pricing/promotion strategies to relate benefits and features of this new service to needs of prospective clients.

Similarly, the repositioned hotel would also perceive sets of business and marketing objectives mandated by its mission statement. Among the business objectives would be the need to redesign and reappoint its traditional hotel image and accommodations to meet the needs of business and professional people, including, for example, meeting and training rooms with hightech communication and education facilities, and study suites to replace traditional hotel room accommodations.

As in the case of the TV network, marketing objectives would focus on profitability, positioning, pricing, and promoting this new service.

3. a. Briefly, here are a few observations, from an infinite number of possibilities, that might be noted in reference to the role of the strategic planning process in the creation of the Bartles and Jaymes' success story:

• *Defining the company mission:* Unlike the statements of many of its competitors, Gallo's mission statement does not restrict it to a narrow product market focus (for example, only wines for the relatively small wine drinker market). Wine coolers obviously represent an innovative new product entry aimed at a totally new, and much larger, market than traditional wine drinkers. As the article makes clear, Gallo is an innovator in a broad spectrum of wine-related product areas, from the low-priced to the premium.

• *Setting company objectives and goals:* The effectiveness of Gallo's positioning and promotional campaigns ("clever advertising" . . . "brute force sales and marketing" . . .) suggests realistic, integrated marketing programs that encompass all its product lines and derive from broader business objectives specifying profit objectives and the sales and cost goals sequenced to achieve these objectives.

• *Designing the business portfolio:* Gallo's consistent record of growth and profitability, based on a broad spectrum of mission-related product lines, suggests a continuing, systematic appraisal of each line in terms of its growth and profit potential, and implementation of invest, hold, and harvest strategies consistent with these appraisals. A continual search for new product/market opportunities, like the Bartles & Jaymes wine cooler, is also suggested.

• *Planning marketing and other functional strategies:* The article emphasizes the strong, effective, goal-oriented marketing strategies and tactics characterizing Gallo's marketing program. Not noted, but of signal importance to the winery's growth and profitability, are the other functional strategies, in such areas as production, distribution, finance, and research and development, which must be effectively integrated with its marketing program.

b.

Strategy	Defined	Example
Penetration	persuade present accounts to use more of product, change "undecideds" to customers, attract customers from competition	Bartles & Jaymes wrests market leadership from California Cooler wine coolers
Product Development	new firm develops products of interest to present or prospective customers, or new ways to package or distribute existing products	Andre champagne, an inexpensive sparkling wine, joins Gallo's line of inexpensive wines
Market Development	firm develops products to attract members of new markets (geographic, consumer, institutional)	Bartles & Jaymes wine cooler attracts the "Yuppie" segment not associated with wine drinking

c. From its position of leadership, Gallo might employ either a leader strategy that builds the size of the overall market, for Gallo and its competitors, by introducing new products, and finding new uses, and users, for existing products; or a leader strategy that gains additional market share by attracting customers from competitors. Both strategies are implicit in the facts of the Gallo case: The success of the Bartles & Jaymes wine cooler is effectively creating huge new markets for all cooler producers; meanwhile, Gallo has successfully positioned its cooler against California Coolers, and replaced this product in its leadership position.

R. Stuart Bewley, president of California Coolers, might attempt to regain its lost leadership position by employing *frontal attack, flank attack,* or *follower strategies.* Given Gallo's solid leadership position in a variety of product lines, a frontal attack strategy against this entire product line hardly seems feasible; however, a flank attack strategy against perceived weaknesses in B & J's offering, or a by-passing strategy focusing on market segments not attracted to B & J (a gourmet cooler, for example) might succeed.

4.

Failed Strategy	Strategic Option
d) Sales of Caprice nosedive	Product development (new products of interest to present and prospective customers)
b) Ross Perot takes none	Penetration strategy (persuade target market members to purchase more of product or service)
c) Sprint introduces MORE	Concentric diversification (related product/service to attract new segments)
d) Carvel loses in California courts	Challenger strategies (frontal attack on Carvel's offering)
e) OPEC	Follower challenger strategies by cooperative members of OPEC, flank attack challenger strategies by non-cooperative members

What all these failures seem to have in common is general lack of understanding of the nature and needs of markets served, and how members of these markets will respond to new, or changing, marketing mixes.

3
THE MARKETING ENVIRONMENT

KEY TERMS

macroenvironment the larger economic, demographic, social/cultural, political/legal, competitive, and technological forces that affect an organization's microenvironment

microenvironment forces in the organization's immediate environment that affect marketing planning, including company mission, objectives, and policies; suppliers; customers; marketing intermediaries; and welcome, unwelcome, and sought publics

---

HOW ENVIRONMENTAL VARIABLES INFLUENCE STRATEGIC PLANNING

In the previous chapter, we examined the role of the marketing manager in developing long- and short-range strategic marketing plans to achieve profitable matches between marketing mixes and target markets.

However, strategic marketing plans are never made in a vacuum. External to the planning process are changing, interrelated environmental forces that present threats and opportunities, and influence the marketing manager's ability to develop and maintain successful transactions with target market customers. The marketing manager has little or no control over these forces; the best he or she can usually do is understand their nature, forecast their direction and intensity, and respond to them by manipulating marketing mix variables that can be controlled.

In this chapter we will examine the nature, scope, and impact of these environmental forces on the marketing planning process, using the Merton Electronics Company case for illustrative examples:

The **Merton Electronics Company**: This large manufacturer of advanced electronic components and systems faces a dilemma. The firm's research and development department, working with its engineering and product design departments, has developed a lightweight notebook computer system tentatively called the Mini. Weighing less than four pounds, the Mini could be used with a diversity of spreadsheets, electronic mail, and word processing programs, and comes with an expansion face that connected into a desktop model with as much as 10 additional megabytes of memory. However, Merton's mission has always been to market its products exclusively in the industrial market, to firms that use Merton products in computers they sell to consumers. Now, if Merton embarks on a diversification strategy to market this new product in the unfamiliar consumer market, it will be competing with its own best customers, and at conflict with its basic mission.

To resolve this dilemma, Merton's senior management retains a consultant to explore and report on problems and opportunities involved in establishing a new consumer products division to make and market a complete line of consumer electronic products spearheaded by the Merton Mini.

It is understood that if the consultant's report recommends the new division, she will stay on as the division's marketing manager.

In developing her report, the consultant began with an analysis of the impact of environmental factors that would influence the success of the proposed new consumer products division. Initially, her focus was on broad macroenvironmental factors, including economic, demographic, social/cultural, competitive, legal/political, and technological variables.

Then, her focus changed to microenvironmental factors affected by the macroenvironment. These included the company itself, with its missions, objectives, and policies; suppliers of resources to make and market consumer products; customers who would purchase these products; market intermediaries who would help finance, promote, and distribute products to customers; and various publics that could help or hinder Merton's marketing efforts.

Figure 3.1 shows the route of the consultant's analyses, from macro- to microenvironmental factors, to marketing mix variables, to targeted markets.

Figure 3–1. Factors affecting company marketing strategy.

THE MACROENVIRONMENT: THREATS, OPPORTUNITIES, AND RESPONSES

Starting with the economic component of the macroenvironment, the consultant analyzed, in turn, demographic, competitive, social/cultural, legal/political and technological environments. Following are her findings regarding the impact of each component on Merton's consumer marketing plans.

THE ECONOMIC ENVIRONMENT

This analysis focused first on broad economic trends and developments affecting Merton's marketing opportunities and then on the economic dynamics of Merton's market.

• *TRENDS AND DEVELOPMENTS*
The two broad economic determinants of demand for Merton's consumer products were ability and willingness of consumers to buy products. Here, the consultant's findings were generally favorable in both domestic and foreign markets.

Domestically, government fiscal and monetary policies were mainly responsible for a number of trends favorable to consumer markets. Employment was up, and taxes, inflation, and interest rates were down, so people had more **disposable** income (left after taxes are paid) and **discretionary** income (left from disposable income after necessities are paid for) to spend on products like the Mini.

According to Engel's laws, published by the German statistician Ernst Engel in 1857, this increase in disposable and discretionary income means increased ability and willingness to purchase relatively expensive products like the Mini. Engel's laws state that, as family spendable income increases, the percentage:

- spent on food decreases

- spent on housing, housing operations, and clothing remains constant

- spent on other items, such as recreation, education, self-help, and luxury items, increases

Most of the products that Merton would make and market in its new consumer products division fell into Engel's "other items" category, and hence should benefit from the increased percentage of higher incomes spent in this category.

In foreign markets, the consultant saw many of the same favorable trends she had seen in the domestic market, especially in developed free world economies and the integration of common markets: inflation and interest rates were moving downward, while productivity and real income were increasing. Additionally, income distribution in many less-developed countries was becoming more equitable, increasing the number of people able to afford Merton products.

• *MARKET DYNAMICS*

In this area of inquiry, the consultant's main concern was the degree of **demand elasticity** that would characterize Merton's consumer market products. Demand is elastic if a small change in a product's price produces a disproportionate change in demand; *in*elastic if the price change doesn't produce this disproportionate demand change. The three conditions depicted in Figure 3.2 illustrate demand elasticity concepts.

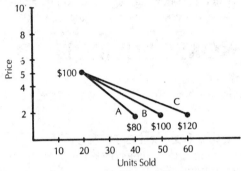

Figure 3–2. Demand curves.

In condition *A*, raising the price from $2 to $5 a unit causes sales to decline from 40 units to 20 units. However, total revenues increase from $80 (40 × $2) to $100 (20 × $5). This desirable condition means that raising prices will produce more revenue dollars.

In condition *B*, revenues remain constant regardless of price changes. At a price of $2 per unit, 50 units are sold, producing $100 in revenues. At a price of $5 a unit, 20 units are sold, also producing $100 in revenues. This is referred to as a condition of unitary elasticity.

In condition *C*, raising the price from $2 to $5 per unit produces a revenue *decrease* from $120 to $100. Thus, if increased revenues are the marketer's main objective, prices should be set at a lower level. This is a condition of elastic demand, with the demand response line stretching more than it does in conditions *A* and *B*.

Products for which few substitutes exist, and which are perceived as necessities, generally develop the inelastic demand pattern of line *A*. Products with many substitutes, which are not perceived as necessities, develop elastic demand curves (line *C*). Hamburger, for example, exhibits an elastic demand pattern because if its price goes too high, there are many substitute products (pizza, frankfurters, etc.) that can replace it. So demand and revenues will both decline as prices rise. However, there are few substitutes for the salt that gets shaken onto the hamburger, so salt, typically, displays an inelastic demand pattern: People will continue to purchase the same amount even if its price rises. Of course, people will only pay so much for a box of salt, or only buy so many pounds of hamburger no matter how low the price gets, so few demand curves remain either elastic or inelastic over their entire length.

As shown in Figure 3.3, elasticity concepts also apply to supply curves.

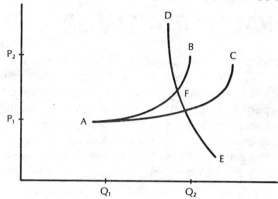

Figure 3–3. Equilibrium of Supply and Demand.

Supply curve AB is inelastic because quantity offered doesn't stretch much as price is increased. For example, Merton might find demand for its Mini so great that it can be priced at point P_2. However, because Merton is only set up to produce B quantity of Minis, output only stretches from Q_1 to Q_2 as the price increases from P_1 to P_2. An elastic supply curve, like an elastic demand curve, would be much flatter, like AC.

When a demand curve, like DE in Figure 3.3, is superimposed on a supply curve, an **equilibrium point** (F) is reached at which the quantity and price sellers are willing to offer equal the quantity and price buyers are willing to accept. This is the **market price** for the product.

Understanding demand and supply relationships is important to marketing managers for a variety of reasons covered in this book, including appraising the economic climate characterizing different markets; devising product, price, promotion, and place marketing mix strategies; and anticipating competitive responses to these strategies.

In applying supply/demand concepts to her analysis of the market for Merton's consumer product line, the consultant assumed its demand pattern would be inelastic. Specifically, she perceived that its unique features and benefits would position it as a "no substitute" necessity among members of many target markets, such as engineers and accountants.

This inelastic demand pattern, in turn, would translate into an excellent profit opportunity: within limits, total demand and revenues would increase as prices increased; furthermore, as output increased to meet increased demand, costs for making and marketing each Mini would decline as economy of scale savings spread these costs over more units.

YOU SHOULD REMEMBER

Economic trends and developments, on both national and international levels, influence strategic marketing planning in two ways.

First, they influence marketing planning by affecting the ability and willingness of people to buy products. For example, high interest, inflation, and unemployment rates stifle economic growth and reduce disposable and discretionary income. Engel's laws are useful in relating income patterns to purchasing patterns, showing that, as income increases, smaller amounts are spent on food, and larger amounts on housing, recreation, and other products.

Second, economic trends and developments influence marketing planning by shaping supply-demand relationships which define competitive climates. In particular, it is important for the marketing manager to understand the nature of **elastic** and **inelastic** supply and demand patterns, and interactions among them that determine market prices and affect other marketing mix elements.

THE DEMOGRAPHIC ENVIRONMENT

The consultant's analysis of economic factors in the macroenvironment showed that prospective customers would have discretionary income to buy Merton products, and a willingness to spend this income. Her analysis also showed a great profit opportunity if supply could keep up with this demand.

Now, she turned her attention to the **demographic** environment to find out where, and in which age groups, this spendable income was most likely to occur. Specifically, she focused on "state of being" trends and developments pertaining to population, income, and expenditures.

• *POPULATION TRENDS AND DEVELOPMENTS*

Of particular concern to the success of Merton's new consumer products division were trends and developments pertaining to domestic population **growth** and **composition**. For example:

- Population growth rate was declining toward zero percent in the 90s, which meant fewer people available to purchase Merton products.

- However, average age of the population was increasing, which meant people would be around longer to buy Merton products.

- When analyzed by age-group category, the population growth rate for Merton products would actually increase dramatically. Thus, while the teen-age segment, only a marginal market for Merton products, declined greatly, the 20–34 and 34–54 age groups would show appreciable increases, and these were the two most potentially profitable age group segments.

- After the 34–54 age group, the over–65 age group would experience the second-largest growth of all age-group segments (20 percent). The consultant made a note to consider developing products targeted to this group.

After analyzing age-group growth patterns, the consultant examined the geographic dispersion of the population for market opportunities. For example, as shown in Figure 3.4, the most rapid population growth would occur in Sunbelt states in the south and west.

U.S. + 7.1%

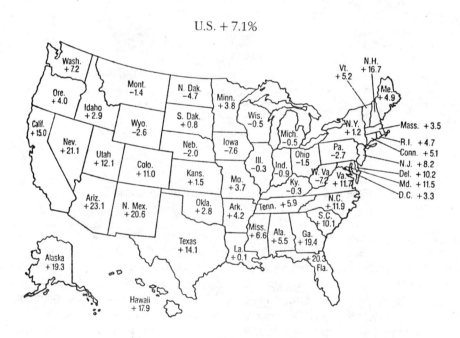

Figure 3–4. Projected population growth rates, 1990–2000. (Source: U.S. Department of Commerce, Bureau of Census)

• *INCOME TRENDS AND DEVELOPMENTS*

Here, the consultant's starting point was the Gross National Product (GNP), defined as the total market value of all goods and services produced in this country in a year.

Viewed as a trend, GNP figures, like population growth figures, had grown at a rate of roughly 3 percent a year over the past century; also, like population growth, many forecasters anticipated a no-growth future for GNP, resulting from trends like a reduced birth rate, rising debt and energy costs, and new thinking about the desirability of growth.

Viewed in terms of its distribution among families and households, however, this no-growth trend looked much more favorable. Thus, between 1930 and 1980 the pyramid depicting the proportion of families with various levels of buying power had turned over completely:

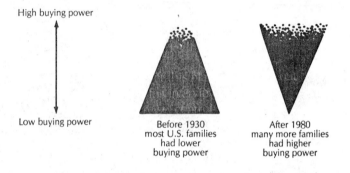

Figure 3–5. Redistribution of income—a revolution.

This reversal meant that more families and households were now important customers for Merton consumer products, although further analysis showed that wealth became more concentrated during the decade of the 1980s, as share of net worth held by the top one percent of households jumped from less than 20 percent in 1979 to more than 36 percent in 1990. Specifically, the consultant concluded that only about 25 percent of total households had sufficiently high discretionary income to purchase Merton products, especially considering that, in 1990, it cost the average urban American family of four $15,000 a year just to maintain an austere living standard. Fortunately, the two age groups that comprised the largest target markets for Consumer Division products (20–34, 34–54) each had a much higher than average representation in the over $30,000 income category.

YOU SHOULD REMEMBER

Since people with money create markets, demographic studies of population and income trends are of particular interest to marketing managers planning strategies to penetrate these markets. Population trend studies focus on overall population growth trends, growth trends in specific age-group categories, and the geographic dispersion of the population. Income trend studies focus on gross national product (GNP) growth rates, and how wealth is distributed among families and households. Although overall population growth rates are declining toward zero, certain age-group categories, such as the 34–54 group, are experiencing strong growth, as are certain geographical areas, such as suburban and urban areas, and the Sunbelt and Southwestern states. Income distribution trends show a dramatic reversal over the past fifty years, resulting in many more families with much more disposable and discretionary income.

THE SOCIAL-CULTURAL ENVIRONMENT

At this point in her analysis, the consultant had profiled prospective target markets in terms of economic and demographic forces that defined the nature, scope, and location of demand for Merton consumer division products. Now, her focus changed to social and cultural trends which would shape and direct this demand.

Of special interest were **core values** and **secondary values** affecting how and why people behave as they do. Core values are highly persistent; secondary values are much more likely to change and to force changes in marketing plans. As examples, persistent core values include getting married and raising families; secondary values include getting married later in life and raising smaller families.

These secondary values, and the various subcultures which share them (teenagers, career women) would prove a rich source of ideas for positioning and marketing Merton products in different target markets. The following cultural changes, for example, suggested ways to market the Mini to the Young Urban Professional family target market:

- from a work ethic to a self-indulgent ethic

- from emphasis on quality of goods to quality of life

- from husband-dominated families to husband-wife equality

- from postponed to immediate gratification

• from a thrift to a free-spending ethic

• from the artificial to the natural

Taken together, these values suggested a family Mini personal computer with special software programs designed to improve a typical family's health and happiness through customized diets, proper exercise regimes, effective financial planning and other self-help programs.

YOU SHOULD REMEMBER

Social/cultural environment forces are of interest to marketing planners because they shape attitudes and behavior patterns which shape target markets and determine how members of these markets will respond to marketing mix variables. Of particular interest are **secondary** cultural values and the subcultures that adopt these values—for example, the yuppie subculture adopting physical fitness values. These secondary values are much less persistent than the core values from which they emerge, and should be closely monitored to identify new marketplace threats and opportunities.

POLITICAL/LEGAL ENVIRONMENT

Like the social and cultural forces that produce them, political and legal forces tend to change slowly, and can yield helpful clues for positioning and promoting products. In analyzing the influence of these forces on Merton's proposed new consumer products division, the consultant identified five areas where government legislation and policies established by government regulatory agencies would most affect strategic marketing plans:

1. general monetary and fiscal policies, which determine how much the government will spend for goods and services, how much money is made available to consumers, and how much money people will have left after taxes are paid

2. broad social legislation and accompanying regulatory agency policies, such as civil rights and environmental protection laws

3. government relationships with individual industries, such as subsidies for agriculture and shipbuilding, and import quotas on Japanese automobiles

4. legislation relating to marketing, including laws and statutes to either regulate and maintain competition or protect the consumer (Figure 3.6 summarizes the main laws in each group; Figure 3.7 shows how selected laws to regulate and maintain competition relate to each of the four marketing mix elements.)

Major legislation affecting marketing
1. *Sherman Antitrust Act* (1890). Prohibits monopolies and combinations in restraint of trade.
2. *Federal Trade Commission (FTC) Act* (1914). Prohibits unfair competition.
3. *Clayton Antitrust Act* (1914). Regulates price discrimination, exclusive dealing, tying contracts, and interlocking corporate directorships.
4. *State Unfair Trade Practices Acts* (1930s). Prohibit "loss-leader" pricing (selling below cost). Laws still in effect in about half the states.
5. *Consumer Goods Pricing Act* (1975). Repeals *federal* laws supporting *state* fair-trade laws. Does away with state laws allowing manufacturers to set retail prices.
6. *Robinson-Patman Act* (1936). Amends the Clayton Act by strengthening the prohibition of price discrimination. Regulates price discounts and allowances.
7. *Wheeler-Lea Act* (1938). Amends the FTC Act; broadens and strengthens regulation of unfair or deceptive competition.
8. *Lanham Trademark Act* (1946). Regulates brands and trademarks.
9. *Celler-Kefauver Antimerger Act* (1950). Amends the Clayton Act; prevents corporate mergers where the effect may be to substantially lessen competition.

Designed Primarily to Protect Consumers
1. *Pure Food and Drug Act* (1906). Regulates labeling of food and drugs and prohibits manufacture or marketing of adulterated food or drugs. Amended in 1938 by Food, Drug, and Cosmetics Act.
2. *Meat Inspection Act* (1906). Regulates meat-packing houses and provides for federal inspection of meats.
3. Various *textile labeling laws* that require the manufacturer to indicate what the product is made of:
   a. Wool Products Labeling Act (1939)   c. Textile Fiber Products
   b. Fur Products Labeling Act (1951)   Identification Act (1958)
4. *Automobile Information Disclosure Act* (1958). Requires manufacturers to post suggested retail prices on new passenger vehicles.
5. *Kefauver-Harris Drug Amendments* (1962). Requires (a) that drugs be labeled with their generic names, (b) that new drugs be pretested, and (c) that new drugs get approval of Food and Drug Administration before being marketed.
6. *National Traffic and Motor Vehicle Safety Act* (1966). Provides for safety standards for tires and autos.
7. *Fair Packaging and Labeling Act* (1966). The "truth in packaging" law that regulates packaging and labeling.
8. *Cigarette Labeling and Advertising Acts* (1966, 1969). Require manufacturers to label cigarettes as being hazardous to health and prohibits TV advertising of cigarettes.
9. *Consumer Credit Protection Act* (1968). The "truth in lending" law that requires full disclosure of interest rates and other financing charges on loans and credit purchases.
10. *Fair Credit Reporting Act* (1970). Regulates the reporting and the use of credit information.
11. *Consumer Product Safety Act* (1972). Establishes the Consumer Product Safety Commission with broad powers to regulate the marketing of products ruled unsafe by the Commission.
12. *Consumer Product Warranty Act* (1975). Increases consumers' rights and sellers' responsibilities under product warranties.
13. *FTC Improvement Act* (1980). Reduces power of the FTC to implement industrywide regulation.
14. *Toy Safety Act* (1984). Gives government power to recall dangerous toys quickly.

Figure 3-6. Summary of selected legislation and policies affecting strategic marketing plans

Figure 3-7. Effect of federal antimonopoly laws on the four Ps.

Law	Product	Place	Promotion	Price
Sherman Act (1890) Monopoly or conspiracy in restraint of trade	Monopoly or conspiracy to control a product	Monopoly or conspiracy to control distribution channels		Monopoly or conspiracy to fix or control prices
Clayton Act (1914) Substantially lessen competition	Forcing sale of some products with others —tying contracts	Exclusive dealing contracts (limiting buyers' sources of supply)		Price discrimination by manufacturers
Federal Trade Commission Act (1914) Unfair methods of competition		Unfair policies	Deceptive ads or selling practices	Deceptive pricing
Robinson-Patman Act (1936) Tends to injure competition		Prohibits paying allowances to "direct" buyers in lieu of middlemen costs (brokerage charges)	Prohibits "fake" advertising allowances or discrimination in help offered	Prohibits price discrimination on goods of "like grade and quality" without cost justification, and quantity discounts limited
Wheeler-Lea Amendment (1938) Unfair or deceptive practices	Deceptive packaging or branding		Deceptive ads or selling claims	Deceptive pricing
Anbmerger Act (1950) Lessen competition	Buying competitors	Buying producers or distributors		
Magnuson-Moss Act (1975) Unreasonable practices	Product warranties			

5. information which helps marketers, including census information which helps marketers define markets demographically and geographically.

Later, when strategic plans for marketing Merton consumer products were formulated and implemented, these areas of political and legal influence would help identify key markets (including the government itself); key areas where government could serve firms like Merton (such as enforcing measures to restrict unfair competition); and important constraints in marketing these products (such as uniform distribution policies).

YOU SHOULD REMEMBER

Political/legal environmental forces, deriving from government legislation and regulatory agencies, affects the marketing planning process when

(1) monetary and fiscal policies define demand patterns

(2) social legislation influences social/cultural attitudes and behavior

(3) government subsidies enhance the competitive strength of individual industries

(4) government legislation helps constrain or maintain freemarket competition and

(5) government agencies, such as the Census Bureau or Department of Commerce, provide information helpful to marketers

---

THE TECHNOLOGICAL ENVIRONMENT

In modern economies, a strong technological base, fueled by public and private research and development expenditures, supports competitive competence and a solid growth rate. Technological advances need not be major discoveries, like the chip circuitry which led to modern computer systems; indeed, the history of technological growth shows few big leaps, but many small steps, like the Merton Mini, between those leaps.

Technology affects marketing in two ways. First, it affects living styles and standards, and creates products that reflect these lifestyles. For example, computer-induced efficiencies made people more productive and affluent, and better able to afford products like personal computers.

Second, technology, like the political and regulatory environment, affects all elements of the marketing mix. Technology produces new products like the Mini and new ways of making, promoting, and distributing these products. Together, these advances can reduce the price paid for products by improving efficiencies and reducing costs.

In analyzing the technological environment surrounding the Mini, the consultant perceived many opportunities to benefit from such technological advances as telemarketing, TV-computer home shopping, and target market opportunities created by cable television.

YOU SHOULD REMEMBER

The technological environment affects marketing planning in two significant ways. First, technological advances cause dramatic changes in living styles and standards, and associated product wants and needs. For example, modern computers help produce the affluence and leisure which created new demand patterns.

Technological advances also affect all elements of the marketing mix, improving products and the way products are manufactured and distributed.

THE COMPETITIVE ENVIRONMENT

Having identified threats and opportunities in the economic, demographic, social/cultural, political/legal, and technological environments, the consultant next turned her analytical attentions to threats and opportunities in the **competitive environment.**

The consultant's analysis of the competitive environment followed the same pattern as her analysis of the other components of the macroenvironment. First, she examined major trends and developments; then she examined their implications for Merton's consumer products.

In the broad competitive context, the consultant perceived four kinds of competitors for Merton customers:

- Brand competition would encompass other manufacturers of the marketed product. For example, IBM, Apple, and the Japanese giants would sooner or later introduce products with the same features and benefits as the Merton Mini.

- Form competition would encompass other forms of the marketed product. Desktop personal computers that do everything the portable Merton Mini do would be an example of form competition.

- Generic competition would encompass products other than the marketed product which could perform essentially the same functions. For example, an airline would represent generic competition for a bus line.

- Desire competition would encompass all other desires consumers might satisfy before satisfying the desire to purchase Merton products. For example, a consultant might satisfy a desire to set up a home office before purchasing a Mini.

Initially, at least, the consultant did not think that form, generic, and desire competition would be important factors in setting up Merton's consumer products division, which would develop around the Mini. The main problem would be brand competition, so this is where she now directed her attention.

To identify and respond to brand competition threats, she consulted a matrix (Figure 3.8) that identified components and characteristics of possible competitive situations Merton would face. At various stages of development, consumer division products could be in any of the four divisions in the matrix:

Important dimensions \ Types of situations	Monopoly	Oligopoly	Pure competition	Monopolistic competition
Uniqueness of each firm's product	Unique	None	None	Some
Number of competitors	None	Few	Many	Few to many
Size of competitors (compared to size of market)	None	Large	Small	Large to small
Elasticity of demand facing firm	Either	Kinked demand curve (elastic and inelastic)	Completely elastic	Either
Elasticity of industry demand	Either	Inelastic	Either	Either
Control of price by firm	Complete	Some (with care)	None	Some

Figure 3–8. Some important dimensions regarding market competitors.

- **A monopoly** exists when a product or service is provided by the government (the U.S. Post Office), a private regulated monopoly (an electric utility), or a private monopoly (DeBeer's diamonds). During its introductory stage, the Merton Mini's unique features and benefits might create a monopoly situation with no brand competition and a generally inelastic demand pattern. Up to a point, revenues would increase as prices were raised, although Merton would have to use some discretion: too high a price could attract competition, or bring charges of gouging the public.
- **An oligopoly** consists of a few large sellers of similar products dominating the market, with many smaller sellers following their lead. In the portable computer systems field, the consultant envisioned that Merton might find

itself in an oligopolistic situation, competing mainly with IBM and a few other large sellers. The fact that each competitor could keep close watch on the others would lead to the **kinked demand curve** phenomenon, whereby price increases produce elastic demand, price decreases inelastic demand. This is illustrated in Figure 3.9.

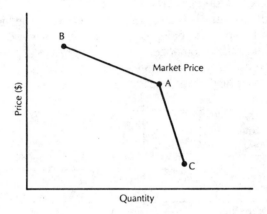

Figure 3–9. Oligopoly: kinked demand curve situation.

Assume that all firms priced their systems at point *A*. Should Merton decide to increase its price to point *B*, the other firms, to gain Merton's market share, will keep their prices at lower point *A*, thus assuring a falloff in demand for Merton's higher priced systems. If, on the other hand, Merton *lowers* its systems price to point *C*, the other firms, not wanting to lose market shares to Merton, will do the same, so Merton's overall sales won't increase much, if at all.

In this situation, the consultant realized, it is important to find the kink, or market price, and to stay there.

• **Pure competition** means many sellers offering similar products to many buyers, each with immediate, full knowledge of market transactions. The commodity market is an example of pure competition, with buyers and sellers aware, via ticker tape, of the exact price pork bellies and other commodities are fetching at any point in time. In this situation, sellers face an almost flat demand curve. The slightest increase above the bid price for a product will practically eliminate demand for this product. This low-profit situation, shown in Figure 3.10, was one the consultant wished to avoid for any of Merton's consumer division products. Even when these products were practically identical to competitive products, she would at least try to get them into the next competitive category, monopolistic competition.

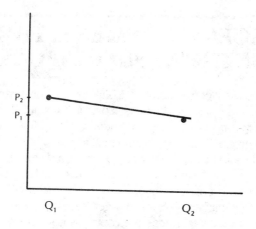

Figure 3–10. Demand curve: pure competition

- In a monopolistic competition situation, few, or many, firms offer products which, at least, are perceived as different by customers. For example, the consultant could easily envision a situation in which IBM, APPLE, and dozens of other foreign and domestic competitors were offering practically identical versions of the Mini. However, by effectively designing and combining marketing mix elements, Merton might create a niche for its Mini in which it is perceived as unique by target market members. Thus, in effect, Merton would have a small monopoly for its Mini in this competitive market.

YOU SHOULD REMEMBER

Competition is broadly defined as any way a buyer can spend money other than on the product marketed. Thus, in addition to obvious **brand** competition, competitors exist on the **form, generic,** and **desire** levels. Although in some circumstances all these forms of competition should be taken into account in market planning, emphasis is usually on brand competition and the characteristics of the climate in which this competition takes place. Number of competitors, similarity of products, and supply/demand patterns are the main determinants of competitive climate, generally referred to as **monopoly, oligopoly, pure competition** and **monopolistic competition.**

THE MICROENVIRONMENT: THREATS, OPPORTUNITIES, AND RESPONSES

In her analytical assessment of the macroenvironment, the consultant was dealing with forces over which Merton would have no control, but would have to respond to in devising and implementing strategic marketing plans. Now, the consultant's attention turned to a group of microenvironmental forces influenced by macroenvironmental forces, including the company itself, customers for Merton products, suppliers and marketing intermediaries who could help make and market these products, and publics with potential influence over the success of Merton's marketing efforts. Although marketing managers generally have more control over micro- than macroenvironmental forces, the control is nowhere as complete as it is for the marketing mix elements shaped by these forces.

THE COMPANY

The consultant realized that the company would encounter a diversity of interdepartmental conflicts, summarized in Figure 3.11, once the consumer products division began operations. These conflicts would be based largely on differing views as to which publics and company resources were most important in making and marketing the Mini and related consumer products.

For example, marketing's emphasis on sales features, custom components, many models, and frequent model changes would conflict with the emphasis of other departments on things like functional features, few models, and few model changes. Marketing's emphasis was based on the primacy of customer wants and needs, while conflicting viewpoints tended to focus more on the product or on production methods.

Thus, an important task of Merton marketing management would be to get all departments to view their activities through the *consumer's* eyes, consistent with the marketing concept of coordinating different functions toward consumer satisfaction. She envisioned working closely with managers of these other departments, and considering their differing viewpoints, in developing marketing plans under which the different departments could work together to accomplish overall company objectives.

However, well before the consumer products division became operative, the consultant anticipated other conflicts over missions, objectives, strategies, and policies. Since its inception, Merton's mission had been to make and market quality electronics products to industrial market customers; now, this proposed new diversification strategy would divert resources toward the relatively unfamiliar consumer market. All the consultant's analyses pointed toward success, but she realized Merton management would need a lot of persuading.

Department	Emphasis	Marketing Emphasis
R&D	Basic research Intrinsic quality Functional features	Applied research Perceived quality Sales features
Engineering	Long design lead time Few models Standard components	Short design lead time Many models Custom components
Purchasing	Narrow product line Standard parts Price of material Economical lot sizes Purchasing at infrequent intervals	Broad product line Nonstandard parts Quality of material Large lot sizes to avoid stockouts Immediate purchasing for customer needs
Manufacturing	Long production lead time Long runs with few models No model changes Standard orders Ease of fabrication Average quality control	Short production lead time Short runs with many models Frequent model changes Custom orders Aesthetic appearance Tight quality control
Inventory	Fast-moving items, narrow product line Economical level of stock	Broad product line High level of stock
Finance	Strict rationales for spending Hard and fast budgets Pricing to cover costs	Intuitive arguments for spending Flexible budgets to meet changing needs Pricing to further market development
Accounting	Standard transactions Few reports	Special terms and discounts Many reports
Credit	Full financial disclosures by customers Low credit risks Tough credit terms Tough collection procedures	Minimum credit examination of customers Medium credit risks Easy credit terms Easy collection procedures

Figure 3–11. Point of view differences between marketing and other departments.

CUSTOMERS

Although individuals and households comprising the consumer market would be the primary customers for Merton's new consumer products division, the consultant did not overlook other market aggregates that could represent target markets for this new division's products, including:

- the producer market, comprising organizations that buy products for use in producing other products

- the reseller market, comprising firms that buy products to resell at a profit

- the government market, which could purchase Merton products for use in producing public services or transferring goods and services to others

- the international market, comprising consumers, producers, resellers, and government market aggregates in foreign countries.

Each of these aggregates would have to be evaluated in terms of its potential purchases of Merton products and, when worthwhile potential existed, further divided into market segments. Each segment, in turn, would have to be defined in terms of unique characteristics affecting the buying decision process. (Market segmentation approaches and techniques are covered in Chapter 10.)

SUPPLIERS

Although Merton was capable of designing and developing many of the products and product components produced by the new consumer products division, the consultant realized the firm would find it more economical to have other firms make other products and components. Then, in situations where Merton decided to make rather than buy, the firm would have to locate suppliers of products and services needed to produce and market these made products. An important part of Merton's planning efforts would involve first establishing quality control and other standards for selecting the best suppliers, and then planning for such contingencies as rising prices and product shortages.

MARKETING INTERMEDIARIES

In addition to selecting suppliers of products and services needed to produce its consumer product lines, the consultant realized that a broad diversity of marketing intermediaries would also have to be selected. These intermediaries would play a supportive role during all stages of the life of Merton's products:

- Financial intermediaries, such as banks, insurance companies, and credit companies, would help finance the development, production, and marketing of consumer products.

- Middlemen, such as agents, brokers, wholesalers and retailers, would help move Merton products through channels to ultimate users, finding customers, closing sales, and creating time, place, and possession utilities in the process.

- Physical distribution intermediaries, such as warehouses and rail, truck, and airline transporters, would stock and move Merton products through channels to final target market destinations.

- Marketing service agencies, including marketing research firms, advertising agencies, and media consultants, would help identify and define target markets for Merton products, and develop marketing programs to penetrate these target markets.

As with suppliers, the consultant realized that policies and procedures would have to be established to identify intermediaries best able to help Merton achieve its objectives, and develop mutually profitable working relationships with these intermediaries.

PUBLICS

The final microenvironmental influence considered by the marketing manager was all the **publics** with actual or potential influence on Merton's ability to achieve strategic marketing objectives. Properly handled, these publics could spell opportunity; ignored, they could represent crippling threats.

As examples, financial publics, including investment banks, brokers, and stockholders, might be the key to financing the new consumer products division; media publics might provide publicity needed to assure marketing success; government and citizen action publics might stimulate laws and regulations (truth in advertising, minority rights, environmental legislation) which could help or hinder product sales.

Even local publics, in areas where the Mini would be manufactured; internal publics, comprised of Merton managers and employees; and the general public, which would help create the "corporate image" of the new division, could affect, positively or negatively, Merton's success.

To help in assessing the potential impact of each public, the consultant categorized them as welcome (such as stockholders in the new venture); unwelcome (such as citizen action groups lobbying against computers in public schools), and sought (such as consumer computer magazines favorably publicizing the Mini). Then she assessed the impact of each public, and the cumulative effect of all these publics, on Merton's plans and made plans herself to communicate with each public and help assure a favorable response to the new division and its products. For example, special Press Kits would be prepared for members of the sought media public, and newsletters about division products and progress sent to stockholders and staff members.

YOU SHOULD REMEMBER

Microenvironmental forces, much closer to home than the macroenvironmental forces which shape them, are also easier to respond to and control in developing and implementing strategic marketing plans. They start with the company, where marketing planning must account for organizational missions, objectives, policies, and procedures, and conflicts arising from differing perceptions of the roles and needs of different departments. Other microenvironmental forces that are usually accounted for in marketing planning include customers, who must be identified and defined; suppliers and marketing intermediaries, which must be located and evaluated, and publics, which have a strong actual or potential impact on the success of marketing plans.

KNOW THE CONCEPTS
DO YOU KNOW THE BASICS?

1. Distinguish between disposable and discretionary income.

2. Using actual dollar and quantity figures, diagram the difference between elastic, inelastic and unitary demand patterns.

3. On the diagram you drew for question 2, indicate a supply curve and an equilibrium point.

4. Explain why a marketing manager might be more interested in the growth rate of a single population age group than in the growth rate of the overall population.

5. Distinguish between cultural core and secondary values, with an example of each. Why are secondary values more likely to adversely influence a marketing plan?

6. Differentiate between legislative and regulatory influences on marketing plans with examples of each.

7. From your own perspective as a consumer interested in setting up a program of vigorous exercise, distinguish between brand, form, generic and desire competition for a rowing machine.

8. From a buyer's viewpoint, what is the main advantage of a pure competition climate? From a seller's viewpoint, what is the main advantage of an oligopolistic climate?

9. In what sense is monopolistic competition a form of monopoly? In what sense do they differ? Give an example of each form.

10. Briefly describe how interdepartmental conflict conflicts with marketing concept precepts.

11. Are factors which lead to inelastic demand and supply curves likely to be found together in the same situation?

12. Assume an individual decides to quit a good job selling computer systems to set up shop as an independent sales representative selling these systems for a number of manufacturers. Give examples of how forces in the microenvironment and macroenvironment might work for, or against, the success of this venture.

TERMS FOR STUDY

brand competition
demographics
desire competition
discretionary income
disposable income
elastic demand
Engel's Laws
environmental threat
equilibrium point
form competition
generic competition
inelastic demand

inelastic supply
kinked demand curve
macroenvironment
marketing intermediaries
microenvironment
middlemen
monopolistic competition
monopoly
oligopoly
publics
pure competition
supply curve

PRACTICAL APPLICATION

1. Assume that a community loses its main employer and is thrown into a depressed state. In terms of Engel's Law, how might the following businesses be affected: (a) a lumberyard? (b) a Computerland outlet? (c) a grocery store?

2. When the Polaroid Company introduced Polarvision—an instant movie camera that could be used to shoot and view home movies within minutes—it discovered that, even at $700, it could sell as many cameras as it could produce. Only when the price exceeded $900 in test markets did revenues begin to decline. Diagram and describe this situation, indicating the elasticity of supply and demand, and the equilibrium point.

3. According to the Monitor series of the Yankelovich marketing research firm, the following are significant secondary cultural values characterizing the large youth and young adult population segments: anti-bigness, mysticism, living for today, less emphasis on possessions, sensuousness, equality of the sexes, and physical fitness. To what extent, and in what ways, do you attribute these values to the success of Club Med? The Terminator films?

4. Speculate on the significance of the following demographic trends in the following industries. Specifically, which industries would benefit most from which trend, and why?

Trend	Industry
Baby boom generation matures	Travel & leisure (travel agencies, airlines, hotels, etc.)
More women are working	Expensive apparel
More over-65 members of population	Consumer electronics (stereo, electronic entertainment)
Smaller family units	

5. Describe how any two of the five political/legal environmental forces listed in the left-hand column, below, might influence each of the marketing situations listed in the right-hand column:

Forces	Situations
general monetary/fiscal policies	renting empty office space in Houston, Texas
social legislation and accompanying regulatory policies	General Electric purchases RCA
government relationships with individual industries	Tobacco farmers make plans to market next year's crop
legislation relating to marketing	Lockheed competes for a large commercial aircraft order
information that helps marketers	

ANSWERS
KNOW THE BASICS

1. Disposable income is the amount of money people have left after paying their taxes. For example, an individual earning $30,000 in the 15 percent tax bracket would have $25,500 disposable income. Discretionary income is money left after necessities are paid for from disposable income. For example, if this individual had to pay $20,000 for rent, food, and clothing, discretionary income would be only $5,500.

2. Here is one possible way to illustrate, graphically, differences between elastic, inelastic, and unitary demand patterns:

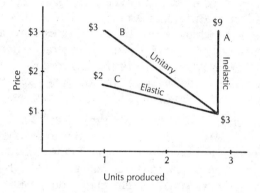

Note that, for line *C*, revenues increase as price drops, showing an elastic demand pattern; in line *B*, revenues remain constant as price drops, indicating a unitary demand pattern; in line *A*, revenue goes down as prices are lowered, indicating an inelastic demand pattern.

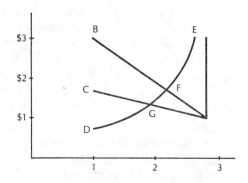

3. In this diagram, line *DE* is a supply curve which intersects with line *C* at point *G*, the equilibrium point at which the market will clear.

4. The single population age group might comprise a target market whose members consume a disproportionate amount of total product output. For example, if 80 percent of all cereals sold are consumed by children in the 5–12 age group, the marketing manager would be more interested in this group's growth rate than in that of the rest of the population.

5. Cultural core values, basic determinants of individual wants and behavior, have a high degree of persistence, such as the strong tendency of people in all periods of our history to marry and raise families. Secondary values, arising from these core values, are much more subject to change. For example, a relatively recent tendency is for people to get married later in life, and have smaller families.

6. Legislative influences on marketing plans refer to laws and statutes enacted by governing bodies, such as congress, that influence, for better or worse, options open to the marketing manager. Regulatory influences pertain to agencies set up to carry out the mandate of these laws and statutes, and the manner in which they are carried out. For example, agencies like the Federal Trade Commission (FTC) and the Federal Communications Commission (FCC) have often been criticized by advertisers and broadcasters for exceeding their mandate in carrying out congressional legislation pertaining to fairness in advertising and licensing standards for broadcasters.

7. Brand competition would be rowing machines manufactured by other firms similar in design, structure and function to the one you are considering. Form competition would be other forms of the basic rowing machine, such as an actual rowboat, rather than the in-place machine. Generic competition would be different products which provide essentially the same benefits as the rowing machine (or rowboat)—for example, a Nautilus gymnastic unit. Desire competition would encompass all the other things you could do with your money other than buy a rowing machine. For example, you might save it, or splurge it on a Caribbean vacation.

8. From a buyer's viewpoint, the main advantage of a pure competition situation is the low market price he or she pays, since marketers lack the pricing protections of other competitive climates. The seller might prefer the relatively high market price received by the few competitors comprising an oligopoly, from which there is little incentive to depart. (As the kinked curve shows, if prices in an oligopoly are increased, revenues will decline rapidly.)

9. Monopolistic competition is a form of monopoly in the sense that the product is perceived as having the unique features of a monopoly product. Hence, the marketer of this product has, in effect, a "monopoly" among members of markets which share this perception. Monopolistic competition differs from a monopoly in that, despite this perception, there are other competitors capable of making essentially identical products. For example, there are many manufacturers of fine china, but Wedgewood

china is perceived of as unique by many collectors. In a true monopoly, such as for diamonds (DeBeers) or mail delivery (the Post Office), there is literally only one supply source.

10. A key precept of the marketing concept is that all the firm's departments and functions should work together cooperatively and harmoniously to satisfy the needs of target markets profitably. For example, if a certain product feature will attract members of a profitable new target market, then purchasing, production, and marketing should work together to assure that this feature is incorporated into the product and promoted as such. Interdepartmental conflict, however, might arise because it is difficult for purchasing to procure this feature, or for production to retool to build it into the product. Hence, the cross purposes of individual departments frustrate the purposes of the marketing concept.

11. Gasoline is an example of a product with an inelastic demand curve because it is perceived of as a unique necessity. Customers will continue to buy gasoline in approximately the same quantities even if its price doubles. An inelastic supply curve would result if the supplier were unable to expand supply to keep up with expanding demand. For example, if a shortage of gasoline were to cause its price to double and demand to expand, an individual dealer, and the industry as a whole, would have only a limited capacity to satisfy this need. Hence, long lines of cars waiting for gas and an inelastic supply curve.

12. Before setting up in business as an independent sales representative, the individual might arrive at these optimistic conclusions regarding the *macroenvironmental influences:* demographically, the business and professional people will be selling products to represent a large and growing market segment; economically, they have sufficient disposable income to afford these products; technologically, these products represent the state of the art in electronics; and competitively, these products offer benefits to my target market which will give them a strong edge; and the *microenvironmental influences:* customers, a number of my previous accounts have assured me they will continue to buy from me in my new position; suppliers, I have already received commitments from six manufacturers of computer systems to let me represent them; market intermediaries, a local bank thinks so well of my prospects for success that it will extend a $50,000 line of credit to get started.

PRACTICAL APPLICATION

1. When the community was thrown into a depressed state, it can be assumed that discretionary income (left after payments for taxes and necessities) would decline appreciably. Thus, based on Engel's Law concepts, the grocery store would probably lose least business, since groceries are a necessity purchased from disposable income. The lumberyard would probably

lose a larger percent of its business than the grocery store, since home operations are closely related to increases, or decreases, in discretionary income. The Computerland outlet would probably lose the most business, since recreation products are purchased, according to Engel, almost solely from discretionary income.

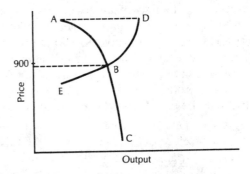

Line *ABC* shows an inelastic demand pattern for the Polaroid camera between points *B* and *C*, i.e., demand doesn't change much regardless of price increases. Line *AB* could be elastic or inelastic, depending on the extent to which sales, and revenues, fall off as price exceeds $900. *EBD* is a possible supply curve, showing the quantity of the product Polaroid is willing to make available at various prices. If the firm could get more than $900 for the camera, it would gladly construct a new factory to make quantity *B...D* available. However, at these prices, demand would decline, leaving the firm with surplus inventory. At point *B*, the amount Polaroid is willing to make available just equals the amount the public will purchase. The $900 price at this point is the market price at which the market clears.

3. Although the Yankelovich study findings relate these secondary cultural values to the youth and young adult population segments, they can be assumed to influence all segments of the consumer population; indeed, a focus on the values of youth is another pervasive value characterizing the American culture.

   Given the pervasive influence of these values, it could probably be argued that all the values noted are evidenced, in all the products listed, with some assuming more importance than others. For example:

   • The Club Med concept of back–to–nature vacations in exotic, unspoiled locales might reflect, mainly, values pertaining to less emphasis on possessions, sensuousness, equality of the sexes, anti-bigness, and living for today.

- The *Terminator* concept of the invincible cyborg moving back to the present might reflect values pertaining to physical fitness, mysticism, and less emphasis on possessions.

It can also probably be argued that the stronger the association between a product and dominant cultural values, the more likely this product is to succeed, assuming this association is persuasively communicated in positioning and promoting the product.

4. Again, it can probably be argued that all the demographic trends listed affect all the industries listed, so the task of marketing managers associated with each industry might be to identify the strongest associations, and use these associations to identify target markets and communicate values. For example:

- The travel and leisure industry might benefit mainly from the maturing of the baby-boom generation, which means more people with more money for business and vacation travel, and from more over-65 members of the population, which means more retired people with more time and money for travel.

- The expensive apparel industry might benefit most from more women working, which means more women managers dressing to express their status, and from smaller family units, which means more family discretionary income to purchase expensive apparel.

- The consumer electronics industry might also benefit mainly from higher discretionary incomes to purchase these products, and from the maturing of the baby-boom generation, who represent a strong target market for these products.

5. Following are some ways in which each of the listed political/legal environmental forces might influence each of the listed marketing situations:

- Renting empty office space in Houston: Government social legislation pertaining to energy conservation, which adversely affected the Houston economy, might help explain why the office space is empty; government monetary and fiscal policies, as reflected in new tax legislation, might explain why owning office space in the first place is no longer the desirable writeoff it once was.

- General Electric plans to purchase RCA: Social legislation, pertaining to monopolistic practices in restraint of trade (which also qualifies as legislation relating to marketing) was certainly considered before this merger actually took place.

- Tobacco farmers plan to market a crop: Paradoxically, political/legal forces both help and hinder the marketing efforts of tobacco farmers. Hindering these efforts is social legislation designed to discourage consumption of tobacco products; helping these efforts is the government's relation to the agricultural segment (often resulting from government fiscal and monetary policies), which mandates subsidy supports for this industry.

- Lockheed competes for a large aircraft order: Government legislation relating to marketing might force Lockheed to use different ground rules in competing with foreign aircraft manufacturers for this order (for example, no under the table payments); however, government relationships with individual industries—especially defense industries—provided the massive loan subsidies which make it possible for Lockheed to compete.

4
MARKETING SYSTEMS

KEY TERMS

control subsystem establishes objectives and feedback processes that help marketing managers learn how actual performance compares to standards and how to plan for the future

marketing system a regularly interacting group of entities forming a unified whole. These entities include the organization that is doing the marketing, the product that is being marketed, the target market, marketing intermediaries that facilitate exchanges, and environmental constraints

organizational subsystem provides guidelines for assuring that goals, policies, procedures, status structures, and lines of communication and authority are consistent with the nature, needs, and goals of the organization

planning subsystem provides guidelines for identifying and assessing marketing opportunities and threats, and preparing strategic marketing plans calculated to achieve organizational objectives

synergism the coordinate action of separate elements such that the total effect is greater than the sum of the effects of the individual elements acting independently

In the previous two chapters, we examined the dynamics of the marketing management process, with emphasis on the role of the marketing manager in identifying threats and opportunities in the micro- and macroenvironments, and devising strategic plans to seize opportunities and avoid threats.

In this chapter, we will examine the marketing system, and its component subsystems, through which the marketing manager develops strategic plans and transforms plans into realities.

Again, we will use the Merton Electronics Company as a source of illustrative examples, assuming that the consultant's recommendations for a new consumer products division have been accepted; she has taken over as the first marketing manager for this new division; and she is presently setting up the systems through which she will manage the marketing process.

SYSTEMS THEORY EXPLAINS THE MARKETING PROCESS

According to *Webster's New Collegiate Dictionary*, a system is a "regularly interacting or interdependent group of items forming a unified whole." An automobile engine, for example, is a system of interacting, interdependent items, like fuel pumps and carburators, that work together as a unified whole to generate and transmit power. Characterizing this system is **input** (fuel), a series of **flows** (of fuel, exhaust, etc), and **output** (the power generated). If the system functions efficiently, **synergy** is also generated, defined as "cooperative action of discrete agencies such that the total effect is greater than the sum of effects taken separately."

Similarly, in an efficient marketing system, operating according to marketing concept precepts, all departments interact synergistically to achieve organizational goals by meeting the needs of target customers. In the process, the output of one department becomes input for other departments: sales reports, for example, provide fuel for activities in accounting, marketing research, and advertising/sales promotion departments.

Included in this marketing system are the organization itself, the product being marketed, the target market receiving the marketing mix output, and marketing intermediaries, such as banks, retailers, and transport agencies, which facilitate the flow of exchanges between the marketing organization and its markets.

As illustrated in Figure 4.1, two sets of flows characterize these exchanges: the first set—communications and products—flows between the company and its target markets. For example, a businessman, responding to a direct mail promotion, might purchase a Merton Mini portable computer.

The second set—payments and market information feedback—flows between target markets and the company. The businessman's payment for the Mini, and information he provides on how, where, and why he purchased it, illustrate these flows.

Multiply this single transaction by all the exchanges with target markets generated by Merton's marketing system, and a picture of the complexity of marketing processes and systems begins to emerge. Further complicating this complexity are all the functions, activities, and alternative approaches involved in carrying out marketing plans; differing, often conflicting, objectives these plans seek to achieve; and all the interacting, uncontrollable elements of the macro- and microenvironment these plans must account for.

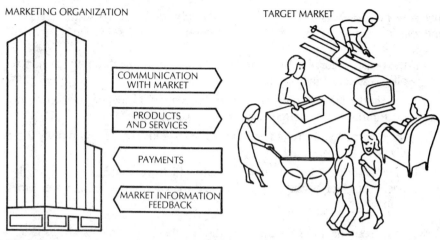

MARKETING ORGANIZATION

TARGET MARKET

COMMUNICATION WITH MARKET

PRODUCTS AND SERVICES

PAYMENTS

MARKET INFORMATION FEEDBACK

Figure 4–1. In the simplest marketing system, the interacting elements—the marketing organization and the target market—are connected by two sets of flows.

YOU SHOULD REMEMBER

A marketing system comprises the organization itself, the product being marketed, the target market, and marketing intermediaries which facilitate exchanges. Like systems in general, marketing systems have inputs, flows, and outputs. Thus, the marketing manager's strategic plans represent **input** into the system, where these **flows** take place:

(1) communication and products between the company and target markets

(2) payments and information between target markets and the company

The **output** of this system are marketing mixes designed to profitably satisfy target market needs. If the system functions efficiently, a **synergism** is created whereby the total effect is greater than the effects of the individual elements acting independently.

SUBSYSTEMS WITHIN THE MARKETING SYSTEM

Amid this complexity, the major job of Merton's new marketing manager was to make a total system of interacting departments and functional activities work together harmoniously to meet target market needs. To do so, her first task in her new position was to design four major subsystems which would comprise the total marketing system for Merton's consumer products division:

(1) the **organizational subsystem**, which would hold together, and harmonize, all the system's interacting elements

(2) the **marketing planning subsystem**, which would identify marketing opportunities and generate customer-oriented strategic plans

(3) the **marketing control subsystem**, which would monitor and modify these plans

(4) the **marketing information subsystem**, which would generate information needed to fuel all the subsystems, and the overall marketing system they comprise

We will examine the first three of these subsystems in this chapter, and devote chapters 5 and 6 to the fourth subsystem.

THE ORGANIZATIONAL SUBSYSTEM INTEGRATES OTHER SUBSYSTEMS

In a modern marketing organization, the organizational subsystem provides a structural framework within which marketing analysis, planning, implementation and control activities are carried out. In small firms, such as a job shop or hardware store, one person performs these functions. Then, as the firm grows larger, the workload is divided into functional activities, such as sales and market research, which are assigned to people who specialize in these activities. If the area to which the person is assigned involves responsibility for generating profits by directing, motivating, and coordinating the activities of other people, it is called a **line** position; Merton's marketing manager, for example, is a line manager.

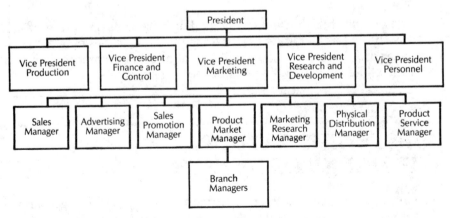

Figure 4–2. Formal line and staff marketing organization.

If the area of responsibility is highly specialized and advisory in nature, with little direct responsibility for profits, it is called a **staff** position. For example, in Figure 4.2 the advertising manager and marketing research manager reporting to the marketing vice president of Merton's industrial products division would both hold staff positions:

As the chief line executive in the industrial products marketing department, Merton's marketing vice president performs two important administrative jobs: he coordinates the work of all marketing personnel reporting to him; and he works with the vice presidents of production, finance and control, research and development, and personnel to integrate and coordinate all company activities and achieve customer-oriented profit goals.

• *ORGANIZATIONAL CHARTS SPELL OUT LINE AND STAFF RESPONSIBILITIES*

A formal organization chart, like the one on page 78, supplemented by job descriptions that spell out duties and responsibilities of all line and staff personnel, is the nerve center of the organizational subsystem. In addition to assigning responsibilities, these documents establish lines of authority and communication through which managers on all levels accomplish their administrative work.

To operate at its synergistic peak, an organizational subsystem should exhibit two important characteristics which preoccupied the new marketing manager as she planned the four subsystems for the consumer products division:

- It should incorporate policies and procedures for effectively selecting, training, directing, motivating, and evaluating line and staff people.

- It should reflect the strategic objectives and approaches of the organization it integrates.

In terms of the strategic objectives and approaches of Merton's industrial products division, the organizational structure depicted above did its job well. Each staff member understood his or her responsibilities and was delegated sufficient authority to fulfill these responsibilities. Activities required to fulfill these responsibilities were clearly defined and specialized in terms of what each staff member, from the newly-hired salesperson to the company president, did best. People were effectively selected, trained, motivated and evaluated.

The organizational structure also worked well from the marketing manager's perspective: There was neither an unmanageably large number of people reporting to him, nor too many layers of authority between his position and the ultimate marketplace. Thus, decisions were usually carried out with efficient dispatch.

From the perspective of the new marketing manager of Merton's consumer products division, however, this structure was not an effective long-range model for generating and carrying out strategic plans.

• *SUCCESSFUL COMPANIES TEND TO*
"THINK SMALL" ORGANIZATIONALLY

The marketing manager of Merton's new industrial products division had just finished reading the Peters/Waterman study[1] of 43 successful firms, many in the high tech environments that would characterize the consumer products division. She noted, in particular, what these successful firms had in common from an organizational viewpoint. For one thing, they tended to think small organizationally. Instead of one centralized authority, as in Merton's industrial products division, authority and responsibility tended to be decentralized and dispersed. Flexibility was important, with temporary task forces forming and reforming to address different problems.

Even relatively permanent components of the organization tended to be lean and simple and designed around a single entity, such as a single product or group of related products. In these small, flexible groups, authority was delegated as low as possible to encourage an entrepreneurial spirit. Communication within and among these groups tended to be informal, roles less specialized, and intragroup competition encouraged and rewarded.

With their emphasis on motivation and innovation, these small, dynamic entrepreneurial groups would permit the new division to adapt quickly to threats and opportunities in the high tech consumer marketplace.

• *GE's SBUs: SMALL BUSINESSES*
WITHIN THE BIG BUSINESS

The model the marketing manager had in mind to achieve the new division's strategic objectives was the Strategic Business Units (SBU) concept pioneered by the General Electric Company. According to this concept, an organizational unit could be built around a single product or business with these characteristics:

- a distinct mission

- outside competitors

- a manager responsible for achieving specific profit objectives

- strategic planning capabilities of the sort discussed in Chapter 2

- operational planning capabilities and control over resources required in operations activities

In terms of this definition, any product, group of related products, or business could qualify as an SBU in Merton's new consumer products division. Even the division's proposed in-house advertising agency would qualify as an SBU: it would have external competition in the form of outside agencies that could create advertising campaigns; it would have a distinct mission (to build markets); it would create strategic advertising plans; and it would have operational capability to implement these plans.

---

1. Thomas J. Peters and Robert H. Waterman, Jr., *In Search of Excellence: Lessons from America's Best-Run Companies* (New York: Harper & Row, 1982)

YOU SHOULD REMEMBER

A modern marketing system encompasses four major independent, but interacting, subsystems: the **marketing organization** subsystem, which integrates all the subsystems; the **marketing planning**
subsystem, which generates goal-oriented plans in response to marketplace threats and opportunities; the **marketing control** subsystem,
which helps keep these plans on track; and the **marketing information** subsystem, which processes the information that fuels all the
subsystems.

The marketing organization subsystem creates a framework for
defining and delegating activities that help achieve the firm's strategic objectives in the face of competitive and other environmental
threats. One model for such a structure, the Strategic Business Unit
(SBU), has many of the organizational characteristics of successful
firms described in the Peters/Waterman study, *In Search of Excellence.* Unlike more traditional organizational structures, with their
centralized authority and clearly defined responsibilities and lines
of authority, SBUs are smaller and more decentralized, with areas
of authority and responsibility much less clearly defined and delin-
eated. Presumably, even in large organizations like General Electric,
such a structure facilitates quicker recognition of and response to
marketplace threats and opportunities.

THE PLANNING SUBSYSTEM HELPS
DEFINE AND EXPLOIT OPPORTUNITIES

In firms which make and market a variety of products in highly competitive
markets, marketing planning subsystems perform two important jobs:

1. They continually and systematically monitor the firm's products, businesses,
   and environments, identifying new opportunities, nurturing worthwhile existing opportunities, and phasing out those in a state of decline.

2. They assist in the development of detailed product-price-place-promotion
   marketing mixes, and assist in the development and documentation of formal marketing plans and programs.

• *IDENTIFYING PRODUCT AND*
BUSINESS OPPORTUNITIES

At Merton, the marketing planning subsystem in place in the industrial division
focused on Return on Investment (ROI) as the main criterion for assessing new

and existing opportunities. Using this approach, anticipated net profits on sales was divided by total assets (including cash, inventory, receivables and fixed assets) required to generate these net profits. To illustrate:

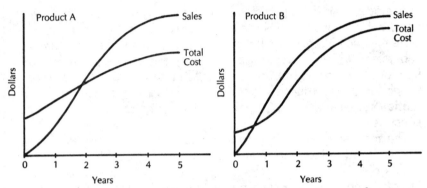

Figure 4–3. Expected sales and cost curves of two strategies over five-year planning periods.

In this exhibit, total costs and revenues involved in developing a new product are projected to the time when the product returns a profit. Note that, in this example, product *A* doesn't return a profit until year two, a reflection of the huge asset investment needed to make and market this product. Product *B*, on the other hand, begins to generate a profit after six months. After five years, however, product *A* is much more profitable than *B*.

In evaluating opportunities, management in Merton's industrial products division tended to adopt a conservative philosophy, favoring product or business opportunities like *B*, which generated fast, if not necessarily large profits.

From the perspective of the new consumer products marketing manager, however, this ROI approach to assessing opportunities would hardly suffice.

Specifically, she felt that, in placing so much emphasis on profit return for deciding among alternatives and allocating resources, the ROI approach put too much pressure on managers to think in terms of short-run results, and to overlook other important criteria for allocating resources to meet customer needs. For example, it would probably take Merton's showcase product, the Mini PC, at least three years to return a profit, and some *un*profitable products might be deliberately introduced by the consumer products division to enhance the profitability of products like the Mini. A line of unprofitable, low-priced software programs, packaged with each Mini purchase, might dramatically increase Mini sales.

GE's STRATEGIC PLANNING GRID
HELPS ASSESS MARKET OPPORTUNITIES

In building a marketing planning subsystem that would avoid the shortcomings of the ROI criterion, the marketing manager again looked to the General Electric Company, and to that firm's Strategic Business Planning Grid:

Business Strength

		Strong	Average	Weak
Industry Attractiveness	High	G	G	Y
	Medium	G	Y	R
	Low	Y	R	R

Figure 4–4. General Electric's strategic business-planning grid.

This grid provides a framework for analyzing a prospective new product or business opportunity in terms of the attractiveness of the industry of which it is a part, and the business strengths of the firm assessing the opportunity.

Green light opportunities, in the *G* boxes in the grid, indicate an invest and grow planning strategy. Yellow light opportunities, in the *Y* boxes, indicate a cautious planning strategy: In the case of a new product like the Mini, weaknesses should be strengthened before the product is launched; with an existing product, the present level of investment should be retained, without committing additional resources.

Red light opportunities, in the *R* boxes, indicate no go strategies: *don't* launch proposed new products; harvest or divest existing products.

To illustrate how this grid is used to assess opportunities, here are key conclusions from the marketing manager's analysis of the Mini as a potential product launch.

Industry Attractiveness:

• Market size was large.

• Market growth rate was among the highest of all technology fields.

• Profit margin potential was high.

• Competitive intensity was weaker than in many more mature technological fields, due largely to the relative newness of the miniaturized personal computer technology.

• Cyclicity and seasonality were weaker factors than in other industries, since they had little to do with the reasons people purchased personal computers.

• The technological role in developing and manufacturing the product was high.

- Macroenvironmental constraints were not as significant a factor as in other industries.

Unlike the industry attractiveness analysis of the Strategic Business Planning Grid, the business strengths analysis revealed weaknesses which would have to be addressed before the Mini was launched.

Business Strengths:

- Relative market share: Weak. Merton's consumer goods division products would start from a position of zero market share, a powerful disadvantage.

- Price competitiveness: Strong. Merton mass-produced many of the components in the Mini, producing economics of scale which would permit a low, market penetration pricing strategy.

- Product quality: Strong. This had traditionally represented Merton's main competitive edge.

- Market/consumer knowledge: Weak. Merton had no experience in the consumer market.

- Sales effectiveness: Weak. Merton's sales force, admirably knowledgeable in the industrial market, had no experience in the consumer market.

- Geography: Weak. Merton had no distribution network to cover the huge market envisioned for the Mini.

BCG's GROWTH-SHARE GRID SHOWS PRODUCT RELATIONSHIPS

In addition to GE's strategic business planning grid, the marketing manager also incorporated the Boston Consulting Group's (BCG) Growth-Share Grid into the planning subsystem. This grid focused on portfolios of products and the relationships among them.

Using the BCG Grid, all company products and businesses are classified according to their positions on two axes: a horizontal axis labelled "relative market share," and a vertical axis labelled "market growth rate."

Relative market share is measured relative to that of the firm's nearest competitor. For example, a product with 50 percent of a market would be at the far left (10x) if its main competitor had only a 5 percent share of this market. This was the first year's position the marketing manager anticipated for the Mini, since she didn't anticipate much competition for at least a year. She also anticipated a market growth rate of at least 20 percent this first year, so the Mini would be positioned in the "high high" upper left quadrant of the grid.

Products in this high high quadrant, called **stars**, typically require considerable cash to finance their rapid growth. As in the case of the Mini, this cash requirement is frequently in excess of the revenues the product will generate.

Key sources of this cash are products, called **cash cows**, which occupy the lower left-hand quadrant. Although their market isn't growing at nearly the rate of the stars, these products occupy a strong leadership position which leads to

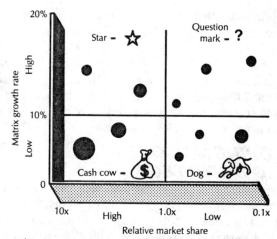

Figure 4–5. The BCG growth-share matrix.

positive profits and cash flows. The marketing manager envisioned that the Mini would be a cash cow within five years, ready to subsidize other consumer division products. Meanwhile, cash cows would have to be found among industrial division products to subsidize the Mini and other consumer division products.

The marketing manager could also envision that, as more and more products were introduced into consumer markets, some would achieve **question mark** status (low relative market share in a high market growth rate industry), and some **dogs** (low share, low growth rate) would never succeed. The strategic planning task was to avoid, or dispatch, the dogs, while making the correct decisions as to which question marks were potential stars, and should be nurtured.

In the context of product portfolio interrelationships on the BCG Grid, marketing managers have four strategic planning options:

1. Build market shares, often foregoing short-term earnings in the process. This strategy is usually appropriate for stars and for question marks that must grow if they are to become stars.

2. Hold existing market share. This strategy is appropriate for strong cash cows which must continue to yield a positive cash flow.

3. Harvest short-term cash flow, regardless of long-term consequences. This strategy, involving sharp reduction of expenses to increase profit return, might be appropriate for weak cash cows or question marks about to slide into the dog quadrant.

4. Divest the product because resources invested in it can be employed more productively elsewhere. This strategy is appropriate for dogs and for question marks that the firm cannot afford to finance.

By depicting threats and opportunities in terms of competitive situations facing individual products, and interrelationships among all products in the firm's portfolio, the BCG grid would help Merton's new marketing manager make build, hold, harvest, and divest decisions as more and more products came on-line.

In using the GE and BCG grid approaches, the marketing manager also recognized their limitations. Essentially, they aid decision making; they don't replace the managerial judgments required to make decisions. Thus, decisions as to what strategic goals best suited the firm's situation, or what constituted an optimal portfolio, or which criteria best defined an SBU or attractive industry, still had to be made by management.

• DEVELOPING MARKETING MIXES AND STRATEGIES

The second important task of the planning subsystem, after assisting in the strategic planning process by helping to identify and define threats and opportunities, is to provide a framework for preparing formal marketing plans. In the diversified firm that Merton is becoming, plans might be written for all products, product lines, brands, and markets, with product or brand plans generally containing the following sections.

EXECUTIVE SUMMARY

This section includes a short summary of the main goals and recommendations contained in the overall plan and gives top management an overview understanding of the plan's thrust and scope. In the Executive Summary for the Merton Mini plan, for example, first-year market share goals were summarized, as were recommended marketing mix activities needed to create this market share; costs, revenues, and expected losses anticipated; and key dates leading up to the product launch.

CURRENT MARKETING SITUATION

This first major plan section describes the current situation with respect to target markets, competition for share of these markets, and company plans to counter this competition. In the Mini plan, this section focused on:

- large, growing business and professional market segments, with geographic, demographic, and lifestyle characteristics of each segment

- features and benefits of the Mini as they related to target market needs

- the general lack of activity by other firms competing for shares in business and professional target markets

- planned strategies and tactics for distributing Minis to markets

THREATS AND OPPORTUNITIES

This section, which summarized key conclusions deriving from the marketing manager's analysis of macro- and microenvironmental factors affecting the success of the Mini, forced management to focus on long-range consideration, rather than on current costs and problems. For example, the strong threat of competition from American and Japanese computer manufacturers who were developing minis of their own suggested a near-term launch of the Merton Mini to take full advantage of opportunities represented by unsatisfied target market needs.

To put both threats and opportunities into perspective, this section of the report analyzed each in terms of potential for harm or good, and likelihood of occurrence, according to the matrix in Figure 4.6.

On the matrix, the threat of a Japanese firm introducing a competitor for the Mini within a year was shown at point 1 as having a low likelihood and a potentially severe consequence. The opportunity represented by the government purchasing huge quantities of the Mini for the defense program was shown at point 2, as being extremely probable and profitable.

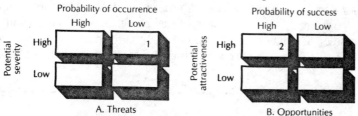

Figure 4–6. Threats and Opportunities.

OBJECTIVES AND ISSUES

This section spelled out long- and short-range objectives the Mini launch was designed to achieve in such areas as sales, costs, revenues, and profit return. In writing this section, the marketing manager made sure to state objectives specifically, explain how they derived from the situation analysis, and schedule them over long- and short-range periods. Also covered were issues that could have a positive or negative impact on achieving objectives. For example, positive profit objectives beginning in year three might never arrive if the threat of competition materialized faster than anticipated.

MARKETING STRATEGIES

This section focused on specific marketing mix strategies for each defined target market designed to achieve long- and short-range objectives. For example, in marketing minis to the government market, greater emphasis would be placed on the price element of the mix, in contrast to marketing to the business and professional segment, where product features and promotion would be emphasized. Also discussed was how each marketing mix strategy responded to threats and opportunities identified in earlier sections of the report.

ACTION PROGRAMS

This section presented a comprehensive schedule of activities, in table form, that would be undertaken during the year covered by the plan, and indicated when they would be performed, and by whom. For example, specific promotional programs would be initiated at different times to encourage distributors to carry the Mini, and to encourage end users to buy the Mini. Provision was also made for changing these action programs as new problems and opportunities arose.

BUDGETS

This section specified revenues anticipated from sales of Minis, and all costs, including production, physical distribution, and marketing, anticipated in generating these sales. The difference between the two figures was the net profit figure which, in the case of the Mini, would not be on the plus side of the profit and loss ledger until year three.

This section also listed other budgeted outcomes in the event that certain threats or opportunities did or did not materialize.

CONTROLS

This final section lists controls used to monitor progress. Goals and budgets were outlined for each month or quarter, with the understanding that the marketing manager would have to take action when actual results deviated significantly from planned results. The nature and scope of the control process are spelled out more specifically in the next section of this chapter, describing the control subsystem.

YOU SHOULD REMEMBER

Both GE's Strategic Business Planning Grid (SBPG), and the Boston Consulting Group's (BCG) Growth-Share Grid, illustrate components of the marketing planning subsystem designed to assess product or business ventures, and develop strategic plans consistent with these assessments. Both grids base their assessments on multiple criteria, as against the Return on Investment (ROI) single criterion approach. In the case of the BCG Grid, assessment criteria pertain to market growth and relative market share; in the case of the SBPG, to industry attractiveness and company strengths. A key difference between the two grid approaches is the portfolio focus of the BCG grid, which categorizes individual products as dogs, stars, cash cows, and question marks in the context of other products so categorized. Typical strategies resulting from single or multiple criteria assessments are build, hold, harvest, and divest. As part of its role, the planning subsystem also generates formal marketing plans incorporating these strategies.

THE CONTROL SUBSYSTEM KEEPS PLANS ON TRACK

Having decided how organizational and planning subsystems would be structured, the marketing manager next turned her attention to the **control subsystem** within the consumer division's total marketing system.

Simply stated, control means that some kind of action is taken to assure that performance meets expectations. Implicit in this definition is the notion that a standard has been established—the expectation—and procedures are in place for measuring the extent to which performance actually meets this standard, such as sales analysis figures. Also implicit is the notion that appropriate actions will be taken if performance doesn't match the standard. For example, if revenues for the Mini fall 10 percent short of budgeted expectations, the marketing manager will probably do something about it, such as improving marketing programs or, perhaps, just lowering the standard for the next period. She will also do something if revenues *exceed* expectations by 10 percent, such as taking measures to see that it keeps happening.

Marketing standards assume a variety of forms, including a salesman's quota, the value of an average sale, the budget for an entire company, or the average profit margin achieved by an entire industry.

To assure that her managers take these goals seriously, the marketing manager planned a "goals down, plans up" approach which would directly involve these managers in the budget building process.

In the case of the Merton Mini, the budgets the marketing manager planned would also serve as goals for each product and department in the consumer products division. To establish the marketing budget for the Mini, the marketing manager would first forecast sales revenues for each year, using approaches covered in Chapter 11. She would then determine desired profit for the year, and leave it largely to her sales, advertising, sales promotion, and marketing research managers to create plans for achieving these target profits.

In addition to the overall budget for the marketing department, budgets were prepared for individual consumer division products and territories. Even the efforts of individual salespeople were budgeted, with each one assigned sales and profit goals, and costs required to achieve these goals. When the overall budget for the marketing department was combined with budgets for all other Merton departments, it became the overall company budget.

Performance analysis techniques would be used to monitor revenues and costs each month and each quarter, and match these figures with budgeted figures to pinpoint significant deviations from budgeted expectations.

In situations where performance and expectations didn't match, the appropriate manager would be expected to act. For example, if feedback sales analysis shows that revenues on the Mini were only $2,000,000 instead of $2,500,000, and sales costs were $600,000 instead of an anticipated $500,000, the sales manager would be called on to justify these figures to the marketing manager who, in turn, would have to justify them to Merton's president and Board of Directors.

Whatever the justification, some kind of action would be required by the marketing manager to retain control over the marketing effort in the next period. If unanticipated uncontrollables were the obvious cause, budgeted figures would be lowered for the next period. If controllable factors explain the difference, actions would be taken to eliminate their influence. For example, sales training and motivation programs might be improved.

YOU SHOULD REMEMBER

The **control subsystem** establishes goals to be achieved by the marketing system and feedback mechanisms or checkpoints to measure progress toward these goals. The formal document that expresses these goals and facilitates comparison of performance with these goals is the budget, which also helps to coordinate and motivate staff members. Actual control takes place when performance deviates significantly from budgeted expectations, and some kind of action is taken to account for this deviation in future planning.

KNOW THE CONCEPTS
DO YOU KNOW THE BASICS?

1. Explain how the adoption of the marketing concept relates to the view of a modern organization as a total system.

2. How does a family planning a vacation trip to the shore operate as a system, with input, flows, output, and controls?

3. A salesman of telecommunications equipment is planning his daily presentations to prospective customers. Would this individual qualify as a marketing system? Why?

4. Assume the efforts of the salesman in question 3 are supported by a comprehensive promotional program which includes inside telephone salespeople generating leads, advertising in business magazines, and direct mail to selected prospects. Would this qualify as a marketing system? How does it illustrate synergy?

5. Distinguish between a traditional line and staff organizational structure and the more fluid, flexible SBU organizational model which characterizes many modern consumer-oriented firms.

6. A management consultant claims that an effective manager sees to it that subordinates perform jobs that are logically related to each other (specialization); sees to it that these jobs test the best abilities of these staff members (highest action); delegates to others responsibility and authority to perform jobs that don't test the manager's best abilities (delegation); and only gets involved in the activities of subordinates when they can't

carry out a job or solve a problem themselves (management by exception). How does a traditional line/staff, organizational model help bring out these characteristics?

7. From the customer's perspective, what are the advantages of the SBU model over the traditional line/staff model, where authority and responsibility are more centralized?

8. Distinguish between GE's strategic business planning grid and the Boston Consulting Group's growth share matrix as tools for identifying opportunities. Under what product/market conditions would a marketing manager be most likely to use each approach? What drawbacks do they have in common?

9. Distinguish between the Return on Investment and the grid approaches for identifying business opportunities. Which would be more appropriate in the following situations:
   (a) General Dynamics, one of the largest defense subcontractors, is preparing to bid on a government missile system contract.
   (b) The Knox Gelatine Company is considering the possibility of entering the chocolate breakfast drink market.

10. Using professional sports as an illustrative example, apply the growth share matrix to identify a star, cash cow, question mark, and dog. Do other parallels exist between this sports team and a typical consumer-oriented business in respect to the function of each?

11. Define the control process in terms of a student planning for an A in a marketing course.

TERMS FOR STUDY

authority	product portfolio
budgets	question marks
build strategy	red light opportunity
cash cow	relative market share
control	responsibility
decentralization	return on investment (ROI)
delegation	sales response function
dog	specialization
green light opportunity	star
growth share grid	strategic business unit (SBU)
hold strategy	strategic planning grid
organization	synergy
planning	yellow light opportunity

PRACTICAL APPLICATION

1. With divestiture legislation passed, the president of AT&T announced that this telecommunications giant would become "a marketing company." Speculate on how and why the systems concept might help AT&T achieve this status.

2. The Sony Corporation faced these product/market situations:

   • The SONY BetaMax videocassette players, once the leader, were losing market share at an accelerating rate to VCR hardware and prerecorded tapes marketed by RCA, GE, and most other manufacturers in the field.

   • The original SONY Walkman, introduced seven years earlier, was still a highly profitable product, in spite of competitive pressures which forced the price of the Walkman down to $39 in some markets, where competitive versions of these lightweight cassette players were selling for up to 40 percent less.

   • An innovative new version of the Walkman, smaller, with a new earphone concept and vastly improved sound quality, was selling extremely well in selected markets, at a price of $100. The Sony Watchman, a personal handheld or vest-pocket black and white TV priced to sell at $200, but heavily discounted in many areas, and with "big picture" brightness and luminance on its two-inch screen, was not doing as well as anticipated, in spite of a general lack of competition.

   Using the BCG Growth Share Matrix as your model, position each of these products as either a dog, star, question mark, or cash cow, and recommend a marketing program strategy based on the interrelationship among them.

3. Speculate on the role of marketing systems in each of the following product/market situations, and explain which of the four flows would be most important in each situation:

   • Quaker Oats wants to increase sales for Gatorade. Presently, 85 percent of the purchases of the thirst quencher are made by heavy users, mostly in Sunbelt states during the summer months.

   • The Henry Ortleib brewing company has three profitable years in a row, in spite of competition from the likes of Miller and Budweiser beer in a field which has dwindled from 125 breweries to 45 in 25 years. The Philadelphia brewer advertises its beer as "more full-bodied... maltier..."

4. Show how GE's Strategic Planning Grid might help marketing management arrive at go-or-no product launch decisions in the following situations:

- Kodak, a leader in the photography field, contemplates bringing out another format to compete with the RCA VCR and the Sony Betamax in the videocassette player field. This new format would be a smaller width tape better suited for home movies on TV screen showing.

- Levi Strauss contemplates broadening distribution of its jeans to include large chains like J.C. Penny and Sears to reduce reliance on jean specialty stores and upscale department stores. Consideration is also being given to discount and off-price outlets.

5. In each of these situations, would a BCG matrix help? How?

6. Evaluate the consultant's recommendation to launch the Executive Learning Institute (Chapter 2) in terms of the Strategic Planning Grid dimensions.

ANSWERS
KNOW THE BASICS

1. The marketing concept is based on the notion that profits result when a firm identifies and satisfies needs of target markets more efficiently and effectively than its competitors. The total systems concept is based on the notion that the marketing concept works most efficiently and effectively to identify target markets and develop marketing mixes to satisfy these markets through the synergistic interaction of subsystem components for organizing, planning, controlling and informing the marketing effort.

2. As an example, the input might be the plan for the trip, including assigned activities and items (beach chairs, insect repellent, clothing, food, etc.) to be purchased or brought along. This plan might trigger a series of flows, as each family member performs scheduled activities to get the trip underway and does what he or she does best during the vacation itself. The synergistic output would be a vacation in which each person has a better time than he or she would have had alone. The control aspect would focus on reasons why the actual vacation didn't live up to expectations, which would be programmed into next year's planning.

3. Yes. Input into this system would include the information the salesman absorbs from such sources as past call reports, sales analysis figures, and

customer complaints. Flows would be the two-way communication between the salesman and his customers and prospects, based largely on his appraisal of information received, and the plan he devises for relating his products to customer/prospect needs. Output would be the sales and profits generated, and new information cycled back into the system, which will help him plan next month's calls.

4. The promotional program supporting the salesman's efforts would qualify as a system in that input is needed to plan a well-integrated promotional campaign, with direct mail, media advertising, and the efforts of inside salesman all planned and timed to support the efforts of the outside salesman. Synergy means that the combined impact of these coordinated elements—in terms of such outputs as sales and profits—would be considerably greater than if each element was acting independently of the others.

5. The traditional line and staff structure can be envisioned as a single, centralized structure, with a number of layers of authority (middle managers, supervisors, etc.) between the uppermost layer, and the layer closest to the customers. Clearly defined lines of authority mean that each individual knows his or her responsibilities, and to whom he or she reports. Tasks are specialized in terms of what each individual does best, and communication routes are relatively fixed. The SBU organizational model, on the other hand, can be envisioned as many smaller structures, each organized around a single product, business, or group of related products. Managers atop each of these structures are much closer to the market, and individual authority and responsibilities, along with communication flows, are much less formally defined: people are likely to be involved in many different activities, often with members of other SBUs. As compared to the more traditional structures, these SBUs can frequently respond faster to marketplace problems and opportunities, and reform or regroup to address these problems and opportunities.

6. By its very nature, a traditional line and staff organizational structure facilitates these attributes of an effective manager. With each person doing what he or she does best (specialization), with sufficient responsibility and authority assigned to carry out these tasks (delegation), each member of the organization will presumably be operating at his or her level of highest action. With a group of able people all doing their best work in a supportive environment, the manager doesn't have to get involved in all the activities going on below, and can step in only when results fall short of expectations, or an exceptional problem arises which only the manager can solve (management by exception).

7. In the typical SBU organizational format, many smaller structures, each organized around a single product, business, or product group, usually means that SBU personnel are closer to the marketplace. Along with the flexibility and looser communication lines characterizing the typical SBU

model, the result is greater attention to marketplace needs than typically results with fixed, formal, traditional line/staff models. In addition to this faster response to changing customer needs, built-in competition among SBUs frequently means that customer needs are served more effectively and economically.

8. The General Electric Strategic Business Planning Grid focuses on a single product/market opportunity, identifying red, yellow, and green light opportunities in terms of the relative attractiveness of the market, and the extent to which the company has the resources and expertise to successfully penetrate this market. The Boston Consulting Group (BCG) model, on the other hand, substitutes two success factors—relative market share and market growth rate—for the diversity of success factors comprising the GE grid. An even more compelling difference between the two models is the BCG's emphasis on a portfolio of product/market opportunities, categorized as stars, cash cows, dogs, and question marks, and the interrelationships among them. Thus, for example, a green light opportunity on the GE matrix might be a question mark on the BCG matrix in terms of its relationship with all the other products comprising the firm's portfolio. Both approaches present potential drawbacks in that their defining criteria (relative market attractiveness or growth rate, etc.) are, in themselves, defined by fallible human judgment, and the models are often used to replace human judgment.

9. The Return of Investment (ROI) approach applies a single criterion for assessing the attractiveness of a product/market opportunity: the discounted dollar value of the cash stream produced by the opportunity over a certain period of time. As such, ROI is useful for comparing the relative attractiveness of alternative investments, indicating at what point each will produce a profit, and the size of this profit. The two grid approaches use a variety of criteria to evaluate the relative attractiveness of a product/ market opportunity. In the case of General Dynamics, where most of the variables comprising the GE and BCG grid approaches are known to be favorable (since, typically, General Dynamics has a monopoly situation for certain government contracted products), these grid approaches can be bypassed in terms of a simple ROI calculation. In the case of Knox Gelatine, entering a risky, relatively unfamiliar marketplace, all of the factors in the GE and BCG grid defining Knox strengths, industry attractiveness, and the influence on other products of Knox's entering this market might appropriately be used to assess this opportunity.

10. Using professional baseball to illustrate an application for the BCG matrix, a star might be the team that surprisingly wins the World Series, setting off speculation that it will continue to win in subsequent years. The cash cow is the team that, year in and year out, draws huge crowds and helps (through shared television and gate receipts) to subsidize all the other teams in the league, although it may not win more pennants or world

championships than the others. The dog is the team that hasn't won a pennant in 40 years, draws poorly at the gate, and continues to sell off its best players to the stars and cash cows. The question mark is the team that just moved to a new city where it may achieve stardom or dogdom.

Note: Two interesting assignments could be based on this situation:

1. Assign team names to each category above.
2. Make the same kind of analysis for the *members* of one of these teams.

Since professional baseball is a consumer-oriented business, there are very strong parallels between this sport and other consumer-oriented businesses. All can use the BCG matrix to define products (i.e., teams) in their portfolio, plan future acquisitions based on the relationships among these products, and take necessary steps to change a product's status (for example, get rid of dogs by encouraging them to relocate, and clarify the status of the question marks).

11. As noted in this chapter, control implies that a goal, or standard, has been established; that progress toward this goal or standard can be monitored and measured; and that appropriate action is taken when progress falls short of expectations. In the case of this student, the "A" would be the goal; progress toward this goal might be monitored and measured by the marks he or she receives on exams or class projects; and the appropriate action might be to study harder when these marks indicate an "A" will not be forthcoming under his or her present rate of progress.

PRACTICAL APPLICATION

1. A key difference in AT&T's status before and after divestiture has to do with its competitive situation. Before divestiture, as a regulated utility, it had achieved monopoly status, with captive markets, virtually guaranteed profits, and practically no competition. With divestiture, these comfortable conditions no longer exist. AT&T must now identify, define, and satisfy new customers for its diverse products and services in an intense competitive climate that is encouraged, and even subsidized, by the government. In this climate, the firm will certainly require a sophisticated marketing information system to identify marketplace opportunities and competitive threats; a planning system to make productive use of this information in evolving marketing goals, strategies and tactics; a control system to monitor and measure the progress of planned activities toward achieving goals; and an organization subsystem to help assure that AT&T's structure remains attuned to marketplace wants and needs, and can respond quickly to competitive initiatives.

2. Defined in terms of the two dimensions of the BCG Growth Share Matrix, the four SONY products described seem to fall into the following quadrants:

- The BetaMax videocassette players were probably question marks, descending rapidly toward "dog" status.

- The old Walkman was probably a cash cow, maintaining its leader status, large share of market, and profitability associated with these conditions.

- The new Walkman was probably a star, with sales and profits growing rapidly in selected markets which it dominated.

- The Watchman was probably a question mark that could achieve either dog or star status, and bore close watching.

A marketing program strategy, encompassing strategic plans for each product, might encompass strategies to phase out the BetaMax, milking it for any remaining profits in the process; building up sales and profits on the new Walkman with profits from the old Walkman, and funds that had previously been used to support the BetaMax. These surplus funds might also be used to help the Watchman achieve star status.

3. Following are possible market system roles and dominant flows in each product/market situation:

- Increasing Gatorade sales: Marketing system roles would probably entail setting up and staffing an organization to market the new product (organizational system); developing profiles of other target market groups, in addition to heavy-user Sunbelt group (marketing information system); developing marketing plans to penetrate profitably these new target markets (marketing planning system); and monitoring, measuring, and, if needed, modifying plans when actual performance deviates from expectations (control system). Flows emphasized would probably be market information feedback flow to identify and define new target markets and communication-with-market flow to sell Gatorade in these markets.

- Ortleib Brewing Company thrives: Ortleib's profitability, which seems to derive from effective positioning and promotion in a highly competitive dwindling market, suggests an effective marketing information system to identify and define target market needs, an effective marketing planning system to persuasively convey its promotional message, and an effective control system to keep the plan on track. Flows emphasized would probably be the market information feedback flow to generate information on market needs and products and services flow to keep delivering its popular product.

4. Kodak, after applying Strategic Planning Grid (SPG) criteria to its proposed product entry in the videocassette player field, might opt for a "Go" strategy based on the following conclusions:

Industry attractiveness: The videocassette home movie field is profitable, fast growing, generally unencumbered by macroeconomic constraints, technologically advanced, and not overly subject to seasonal and cyclic constraints—all positive signs. The only strong negative is its competitive intensity.

Business strengths: Through our dominance of the photography market, we begin with a strong relative market share, to which are added these plusses: excellent geographical market coverage and sales effectiveness; strong quality control and market/consumer knowledge. Against these plusses, the major negative might be an inability to compete on price against Japanese imports.

• Levi Strauss, after applying SPG criteria, might also arrive at a "Go" decision, in spite of possible industry attractiveness drawbacks (smaller profit margins and seasonal constraints) and business strength negatives (unfamiliarity with discount and off-price distribution outlets might limit Strauss' sales effectiveness and ability to compete on price).

5. The BCG Growth-Share Matrix (GSM) would probably help in both of these situations by indicating the relationship between the proposed new product venture and other products in each firm's portfolio. In the Kodak case, for example, a GSM analysis might indicate an insufficient number of cash to finance this prospective new "star"; in the Strauss case, it might show that a successful star here will have the effect of converting some promising question marks into dogs (or, maybe, stars).

6. In terms of the two dimensions of GE's Strategic Planning Grid, the recommendation to launch the Executive Learning Institute (ELI) was conceptually similar to the decision, in this chapter, to launch the Merton Mini. In both situations, the Industry Attractiveness dimension was highly favorable; for example, as Porter's analysis (page 32) indicates, the market was large and expandable, with few macroeconomic constraints, little anticipated competition, and huge profit potential. However, as with the Mini, company strengths were lacking; at the outset, for example, ELI had no share of this new market, and generally lacked market knowledge and distribution facilities. As with the Mini, these weaknesses highlighted areas of managerial concern.

5
MARKETING INFORMATION SYSTEMS AND MARKETING RESEARCH

KEY TERMS

marketing information system a continuous and interacting structure of people, equipment, and procedures to gather, sort, evaluate, and distribute pertinent, timely, and accurate information for use by marketing decision makers to improve marketing planning, execution, and control

marketing research the systematic design, collection, analysis, and reporting of data and findings regarding a specific marketing situation facing a company

---

In Chapter 4, we focused on the efforts of Merton's consumer products division's marketing manager to establish a total system of people and processes for making and marketing a line of consumer electronic products, spearheaded by the Merton Mini personal computer.

This total marketing system had four interrelated subsystems: a planning subsystem, an organizational subsystem, a control subsystem, and a marketing information subsystem. The first three of these subsystems were discussed in Chapter 4.

THE MARKETING INFORMATION SYSTEM FUELS OTHER SYSTEMS

Now, the marketing manager turned her attentions to the fourth subsystem, a marketing information subsystem to gather and interpret information from both within and outside the organization. Properly processed, this information would help managers solve problems and make better decisions during all stages of the strategic marketing planning process: it would help managers make better plans to match marketing mixes with target market opportunities, develop more productive organizations to activate and motivate people in carrying out these plans, and provide performance review information for exercising control when performance didn't match expectations.

WHAT AN MIS IS AND DOES

A marketing information system is:

> A continuous and interacting structure of people, equipment and procedures to gather, sort, evaluate and distribute pertinent, timely, and accurate information for use by marketing decision makers to improve marketing planning, execution and control.

Figure 5.1 shows the MIS envisioned by the marketing manager. To see how the various parts of this system might interact to fuel Merton's strategic planning effort, assume that the marketing manager, occupying *Box 1,* needs information about the best way to position and promote the Mini to the engineering market segment.

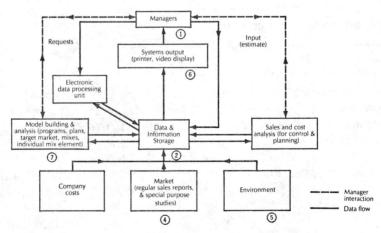

Figure 5–1. MIS as envisioned by the marketing manager.

From *Box 4* (Market) comes information which profiles this market in terms of pertinent demographic and psychographic characteristics: jobs held, income, career goals, continuing education requirements, and so on.

From *Box 5* (Environment) comes information on competitive offerings, new technologies affecting the engineering profession, and the effect of anticipated economic changes on professional spending patterns.

Data from these sources are pulled together, focused, and transformed into information in *Box 2* (Data and Information). This information is then presented in printout form by *Box 6* (Systems Output).

If the marketing manager needs additional information not available from the data and information storage complex, she might commission a special purpose study from this complex, or from *Box 7* (Model Building and Analysis). For example, she might commission a marketing research study to estimate the effect on sales of different prices for the Mini.

Information provided by Merton's MIS would be incorporated into all the strategic marketing plans that make up the marketing program for the consumer products division. Then, as each planned campaign progresses toward projected goals, information is fed back into the MIS for present and future use. For example, feedback on sales, cost, and profit performance would be compared to budgeted standards as a means of controlling campaign performance. This same information might later be used in the preparation of new marketing campaigns.

BUILDING THE MIS DATA BASE

To help assure that the consumer division's MIS would fulfill company needs, her own needs, and needs of managers reporting to her, the marketing manager first designed and distributed a questionnaire to her managers covering these areas:

- types of decisions each manager regularly made

- types of information required to make these decisions

- types of information that each regularly received

- types of special studies each periodically requested

- types of information each would *like* but didn't have

- frequency requirement for each type of information (daily? weekly? monthly? yearly?)

- publications or trade reports each would like to receive on a regular basis

- specific topics each would like to be kept informed of

- types of data analysis programs each would like made available

Responses to the questionnaire from her managers were first edited to eliminate duplicate or irrelevant information, then integrated into a data base to effectively serve each manager's needs as well as overall organizational and departmental needs. In general, information for each manager pertained to the planning, organizing, implementing, and controlling activities that characterized the marketing system as a whole. The sales manager, for example, needed information to plan the most efficient allocation of resources—human and otherwise—to enhance the profitability of Merton's consumer division sales force. To accomplish this, his primary need was for information pinpointing the relative profitability of consumer division products, territories, target markets, and salespeople. With this information, he could direct and control the consumer division sales force to bring together profitable products and high-potential customers in high-potential territories.

Similarly, the advertising manager received information that would help plan, implement, and control productive promotion campaigns to support the sales force; the various product managers, information that would help them plan, organize, implement, and control marketing strategies for their product groups; and the marketing manager, information that would help her recognize worthwhile marketplace opportunities, develop productive marketing programs, and monitor the performance of her other managers in carrying out these programs.

The role of the marketing research manager in this information scheme was to generate and distribute the information required by other managers to solve problems and make better decisions. In this role, he contributed a knowledge of marketing research approaches and techniques, while the marketing manager contributed a general understanding of marketing research approaches and limitations, and the ability to interpret, evaluate, and act on marketing research findings and conclusions.

The remainder of this chapter, and all of Chapter 6, will explore the nature and scope of this partnership between marketing managers and the marketing research manager.

YOU SHOULD REMEMBER

The marketing information subsystem gathers and manages data from internal and external environments to fuel the three other subsystems comprising the marketing system (planning, organization, control), and help marketing managers make better, faster and less risky decisions during all stages of the planning process. Building a typical MIS begins with summaries of the information needs of individual marketing managers, from which emerges an integrated system for gathering, sorting, evaluating and distributing this information. An important role of the marketing research manager is to relate the capabilities of the MIS to the needs of individual marketing managers.

THE MARKETING RESEARCH PROCESS: SYSTEMATIC PROBLEM SOLVING

In the remainder of this chapter, we describe the marketing research process, defined as "the systematic design, collection, analysis and reporting of data and findings regarding specific marketing problems and situations facing a company."

Although the marketing research process and marketing information systems have the common objective of improving managerial decisions, there are significant differences between the two. The marketing research process tends to operate on a project-to-project basis, rather than continuously; and to focus on solving problems rather than on preventing them. Beyond these differences, however, both systems work closely together to facilitate the marketing research process in a broad range of applications.

APPLICATIONS FOR MARKETING RESEARCH

Table 5.1 from a survey of marketing research activities of 599 companies by the American Marketing Association, shows that most of these activities occur in the following areas: advertising research, business economics and corporate responsibility research, product research, and sales/marketing research. Following are examples of marketing research studies in these areas carried out at the Merton Company:

- **Advertising Research** studies were used to define needs that could be fulfilled by consumer electronics products, test the effectiveness of various promotional appeals and media channels for relating Merton's offerings to these needs, and monitor the effectiveness of advertising and sales promotion campaigns.

- **Business Economics and Corporate Research** studies helped Merton forecast long- and short-range sales and profits for consumer division products, and identify economic threats and opportunities in the external environment.

- **Corporate Responsibility Research** helped Merton identify legal and ecological constraints on Merton's marketing initiatives such as consumer "right to know" legislation, and legislation safeguarding the environment.

- **Product Research** studies were useful in predicting new product acceptance, measuring market potential for these products, studying features and benefits of competitive products, and developing competitive marketing strategies.

- **Sales and Marketing Research** were used to measure overall market potential and market share for consumer division products; develop demographic and psychographic profiles of target markets to help position and promote these products; establish sales territories and quotas; and analyze sales and profit results by product, territory, customer group, and distribution channel.

Table 5.1: Major categories of corporate market research studies

TYPE OF RESEARCH	PERCENT DOING IT
Advertising Research	
A. Motivation research	47%
B. Copy research	61
C. Media research	68
D. Studies of ad effectiveness	76
E. Studies of competitive advertising	67
Business Economics and Corporate Research	
A. Short-range forecasting (up to 1 year)	89
B. Long-range forecasting (over 1 year)	87
C. Studies of business trends	91
D. Pricing studies	83
E. Plant and warehouse location studies	68
F. Acquisition studies	73
G. Export and international studies	49
H. MIS (Management Information System)	80
I. Operations Research	65
J. Internal company employees	76
Corporate Responsibility Research	
A. Consumer "right to know" studies	18
B. Ecological impact studies	23
C. Studies of legal constraints on advertising and promotion	46
D. Social values and policies studies	39
Product Research	
A. New product acceptance and potential	76
B. Competitive product studies	87
C. Testing of existing products	80
D. Packaging research: design or physical characteristics	65

Table 5.1: Major categories of corporate market research studies

TYPE OF RESEARCH	PERCENT DOING IT
Sales and Market Research	
A. Measurement of market potentials	97
B. Market share analysis	97
C. Determination of market characteristics	97
D. Sales analysis	92
E. Establishment of sales quotas, territories	78
F. Distribution channel studies	71
G. Test markets, store audits	59
H. Consumer panel operations	63
I. Sales compensation studies	60
J. Promotional studies of premiums, coupons, sampling, deals, etc.	58

Source: Dik Warren Twedt, ed., *1983 Survey of Marketing Research* (Chicago: American Marketing Association, 1983), p. 41

• *HOW MARKETING RESEARCH APPLICATIONS DIFFER*

The extent to which a firm uses marketing research, and for what purposes, differs considerably within and between organizations. Within organizations, MR applications differ by management level. For example, senior management at Merton would be more interested in research studies pertaining to long-range business trends and opportunities, while lower echelon managers would be better served by focused studies in such areas as sales analysis or advertising effectiveness.

Between organizations, marketing research scope and emphasis differ by markets served and offerings made in these markets. Consumer-oriented organizations place stress on MR studies designed to identify and profile target markets and build promotion programs (including test market and store audit studies) attractive to these target markets. Organizations serving industrial markets, which place less emphasis on advertising and more on personal selling, would also place greater MR emphasis on economic trends and developments which influence the higher decision process.

These differences in emphasis between organizations are reflected in the size of marketing research budgets, which usually range from .01 to 3.5 percent of sales, with higher budgets in highly competitive, consumer-oriented firms. Between one half and three quarters of this money is spent directly by the marketing research department, with the remainder used to buy services from three categories of outside firms:

1. Syndicated-service research firms gather and sell consumer and trade information. For example, A. C. Nielson Company reports on television audiences, Selling Areas–Marketing Incorporated (SAMI) reports on warehouse movements, and Simmons reports on magazine audiences.

2. Custom marketing research firms carry out specific research projects. Examples would include the consulting firms that did research leading to ELI (Chapter 2) and Merton's consumer products division.

3. Specialty-line marketing research firms provide specialized services to other marketing firms and company research departments. An example would be firms which conduct store audits or sell field interviewing services to other firms.

KEY CONSIDERATIONS: VALIDITY, RELIABILITY

Depending largely on what they aim to achieve, MR studies are subject to a diversity of constraints that should be taken into account in building marketing information systems or initiating individual MR projects.

To understand the nature and scope of these constraints requires an understanding of two key concepts—validity and reliability. **Validity** is the extent to which a research study measures what it is supposed to measure. For example, test market research occasionally shows a strong preference for a product, such as "new formula" Coca Cola, which never materializes in the marketplace. When study findings don't accurately measure what they set out to measure, they are said to be invalid. When findings apply only to the population surveyed (for example, they love new formula Coke in Peoria, where the survey was conducted, but nowhere else), they are said to have *internal* validity.

Reliability is the likelihood that research results can be repeated. Assume, for example, that the new formula Coca Cola study, above, indicated a strong preference for the new formula among residents of Peoria. To be reliable, the study should produce similar preference findings among groups in other cities who are similar in all pertinent respects to the Peoria population (matched populations). Note that it is possible for a research study to be reliable (each population surveyed loves the new formula) without being valid (the results don't really measure the preferences they set out to measure).

Validity and reliability are especially important to marketing managers, because many marketing research studies entail considerable cost and risk, and can create expensive problems if misapplied or misdirected. A wrong price, an unpopular product feature, a poorly conceived marketing effort, an inefficient distribution channel—any of these can put a firm at a competitive disadvantage from which it never recovers. Given this cost and risk, it helps to understand and factor MR limitations into MR plans.

MARKETING RESEARCH METHODS

As compared to research in the physical sciences, marketing research, like research in the social sciences in general, exhibits a variety of built-in limitations which reduce validity and reliability:

- **Fewer controls** In a typical research study in the physical sciences—for example, measuring the boiling point of water at various stratospheric levels—conditions can be very precisely controlled. In a typical marketing research study—for example, a two-city test market study to measure the effect of a price reduction on Mini sales—conditions are typically much too diverse and complex to control with any degree of precision. Even in marketing research situations where they can be controlled, they can usually be expected to change shortly to make exact duplication impossible.

- **Complex phenomena** In the physical sciences, phenomena being studied tend to be stable, predictable, and unchanging. A typical marketing research study, on the other hand, deals with human variables like feelings, attitudes, and beliefs, which are difficult to define and measure. Even when they can be precisely pinned down, these variables can change quickly.

- **Crude instruments** In the physical sciences, precise, finely calibrated instruments measure phenomena like weight, height, temperature and pressure with a high degree of precision. A typical marketing research study uses measurement instruments—like questionnaire surveys delivered by mail or phone, or face-to-face interviews—that contain many built-in biases, inaccuracies and ambiguities.

- **Time constraints** In the physical sciences, there is usually time to make sure research findings and conclusions are valid and reliable. In marketing research, competitive pressures and the pressures of a changing environment create pressures for fast results that often sacrifice validity and reliability for speed.

- **Less objectivity** Marketing research is more likely to be biased and self-serving, as when conclusions are generated to prove a promotional point.

RESEARCH STEPS: DEFINE, ANALYZE, IDENTIFY, IMPLEMENT

To illustrate the workings of a systematic marketing research approach designed to optimize validity and reliability, and to produce findings and conclusions whose value exceeds the cost of the research itself, we will refer again to the problem

YOU SHOULD REMEMBER

In systematically designing, collecting, analyzing, and reporting on data and findings relevant to specific marketing situations, most marketing research (MR) studies focus in the areas of advertising research, business economics and corporate research, corporate responsibility research, product research, and sales/marketing research. Level of management and markets served are key determinants of research emphasis, with senior management requiring broad research into long-range trends and developments, and consumer marketing research focusing on target markets and promotional mix components. Differences in emphasis are reflected in MR budgets, which tend to take a larger percent of sales in consumer marketing firms than in industrial marketing firms. These differences in emphasis also determine the extent to which outside firms—including syndicated-service research firms, custom marketing research firms, and specialty-line marketing research firms—are used to supplement MR programs. Validity and reliability, the two main determinants of research accuracy and objectivity, are generally difficult to achieve in marketing research because of crude measuring instruments, complex phenomena investigated, and built-in biases.

noted earlier: disappointing sales of a Merton Mini PC model designed to fulfill the computational needs of engineering professionals. This problem is especially vexing because sales of Minis designed to fulfill needs of other segments in the business/professional market generally exceed expectations.

During the course of the marketing research study designed to solve the problem of the disappointing sales, the following activities were performed:

1. The research problem was defined, and realistic research objectives were established.

2. The situation provoking the problem was examined and analyzed.

3. An informal investigation identified possible reasons (hypotheses) for the problem identified.

4. A formal research study was designed and carried out to test the hypotheses.

• *STEP ONE: DEFINE THE PROBLEM AND RESEARCH OBJECTIVES*

Problems are broadly defined as unexpected occurrences that adversely affect efforts to achieve objectives, and that can be dealt with.

In defining problems, marketing researchers usually distinguish between major (primary) problems and symptomatic (secondary) problems. For example, the fact that sales of the engineers Mini are below expectations might be only a symptom of other, primary problems causing this decline. Thus, the primary problem may be "Why are sales declining?" not "How can we stop the sales decline?" Frequently, a good way to begin a research study is to list as many causative primary problems as possible; each then becomes a hypothesis to be accepted or rejected during later stages of the research process. For example, in the Merton "Engineering" study, each element comprising the product's strategic planning framework, including the target market and marketing mix components, was examined to find hypotheses to be tested.

Once potential primary problems have been identified, research objectives can be established which will define types of research and research methodology to be emphasized in solving problems. Sometimes the objective is exploratory—to gather preliminary information that will help define the problem and suggest solutions. Sometimes it is descriptive—to describe situations statistically and infer problem definitions and solutions from these descriptions. Less frequently, causal objectives will be projected to identify and define cause-effect relationships.

Frequently, objectives will change during the course of a research study. For example, exploratory research might reveal all the researcher wants to know or might suggest the need for additional descriptive or causal research.

• STEP TWO: CONDUCT A SITUATION ANALYSIS

The main objective of this second exploratory stage of the research process is to find reasonable explanations or hypotheses for unexpected events. This exploratory stage is less expensive and less disciplined than later, more conclusive stages of the research process, when hypotheses are evaluated and tested.

During this situation analysis, the focus is on sizing up the situation through surveys of knowledgeable people and surveys of secondary data.

- **Survey of knowledgeable people** This survey is usually restricted to informed executives and others in the company with a presumed knowledge of primary problems. Later, if this inside information isn't sufficient, the research study will seek information from outside sources. Since the Mini was a new product just introduced into a new market segment, this approach didn't prove useful in defining and solving the problem of falling sales in the engineering segment.

- **Survey of secondary sources** Secondary data is information which has already been published or collected for purposes other than those of the researcher. Hence, its usefulness for the researcher's purposes should be suspect, and carefully evaluated in terms of its relevance to the current research project, its accuracy in terms of the validity and reliability of its controls, its timeliness, and its impartiality. For example, a three-year-old article prepared by a computer manufacturer's public relations firm, describing the overwhelmingly favorable response among engineers to its personal computer, would probably fail in all four criteria areas.

Secondary data sources are classified as either internal or external. Internal sources include documents generated within the organization, such as sales figures, balance sheets, inventory records, and profit and loss statements. For example, sales figures comparing Mini sales volume in different target market segments revealed the secondary problem of falling sales that precipitated the marketing research study.

External sources include documents generated outside the company, such as publications by federal, state, and local governments (including *The Statistical Abstract of the United States,* which lists more than 1000 summary tables from public sources, Department of Commerce reports, and State Industrial Directories); reference books and periodicals published by private sources like associations, advertising agencies, newspapers, and magazines; and commercial sources, like those published by the Marketing Research Corporation of America (MRCA) and the A. C. Nielsen Co. MRCA, for example, maintains a consumer panel of more than 7500 families throughout the United States, and the Nielsen organization provides radio and television audits and ratings.

YOU SHOULD REMEMBER

A systematic marketing research process, designed to optimize validity and reliability, should

1. define research problems and establish realistic research objectives,

2. examine and analyze the situation provoking the problem,

3. identify possible reasons (hypotheses) for the problem, and

4. design a research study to select the best hypotheses.

During the first stage, it is important to distinguish between primary problems and secondary problems; primary problems should be the subject of the study. Research objectives, subject to change as the study progresses, are usually either exploratory, statistical, or experimental in nature.

In conducting the second step, two sources of information help explore situations provoking primary problems: secondary sources and knowledgeable people. Secondary sources can be internal or external, and should be evaluated for relevance, accuracy, timeliness and impartiality. During this second stage, knowledgeable people consulted have close association with the problem and are usually members of the organization conducting the research study.

• *STEP THREE: CONDUCT AN INFORMAL INVESTIGATION*

Having exhausted internal sources, researchers now turn their attentions to sources outside the company, sources like informed members of target markets. In the Mini research study, it was assumed that engineers would have this informed knowledge, so a series of *focus group* interviews was set up with selected members of the target market to elicit possible explanations for the sales volume differences between this segment and all other segments of the business professional market.

• *STEP FOUR: PLAN THE FORMAL RESEARCH PROJECT*

If exploratory and informal research have failed to identify and solve primary problems, then a formal research project is planned to gather primary data required to test hypotheses developed during the two preceding steps. Primary data is information collected for the specific purpose at hand.

This formal research project, also called conclusive research, differs from exploratory and informal research in four significant respects:

1. It is guided by hypotheses, rather than seeking to find these hypotheses.
2. It applies much more rigorous controls.
3. It deals with larger numbers and leads to mass data analyses covering classes, averages, percentages and dispersions.
4. It leads to predictions (i.e., if this hypothesis is true, then such and such will happen). These characteristics of conclusive research are illustrated in the sample study examined in Chapter 6.

The two most frequently used conclusive research approaches are statistical methods and experimental methods. Each was used as follows in the Mini study.

Statistical methods classify data in such a way that inclusion in one category implies inclusion in one or more other categories, often revealing significant relationships among the data categories.

Thus, the following statistical analysis in the Mini study revealed significant relationships between the professional group an individual belonged to, the likelihood that he or she would be subsidized by an employer, and the likelihood that he or she would purchase a personal computer. This analysis seemed to confirm the hypothesis that purchases of Minis are related to degree of subsidization. Note first that 80 percent (40 out of 50) of the members of the business/professional sample are subsidized, as against only 25 percent of members of the engineering group. Also note that, among subsidized members of the engineering group, 70 percent purchased Minis, as against only 50 percent of the subsidized members of the other group.

Table 5.2 Comparison of personal computer purchases among subsidized and non-subsidized members of engineers market and business/professional market

Decision variables	Engineers market				Business/professional market			
	Subsidized		Non-subsidized		Subsidized		Non-subsidized	
	Number	Percent	Number	Percent	Number	Percent	Number	Percent
Purchased mini computer	7	70%	4	10%	20	50%	3	30%
Didn't purchase personal computer	3	30	36	90	20	50	7	70
Total	10	100	40	100	40	100	10	100

While indicative, statistical research is rarely, if ever, conclusive; in the Merton study, it is at least conceivable that other factors, such as the fact that most members of the engineering segment work on certain kinds of projects, might explain both the subsidy and purchase rate results. Also, as additional classifications are brought into a statistical analysis, figures get smaller and results become less valid and reliable. In the above matrix, for example, note that there are only four members in one engineer-nonsubsidized cell—hardly enough to produce significant mass data conclusions.

For most practical marketing research purposes, however, statistical results are sufficiently conclusive. For example, if a particular promotional appeal or pricing strategy or distribution channel is shown to be more effective or profitable through statistical analysis, the marketing manager will usually let it go at that; to go further can cost a lot of money, consume a lot of time, and incur unnecessary risks.

Experimental methods, in which one or more variables are manipulated under conditions that show the effects of these variables in an unconfused manner, is the only sure research approach for identifying and defining cause-effect relationships.

For example, in the Merton research study, the "Before-After-with-Control-Group" experiment shown in Figure 5.2 was conducted to determine if a causal relationship between subsidization and Mini purchases really existed. Note that in the left-hand side of this model, a before measurement is taken (only 10 percent of the sample of engineers purchased the Mini). Then an experimental variable is manipulated (this group is given a subsidy equal to the subsidy given business people), and an after measurement is taken. This result seems to indicate that the effect of this subsidy is to increase sales from 10 to 50 percent of the sample.

To account for potentially biasing factors, a control group is also incorporated into the right-hand side of the experimental model. For this group, however, no

	Experimental Group (sample receives a subsidy)		Control Group (Matched sample doesn't receive subsidy)	
Before measurement (x_1) (% that purchased personal computer)	10%		(y_1)	10%
Experimental variable (incentive subsidy offered)	Yes			No
After measurement (x_2) (% that purchased personal computer)	50%		(y_2)	10%
Effect of experimental variable	$(x_2 - x_1) = 40\%$ $(x_2 - x_1) - (y_2 - y_1) = 40\%$		$(y_2 - y_1) = 0$	

Figure 5-2. Model of Before-After-with-Control-Group experiment to measure effect of a subsidy or personal computer purchases among members of engineers market

experimental variable is manipulated, i.e., these engineers, matched in all significant respects with the experimental group, are not offered a subsidy incentive. An after measurement indicates that only 10% of unsubsidized engineers will purchase the Mini, reinforcing the validity of the hypothesis that Mini purchases are related to subsidies.

However, at least six variables can invalidate this finding: selection, mortality, pretest effect, history, maturity, and measurement variations.

Selection means that, consciously or not, different criteria might have been used to select members of each group, so the groups are never truly matched. Actually, no two groups will ever be identical, and the extent of this difference will always bias any experiment's findings.

Pretest effect refers to a rather common biasing influence that occurs when people know they are being selected to participate in a special event of some kind. Frequently, this recognition alone can motivate them to behave in an unnatural manner, perhaps purchasing more of the product because they feel it is expected of them.

Mortality refers to the likelihood that members of one group—usually the control group, which isn't being recognized—will desert its ranks in greater numbers, so even if both groups begin as matched, they might not stay that way.

History means that events outside the sphere of the experiment might bias the results. For example, the only manufacturer of a similar competitive mini-computer might stop producing this model, leaving the entire market to Merton.

Maturity refers to biological or psychological changes that might influence experimental results. For example, word-of-mouth promotion by Mini users might persuade more engineering students to purchase it in spite of its high price.

Measurement variation refers to different ways of measuring before and after findings, or findings from each of the groups participating in the experiment.

WHY MARKETERS SHUN TEST MARKETS

A typical test market study illustrates a marketing application for the experimental approach. A manufacturer might test, and predict, the effect of a price or promotional strategy (the intervening variable) by changing this strategy in one city (the experimental group) while leaving it alone in another city (the control group). Sales increases, or decreases, in the experimental city might then be attributed to this pricing strategy change.

Unfortunately, the biasing effects of selection, pretest effect, mortality, history, and maturity would probably be working on both groups to reduce the validity and reliability of findings and conclusions. Furthermore, test market studies are usually quite expensive and time-consuming, and provide competitors with both a blueprint of marketing plans and an opportunity to distort the test results by manipulating their own variables in one or both of the test cities.

The high cost in time, risk, money, validity, and reliability have led many marketing managers to place greater emphasis on consumer panels to generate hypotheses and describe situations about markets and products. Panels also assure a much higher degree of secrecy than do test markets, important when a new product, or product concept, is being tested.

The size of these panels can range from the 4300 homes hooked into A. C. Nielsen's polling system to indicate what America's 86 million television households are watching, to small focus groups that provide feedback on new product or promotion concepts.

YOU SHOULD REMEMBER

The third stage of the marketing research process—after problems and objectives have been defined and the situation causing the problems has been examined and analyzed—involves conducting an informal investigation to identify possible reasons for the problem. Many studies terminate at this third stage, with sufficient information generated through interviews with members of the external environment to solve the problem to the satisfaction of management. If the problem isn't satisfied in this stage, a fourth stage of conclusive study is usually implemented, guided by hypothesis and dealing with larger numbers and more rigorous controls than exploratory research. Statistical conclusive studies indicate, but never conclusively prove, cause-effect relationships; experimental conclusive studies can prove these relationships to the extent that a diversity of biasing influences are accounted for in the experimental design.

KNOW THE CONCEPTS
DO YOU KNOW THE BASICS?

1. Discuss problems facing a small firm unable to afford an MIS system.

2. In what ways are marketing research and marketing information systems similar and different? What do the differences mean in terms of the information needs of marketing managers?

3. What are the advantages and disadvantages of marketing research as compared to intuitive decision-making?

4. What are the major shortcomings of marketing research as compared to research in the physical sciences?

5. Distinguish between exploratory and conclusive research. Under what circumstances will the research effort end in the exploratory stage?

6. Distinguish between validity and reliability, and give an example of how marketing research shortcomings might limit both in a typical study involving conclusive research.

7. Distinguish between primary and secondary data, and explain how both might be used in selecting a good place to eat in a strange town. Give two reasons why both sources might prove to be invalid.

8. What is the difference between defining the research problem and developing a hypothesis?

9. Under what circumstances would a researcher be justified in assuming a causal relationship among variables?

10. List the steps in the research process, and describe how each might come into play in arriving at, and testing, a hypothesis.

TERMS FOR STUDY

advertising research
causal research
conclusive research
corporate responsibility research
experiments
focus groups
hypotheses
internal validity
marketing information system
marketing research
mass data

primary problems
product research
reliability
sales research
secondary problems
secondary sources
situation analysis
specialty line research firms
statistical methods
syndicated services
validity

PRACTICAL APPLICATION

1. Describe, with examples, how the following MIS components might help a used car dealer decide which automobiles to promote as specials this month: environment database; market database; company costs database; sales and cost analysis database; data and information storage processor.

2. What types of research (exploratory, descriptive, causal) would be most appropriate in the following situations?
   a. The campaign manager for a candidate for a hotly-contested U.S. Senate race wants to identify major issues among 50 different demographic groups.
   b. The Ford Motor Company wants to determine the relationship between income and type/brand of automobile purchased.
   c. A small jogging shoe boutique in a large shopping mall wants information on customer attitudes toward merchandise and service provided.

3. Assume you are a real estate agent selling residential properties in a highly competitive environment. List at least five specific types of information from your firm's MIS that would help you do a more effective job, and an annual special study you would commission using marketing research tools and techniques.

4. Listed below, in column one, are objectives for five marketing research studies which might have been performed by the insurance company. Match up each study with the general area covered in this study in column two, and the title(s) of the individual(s) at the insurance company who would be most interested in findings and conclusions emerging from each study.

Study Objective(s)	Study Area	Interested Party
a) To test the response in the corporate marketplace of a new kind of integrated medical insurance policy.	1. Corporate Responsibility Research	1. President
	2. Business Economics and Corporate Research	2. Marketing Manager
		3. Sales force members
		4. Advertising Manager
b) To develop information that will help the firm defend itself in a class action suit claiming company salespeople are overselling insurance to senior citizens.	3. Product Research	5. National sales manager
	4. Sales and Marketing Research	6. Financial vice president
	5. Advertising Research	

Study Objective(s)	Study Area	Interested Party

c) To determine the best
instruments in which
to invest the firm's
surplus over the next
decade, with
emphasis on safety,
growth, and return.

d) To determine the
most effective appeal
for an advertising
campaign supporting
a new homeowner's
insurance coverage,
as well as the best
media mix for
carrying this
campaign.

e) To establish equitable
sales quotas for each
salesperson by
measuring the sales
volume generated by
each salesperson
over the previous
year as compared to
the potential in each
salesperson's territory.

5. Referring to the study in question 4, to determine the most effective appeal
   and media mix, show how an experiment might have been used to indicate
   the most persuasive appeal for the campaign, and a statistical study might
   have been used to indicate the relative efficacy of television versus magazines to carry this appeal.

ANSWERS

KNOW THE BASICS

1. A Marketing Information System generates and distributes information on
   marketing opportunities and threats, such as prospective new customers
   in a territory or competitive attempts to attract these prospects, that can

be much more important to the survival of a small firm with limited resources than to a well-cushioned large firm. A number of studies have shown that lack of such information, which could be provided on a continuing basis by an MIS, is invariably among the top two reasons for the high failure rate among small companies.

2. Marketing information systems are designed to develop and disseminate information, on a continuous basis, that will help managers anticipate and respond to threats and opportunities in both internal and external environments before they assume crisis proportions. In performing this continuing role as the eyes and ears of the firm, MISs rely on information from the past which has already been programmed into its data base. Marketing research, on the other hand, is much more likely to focus on problems or situations that were not anticipated and that can have a positive or negative influence on company operations. In addressing these problems and situations, marketing research must typically generate new data and information, which is more likely to focus on the current situation, and future prospects than on past history. Also, unlike MIS, which tends to function on a continuing basis, marketing research studies are usually created for a limited and specific purpose.

From the perspective of the marketing manager, these differences mean that each can supplement the other in developing, implementing, and controlling marketing programs. For example, the MIS can reach into its data base for information on which target markets and marketing mixes represent the best match, while MR develops more timely information to fill gaps in the MIS data base, or to produce and test hypotheses to explain why marketing programs aren't performing as expected.

3. A well-conceived and planned marketing research study, unlike intuitive decision making, systematically takes into account most of the significant variables involved in solving a problem (such as people in the best position to define the problem, or historical developments which caused the problem), and can provide an index of the relative validity and reliability of the emerging solution to the problem. A number of research studies have shown rather conclusively that proper information, properly organized and analyzed, produces better decisions than sheer hunch or intuition.

4. Compared to research in the physical sciences, marketing research usually deals with much less stable and predictable phenomema, relies on much less accurate measuring instruments, can't implement the same tight controls, and operates under severe time constraints and, often, pressures to make sure research results are consistent with preconceptions.

5. In general, exploratory research represents a search for hypotheses, or good reasons, to explain a problem or situation, and is much less controlled and focused than conclusive research, when these hypotheses are tested. The research effort will end in the exploratory stage if the researcher is satisfied that sufficient information has been developed to

achieve the objectives of the research study, and/or it is apparent that the cost of continuing the research study will exceed any possible benefits from this study.

6. Validity addresses the question: Did this study measure what it was supposed to measure? Reliability addresses the question: Are we likely to get the same results if we conduct another study with the same conditions and controls? To illustrate how marketing research shortcomings might limit both validity and reliability, consider some of the reasons why election forecasts—a form of marketing research—are frequently so far off the mark in terms of validity (they often *don't* measure people's real beliefs or intentions) and reliability (these beliefs and intentions can change with the next debate, producing completely different results from the last survey). People are unpredictable, survey instruments suffer all the imprecisions and ambiguities of our language, time pressures are intense, and—simply judging from differing interpretations of the same results by opposing candidates—the purpose of the research is often subjectively self-serving.

7. Secondary research data is data that was produced by other people for purposes other than that of the present research study. Primary data is data gathered for the specific research purposes at hand. Secondary sources referred to in locating a good restaurant in a strange town would include a directory of restaurants or listings in a telephone book. Primary sources might include the bellhop in your hotel, or the proprietors of restaurants named in the directory. A restaurant display ad in the local yellow pages would probably prove invalid to the extent that it is probably biased, possibly dated, and not based on sound research. The same comments might be made with respect to the evaluations by the bellhop or the proprietor.

8. The process of defining the research problem usually culminates in a question that the research process will attempt to answer. Why are sales falling? What will happen to profits if we raise our price? Developing a hypothesis, or series of hypotheses, usually involves coming up with an answer or series of answers, to these questions, which are then tested during exploratory and/or definitive stages of the research process. If you don't come up with the proper research question, you will not test the proper hypotheses.

9. A causal relationship among variables can be assumed if, in a controlled experimental situation, an intervening variable changes the after measurement in an unambiguous manner. For example, if a 10 percent price decrease (the intervening variable) increases sales by 20 percent (the after measurement), then a causal relationship can be assumed between price and sales, i.e., reduced prices cause sales increases. To reduce the ambiguity of this causal conclusion, the experiment should probably include a matched, control group, which would not be subject to the influence of

the intervening variable. Thus, any biasing influence of selection, history, mortality, maturity, or pretest effect, which would presumably influence both groups, would tend to be cancelled out.

10. The steps in the research process entail defining the problem and research objectives, conducting a situation analysis, conducting a formal investigation, and planning the formal research project.

   To illustrate how these steps might be involved in arriving at, and testing, a hypothesis, assume a problem of falling sales in a particular territory for which there is no apparent reason.

   During the first stage, the problem would be defined (What are the causes for falling sales?), and a number of hypotheses promulgated to explain the reason for the sales decline (competitor's initiative, changing consumer attitudes, poor distribution, etc.). Each of these hypotheses would then be ranked from most likely to least likely, and, in turn, tested during subsequent stages of the research process. For example, one most likely hypothesis might explain the falloff as a consequence of a competitor's price cut, which further exploratory investigation (observation, a survey of knowledgeable people, etc.) might confirm. If not, then this hypothesis might be tested, and shown to be correct, during a formal research project of either the statistical or experimental variety.

PRACTICAL APPLICATION

1. The *environment database* might indicate that a certain make of automobile was just chosen as "Car of the Year," or that tight economic conditions were stimulating demand for smaller economy cars. The market database might show that sales of a particular model or make were declining, so that automobile might be given "special" status to reverse this trend, or this database might indicate that a larger local competitor is gaining market-share, so an extremely popular automobile might be given "special" status to reverse this trend. The company cost database might indicate that a particular make/model is much more profitable than others (because of higher markups or lower handling costs associated with this model), so this auto might be given "special" status with the understanding that its price can be reduced somewhat and still produce a better-than-average profit. The sales and cost analysis database might show a correlation between high sales for a given period and luxury automobiles that require many options.

2. **a.** A descriptive statistical research study that cross-references issues and defined demographic groups.
   b. Another descriptive statistical research study, in this case cross-referencing buyer income groups with automobiles purchased.
   c. An exploratory survey of knowledgeable people who had patronized the store.

3. Types of information provided by MIS data bases which would help the real estate agent do a more effective job include: sales trends of residences in different price and age categories, numbers of new listings by geographic area, interest rate projections, competitor's share of market figures, and projections of new housing starts. An annual special study which might be commissioned using marketing research tools and techniques might develop a statistical profile correlating sales of homes in various age, price, and location categories with variables presumed to influence these sales (such as disposable income, interest rates, or housing starts). Based on multiple regression techniques, such a profile would indicate the relative influence of each variable on sales.

4. Before suggesting responses to this exercise, it should be noted that, in a modern, marketing-oriented organization, all the titles in Column 3 would have some degree of interest, even if indirect, in the studies in Column 1, and the marketing manager would probably have a direct interest in all of them. Also, more than one study area (Column 2) is implicit in some of the objectives in Column 1. Thus, response below refers to the study areas and titles most directly related to each objective:

Objectives	Areas	Parties
a) test response in marketplace	product	marketing manager
b) help firm defend itself	corporate responsibility	president
c) best investment instruments	business economics/corporate	financial vice president
d) effective advertising appeal	advertising research	advertising manager
e) equitable sales quotas	sales/marketing research	national sales manager

5. **a.** A before-after-with-control-group experiment might be used to indicate the most persuasive appeal by varying the experimental variable (i.e., the appeal itself) for the experimental group but not for the control group. Any difference in response (as measured, say, by responses to a direct mail request for information) from members of the experimental group might then be assumed to be related to the effectiveness of the appeal.

   b. A statistical study might summarize the relative impact of advertising campaigns (presumably using the most effective appeal uncovered in the experimental study) carried in television and magazine media. This statistical summary might profile viewers of the television program and readers of the magazine along a number of significant demographic and psychographic dimensions (age, income, attitudes toward insurance, etc.) and indicate what proportion of each population was motivated by the campaigns to take some kind of action, such as inquiring about various advertised coverages or actually buying insurance.

6 MARKETING RESEARCH: TOOLS AND TECHNIQUES

In Chapter 5, we examined the structures of marketing information systems (MIS) and the stages of the marketing research process. In this chapter, we will examine more closely three areas of particular importance in designing and conducting marketing research studies:

1. sampling
2. gathering information
3. processing information

We will continue to refer to the engineer's marketing research study for illustrative examples. This study was designed to define and solve the problem of disappointing Mini sales among engineers.

SAMPLING TECHNIQUES

A sample is defined as "a limited portion of a larger entity." In the engineers' study, for example, the larger entity, or population, consisted of all engineers who might use the customized Merton Mini. The limited portion, or sample, could be any number up to one less than the total number comprising the entire population.

All samples observed or surveyed during marketing research studies represent either probability or non-probability samples. In a **probability sample**, each member of the population has the same likelihood, or probability, of being chosen. For example, each member of a classroom population of 40 students would have one chance in four of being chosen for a probability sample of ten students. A **non-probability sample** is selected on the basis of criteria which assure that some members of the population will have a greater probability of being selected than others.

NON-PROBABILITY SAMPLES

The three most common kinds of non-probability samples are **judgment, convenience**, and **quota** samples. In the engineers' study, these samples might have been selected as follows:

- **Judgment**: Engineers are selected for the sample based on the researcher's judgment that they have a superior understanding of engineering applications for personal computers.

- **Convenience**: Engineers are selected for the sample because they are conveniently located close to research facilities.

- **Quota**: Engineers are selected for the sample based on their representation in the population. For example, if mechanical engineers represent nine of ten engineers in the population at large, they will comprise this proportion in the sample.

Non-probability samples are most often used during exploratory research in order to define problems and develop hypotheses and as a second-best alternative when information on which to build a probability sample is not available.

PROBABILITY SAMPLES

During later, more conclusive stages of the research process, when objective, accurate information is required, probability sampling methods offer a number of advantages over non-probability sampling methods:

- **Less information is required.** Basically, all that is necessary to construct a probability sample is a way to identify each universe element (e.g., each engineer), and knowledge of the total number of universe elements.

- **Measurable Accuracy:** Probability sampling is the only sampling method that provides measurable estimates of accuracy.

The Neilsen television rating service illustrates the precision possible with probability sampling. Because the sample comprising "Nielsen households" is a randomly selected probability sample, it is possible to summarize its findings along these lines:

> In 99 of 100 situations where a random sample of 4300 households, selected from a population of 86 million TV viewing households, is polled, results will show that between 29.6 and 30.2 percent of sample members, *and the entire viewing population* watched the television show "Sixty Minutes" on Sunday, May 11.

Marketing managers who can have this degree of confidence in the accuracy of their research conclusions can also have considerably greater confidence in the reliability of decisions emerging from these conclusions. Impressive cost savings are also possible using random sampling methods; note, for example, that the Neilsen organization surveys only one household out of each 20,000 to achieve these accurate results.

YOU SHOULD REMEMBER

Sampling and information-gathering techniques, properly understood and applied, help assure more accurate, valid results during all stages of the marketing research process. **Non-probability samples**—for which certain members of a population have a greater chance of being chosen based on researcher *judgment*, or *convenience*, or a prescribed *quota* requirement—are more likely to be used during exploratory research to develop hypotheses. **Probability samples**, for which all members of a population have an equal chance of being selected, can assure measurable degrees of validity, applicable to entire populations, at a relatively small cost. Probability samples are used to test hypotheses during conclusive stages of the research process.

QUESTIONNAIRE DESIGN

There are many reasons why a poorly designed questionnaire can invalidate the findings of a well-conceived sampling plan. These include

1. a misunderstanding of study objectives
2. inappropriate or poorly worded questions
3. improper question sequence
4. failure to account for the needs and perceptions of people being surveyed (i.e., respondents)

The following step-by-step approach for designing a questionnaire will help you avoid these problems and achieve the validity and reliability implicit in a good sampling plan:

1. Establish research objectives
2. Determine desired information
3. Determine type of questionnaire to use
4. Determine mode of questionnaire communication
5. Determine question content, wording, and format
6. Determine questionnaire sequence

(We will continue to use the engineering study for illustration.)

DETERMINE OBJECTIVES AND DESIRED INFORMATION

The primary purpose of a questionnaire survey is to translate research objectives into specific questions. Thus, a good starting point in designing a questionnaire is to briefly summarize these objectives. For example, an important objective of the engineers' survey was to generate data on occupational and other demographic criteria that might motivate market members to purchase a Mini.

A comprehensive but specific statement of research objectives will suggest the information required. For example, objectives of the engineers' survey would surely mandate questions pertaining to on-the-job use of computers.

DETERMINE TYPE OF QUESTIONNAIRE TO USE

• *FACTORS TO BE CONSIDERED*

Major determinants defining questionnaire type include the kinds of information desired, the degree of validity/reliability required, and the ability of respondents to provide the desired information.

KINDS OF INFORMATION DESIRED

A simple, structured questionnaire can be developed to obtain simple, straight-forward information, such as might be elicited by a job application questionnaire. As desired information becomes more complex and variable, and respondents are less willing or able to provide it, more sophisticated questionnaire formats are required, often calling for trained professionals to motivate and control the information flow from individuals or groups.

DEGREE OF VALIDITY AND RELIABILITY REQUIRED

Validity and reliability refer to the likelihood that biasing factors built into the questionnaire or communication mode will not enable the questionnaire to measure what it was designed to measure (validity), or make it possible to repeat questionnaire results (reliability). Types of biases that frequently arise in marketing research include:

- **Interviewer and interviewee biases,** whereby the attitudes and actions of either the interviewer or the respondent distort questionnaire findings. For example, perceived socioeconomic differences between the interviewer and the respondent can color the interviewer's interpretation of responses, or motivate the respondent to distort his or her responses to impress the interviewer.

- **Halo effect bias,** the tendency to generalize from a single aspect to multiple aspects of an object. For example, a surveyed engineer who has had favorable experiences with some Merton products might comment favorably on the Merton Mini without knowing anything about it.

- **Non-response bias,** which occurs when people fail to respond to a questionnaire survey, thus altering survey results. For example, 20 percent of engineer respondents who did not return questionnaires asking about personal computer preferences might have failed to respond because of neutral or negative attitudes toward PCs. If they had responded, these attitudes would have changed survey findings by making them more positive or negative.

- **Self-selection bias,** which occurs when people respond to a questionnaire survey but in a way that might bias survey results. For example, members of a group of engineers who volunteer comments about the Mini PC might have some first-hand knowledge of this product not shared by the other members. Comments from these other members could change survey findings considerably.

- **Hawthorne effect bias,** which is the bias introduced by psychological responses to the nature or conditions of a research study. For example, the realization that an individual has been selected to participate in a survey might favorably bias his or her attitudes and answers. (A classic early study in motivation done at the Western Electric Hawthorne Works in Illinois showed the importance of individual worker or participant attitude.)

Other biasing factors pertain to the wording and sequencing of survey questions, and will be covered during our discussion of problems involved in actually preparing the questionnaire.

Note: Although most marketing research studies are designed to reduce the influence of these biases, it must be recognized that there are situations, usually involving product promotion research, when they are actively encouraged. For example, a television commercial featuring the favorable comments of a "self-selected" housewife toward a detergent or floor polish could easily reflect all the above biases.

ABILITY AND WILLINGNESS OF RESPONDENTS TO PROVIDE INFORMATION

Three levels of ability/willingness to provide information help determine the choice of questionnaire type:

- On the first level, respondents are able and willing to provide the information desired, as in a job application, for example.

- On the second level, respondents are able to provide the desired information but are unwilling to do so, for example, where questions pertain to "private" matters such as income, family life, political orientation, or religious beliefs.

- On the third level, respondents are unable to provide the desired information because it is buried in their subconsciouses. Followers of Freud and proponents of modern motivational research theory claim that many of our needs and drives derive from early childhood, and are repressed or suppressed because they seem illogical or irrational to us as adults. However, they maintain, these needs and drives still exert a potent motivational influence on our adult behavior.

• TYPES OF QUESTIONNAIRE

In terms of the information desired and the respondents' ability or willingness to provide this information, questionnaires can be designed in terms of **degree of structure** and **degree of disguise**. A highly structured questionnaire, with unchanging content/sequence characteristics, generally elicits uncomplicated information which the respondent is both willing and able to provide. A questionnaire with a *disguised* intent attempts to elicit information on the second and third levels, i.e., that information which people have but are unwilling to provide, or that they are not aware they have. Using these "structure/disguise" criteria, four types of questionnaires emerge, ranging from highly structured/non-disguised to unstructured/disguised.

Table 6-1 briefly examines each questionnaire type in terms of the characteristics, applications, costs, degree of control, flexibility, validity/reliability, and ease of interpretation associated with each.

YOU SHOULD REMEMBER

Well-designed questionnaires translate research objectives into questions that are clearly understood and motivate responses. A step-by-step procedure for designing such questionnaires begins with a summary of research objectives followed by decisions pertaining to (1) the information needed to achieve these objectives, and (2) the types of questionnaires best calculated to generate this information. For example, if people are likely to be willing to provide the information, a structured format might be best. If the needed information requires deeper probing, an unstructured format might be more appropriate. Another consideration in selecting questionnaire type is the degree of validity/reliability desired. Some types of questionnaires are more susceptible to interviewee, interviewer, non-response, halo effect, self-selection, and other biases.

DETERMINE MODE OF COMMUNICATION

Three different methods of communication are available: personal interviews, telephone interviews, and mail surveys. For years, most marketing research surveys were conducted by personal interview, but in recent years advanced techniques and technologies have dramatically improved the efficiency and productivity of telephone and mail approaches.

Table 6-2 summarizes and analyzes each communication approach in terms of the criteria used in our examination of questionnaire types: cost, control, flexibility, validity/reliability, and ease of interpretation.

YOU SHOULD REMEMBER

The choice of questionnaire type depends on the kinds of information and degree of validity desired, as well as the ability and willingness of respondents to provide this information. Questionnaires become less structured as more complex, in-depth information is desired, and more disguised as respondents become less willing or able to provide this information. The mode of questionnaire communication can be personal interviews, telephone, and mail. Criteria for selecting both the questionnaire type and the mode of communication include cost, control, flexibility, validity/reliability, and ease of interpretation.

Table 6-1. Comparison of Questionnaire Type by Structure/Disguise Characteristics

	Structured/Non-Disguised	Non-Structured/Non-Disguised	Non-Structured/Disguised	Structured/Disguised
Key Characteristic	Question content and sequence identical on each questionnaire	Question content and sequence vary at interviewer's discretion	Study objectives disguised to overcome unwillingness or inability of respondent to answer personal questions	Questionnaire content fixed, but questionnaire objectives are disguised. Real attitudes are inferred from answers
Typical Applications	During exploratory research, develop hypotheses to be tested later, during conclusive stages	"Depth interviews" during exploratory research stage to generate hypotheses and relationships	Exploratory research probes for subconsciously held attitudes, motivations	To elicit "private" information (on religion, politics, etc.) respondent would otherwise be reluctant to provide.
Cost Elements	If by phone, line charges and interviewer expenses; if by mail, recipient list and costs for mailing questionnaire, processing responses	recruiting, training, administering interviewers, setting-up focus groups	Essentially the same as for non-structured non-disguised type	Essentially the same as for structured/non-disguised
Control	Difficult to control accuracy of recipient list, size of response	Difficult to control questionnaire content, sequence, and quality of responses	Essentially the same as for non-structured, non-disguised	Essentially the same as for structured/non-disguised

Flexibility	Question content and sequence difficult to change, except by rotating questions and directing respondents to skip irrelevant questions	Question content and sequence easily changed at discretion of interviewer	Projective materials (such as word association and picture completion surveys) are difficult to change, but interviewer questions can be changed	Essentially the same as for structured/ non-disguised
Validity & Reliability	No interviewer or interviewee bias with mail surveys, but possible halo, Hawthorne, self-selection and non-response biases	Interviewee, interviewer, halo, non-response and self-selection biases all possible	Disguised nature of questions reduces interviewee bias, although all other biases associated with non-structure non-disguise are possible	Essentially the same as for structured/ non-disguised, less-ened somewhat because of disguised nature of probe
Ease of Interpretation	Responses easiest of all to tabulate, organize and analyze	Different interviewer styles and subjective responses make responses difficult to tabulate and interpret	Essentially, same problems as associated with non-structured, non-disguised	Generally as easy as structured/ non-dis-guised responses, with some room for error in making subjective inferences from objective answers.

Control refers to the extent to which the questionnaire can be monitored and corrected. For example, the activities of field researchers conducting face-to-face interviews are more difficult to control than those of supervised telephone interviewers.

Flexibility refers to the extent to which questionnaire content and sequence can change in response to answers.

Validity and reliability refer to the likelihood that biasing factors built into the questionnaire will prevent the questionnaire from measuring what it was designed to measure or make it difficult to repeat survey results.

Ease of interpretation refers to the degree of cost and effort involved in processing questionnaire responses after interviews are completed. For example, drawn-out responses elicited during an unstructured, focus-group interview would be much more difficult to organize and analyze than short answers to true or false questions.

Table 6-2. Comparison of Questionnaire Communication Modes

	Personal Interview	Telephone	Mail
Key Characteristic	Obtains information in face-to-face settings.	Most widely used and fastest. Higher quality, but less information obtained as compared to personal interviews.	With no interviewer to stimulate and record answers, emphasis is on questionnaire design, effective cover letter.
Common Applications	Usually during exploratory research, when "depth" information is required.	For more structured interviews than required with personal interviews; also, in situations where shorter answers will suffice, and no observation is required.	To elicit less timely and detailed information; also, "personal" information not as obtainable with two other modes.
Cost Elements	Highest of three modes. Main elements: recruiting, administering field interviewers; controlling, processing feedback.	Less expensive than personal interviews, especially with WATS line rates.	Lowest of three modes. Main costs: recipient list, mailing, processing responses.
Control	Difficult to control activities of field interviewers, or quality of calls and responses.	Easier to control, monitor telephone interviewers, who usually call from single location. Interview content also easier to control with computerized systems.	Total over questionnaire preparation and mailing; less over quality of list, quantity of answers.

Table 6-2. Comparison of Questionnaire Communication Modes

	Personal Interview	Telephone	Mail
Flexibility	High. Interview can be stopped, question content and sequence changed, props and observations used.	Same as personal interviews, without props or observations, and with greater geographic flexibility, easier callbacks.	Difficult to change question content and sequence, but best geographic coverage of three modes (can't reach 10% illiterate population).
Validity/ Reliability	High interviewer and interviewee bias, but better designation of sample, higher completion rates than with mail survey.	Essentially same as for personal interviews, except that more standardized stimuli and shorter responses make results more comparable.	No interviewer/ interviewee bias, but big non-response problem (however, effective design of mailing, and callbacks, can produce 50% and better response rate).
Ease of Interpretation	Most difficult to record, tabulate and analyze because of problems in gathering data, and length of responses.	Shorter answers make tabulation easier than with personal interviews, not as simple as with mailed surveys.	Of all methods, easiest to edit, code, tabulate.

DETERMINE QUESTION CONTENT

Once questionnaire objectives have been clearly stated and the decision has been made as to questionnaire type and communication method, the stage is set for preparing the questionnaire. This process involves first determining the content of individual questions, then deciding how those questions will be worded.

The following guidelines will help assure that questionnaire content is clearly stated, that it furthers the purpose of the study, and that it motivates respondents to respond:

- **Make sure the question is necessary.** If you are not sure the answer to a question will help achieve survey objectives, go back and review those objectives.

- **Make sure the respondent will answer the question.** If a respondent does not want to answer a particular question, he or she may be "turned off" to the entire questionnaire. Generally, respondents do not answer questions that they perceive as embarrassing or that relate to private matters such as personal finances, family life, or political or religious beliefs.

  When it is necessary to ask a potentially embarrassing survey question (generally in an unstructured survey), the question can be communicated more effectively using one or more of these techniques: (1) explain the importance and need for the question; (2) use the projective technique of referring to "other people," so the respondent's ego isn't threatened (rather than a direct question about a respondent's salary, for example, you might ask something like, "What should an engineer working for Acme Company be earning after two years?); (3) "bury" the potentially sensitive question among several innocuous questions; or (4) list categories of answers coded by letter, and have respondents select one of these categories. For example, possible responses to a question about income might be:

☐	CLASS A	Under $30,000
☐	CLASS B	$30,000–$50,000
☐	CLASS C	over $50,000

- **Make sure the respondent has the desired information.** A question that respondents cannot answer is as likely to turn them off to the entire questionnaire as a question that they will not answer. To avoid this pitfall, make sure that (1) the question is within the respondent's experience, (2) he or she will not have to work to get the information, and (3) he or she will remember the information. In general, people are more likely to remember important events (their first automobile), unusual events (a no-hitter baseball game), events that are part of an established pattern (the soft drink they always purchase), or events that interrupt an established pattern (that new soft drink they decided to try).

- **Make sure several questions are not needed instead of one.** Some questions imply two or more answers which, if incorporated into one question, are impossible to interpret and answer. A question like, "Do you regularly use computers in your work or at home?" for example, is really two questions.

DETERMINE QUESTION WORDING

The wording of questions can strongly influence questionnaire validity and reliability, the respondent's willingness to respond, and the accuracy of those responses. Following are some guidelines for wording questions:

- **Define the issue.** Every question should address one or more of the who-what-when-why-where-how questions characterizing an effective news story. Check each survey question against these criteria to make sure you are not leaving something out. For example, a question like, "How much is your income," leaves out an important "what" (what comprises income? salary alone? salary and benefits?), and an important "when" (what period is addressed: weekly? monthly? annually?).

- **Use understandable words.** The average word in a dictionary has nine different meanings, so finding words that have the same meaning to all respondents can be difficult. "Judgment" words, or words whose interpretation is subject to the subjective judgment of different people, usually ensure ambiguity in questionnaires.

- **Avoid leading questions.** As their name implies, leading questions *lead* the respondent to answer the question (and, usually, follow-up questions) in a certain (usually desired) way. Perhaps the primary violation of this guideline in marketing research surveys involves a question that mentions the name of the product; with Hawthorne and halo biases working, such questions (such as, "What is your opinion of the Merton personal computer") usually motivate the respondent to answer in a manner favorable to the sponsor. (If the Merton Mini were listed as only one of a number of PC models, with no indication that Merton was conducting this survey, this problem could be avoided.)

- **Do not ask questions that require generalized answers.** Unless the questionnaire is unstructured and open-ended, and such general answers are desired, questions should be stated as specifically as possible. The question, "What is your opinion of the Merton engineers' PC?" for example, would probably elicit a vague generalization which would be difficult to analyze, and would produce much less useful data than a multiple choice question structured to elicit more specific information.

DETERMINE QUESTION FORMAT

Four types of question formats are available for communicating question content, ranging from the unstructured "open" question to more highly structured "multiple choice," "rating scale," and "dichotomous" questions. Following are summaries of the characteristics, limitations, and applications of each type:

• *OPEN QUESTIONS*

Open questions do not suggest alternative answers and, hence, can be answered as the respondent sees fit. This open question, with which the engineers' survey might begin, illustrates the advantages and disadvantages of such questions:

> "What, in your opinion, are the main advantages and disadvantages of a portable personal computer to a mechanical engineer?"

As the first question on a questionnaire, an open question is frequently a good way to familiarize the respondent with the purpose and content of the survey and prepare the way for more specific questions. It is also a good way to interest and involve the respondent in the survey—particularly if the respondent is flattered by being asked for his or her opinion.

Also, since open questions do not suggest possible answers—as do multiple choice questions, for example—they often produce unexpected responses. This makes them particularly useful during the exploratory stage of marketing research, when ideas are being sought to promote or position products, or hypotheses emerge to be tested during later stages. These answers can also be helpful in designing multiple choice questions for more structured surveys. Also, verbatim answers to open questions have an authoritative "ring" that adds interest, conviction, and concreteness in reporting survey results.

Against these advantages are a number of potential disadvantages associated with open questions, including the difficulty reviewers face in recording and tabulating answers, and the possibility of interviewer bias resulting in the distortion of long, rambling answers. One solution to these problems involves using a multiple-choice format on the interviewer's version of the question. For example, for the question above, the interviewer's version might list the most likely "advantages" and "disadvantages," and leave space for unexpected answers.

Another disadvantage of open questions is the interviewee bias implicit in the fact that more affluent, better-educated respondents tend to give more complete, articulate answers, and hence will have greater weight in the final results.

The disadvantages of open questions, which make them three to five times more costly to process than structured questions, mean that they are rarely used in structured questionnaires; especially in light of the fact that other formats, discussed next, achieve the same goals.

• *MULTIPLE CHOICE QUESTIONS*

Multiple choice questions, which offer respondents a number of specific alternatives from which to choose, address most of the problems of open questions while introducing a few of their own. To illustrate, here is a typical multiple choice question that might appear in the engineers' questionnaire:

Which of the following features would you find most useful in a personal computer?

portability _____
flexibility _____
computational speed _____
memory capacity _____
reliability _____

In addition to the fact that the alternatives are all stated as vague, judgment words and terms that should be defined more specifically (for example, specific degrees of speed or capacity, or definitions of "portability" and "flexibility"), this example also illustrates other multiple choice problems:

- Too many alternatives can cause respondents to lose interest in the entire questionnaire; five are usually considered the limit (and the respondent must be told if more than one can be selected).

- Alternatives may not include all possible categories (so append an "other" category).

- Alternatives may not be mutually exclusive (for example, "portability" and "flexibility" might mean the same thing to some respondents).

Other problems peculiar to multiple choice questions are the two biases they engender: (1) **position bias**, or the tendency for respondents to select the first alternative in a sequence, and (2) **order bias**, or the tendency to select an alternative in the numerical center of a group.

For example, if "memory capacity" were more precisely defined as follows in another multiple choice question on the engineers' questionnaire, respondents would tend to select the middle answer ("512 K"):

How much memory capacity in a personal computer would best suit your purposes?
256K _____
512K _____
768K _____

Both order and position biases can be eliminated by rotating responses on mailed questionnaires. For example, for the six alternatives offered in response to the "PC features" question above, "portability" would appear in each position on one-sixth of the questionnaires mailed out. Also, multiple choice answers practically eliminate interviewer bias, and are relatively easy to edit, classify, code, and tabulate.

• *SCALING QUESTIONS*

Scaling is a variant of multiple choice questions developed mainly to address the problem of comparability in studies measuring subjective variables like motives, attitudes, and perceptions. For example, engineers might be asked to rank various personal computers, including the Merton, in terms of their perception of the memory capacity of each. On the simplest level, an **ordinal scale** would indicate the degree to which memory capacity is better, or worse, among the computers ranked: IBM, AT&T, and Merton.

Although they make no attempt to measure the degree of favorability of the different rankings, ordinal scales are the most widely used of all rating scales in marketing research.

Two variants of ordinal scales which have many marketing research applications are **Thurstone scales** and **Likert scales.**

Thurstone scales present a series of statements from which the respondent chooses those that correspond to his or her attitudes:

1. Use of personal computers actually slows me down
2. Personal computers allow me to be slightly more efficient
3. Personal computers make me much more efficient, etc.

Thurstone scale statements are usually arranged in descending order from negative to positive, and the respondent is permitted to select more than one statement.

Likert scales carry the Thurstone scale a step further by permitting the respondent to indicate the extent of agreement or disagreement with each statement. Thus, an engineer might respond to the first two statements above as follows:

	Agree very strongly	Agree	Undecided	Disagree	Disagree very strongly
1. Use of personal computers actually slows me down					X
2. Personal computers allow me to be slightly more efficient		X			

Interval scales carry ordinal rankings a step further by measuring the distance between rank positions in equal units. For example, a respondent might be asked to rank personal computer memory capacity along the following interval scale:

	POOR	AVERAGE	EXCELLENT
IBM		X	
Merton			X

On this scale, the distance between "poor" and "average" is the same as the distance between "average" and "excellent." However, such a scale does not permit the conclusion that "excellent" is twice as good as "average," since no zero position has been established. For example, if "poor" is 100, "average" might be 120, and "excellent" 140. A scale that permits such absolute measurements is called a **ratio scale**, which, while commonly used in the physical sciences, is virtually never used in marketing research, which generally does not require such fine calibrations of subjective variables.

• *DICHOTOMOUS QUESTIONS*

Dichotomous questions that allow a choice of only one of two alternative answers (yes or no, cash or credit, did or did not, etc.), are the most widely used of all question formats. Sometimes, the alternatives are only implied (Do you use personal computers or mainframe computers in your computational activities? _____), although research shows that results are more accurate if alternatives are stated. In general, the same advantages and disadvantages of multiple choice questions apply to dichotomous questions. On the positive side, they eliminate interviewer bias and are relatively easy to edit, code, and tabulate; on the negative side (as illustrated by the dichotomous question above), both alternatives might be true, and other possible answers might be excluded.

YOU SHOULD REMEMBER

Four major question format options are available: the *open question* format, which permits the respondent to answer as he or she pleases; the *multiple choice* question format, which offers the respondent a choice from among a number of alternative answers; the *rating scale* format, which permits a gradation of responses to subjective questions; and the *dichotomous* question format, which offers only two alternative answers, expressed or implied. The open question format provides a means of interesting respondents in questionnaire content and motivating responses, and often evokes information not available from other formats. This information can add authority and concreteness to questionnaire findings. However, the open format also evokes interviewer and interviewee biases, and produces answers that are much more difficult to edit, code, and tabulate than answers to multiple choice or dichotomous questions. These latter types of questions also reduce interviewer and interviewee bias, replacing them, however, with order and position biases. Bias can be reduced in all formats through tighter controls and better selection and wording of both questions and answers.

Rating scale questions are a version of multiple choice questions designed to introduce a degree of comparability in measurements of such subjective variables as attitudes and perceptions. *Ordinal* rating scales simply ask respondents to rank products against an attribute; *interval* scales provide more precision by measuring the distance between ranks in equal units. Neither scale provides the absolute values that are available with the ratio scales used in the physical sciences.

DETERMINE QUESTION SEQUENCE

Regardless of whether they are communicated via mail, telephone, or personal interview, most questionnaires encompass three major sections:

1. a **basic information** section comprising the actual questions asked

2. a **classification information** section in which the respondent provides demographic data which can be related to the basic information (for example, the respondent's age, income, and education level might all be considered important variables relating to computer usage)

3. an **identification information** section which includes identifying data (names, addresses, code numbers, etc.) for all questionnaire participants: interviewer, interviewee, editor, card puncher, etc.

To help ensure respondent interest and involvement, the questionnaire should follow this basic information, classification, identification sequence. Here are other sequencing guidelines:

- Place questions that the respondent might not wish to answer in the body of the basic information section, to be asked when the respondent is at ease with the interviewer or the questionnaire content.

- Consider the influence of question placement on succeeding questions. Place questions that use the product name at the conclusion of the questionnaire.

- Arrange questions in a logical order, avoiding sudden topic changes that will confuse the respondent.

OTHER DESIGN CONSIDERATIONS

Research studies suggest a variety of approaches and techniques for improving the quality and quantity of responses to questionnaires communicated by personal interviews or through the mail.

- Number questionnaires serially to verify that all are accounted for. Formerly, a code number on a mailed questionnaire was thought to compromise a promise of anonymity, but research has indicated that it influences results little, if at all.

- Make sure the questionnaire is of proper size and length. For a personal interview, the questionnaire should be sufficiently large so that information is not cramped, yet not so large that it is awkward to handle. For most applications, 8½" × 11" letter size is best. Mailed questionnaires of more than two pages show a dramatic falloff in returns, as do personal questionnaires of more than four pages. A questionnaire that runs into several pages should be made into a booklet for easier handling and data entry.

- People are more likely to respond to questionnaires that (1) have interesting titles and first pages; (2) include a cover letter explaining the purpose of the mailing and relating this purpose to the respondent's self interest; (3) are personalized by hand-signing and addressing the respondent by name.

- The use of direct incentives, including cash, trading stamps, lottery tickets, and similar premiums, almost invariably improves response rates. With cash incentives, larger amounts included with each letter increase returns up to about one third, beyond which the percentage of return levels off. Research findings are ambiguous as to the optimal amount to include as an incentive; the figure tends to change with respondent groups and inflation rates. However, research strongly indicates that cash incentives are a cheaper way to assure a desired rate of return than follow-up mailings and phone calls.

- Mechanical and perceptual devices that increase returns include (1) telephone contact with respondents before they receive the questionnaire explaining its purpose and importance; (2) questionnaires sent via special delivery, registered mail, and first class mail; and (3) stamped, self-addressed envelopes included with each mailing for returning the questionnaire.

- Regardless of how the questionnaire is communicated, it should be pretested to eliminate inaccurate, ambiguous phraseology and distortive biases. Pretesting should be conducted under the same conditions that will be used in the actual interview situation.

YOU SHOULD REMEMBER

Questionnaire sequence guidelines aim to reduce the respondent's confusion and enhance his or her motivation to respond. Basic information should precede classification information, which should be followed by identification information. In the basic information section, interest-arousing questions should appear first, with potentially embarrassing questions faced later, when the respondent is likely to be more at ease. Consider the influence of early questions on later questions, and avoid abrupt subject changes.

Direct incentives like cash and premiums, general motivators like personalized salutations, and perceptual devices like pre-mailing phone calls have all been found to increase response rates.

INFORMATION PROCESSING

If appropriate sampling and data-gathering approaches have been used, marketing research data will meet standards for objectivity, rationality, and precision, and will be as valid and reliable as possible.

CODING, TABULATING, AND ANALYZING DATA

For data to be of value to marketing managers in making critical decisions, however, it must be properly processed in a sequence of activities that involve coding, tabulation, and analysis.

To illustrate these activities, assume that part of the engineers' study involved determining the extent to which three engineering subgroups—mechanical engineers, civil engineers, and industrial engineers—made use of personal computers in their work:

- **Coding** is the process of transforming questionnaire responses into interpretable form by assigning responses to categories, and numbers to the categories, to facilitate analysis. Thus, each response from each subgroup would automatically be assigned to a numbered category indicating whether the respondent did or did not use a personal computer in his or her work.

- **Tabulation** is the process of summarizing responses by categories, with results expressed as totals or percentages. For example, the engineers' study tabulation showed that only 20 percent of mechanical engineers, and ten percent of civil engineers, used personal computers, as compared to 60 percent of industrial engineers.

- **Analysis** involves the use of various statistical techniques to evaluate responses in respect to original research objectives. In the engineers' study, for example, (1) statistical tests of significance showed there was virtually no chance that percentage differences among the three groups would arise through sampling error, making them highly significant, and (2) correlation studies showed strong associations between the use of personal computers and certain occupational characteristics. For example, both civil and mechanical engineers worked outdoors much more than industrial engineers, where they perceived personal computer use would be impractical.

MAKING RECOMMENDATIONS

Finally, after findings are coded, tabulated, and analyzed, the marketing research manager must make recommendations that will produce decisions to solve the problem under investigation. Although occasionally overlooked, this is the most important aspect of the entire marketing research process, and should be performed to enable all marketing people responsible for making these decisions to understand and act on recommendations. In the engineers' study, for example, recommendations were made for changes in the design of the Mini to accommodate the working conditions of civil and mechanical engineers.

IMPLEMENTATION AND FEEDBACK

Finally, the marketing research process comes full circle as findings and recommendations are programmed into appropriate MIS subsystems, and used in the subsequent creation, implementation, and control of Mini marketing plans.

YOU SHOULD REMEMBER

Data produced through sampling and survey techniques are coded, tabulated, and analyzed to produce information, in the form of conclusions and recommendations, of use to management in solving problems addressed by the research study. This information is then programmed into the MIS for use in developing, implementing, and controlling marketing plans.

KNOW THE CONCEPTS

DO YOU KNOW THE BASICS?

1. What is the significance of the word "probability" in defining probability and non-probability samples?

2. Why are non-probability samples more likely to be used in the exploratory phase of the marketing research process, while probability samples are more likely to be used during the conclusive stage?

3. Give examples of the kind of information a researcher might elicit on behalf of a political candidate for which the following types of samples would be appropriate: judgment; quota; convenience; random.

4. Give examples of two kinds of bias that might emerge during the process of falling in love.

5. Relate three kinds of questionnaire design (structured/non-disguised, non-structured/non-disguised, etc.) to the level of information desired (know, will divulge; know, will not divulge; know, cannot divulge). Why, as the level gets deeper, is disguise more important? Are there moral implications in administering a test with a high degree of disguise?

6. Briefly describe two circumstances that would work against the use of each of the following survey methods: person-to-person; telephone; mail.

7. Think of a questionnaire (or other example of "junk" mail) that you recently threw away. How might this mailing have been redesigned to make it less likely to be thrown away?

8. Envision a question a prospective employer might ask you pertaining to vices (such as drug or alcohol abuse) you might display on or off the job. Under what circumstances might this question be couched in a highly disguised manner? Under what circumstances would it be presented as a multiple choice or a dichotomous question? How might the placement of this question among other questions in the questionnaire influence your answer?

9. Explain how you would engage in the following activities leading up to a recommendation that a friend go out on a blind date with another of your friends: coding; tabulating; analysis.

TERMS FOR STUDY

analysis
basic information
classification information

coding
confidence levels
convenience sample

degree of disguise
degree of structure
dichotomous questions
direct incentives
halo effect bias
Hawthorne effect bias
identification information
interval scales
interviewer/interviewee bias
judgment sample
Likert scale
mail survey
mechanical devices
multiple choice questions
Neilsen rating services
non-probability sample
non-response bias
open questions
order bias

ordinal scale
personal interview
population
position bias
probability sample
question format
questionnaire
quota sample
ratio scale
respondents
sample
sampling principle
scaling
self-selection bias
survey
tabulation
telephone survey
Thurstone scale

ANSWERS

KNOW THE BASICS

1. "Probability," in sampling, means that every member of a population has an equal chance of being selected for the sample. The significance of this characteristic derives from the nature of findings and conclusions emerging from probability samples: unlike in non-probability samples, these findings and conclusions can be stated with a measurable degree of accuracy. For example, a probability sample designed to determine the average height of students in a classroom might conclude: "There is a 99 percent probability that the average height of students in this classroom is between 5'8" and 5'9". Unless you measure the heights of all members of the population, you will never know the exact average height, but you will have confidence in the upper and lower limits. Futhermore, it is possible to obtain unusually precise, accurate confidence levels from relatively small samples, and at comparatively little cost.

2. The use of non-probability samples means that some members of the sample will have a greater or lesser probability than others of being included in the sample, usually based on some predetermined criterion pertaining to sample composition (quota), access of sample members (convenience), or expertise of sample members (judgment). The qualities that define non-probability samples—such as attitudes of women toward female political

candidates that emerge from a judgment/quota sample—also make them especially useful in developing hypotheses during exploratory research stages. However, testing these hypotheses during conclusive research stages requires the measurable precision of probability samples.

3. A *judgment* sample might include political leaders expressing opinions as to the most important issues in an upcoming campaign (in the researcher's *judgment,* they would be best able to provide this information); a *quota* sample might include young people and senior citizens commenting on the divisive issue: "should we cut back on social security benefits?" Each group would be represented in the sample in proportion to its representation in the entire population; a *convenience* sample would be illustrated by a local newspaper's "man-in-the-street" interview of voter attitudes toward issues or candidates; a *random* sample might be used to predict, within measurable confidence levels, the percent of the entire population who plan to vote for candidate "A".

4. Some examples: "Halo effect" bias would probably be evidenced in the many attributes of the loved one you elevate in light of favorable attitudes toward a few attributes (for example, you love the way he *looks,* therefore you love the way he *acts*); "interviewee bias" might be evidenced in your responses to questions about the loved one (you want interviewers to have as high a regard for her as you have); "Hawthorne effect" bias would be reflected in unnatural behavior patterns (for example, you no longer slurp your soup) in response to the realization that you are "special."

5. If the respondent knows, and is perfectly willing to divulge information, then the structured, undisguised format is probably most appropriate; just *ask* him or her in a direct, undisguised manner. As information required becomes more complex and subjective—for example, attitudes toward a political candidate, or motives for voting for this candidate—an unstructured undisguised format becomes more viable: provide respondents with a free-wheeling format for sharing ideas and stimulating new insights. Finally, in situations where respondents are unwilling or consciously unable to provide the desired information, a disguised format, either structured or unstructured, might be used to develop this information by indirection, i.e., the respondent is commenting on a general situation in a way that does not threaten his or her personal sense of worth. Moral implications of disguised studies probably equate to any event in a democratic, free-enterprise society that fools people, from a politician's lie to a "bait and switch" ad: Should the buyer beware? Should Big Brother protect the buyer from *having* to beware? Do beneficial ends justify deceptive means?

6. *Person-to-person:* When survey questions are simple and uncomplicated, and willingly answered by respondents, then the considerable expense and administrative bother of a person-to-person interview can be avoided by using a telephone or mail survey.
   Telephone: If the information desired is complex and subjective, requiring

long, in-depth interviews or a group sharing of ideas, or if it can be gathered more efficiently and economically through a mail survey, then these other communication modes would be more effective.

Mail: Lengthy or highly subjective information that cannot be obtained in the relatively short, fixed format of a written questionnaire would be more effectively pursued using other information-gathering approaches. (However, in mail surveys people will often provide "personal" information that would not be provided in telephone or person-to-person surveys.)

7. Here is an illustrative example: A publisher solicits a professor's ideas and opinions on a proposed new textbook-publishing venture: (1) a publisher's representative phones the professor to inform him or her that the questionnaire is forthcoming; (2) the envelope containing the questionnaire, and the inside address on the transmittal letter, are typed and personalized; (3) an incentive (such as a book from the publisher's list) is offered to encourage the recipient to respond to the questionnaire; (4) a stamped, self-addressed envelope is included to facilitate the professor's response.

8. Assume the vice referred to is alcohol abuse. A prospective employer's question might be couched in a disguised format if this vice would be considered a detriment to the position (say, an airline pilot). The question would be asked in a direct manner, using a multiple choice or dichotomous format, in the unlikely event the vice was a requirement for the job (perhaps a job participating in an experiment on alcohol rehabilitation measures). If the question was perceived as a threat by the respondent, its placement at the beginning of the questionnaire could influence respondent's attitude toward all the questions, and the likelihood that they will be answered truthfully, or at all.

9. Coding: You might, for example, identify certain important attributes (charm, wit, etc.) that both your friend and the prospective blind date have in common. Tabulating: You might then total the extent to which each possess these attributes (for example, they both score "10" in "good looks" and "interest in Bruce Springsteen"). Analysis: You compare these totals in these key categories, and conclude they are meant for each other.

7
CONSUMER
BEHAVIOR

KEY TERMS

attitude a person's enduring cognitive evaluation, feeling, or action tendency toward a particular object, idea, or person

culture symbols and artifacts created by people and handed down from one generation to another as determinants and regulators of human behavior in a given society

diffusion of innovation a process by which an innovation is communicated within social systems over time

family life cycle the series of stages a family goes through, each characterized by different needs and purchasing behavior patterns

learning changes in an individual's behavior arising from experience

life style a pattern of living comprising an individual's activities, interests, and opinions

motivation the force that activates goal-oriented behavior

perception the process of selecting, organizing, and interpreting stimuli received through the senses; perceptions shape behavior

personality an individual's unique pattern of traits that lead to consistent and enduring behavioral responses

psychographics a system of explaining market behavior in terms of demographics, attitudes, and life styles

social class relatively homogeneous, enduring, and hierarchically ordered social divisions whose members share similar values and behavior

This chapter is the first of five that examine the nature, scope, and structure of product markets. Particular emphasis is placed on pressures that influence decisions to purchase, and on how both market members and marketing managers react to these pressures.

In this chapter and Chapter 8, the focus will be on consumer market behavior. This market encompasses all individuals and households that buy or acquire goods and services for personal consumption. In 1990, the consumer market comprised 240 million people who purchased more than $2 trillion worth of goods and services, almost $9,000 for every person.

A MODEL OF CONSUMER BEHAVIOR

The nature of consumer behavior, focusing on when, why, how, and where people do or do not buy products, is illustrated by the "black box" model in Figure 7-1.

ENVIRONMENTAL FACTORS		BUYER'S BLACK BOX		BUYER'S RESPONSES
Marketing Stimuli	Environmental Stimuli	Buyer Characteristics	Decision Processes	
Product Price Place Promotion	Economic Technical Political Cultural	Attitudes Motivation Perceptions Personality Lifestyle	Problem recognition Information search Alternative evaluation Purchase decision Post-purchase behavior	Product choice Brand choice Dealer choice Purchase timing Purchase amount

Figure 7–1. "Black box" model shows how stimuli, consumer characteristics, and decision processes interact in eliciting consumer responses.

To illustrate the decision-making process implicit in this model, consider the process leading up to an engineer's purchase of a Merton Mini.

First, the engineer might have been exposed to two kinds of stimuli (from the "Environmental Factors" box in the model): **marketing stimuli,** which are largely under the control of the marketing manager, and **environmental stimuli,** which are largely uncontrolled. For instance, the engineer might have been impressed with product features and price when a local dealer demonstrated the Mini; then, the favorable response of associates to the Mini might have further persuaded him to investigate a Mini purchase.

Helping to define and direct this further investigation are a group of "buyer characteristics" (the "Buyer's Black Box" in the model), including the engineer's **perception** of the Mini as compared to competitive products, and motivating goals he feels the Mini will help achieve. Many, perhaps all, of these stimuli would then combine to motivate and direct his decision to purchase the Mini (i.e., "Buyer Response").

In this chapter, we will examine the cultural, social, and personal environmental stimuli that directly influence the consumer decision-making process. These influences can be classified as interpersonal (between people) or intrapersonal (within people). **Interpersonal** influences include family, friends, and other larger social and cultural groups to which people belong or would like to belong. **Intrapersonal** influences include drives, perceptions, attitudes, and habits that shape behavior in general and consumer behavior in particular. The behavioral sciences (sociology, anthropology, psychology) have contributed most of the research findings pertaining to the influence of interpersonal and intrapersonal factors on behavior.

THE IMPORTANCE OF UNDERSTANDING CONSUMER BEHAVIOR

It is particularly important that marketing managers understand consumer behavior in light of marketing precepts which mandate a marketing response geared to marketplace needs. Thus, understanding **consumer behavior** helps the marketing manager to understand marketplace needs and develop marketing mixes to satisfy these needs. The Merton Mini evolved in response to the identification of groups of people who perceived the need for such a product to help them achieve the career goals toward which they were motivated. These groups then became **target markets**, whose needs defined Mini marketing strategies—product features, how the product was priced and promoted, and so on.

To illustrate key concepts pertaining to the nature and scope of consumer behavior and decision-making processes, and their role in building marketing strategies, we will introduce another case:

> **Friendship Camps, Inc.:** This firm operates a chain of eight summer camps situated in four New England states. Each camp offers a traditional camping program for children between the ages of four and 16, including coaching and skill development in such land and water sports as soccer, tennis, swimming, sailing, softball, gymnastics, backpacking, and theater crafts.
>
> Despite the camps' "blue chip" image, excellent word-of-mouth referrals from campers and parents, a spotless safety record, and continuing targeted advertising campaigns, Friendship Camps began experiencing difficulty attracting campers. Beginning in the late 1980s, it experienced a succession of years during which costs progressively exceeded revenues.
>
> To reverse this loss trend Friendship Camps retained the Acme Advertising Agency, which it selected over a number of other agencies competing for the account. Friendship's management was particularly impressed with Acme's successful record working with clients in the "services" industry, and with

its insistence that it be involved in all phases of the strategic marketing planning effort, including identifying target markets and building marketing mixes.

Acme assigned the Friendship account to a team consisting of an account executive and specialists in such areas as media, advertising production, art, copy, and marketing research. The team's first act on behalf of its new client was to conduct a situation analysis to identify primary problems responsible for Friendship's deteriorating situation. This analysis showed that the problems emerged largely from competitive pressures and from the generally negative perceptions and attitudes they engendered toward the "traditional camp" concept.

Next, the team undertook a study of the influence of interpersonal and intrapersonal variables on the behavior of potential consumers of Friendship Camp services. On the interpersonal level, the team was particularly interested in the influence on consumer behavior of various groups people belonged to, or aspired to, in what kinds of information was communicated among people and these groups, and in the processes whereby this information was communicated.

On the intrapersonal level, the team studied the influence on consumer behavior of economic, demographic, and psychographic variables such as income, age, occupation, lifestyle, motivation, and attitudes.

In addition to helping the agency team identify and profile target markets toward which Friendship could tailor its marketing mix offerings, this study of interpersonal and intrapersonal influences also sparked a variety of ideas for changing the traditional Friendship camp offerings, and positioning and promoting the camps so they were more consistent with target market wants and needs.

YOU SHOULD REMEMBER

The study of consumer behavior focuses on how marketing, environmental, and other stimuli influence consumer purchase decisions. Of particular interest to marketing managers are the contributions of the behavioral sciences (notably sociology, anthropology, and psychology) to an understanding of the influence of interpersonal factors, such as cultural and social groups, and intrapersonal factors, such as habits, attitudes and motives, on consumer behavior. By identifying and profiling target markets in terms of these criteria, marketing managers develop useful ideas for developing products and devising price, place, and promotion strategies for marketing them.

HOW INTERPERSONAL VARIABLES INFLUENCE CONSUMER BEHAVIOR

The agency team's analysis started with an examination of the influence of larger groups on consumer behavior—namely, cultures, subcultures, and social classes—then narrowed to focus on the influence of smaller peer and reference groups. In general, smaller groups have greater influence on consumer behavior. For example, you are more likely to attend a movie or eat at a restaurant based on the recommendation of a friend or associate than on a review published in an entertainment magazine.

CULTURE

Culture is broadly defined as a complex of core values and beliefs created by society, handed down from generation to generation, and reinforced by such social institutions as schools and churches. Consciously or unconsciously, cultural values exert pressures on people to behave in certain acceptable ways. Frequently, an effective marketing plan harnesses these pressures in behalf of specific products. For example, in developing the marketing plan for Friendship camps these primary cultural values were considered: achievement and success, creativity and involvement, efficiency and progress, individualism, humanitarianism, and youthfulness.

While these primary cultural values change slowly, secondary values deriving from them change much more frequently. Here are examples of these relatively recent secondary cultural values that the agency team incorporated into its marketing plan:

- Emphasis on quality of life, rather than quantity of product possessions, manifested by (1) a growing appreciation for art, music, literature, and drama; (2) a growing need for value, durability, and safety in products; and (3) a growing concern over crime, inflation, and the quality of the environment.

- The changing role of women, emphasizing their attempts to (1) break from often discriminatory stereotypes in families, jobs, recreation, and product use; and (2) seek greater political, economic, and career opportunities.

- Changing attitudes toward work and pleasure, with emphasis on (1) careers and lifestyles that bring rewards other than status and high incomes; and (2) self-centered, self-fulfilling activities, such as physical fitness and health pursuits.

- Increased leisure time resulting from shorter work weeks, longer paid vacations, and more labor-saving devices.

SUBCULTURES

Subcultures are separate segments of a culture organized around such factors as race, nationality, religion, or geographic location. The common interests and characteristics of each subculture frequently represent marketing opportunities. For example, people sharing a common ethnic background have certain attitudes and preferences (in food, recreation, political attitudes, geographic location, etc.) that identify them as discrete market segments, as do people sharing similar racial, religious, or geographical backgrounds. In analyzing these subcultural groups, however, it is important to recognize that there are usually as many differences as similarities among them. For example, both the Black and Hispanic subculture markets comprise many separate segments with distinct demographic, economic, and social characteristics.

SOCIAL CLASSES

Social classes are defined as relatively homogeneous and enduring divisions in a society whose members share similar values, interests and behavior. A number of studies have shown, among other things, that social classes are hierarchically structured and that similar social class hierarchies exist in all geographical areas, from small towns to large cities. An individual's position in a given hierarchy is not based on income alone, but takes into consideration the type of income, occupation, type of house, and area of residence within the community. Members of a given social class show distinct product and brand preferences in such areas as clothing, home furnishings, and automobiles. Social class membership is a more significant determinant of buyer behavior than amount of income. In the United States, lines between social classes are not fixed; over their lifetimes, people can move up or down among the hierarchies.

Here, from a social class study conducted by Engel, Blackwell, and Miniard, are some characteristics and purchase proclivities of six social classes[1]:

1. *Upper-upper class* (less than one percent of the population): Socially elite, inherited wealth, well-known family name and background; give large sums to charity, maintain more than one home, send children to best schools; excellent market for jewelry, antiques, homes, vacations; often buy, dress conservatively. Serve as reference group for imitation by other social classes.

2. *Lower-upper class* (about two percent of the population): High income or wealth earned through exceptional ability in business or professions; active in social, civic affairs; buy status-symbol products for selves, children (expensive homes, cars, yachts, etc.). Include nouveaux riche, whose pattern of ostentation is designed to impress classes above and below them. Main ambition: to be accepted, or have children accepted, by "upper-uppers."

---

1. James F. Engel, Roger D. Blackwell, and Paul W. Miniard, *Consumer Behavior*, 5th ed. (Hinsdale, Ill., Dryden Press, 1986), pp. 344–348.

3. *Upper-middle class* (about 12 percent of the population): Professionals, independent business people, and corporate managers who possess neither family status nor unusual wealth, are primarily concerned with careers for selves and children. Highly civic-minded joiners, they like to deal in ideas and "high culture," entertain friends and clients at home. Represent a quality market for good homes, clothes, furniture, appliances, and vacation amenities.

4. *Lower-middle class* (about 30 percent of the population): Primarily white collar workers (e.g., office workers, small business owners), "gray collar" workers (mailmen, firemen), and "aristocratic blue collar" workers (plumbers, factory foremen). Concerned with "respectability," they exhibit conscientious work habits and adhere to culturally defined norms. Maintain neat, "pretty" homes, buy conventional furnishings, and do own repairs. Avoid "high style."

5. *Upper-lower class* (about 35 percent of the population): "Blue collar" skilled and semi-skilled factory workers. Seek respectability and security. Husband has "macho" self-image, is a heavy smoker, beer drinker, outdoorsman, sports enthusiast. Wife spends most of her time cooking, cleaning, caring for children, with little time for organizations or social activities.

6. *Lower-lower class* (about 20 percent of the population): At bottom of hierarchy, comprise poorly educated, unskilled laborers, often reject middle-class standards of morality, behavior. Buy impulsively, with little concern for quality. Tend to buy on credit, and pay too much. Large market for food, television sets, used automobiles.

REFERENCE GROUPS

Reference groups have a direct (face-to-face) or an indirect influence on consumer attitudes and behavior. Major reference group categories include (1) **membership groups** the individual belongs to, (2) **aspirational groups** the individual would like to join, and (3) **disassociative groups** whose values the individual rejects.

Membership groups can be primary or secondary. Primary groups, such as the individual's family, friends, or co-workers, are more informal than secondary groups, which include social, religious and professional associations. Interactions among members tends to be more continuous in primary than in secondary groups.

Membership and aspirational groups influence people in a variety of ways of interest to marketing managers; they expose people to new products and behaviors, influence an individual's attitudes and self-concepts, and create pressures to conform to group values. The force of this influence depends on (1) the group itself, with more cohesive groups (such as a strong religious or political group) exerting more influence; (2) the individuals being influenced by group norms and values, with "other-directed" people, who adopt values of reference groups, more likely to be influenced than "inner-directed" people, who act on personal values; and (3) the product over which the group exerts influence.

Research indicates that group influence is strongest in the case of highly visible products which can be seen in use by others. Group influence on product choice also varies with the product class and brand of the product being promoted. For example, Figure 7–2 shows how the motivating force of group influence varies by product class and brand for a selected sample of products. The agency team handling the Friendship account was interested to note that camps fell into the "strong-strong" category, indicating that group influence was strong in motivating both a camping experience (class) and a specific camp to attend (brand).

Brand Type \\ Product Class	WEAK	STRONG
WEAK	Canned peaches Laundry soap Refrigerator	Air conditioner Instant coffee Television
STRONG	Clothing Furniture Magazines	Automobile Drugs Camps

Figure 7–2. Influence of reference groups on product/brand decision.

The extent of group influence on product choice also varies with the product's life cycle stage. For products in the introductory stage, product class influence tends to be strong and product brand influence weak. Products in the growth stage of the product life cycle tend to exhibit "strong-strong" group influence on both class and brand levels, while products in the maturity stage—where Friendship camps were when the agency took over the account—tend to have weak product class and brand group influence.

In working with and through reference groups to market products, marketing managers must first

1. identify relevant reference groups
2. measure the extent of the group's influence on consumer behavior
3. develop a marketing communication program to influence these influential group members favorably toward the offering

YOU SHOULD REMEMBER

Interpersonal influences on consumer behavior are exerted by (1) complexes of socially-created and conditioned values and beliefs called **cultures;** (2) separate segments of cultures called **subcultures;** (3) relatively enduring socioeconomic groups called **social classes,** and (4) primary or secondary groups that people belong to, aspire to belong to, or do not want to join, called **reference groups.** These groups all affect consumer behavior in a variety of ways, depending on such factors as the cohesiveness of the group, the nature of people influenced by the group, and the characteristics of the product affected by group influence. The marketing manager's job in positioning and promoting products involves first identifying the relative impact of each group on consumer behavior, then developing marketing communication plans and programs that work through these groups to favorably influence consumer behavior.

COMMUNICATING TO AND THROUGH GROUPS

Two important areas of research for developing marketing communication programs to influence influential group members are the processes whereby messages are transmitted within groups, and the nature and characteristics of groups and of the individuals that transmit these messages.

The Friendship advertising team developed a strategy to enable them to identify and sell influential people in target reference groups, thus saving time and money by having these influentials do much of the marketing job for them.

HOW MESSAGES ARE TRANSMITTED IN GROUPS

For years it was assumed that information traveled vertically within groups, usually from high socioeconomic levels (the upper-uppers) through and to lower levels. Studies by Katz and Lazersfeld[2], however, show the horizontal nature of opinion leadership. Influence emerges on each level of the socioeconomic scale, moving from opinion leaders to peers in a two-step information flow, as shown in Figure 7–3.

---

2. Elihu Katz and Paul Lazersfeld, *Personal Influence* (New York: Free Press, 1955), especially p. 325; also Elihu Katz, "The Two-Step Flow of Communications: An up-to-date Report on a Hypothesis," *Public Opinion Quarterly*, Spring, 1957, pp. 61–78.

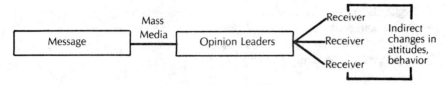

Figure 7–3. Katz Lazersfeld two-stage communication model.

WHO TRANSMITS MESSAGES

Research studies relating to the processes whereby messages are transmitted or diffused within groups typically focus on the new-product adoption process. Unlike socioeconomic group studies, which focus on characteristics and behavior patterns of social systems at a given point in time, these diffusion studies examine behavior patterns of groups over time.

Rogers,[3] for example, identified the following groups involved in the purchase decision process, based on the point in time at which the purchase decision was made and the relative influence of each group in motivating other groups to purchase a product:

Innovators, the first to adopt a new product, tend to be younger and wealthier than other "adopter" groups. They also tend to have higher social status and more cosmopolitan social relations and are more likely to rely on impersonal information sources than on salespeople and other word-of-mouth sources. They average 2.5 percent of the target market.

Early adopters, unlike innovators, tend to be "localites" rather than cosmopolites, and include more opinion leaders than any other adopter group. Better integrated into and respected by members of their social system, this group represents the change agent through which marketing managers can work to speed up product acceptance. They average 13.5 percent of the target market.

The early majority, a more deliberate group, above average in social and economic status, tend to accept an innovation just before the "average" adopter in a social system. Its members rely largely on advertisements, sales people, and early adopters for product information. They average 34 percent of the target market.

Late majority members, generally skeptical, tend to adopt an innovation in response to economic necessity or peer pressure, with late- or early-majority members serving as information sources. Advertising and personal selling is less effective than word of mouth. They also average 34 percent of the target market.

---

3. Everett M. Rogers, "New Product Adoption and Diffusion," *Journal of Consumer Research*, March, 1976, pp. 290–301.

Laggards, of little interest to marketing managers, are the last to adopt an innovation. Suspicious of innovations and innovators, laggards are usually older and at the low end of the socioeconomic scale. They represent about 16 percent of the target market.

• *THE FAMILY*

As the smallest reference group with which the consumer interacts, the family is also the most important buying influence in society. Two kinds of family—the *family of orientation* and the *family of procreation*—exert this persuasive influence:

> **The family of orientation,** consisting of the consumer's parents and siblings, imparts beliefs and values toward religion, politics, and economics, and feelings of personal ambition and self-worth. This family can even influence the buyer's unconscious behavior.

> **The family of procreation,** consisting of the consumer's spouse and children, has a more direct influence on everyday buying behavior than any other social organization.

As with reference groups in general, the nature and impact of family influence on consumer buying decisions can be understood in terms of (1) the nature of the group itself, as regards its location in the family life cycle; (2) the nature of specific products being considered, and (3) the roles of individual family members in making these decisions.

Family life cycle (FLC): This concept assumes a number of distinct stages in the life of a typical family, each with different demographic characteristics, values, and product needs, and each requiring a different marketing strategy. As a major determinant of buying behavior, the FLC is an effective basis for segmenting markets, and is often the only way to account for consumption differences among people of the same age and sex.

Table 7–1 identifies significant demographic and consumption characteristics of nine life-style stages.

Table 7–1. Consumption Patterns During Life Stages

Family Life Cycle Stage	Demographic and Consumption Patterns
1. Bachelor stage. Young, single people.	Don't live at home. Few financial burdens. Fashion opinion leaders. Recreation oriented. Buy: basic kitchen equipment, furniture, cars, vacations, "mating game" equipment.

Family Life Cycle Stage	Demographic and Consumption Patterns
2. Newly married couples	Young, no children. Better off financially than in later stages. Highest purchase rate and highest durables purchases. Buy: cars, refrigerators, stoves, sensible and durable furniture, vacations.
3. Full nest I	Youngest child under age six. Home purchasing peak. Low liquid assets. Dissatisfied with finances. Interested in new, advertised products. Buy: washers, dryers, TV sets, baby food, vitamins, dolls, children's toys.
4. Full nest II	Youngest child age six or over. Better financial position. Some wives work. Less influenced by advertising. Buy larger sizes, multiple units, many foods, bicycles, music lessons.
5. Full nest III	Older married couples with dependent children. Still better financial position. More wives and children have jobs. Advertising has less influence. High average purchase of durables. Buy: new, more tasteful furniture, auto travel, non-essential appliances, boats, dental services, magazines.
6. Empty nest I	Older married couples, no children living with them, head in labor force. Home ownership at peak. Most satisfied with finances. Interest in travel, recreation, self-education. Make gifts, contributions. Little interest in new products. Buy: vacations, luxuries, home improvements.
7. Empty nest II	Older married, no children at home, head retired. Drastic income cut. Keep home. Buy: medical appliances, medical-care products that aid health, sleep, digestion.
8. Solitary survivor, in labor force	Income good, likely to sell home.
9. Solitary survivor, retired	Drastic income cut. Special needs for medical products, attention, affection, security.

Although useful for defining and segmenting markets and developing marketing strategies to meet market needs, the family life cycle concept has been faulted for overlooking significant market segments. For example, according to 1990 census figures, one of four U.S. families falls into the "singles" category, and the size of the "mingles" category (unmarried couples of opposite sexes) more than tripled between 1970 and 1990. Both these groups are unrepresented on most FLCs, yet each group consists mainly of under-25 adults who are more affluent, mobile, experimental, appearance-conscious, and status-sensitive than most other FLC groups. Of particular interest to the friendship agency team was the fact that these two "left out" groups are much more active in leisure pursuits and responsive to promotional appeals.

Products being considered: The agency team was particularly interested in research findings pertaining to which family members make which kinds of decisions pertaining to specific products. Generally, these findings indicate that husbands are more involved in the purchase of **functional products** which are external to family concerns; for example, a personal computer that might be used in the husband's business. Wives, in general, are more involved in the purchase of **expressive products** which are internal to family concerns, such as a new carpet. Wives are generally the dominant buying influence for expressive/internal products purchased for others, such as a daughter's dress.

Where product categories overlap, such as for functional/internal products (a videocassette recorder or a microwave oven, for example), or expressive/external products (such as a donation to a public TV station), both husband and wife tend to combine efforts. The agency team decided that the new Friendship Camps would be perceived as essentially expressive/external.

In addition to relating general product characteristics to family members, researchers have also studied the relationship among specific products, specific family members, and specific stages of the decision-making process.

For example, findings indicate that wives typically take the initiative in purchasing food and clothing, husbands in purchasing television sets and life insurance, while both participate in purchasing vacations, housing, and outside entertainment.

However, when the purchasing process is perceived in terms of its components, a different picture emerges. Thus, while a husband might be the dominant influence in gathering information pertaining to the best value in a color TV set, and influencing the purchase decision, the wife tends to be the dominant influence in initiating the purchase in the first place.

Figure 7–4 shows the relative influence of husbands and wives in the purchase decision process for different product categories. As with the family life cycle model, however, this product-related model of family member influence should be viewed with caution, particularly in light of the changing roles and status of family members, as more wives enter the workforce and more husbands assume in-home responsibilities.

Roles and status: A role consists of the activities a person is expected to perform by other members of his or her reference group. For example, the president of

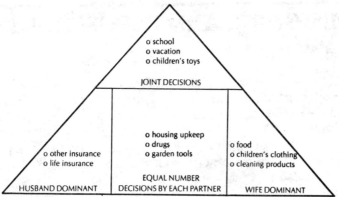

Figure 7–4. Relative influence of husbands and wives in decision process for selected products.

Friendship Camps, Inc., would be expected to assume a different role as a member of his family group (loving father, doting grandparent) than as a chief executive. Each role also carries with it the status reflecting the esteem accorded it by society. People buy products that reflect what they perceive to be their existing, or desired, roles, and the status associated with these roles. The Friendship Camp agency team studied the possibility of positioning the new Friendship Camps as "status symbols" associated with the expected roles of target market members.

YOU SHOULD REMEMBER

Two areas of interest to marketing managers in developing marketing communication programs to influence target market members include (1) processes whereby messages are transmitted between and within groups, and (2) the nature and characteristics of groups and individuals that transmit these messages. The Katz and Lazersfeld studies showed that message transmission is essentially horizontal within socioeconomic levels, rather than vertical between these levels. The Rogers diffusion studies showed that, over time, messages are transmitted from innovators and early adopters through early and late majorities to laggards. As to groups and individuals who transmit messages, studies of families of orientation and procreation indicate that influence is based on family position on the family life cycle, the specific products being considered, and the individual family members involved in making decisions. For example, newly married couples would be more involved in purchasing vacations than groups in other family life cycle stages. These decisions would probably involve both husband and wife, but would be initiated by the wife.

REDESIGNING AND REPOSITIONING THE PRODUCT

The agency team's in-depth exploration of interpersonal factors affecting consumer behavior sparked a variety of ideas for redesigning and repositioning the Friendship Camp offering to appeal to a diversity of potentially profitable new target markets.

Conceptually, the camps, now tentatively renamed "Lifestyle Camps," would comprise six individual camps, each with a distinct mission based largely on subcultural trends and developments.

Integrating all the camps would be:

- a "blanket" mission to help individual campers make the most productive use of their lives by recognizing and nurturing individual capabilities and environmental opportunities.

- operational guidelines based largely on primary cultural values; thus, each camp would present purposeful challenges to campers to test skills and abilities learned at the camp and from life experience. Progress and achievement, both individually and in the group, would be recognized and rewarded.

Consistent with its mission, each camp would be designed to serve the needs of one or another family life cycle group. One camp, for example, was designed to help members of the bachelor group identify and chart individual career paths consistent with their aptitudes and aspirations, which would be evaluated early in each camping session. (Consistent with an important subculture trend, both male and female campers would be treated as equals in all the camps.) Campers would have an opportunity to explore various career options in realistic situations, actually gaining "hands-on" skill in publishing, accounting, teaching, and other business and professional environments. Counselors, representing a diversity of businesses and professions, would serve as teachers and guides, providing feedback on progress and success.

Other camps in the "lifestyle" group would include:

- culture camp, dedicated to an appreciation of the arts and crafts, with artists and artisans serving as counselors, and workshops fostering creative and critical faculties.

- academic camp, dedicated to choosing the best education paths for children of parents in the "full nest" PLC groups, with counselors representing diverse educational institutions and disciplines, and offering opportunities to explore options in real-life academic environments.

- ethnic camp, dedicated to a better understanding of diverse ethnic groups, through exposure to different national, religious, and racial life styles, with a variety of ethnic backgrounds represented among the campers and counselors.

- retirement camp, dedicated to choosing the most satisfying and productive retirement experience, including travel experiences, satisfying hobbies, post-retirement work experiences, and profitable handling of finances. Campers would have opportunities to explore and appraise diverse retirement options, with counselors from retirement fields guiding, advising, and evaluating.

In positioning and promoting the camps, the agency team's analysis of the nature and needs of various socioeconomic classes helped identify target market groups most likely to respond favorably to each camp's offering. For example, team members agreed that the primary appeal of the academic camp would be to members of the upper-upper class socioeconomic group, who are interested in getting their children into fine schools, leading to blue chip careers. In aiming the camp's appeal to this group, however, team members realized they would also attract many children from the much larger lower-upper and upper-middle class groups, whose parents viewed upper-uppers as an aspiration reference group with whom they would want their children to begin networking.

Other camps were aimed at other socioeconomic target markets: the upper-middle and lower-upper members were targeted for the culture camp, whereas the upper- and lower-middle class groups were targeted for the retirement camp. The assumption in both cases was that groups above that particular level did not need this experience.

In planning marketing strategies for all the camps, an effort would be made to identify, and appeal to, "innovator" and "early adopter" groups on each socioeconomic level—often quite different. For example, an innovator group for the education camp, with its elitist viewpoint of "staying within our class," might represent a laggard group for the ethnic camp. The agency team also undertook to identify and define characteristics of opinion leaders in each group capable of influencing others to accept the camp's offering.

HOW INTRAPERSONAL VARIABLES INFLUENCE CONSUMER BEHAVIOR

The agency team first identified major interpersonal variables, common to all members of a target market, that might influence the behavior of market members towards the new Lifestyle Camp concept. It then narrowed its focus to examine the influence of intrapersonal variables, peculiar to each target market member, that might predispose him or her toward the new concept. For example, what would be the effect of the respondents' age and economic situation on a decision to enroll in a camp? Which camp? Might certain motivations, perceptions, and attitudes predispose individual members to enroll? Were lifestyle and personality characteristics predisposing characteristics?

In exploring the nature and impact of these variables on consumer behavior patterns, the team began with **demographic** intrapersonal variables—including age, occupation, and economic circumstances—then explored **psychographic** intrapersonal variables, including motivation, learning, perception, attitudes, personality, and life style.

DEMOGRAPHIC INTRAPERSONAL VARIABLES

Demographic intrapersonal variables can often influence what products are produced and how these products are priced, promoted, and distributed. For example, an elderly population would have greater need for geriatric medicines, an affluent population greater need for expensive homes, and a blue collar population a greater need for work shoes than other groups.

The agency team found a number of obvious correlations between camp interest and all three demographic variables they studied. They found, for example, that the retirement camp would attract a much older age group than the academic or career camps, although their research identified significant crossovers, with many relatively young people planning early retirements and even some elderly "sole survivors" planning academic and career paths. Occupation was also correlated with camp preference in some cases, with people in blue collar occupations more likely to enroll in the career camp and people in white collar occupations more likely to enroll in the retirement camp. Economic circumstances, which included spendable income, borrowing power, and attitudes toward spending and saving, were also found to correlate with intent to enroll at specific Lifestyle Camps.

PSYCHOGRAPHIC INTRAPERSONAL VARIABLES

Psychographic intrapersonal variables can be the most useful of all for building attractive, persuasive offerings, in that they represent motives, attitudes, and perceptions to which marketing managers can relate their product/price/place/promotion offerings. Following are some of the agency team's conclusions pertaining to the influence of motives, learning, perceptions, attitudes, personality, and life styles on responses of target market members to Lifestyle Camp marketing mix variables. For illustrative purposes, we will focus only on the effort to attract "bachelors" (male and female) to the proposed career camp.

• *MOTIVATION*

A motive, or drive, is a stimulated need that an individual seeks to satisfy. For example, a word-of-mouth endorsement might stimulate a need for a bachelor to enroll in the career camp, and until this need is fulfilled (or otherwise eliminated, such as by rationalizing it away), it will generate an uncomfortable tension motivating the bachelor to enroll. Aroused needs can be classified as primary buying motives (associated with broad categories of products, such as camps), or selective buying motives (associated with specific product brands, such as the Lifestyle Career Camp).

Motives can also be classified as **biogenic** (such as needs for food and bodily comfort arising from physiological tension states) or **psychogenic** (such as needs for status or happiness arising from psychological tension states).

Since marketing can be viewed as a way to both stimulate and satisfy motives, marketing managers can profit from an understanding of how motives arise, and the various forms and direction they take.

According to Freudian theory, people frequently don't recognize the real motives (or drives) shaping their behavior; these drives were formed during early childhood, and get repressed as we grow up. As embarrassing as they might seem to us now, as adults, however, they still exert a potent (if subconscious) influence on us. For example, the real motive impelling the bachelor to enroll in the career camp may have more to do with meeting members of the opposite sex than with charting a career path.

Assuming these hidden motives do exert the potent influence claimed by the Freudians (and many marketing managers insist they do not), the problem of identifying them becomes a difficult challenge because they are unrecognized by those who possess them. Usually, projective techniques of the sort described in the Chapter 6 discussion of unstructured disguised surveys are used in this identification effort.

Another useful theory of human motivation, formulated by Abraham H. Maslow, identifies a hierarchy of five levels of needs, arrayed in the order in which an individual seeks to gratify them. This hierarchy of needs is illustrated in Fig-

Source: A.H. Maslow, *Motivation and Personality*, 2nd ed. (Harper & Row, New York, 1970), pp. 80–106

Figure 7–5. The hierarchy of needs.

ure 7–5. According to Maslow, people remain at one level until needs on that level are largely satisfied, at which point new needs emerge on the next highest level. At the lowest level, these needs are primarily biogenic. They become more psychogenic through levels of "ego" needs (belonging, esteem) until they reach the final "self-actualization" level, where the individual's self-centered ego needs are largely replaced by more altruistic needs to develop the whole person through good works and expressive relationships.

Accepting Maslow's theory, the Lifestyle Camp marketing manager would have to attempt to identify the need hierarchy level occupied by bachelor prospects for the career camp. Obviously, the perception of the camp as a means of achieving belonging and love would call for a different approach than its perception as a means of achieving self-actualization.

• LEARNING

Learning is defined as changes in behavior resulting from experience. According to the **stimulus-response model**, a motive, stimulated by an environmental cue, triggers a response which, if continually reinforced, leads to habitual behavior. The stronger a product habit, the more difficult it is for a competitive product to break it.

For example, an advertisement or peer endorsement (the cue) extolling career camp benefits might encourage a bachelor to enroll (the response). If it is a satisfying experience (reinforcement) he might enroll again and again until the behavior becomes habitual, and the camp achieves "brand loyalty" or "brand insistence" status.

In general, it is easier to condition a response in the first place than it is to extinguish habitual behavior later on. This suggests that it is worthwhile to invest considerable expense and effort in the conditioning process, which might involve marketing campaigns over considerable periods of time.

Cognitive learning models generally reject the stimulus-response model as being too mechanistic and animalistic. These theories assume a higher order of information processing activities which involve the human ability to learn by recalling and manipulating ideas. They also assume that attitudes, beliefs, past experience, and goal-oriented behavior enter into the learning of new behavior. For example, a comparative advertising campaign positioning the career camp, point-by-point, against other, competitive approaches for charting career paths might leave it up to the reader to come to his or her own conclusions based on his or her ability to bring past experience into a critical analysis of alternatives, and generalize new insights based on this analysis. (The steps in the consumer decision-making process, discussed in Chapter 8, make use of the cognitive model.)

• PERCEPTION

This is the process by which people derive meaning from the selection, organization, and interpretation of stimuli from within themselves (such as a hunger pang) or from the external environment (such as an advertisement for the career camp).

Three perception-related concepts are of particular interest to marketing managers. Here is how each might influence a promotional campaign for the career camp:

- **Selective exposure** means that people consciously or unconciously select some stimuli and ignore most of the others, simply because we only have the mental ability to process a few at a time. For the marketing manager, this means that stimuli should be designed to be selected for further processing. Stimuli that relate to an anticipated event, help the viewer satisfy current needs, or represent a significant change in intensity have been found to be more likely to be selected. Thus, a full-page ad (intensity change) might announce a special career camp open house (anticipated event) to identify the ten best career options for prospective bachelor campers (current needs).

- **Selective distortion** means that people change the meaning of dissonant stimuli so it becomes consistent with their feelings and beliefs. For the marketing manager, this means that the offering should be consistent with these feelings and beliefs, or its intended meaning will be lost. For example, if the career camp is perceived primarily as a social experience, then any other appeal will tend to be interpreted in this light. The task then becomes to either change people's perceptions or to position the message so it is consistent with existing perceptions. (Note: There are situations where the marketing manager might wish to exploit this tendency for people to distort messages, or generalize from limited stimuli. For example, a few suggestive cues might cause a political candidate to be adversely perceived by an audience that believes "all politicians are crooks".)

- **Selective retention** means that people are more likely to remember stimuli that support preconceived feeling and beliefs, and to forget stimuli that do not. In general, people tend to ignore or quickly forget stimuli which they perceive as either a functional risk (i.e., the product will not perform as claimed) or a psychological perceived risk (the product will not enhance their self-concept or well-being). For the Lifestyle marketing manager, this suggests appeals stressing proofs of performance.

• *ATTITUDES*

Attitudes are relatively stable tendencies to perceive or act in a consistent way toward products or classes of products. They are formed or adjusted by what is learned from families and other social groups, from information received, and from behavior. Although attitudes are second only to intentions as predictors of behavior, they are difficult to define and to relate to specific purchase decisions. In general, they are thought to have three components: the **cognitive** (knowledge or beliefs), the **affective** (feelings or emotions), and the **conative** (intention to act). Thus, a bachelor might believe that the career camp is a good place to play the mating game, and feel this to be desirable, thus motivating an intention to enroll.

One problem in relating attitudes to actions is that it is difficult to determine the relative strength of each of the three components (a bachelor might believe in, and be favorably inclined toward, career camp objectives, but not have any intention of enrolling). There may also be problems in identifying the specific objective of a conative intention (the bachelor might decide to enroll in a competitor's career camp).

Marketing managers often find it helpful to define and attempt to measure the influence of people's attitudes toward the product in regard to four functional areas: **utilitarian**, or the ability of the product to achieve desired goals (i.e., a productive career path); **ego-defensive**, or the capability of the product to defend the person's self-image against internal or external threats; **value expressive**, or the degree of consistency of the product with one's central values or self-image, and **knowledge**, or the ability of the product to give meaning to the individual's beliefs and experiences. For example, a measurement of attitudes among the bachelor market (using the rating scale approaches discussed in Chapter 6) might show weaknesses in ego-defensive attitudes, which promotional literature for the camp could address.

• *PERSONALITY*

Personality is defined as distinguishing combinations of traits that lead to relatively consistent and enduring responses to an individual's environment. Attempts to define and measure such personality trait combinations as "self-confidence," "dominance," and "sociability," then relate them to product and brand choices, have generally proved disappointing.

• *LIFE STYLE*

The distinguishing combinations of activities, interests, and opinions which lead to relatively consistent and enduring responses to the environment comprise an individual's life style. People coming from the same subculture, social class, or even occupation may have quite different life styles. The usual technique for defining an individual's life style, called **psychographics**, involves measuring attitudes, interests, and opinions (AIO) in a variety of areas by soliciting agree/disagree responses to questionnaires that may be as long as 25 pages. For example, the agency research team noted that people interested in enrolling in the culture camp generally agreed strongly with these statements:

- I enjoy going to concerts
- I often have a cocktail before dinner
- I usually dress for fashion, not for comfort

Once distinctive life style groups are revealed through similar (AIO) response patterns, an attempt is made to relate these groups to demographic variables, then to specific products or brand choices. For example, the agency team noted these relationships between similar (AIO) responses, demographics, and camp choice:

Activities	Interests	Opinions	Demographics	Camp Choice
Community Club membership	Food, fashion	Culture, future	Newly married upper, lower middle class	Ethnic
Work, Hobbies	Job, Media	Themselves, business	Bachelor FLC stage upper, lower middle class	Career

This kind of information not only provided useful insights into target market groups that might make use of various life style camps, but also sparked ideas for making camp offerings more attractive to these groups.

YOU SHOULD REMEMBER

Unlike interpersonal variables (social class, cultural group), which exert an external influence on consumer behavior, intrapersonal variables largely emerge from within the individual to influence his or her behavior. Demographic intrapersonal variables such as age and occupation are "states of being" variables that can frequently be related to product and brand choices (for example, work shoes for construction workers). Psychographic intrapersonal variables, including motives, habits, perceptions, attitudes, personality, and life style, are "states of mind" variables that can often be used to identify and profile target market groups. These groups can then be related to demographic variables, and sometimes to specific product and brand choices.

KNOW THE CONCEPTS

DO YOU KNOW THE BASICS?

1. Describe how a successful telethon on behalf of a charity dedicated to eliminating cigarette smoking might make use of the following behavioral sciences in fashioning a persuasive appeal: anthropology; sociology; psychology.

2. Describe how the components of the "black box" model might explain the impulse purchase of a *TV Guide* at a supermarket checkout counter.

3. The successful commercial for the Lincoln town car—which positions this automobile against competitive "look-alike" automobiles—portrays the chaos among a group of upper-upper class members attempting to find their cars on leaving an exclusive social function. Only the patrician Lincoln owner and his wife have no trouble. Describe how the commercial might have made use of social class studies, cultural values, reference groups, and life style studies in developing its appeal.

4. Why do marketing precepts make the study of consumer behavior especially important?

5. Why might the values of religious, geographic, and racial subcultures be of concern to a large record company?

6. Describe how each of the following reference groups might have been instrumental in the success of a political party in a presidential election: primary; secondary; membership; aspirational; disassociative.

7. Using the Katz-Lazersfeld and Rogers theories of how messages are communicated to and through groups, speculate on why the opponent of the candidate in question 6 failed to get elected.

8. Describe products whose purchase might be based on the following key components of family life cycle stages: occupation of head of household; age of family members; size of family.

9. Discuss, in terms of the factors that determine the strength of group influence on individual behavior, why pressure to succeed in college might be greater on the children of a family of Vietnamese "boat people" than on children in a typical suburban American family.

10. At which level of Maslow's hierarchy of needs are the following messages directed?

    - "Schaeffer: the one beer to have when you're having more than one"

    - "Warning: Smoking can be dangerous to your health"

    - "Don't leave home without it" (American Express)

- "Reach out and touch someone" (AT&T)
- "Be all that you can be" (Armed Services)
- "Now you can be taller than she is" (Adler Elevator Shoes)

11. Which learning model—the stimulus-response or the cognitive model—best explains (1) the purchase of a package of gum at a supermarket checkout; and (2) a decision to purchase a Cadillac Eldorado over other luxury automobiles? Justify your answer.

12. How could the marketing managers for the gum and automobile companies mentioned in question 11 promote each product to take advantage of the applicable learning theory?

13. Briefly describe how motives, attitudes, perception, and personality might all come together in a person's selection of a college.

14. Which attitude areas do each of the following appeals reflect?

- a political party seeking new members advocates higher taxes
- a food processor commercial demonstrates how its product can be used to assist in the preparation of an entire meal
- an advertisement promoting a "Great Books" course lauds "the joy of learning"

TERMS FOR STUDY

adoption process
affective
aspirational groups
attitude
behavioral sciences
biogenic needs
black box model
cognitive learning
conative
consumer behavior
culture
decider
demographics
diffusion of innovation
disassociative group
early adopters
early majority
ego-defensive attitudes

environmental stimuli
expressive products
family life cycle
family of orientation
family of procreation
functional products
innovators
interpersonal variable
intrapersonal variable
laggards
late majority
learning
life style
lower-lowers
lower-middles
lower-uppers
marketing stimuli
Maslow's need hierarchy

membership groups
motivation
motivational research
perception
personality
primary values
psychographics
reference groups
reinforcement
role
secondary values
selective distortion

selective exposure
selective retention
social class
status
stimulus-response
subculture
target markets
upper-lowers
upper-middles
upper-uppers
utilitarian attitudes
value expressive attitudes

ANSWERS

KNOW THE BASICS

1. Anthropology, which defines the cultural values of an entire society or a major subcultural subdivision, might have defined a dominant social value, such as physical fitness, toward which the telethon could develop and direct its appeal. Sociology, the study of how human behavior is influenced by groups (such as families and social classes), might have identified "influentials" in the viewing audience toward which the appeal could be directed. Psychology, the study of how human mental processes (motivation, perception, learning, etc.) influence human behavior, might have identified the most potent needs (such as the need for recognition or self-actualization) toward which the appeal could be directed.

2. The "marketing stimulus" was the magazine itself, which might have featured an article capable of fulfilling your social "need" to watch a particular television show. Your response to the influence of these marketing and internal stimuli—the purchase of the magazine—resulted from your mind's "information processing" activities (the "intervening variable").

3. In developing the successful appeal for its town car versus the look-alike competition, Lincoln marketing people might first have identified the cultural values and aspirations of members of the upper-upper, lower-upper, and upper-middle social classes toward which the commercial's appeal was directed. Perhaps, for example, a dominant value among members of these groups is the status and distinctiveness projected by the Lincoln's expensive styling. The tuxedo-wearing patrician and his elitist wife who

"star" in this commercial are reference group models to guide the behavior of the social groups appealed to; and the social function illustrates their lifestyle.

4. According to the marketing concept, a firm profits most in competitive markets by developing marketing mix offerings responsive to the needs of target market members. The application of consumer behavior research findings represents an effective approach for identifying these needs as well as significant characteristics of groups that exhibit these needs, and effective approaches for fulfilling them.

5. Understanding the values of each of these groups, such as an appreciation for country rock in the south and southwest, and for revivalist music among conservative religious groups, would help the record company identify and define its target markets, and develop recorded offerings attractive (in terms of types of recorded music and how records are priced, promoted, and distributed) to these groups.

6. Volunteers for the candidate were brought together in secondary membership groups (e.g., Young Republicans or Young Democrats), to plan in-home presentations to elicit support for the candidate from primary family group members. Meanwhile, the candidate was effectively excoriating disassociative groups ("those crazy big spenders"), while associating his (or her) position with groups reflecting the party platform.

7. According to Katz-Lazersfeld, marketing communication is essentially horizontal in nature, with messages being transmitted, in two steps, from opinion leader influentials to others who defer to these influentials. The candidate might have failed to identify these opinion leaders, or, if they were identified, to properly motivate them to deliver the party line. According to Roger's theory, messages are transmitted, sequentially, through groups of innovators, early adopters, the early majority, the late majority, or laggards. The candidate might not have identified the right group to appeal to (for example, maybe innovators would most effectively have carried the message that was being directed to the late majority, or the message was not clearly understood).

8. The occupation of the head of household may reflect purchases of work clothes or business travel; the age of family members would affect expenditures for vacations and schooling; the size of the family would have impact on purchases of food and furniture, and recreation expenses.

9. The Vietnamese family would probably be more cohesive because its members had suffered great privation together, and face, together, new pressures in a foreign environment. Also, by tradition, members of this family tend to be "other directed" in that they exhibit a disciplined obedience to the wishes of parents and grandparents. Finally, the "product," in this case—a college education—is highly visible in terms of the many successful educated people with whom the Vietnamese family associates, directly or indirectly.

10. Each of these promotional messages may be directed to groups occupying more than one level of Maslow's need hierarchy; however, the most likely target levels are:

    • "Schaeffer is the one beer...": physiological level

    • "Warning: Smoking can be...": safety and security

    • "Don't leave home...": safety and security

    • Reach out...": belonging

    • "Be all that you can be...": self-fulfillment

    • "Now you can be...": ego

11. Habitual buying behavior such as the purchase of the gum is best explained by the stimulus response model; earlier responses that satisfied a need (in this case, to chew something) reinforced this behavior until it became habitual. The purchase of the Cadillac is best explained by cognitive model precepts, which hold that attitudes, beliefs, past experience, memory, goals, and thinking processes are all involved in the decision.

12. In the first case (stimulus-response), the marketing manager could devise a promotion campaign that emphasizes message repetition to induce trial, rewards to generate satisfaction, and reinforcement (for example, a contest or rebate), and easy product access to encourage habitual purchases. In the second, cognitive case, the marketing manager might relate to the prospect's cognitive processes by including in commercials a point-by-point comparative evaluation of the Cadillac and its main competitors so the prospect can make up his or her own mind.

13. An individual might exhibit a distinguishing combination of traits or personality, which predisposes him or her to attend a certain kind of college; for example, a woman might have a studious personality which predisposes her toward a college so oriented and positioned. This studious personality, in turn, would motivate her toward certain colleges which she perceives provide offerings consistent with her personality needs. These perceptions would be reflected in favorable attitudes toward certain colleges and unfavorable attitudes toward others.

14. The political party: value expressive; the food processor: utilitarian; the "Great Books" course: knowledge.

8
THE BUYER'S DECISION- MAKING PROCESS

KEY TERMS

alternative evaluation the application of various criteria to aid in choosing among decision alternatives

choice decision to purchase based on an evaluation of alternatives

information search the active or passive seeking of information that will help in making a buying decision

post-purchase evaluation degree of satisfaction with the purchase decision, which tends to decrease with purchases of strong social or psychological importance

problem recognition a tense awareness, triggered by internal or external stimuli, of a need for action to satisfy a need

In Chapter 7, we examined consumer behavior processes, focusing on the first two segments of the "black box" model to illustrate how marketing and other stimuli, interacting with interpersonal and intrapersonal variables (such as motives, perceptions, and peer group pressures), triggered decisions to try, or buy, products (see Figure 8–1).

In this chapter, we will focus on the third segment of the black box model, the response segment, emphasizing the dynamics of the decision-making process. For this examination, we will expand this third segment into a five-stage model of the decision-making process. This is shown in Figure 8–2.

To illustrate this model, we will refer again to the Merton Mini case, showing what happened in each of the five decision stages when an engineer decided he needed a personal computer.

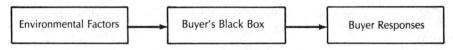

Figure 8–1. "Black Box" model of consumer behavior.

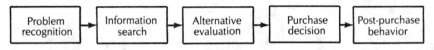

Figure 8–2. Five-stage model of buyer decision process.

UNDERSTANDING THE DECISION-MAKING PROCESS

For marketing managers, the five segments of the decision-making process model serve as a reminder that a prospect's decision to purchase a product is only one step in a process that might have started long before the decision and will have consequences long after. By illustrating the nature and dynamics of the decision-making process, this model also suggests strategies for leading the prospect through to a final, favorable, decision to purchase. For Merton's marketing manager, for example, understanding how an initial need for a personal computer typically arises (problem recognition), and how and where the typical prospect satisfies this need (information search), suggested a number of promotional information ideas to both stimulate and satisfy prospect needs.

EFFECT OF BUYING SITUATIONS ON DECISION-MAKING

In order to understand the extent to which each of the five stages of the buyer's decision-making process can influence favorable decisions, the marketing manager should first understand something about the buying situations in which these decisions are made. These situations, which vary from product to product, are generally defined by (1) the amount of involvement and complexity they entail, and (2) the number of individuals who influence the decision.

Viewed in terms of their degree of involvement and complexity, buyer decisions can be categorized as *routinized, limited,* or *extensive.*

Routinized problem solving characteristically occurs with low-cost, low-risk, frequently purchased, "low-involvement" products, which are usually purchased impulsively or habitually. The liter of 7-Up or the copy of *TV Guide* purchased during a weekly shopping trip are examples of such products, which are also referred to as **convenience goods.**

The marketing challenge in response to routinized problem-solving situations is to (1) keep present customers by maintaining a consistent level of quality and service and making sure products are readily available; and (2) attract new buyers through intensive product development and promotional activities (for example: new versions of Coca Cola—classic, cherry, etc.—supported by intensive "reminder" and coupon promotions).

Limited problem solving occurs when the buyer encounters unfamiliar brands in a familiar product class. This is the situation that occurs, for example, when a new, unfamiliar computer brand—like the Merton Mini—is introduced to compete with familiar brands (like IBMs and Apples) in a familiar product class (personal computers). When such products are relatively expensive and involve comparing other products to arrive at purchasing decisions, they are called **shopping goods.**

To relate to the needs of buyers engaged in limited problem solving, the marketing effort must center around designing communication programs to increase buyer comprehension and confidence, often by positioning the unfamiliar brand against the familiar ones.

Extensive problem solving characterizes situations where the product class itself is unfamiliar, and few if any standards exist on which to base a decision. Such a situation usually prevails with a "break-through technology" product, such as the first Polaroid camera or videocassette recorder. Because of their unique characteristics, such products are usually classified as **specialty goods.** They are also usually classified as "high-involvement" products in that they are comparatively expensive, typically highly visible, and of enduring interest to the buyer. High involvement products also are associated with a diversity of risks. Here, for example, are six risks that might be associated with the "high involvement" Merton Mini:

1. **Performance risk,** or the chance that the Mini, once purchased, will not perform properly

2. **Financial risk,** or the risk of paying the high price of a Mini only to end up with an inferior product

3. **Physical risk,** or the concern that the Mini might somehow cause injury or threaten health (perhaps as a result of staring at its display screen for hours on end)

4. **Psychological risk,** or the risk that the product will not be compatible with the buyer's self-image (an engineer, for example, might consider it a cop-out to do calculations on a computer rather than the old, trusty slide rule)

5. **Social risk,** or the likelihood that the purchase will not meet with peer approval (the engineer might fear being ridiculed by associates for purchasing an expensive "lemon")

6. **Time-loss risk,** or the likelihood that getting the Mini delivered, repaired, or replaced will consume too much valuable time and effort

In responding to extensive problem-solving situations, marketing managers must understand which of these risks (or combination of risks) influence the decision-making process, and how they can be effectively reduced (for example, by offering an unusually strong warranty or a money-back guarantee to mitigate performance, financial, and social risks).

Marketing managers must also understand how, and from what sources, buyers gather information, and how they evaluate this information to arrive at buying decisions. Finally, marketing managers should understand which product features are most important to buyers in motivating favorable buying decisions. These considerations will all be explored shortly, when we examine how each stage of the decision-making process might have affected the engineer's purchase decision.

EFFECT OF ROLES ON PURCHASE DECISIONS

Depending largely on the type of buying situation and its degree of involvement and complexity, a number of people might be involved in the purchase decision, each assuming a unique, distinct role. For example, the following roles were involved in the extensive problem-solving situation leading up to the engineer's decision to purchase a Mini:

- An **initiator,** who suggested the purchase in the first place (in this case, another engineer at the buyer's firm who had purchased and highly recommended his personal computer)

- An **influencer,** whose views carry weight, and who the engineer consulted to confirm the initial recommendation (in this case, the buyer was most influenced by a *Consumer Reports* evaluation of specialized personal computers)

- A **decider,** who ultimately determines any part of the purchase decision (in this case, the engineer's department chief was primarily responsible for deciding, based on her own evaluation of competing makes, whether or not the firm would purchase the Merton Minis for all department members)

- The **buyer** who would actually purchase the Minis (in this case, the firm's purchasing agent who would solicit bids from competing vendors)

- The **user,** or the engineer who initiated the information search in the first place

In working with and through the buyer's decision-making process to motivate favorable purchase decisions, the marketing manager should also understand which of these roles will be involved in this process, and the relative influence of each. In the extensive problem-solving process illustrated, they might all be actively involved; in an impulse-decision situation, they might all be incorporated in a single individual.

YOU SHOULD REMEMBER

Understanding the five-stage consumer decision-making process model, and what happens during each stage to motivate favorable purchase decisions, can help marketing managers develop marketing plans responsive to buyer needs. For example, a promotional program can stimulate an unsatisfied need during the first, problem-recognition stage, and provide information to satisfy this need during the second, information-search stage. Other marketing activities can also be used to shape and direct favorable buyer decisions during the final three stages: evaluation of alternatives, decision to purchase, and post-purchase behavior. The extent to which all five stages actually enter into the buyer's decision-making process is largely a function of the type of decision being made. As purchase decisions move from low-involvement, routinized problem-solving situations through medium-involvement, limited problem-solving situations, to high-involvement, extensive problem-solving situations, all five stages come more actively into play. Also, as decision situations move from routinized to extensive problem solving, (1) more people become involved in purchase decisions, assuming such roles as initiators, influencers, deciders, buyers, and users, and (2) products become more expensive, visible, and risky. Risks typically associated with high-involvement shopping or specialty goods include performance risk, financial risk, physical risk, psychological risk, social risk, and time-loss risk.

THE DECISION-MAKING PROCESS

In relating the sequence of steps in the buyer decision process to the purchase of a single Merton Mini, we will be examining an extensive problem-solving situation, actively involving many roles and risks and all the steps of the process.

PROBLEM RECOGNITION

Regardless of the type of situation, some combination of internal and external stimuli will first trigger the buying decision process by highlighting an unsatisfied need.

The engineer, for example, was motivated to explore a personal computer purchase by a felt need to enhance his career opportunities (internal stimuli), combined with the effects of an associate's endorsement as well as his reading of articles on personal computers in consumer and engineering trade journals (external stimuli).

In relating marketing plans to the dynamics of this first stage, marketing managers should understand what kinds of needs or problems are most likely to motivate an individual toward a particular product class, and how these needs are stimulated in the first place.

INFORMATION SEARCH

If the felt need motivating behavior is strong enough, and the product is capable of satisfying this need quickly and safely, the buyer will probably not reach this second stage of the decision process. If it is reached, however, two levels of search activity are possible: (1) **some search**, during which heightened interest makes the buyer more receptive to product information, and (2) **active information search**, during which the buyer actively solicits such information.

The extent to which buyers engage in active search depends on a variety of considerations, including the degree of motivation toward the product class, the amount of information available, the ease of obtaining additional information, the value placed on this information, and the satisfaction resulting from the search. In our example, the engineer was highly motivated to explore a personal computer purchase, which he saw as a way to satisfy a frustrated need to advance in his profession. Furthermore, he perceived that important information on the use of personal computers in engineering was readily available from professional journals he read, associations to which he belonged, and other engineers with whom he worked.

These information sources can be classified as either **commercial sources** or **personal sources**. Commercial information sources, such as an advertisement for the Merton Mini in *The American Engineer,* perform informative and persuasive functions. Personal information sources, like an endorsement from a respected associate, perform evaluative and legitimizing functions.

The task facing marketing managers is to determine, through marketing research, the relative influence of commercial and personal information sources in the decision-making process, and how this information can be most effectively distributed. In assessing the engineers' target market, Merton's marketing manager decided that both sources were equally important, and that (1) commercial information on the Mini should be disseminated through publicity and advertising in two highly regarded professional journals; and (2) personal information should be disseminated through members of three engineering associations, also highly regarded, whose officers all subscribed to the journals.

As the engineer moved from commercial information to personal information in search of the personal computer best calculated to satisfy his career goals, two things happened: first, the size of his **awareness set** (that is, the set of all personal computer brands of which he was aware) increased; second, certain products were eliminated from this awareness set as being unsuitable to meet his specific goals.

In marketing terms, this narrowing-down process is illustrated as shown in Figure 8–3. From the "awareness set" comprising all the personal computers of which the engineer was aware after consulting the literature, further exposure to commercial and personal information narrowed his **choice set** to three models: IBM, Leading Edge, and Merton. While awareness and choice sets will obviously differ from target market to target market, it is important for marketing managers to understand which brands are most likely to occur in each set for each target market, and why. With this information, the marketing manager can effectively position and promote products to get them into awareness sets, and into and out of choice sets as the final purchase.

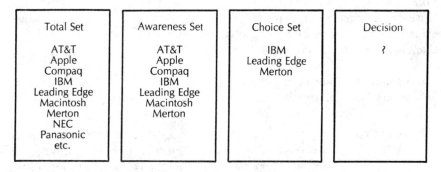

Figure 8–3. Sets involved in consumer decision process.

YOU SHOULD REMEMBER

Marketing managers are interested in the first two stages of the buyer's decision-making process because marketing stimuli can both motivate needs during the problem-recognition stage and help satisfy these needs during the information-search stage. During the information-search stage, buyers engage in either *some search* or *active information search*, depending, mainly, on the buyer's motivation to purchase the product, the amount and accessibility of information, and the value placed on this information. Information sought is either *commercial*, which informs and persuades, or *per-*

sonal, which evaluates and legitimizes. As the buyer is exposed to more and more of this information, his or her *awareness set* first expands, then constricts into a *choice set* containing only those products perceived as able to effectively satisfy the original need. An understanding of which products are likely to occupy awareness and choice sets for different target market groups helps marketing managers plan message/media promotional strategies for getting their products into, and out of, awareness and choice sets.

EVALUATION OF ALTERNATIVES

During this third stage of the decision-making process, buyers evaluate the alternatives remaining in the choice set after exposure to commercial and personal information, before arriving, finally, at the fourth, "purchase decision" stage of the process.

Five product/market concepts help explain the dynamics of this alternative-evaluation stage and the strategic response to these dynamics: product attributes, salient attributes, brand image, utility function, and the ideal product.

1. **Product attributes** are characteristics of the product that relate to buyer needs. For example, the three desired product characteristics in the engineer's choice set were memory capacity, processing speed, and portability.

2. **Salient attributes** are "top of the mind" product attributes that buyers are likely to name when asked to think of the product. Salient attributes are not necessarily the most important attributes from either the buyer's or the seller's viewpoint. For example, during its first year, Merton promoted the Mini's "portability" feature to the point where it became a salient attribute. However, now that many competitors also offered this feature, it was perceived as a liability by Merton's marketing management, overshadowing other, more important features.

3. **Brand image** comprises a set of buyer perceptions, either favorable or unfavorable, about each product attribute. These could be at variance with the true brand image due to selective perception and retention by prospective buyers. For example, because early versions of the Merton Mini were so remarkably compact, the product gained an inaccurate, unfavorable image as a sort of glorified toy, incapable of performing normal personal computer functions.

4. The **utility function** defines the extent to which buyer satisfaction will vary with alternative levels of each attribute. For example, would buyer satisfaction increase if the Mini, already small enough to fit into a thin attache case, were made small enough to fit into a cigar box? If yes, this "smallness" attribute would have a positive utility function. Otherwise, depending on consumer response, the utility function could vary from neutral to negative.

Understanding utility functions is especially useful in designing and positioning products; knowing which attributes can be most profitably changed often means knowing how to gain a fast competitive edge.

5. The **ideal product** is the product which combines attributes with the highest desired utility levels. For example, a Mini with levels of processing speed, memory capacity, and portability beyond which customers will begin to manifest dissatisfaction would be the ideal.

• *DECISION-MAKING MODELS*

Now we will bring together these five concepts in examining four models designed to explain and predict how a buyer arrives at the single best choice from among all the products in his or her choice set.

1. The **expectancy value model** is based on the assumption that buyers consider a number of product attributes in making a decision, assigning weights and values to each attribute and purchasing the product with the highest score. To illustrate, assume the engineer assigned the following weights and values to the three decision attributes he considered most important.

ATTRIBUTES

MINI PC BRANDS	SPEED			MEMORY			PORTABILITY			GRAND TOTAL
	Value	Weight	Total	Value	Weight	Total	Value	Weight	Total	
IBM	7	.4	2.8	8	.4	3.2	7	.2	1.4	7.4
Leading Edge	10	.4	4	8	.4	3.2	4	.2	.8	8
Merton	6	.4	2.4	9	.4	3.6	7	.2	1.4	7.4

Figure 8–4. Expectancy Value Model: Values and weights assigned to personal computers.

The Leading Edge model is perceived as a "10" for "speed," as opposed to an "7" for the IBM Mini and a "6" for the Merton Mini. Since "speed" is considered important to the buyer, it is assigned a weight of .4, as against only .2 for portability, which is only considered half as important as speed and memory. Totalling the products of the weights and values produces a tie, at 7.4, for the IBM and Merton models, with Leading Edge the preferred choice with an 8.

2. The **conjunctive model** assumes that consumers base buying decisions on criteria that satisfy a set of minimum attribute levels. For example, given the values in Figure 8.4, if the engineer insisted that the personal computer he purchased have a memory capacity of at least eight and a speed of at least eight, then only the Leading Edge model would remain in the choice

set. A good illustration of the conjunctive model at work is a typical shopper buying products in a supermarket, with minimum standards required for each choice.

3. The **disjunctive model** assumes an either/or decision, based on high attribute levels. For example, the engineer might decide he will not purchase a personal computer unless it has either a speed of 6 or a memory of 8, in which case all three models will remain in the choice set.

4. The **lexicographic model** assumes people evaluate brands on the basis of the most salient attributes and, in case of a tie, will shift to the second most salient attribute. This model is often offered to explain how many Americans vote in presidential elections, with a "salient" smile being given greater weight than positions on issues.

A research-based understanding of which of these models best explains the decision process for different products and target markets can be extremely useful to marketing managers in planning product/market strategies. In the Merton Mini case, for example, the expectancy value model might explain how the purchasing agent for the engineer's firm chooses the vendor to supply the needed Minis, first evaluating each in a number of areas (service, delivery, reliability, etc.), then ordering from the vendor with the highest "score." The disjunctive model, on the other hand, might characterize the decision-making process of an engineer interested in only a single attribute of the product, such as its memory capacity or processing speed.

• STRATEGY IMPLICATIONS

An understanding of the decision models buyers use to choose products can suggest product/market strategies. The strategies employed by Merton's marketing manager might be based on these assumptions: (1) engineers use the disjunctive decision model, with the primary requirement that memory capacity achieve at least a "9" rating; (2) however, if a memory capacity of "9" is not available, processing speed of at least "9" will serve as a substitute; (3) of the three attributes considered important by engineers, portability is least important.

These criteria, along with the engineer's perceptions of the attributes of the three personal computer models in his choice set, can be diagrammed as shown

ATTRIBUTE

PRODUCT	SPEED		MEMORY		PORTABILITY		TOTAL
	Value	Weight	Value	Weight	Value	Weight	
Leading Edge	8	.4	10	.4	5	.2	8.2
IBM	10	.4	8	.4	7	.2	8.6
Merton	7	.4	6	.4	8	.2	6.8

Figure 8–5. Attribute criteria for personal computer purchase.

in Figure 8–5. Note that, given these engineer perceptions and preferences, the Merton Mini, with its perceived "6" memory and "7" processing speed, is effectively removed from the engineer's choice set.

Here are some strategies the marketing manager might consider to get it back in again:

- **Real repositioning:** Assuming the engineer's perceptions are correct, reposition the Mini so it achieves "10" ratings in "memory" and "speed" criteria categories.

- **Psychological repositioning:** Assuming the Merton Mini *is* actually the equal of its two choice-set competitors in speed and memory capacity, alter the attitudes of engineers to permit them to recognize this fact— perhaps through a promotional campaign featuring an objective, point-by-point assessment of the three models.

- **Competitive depositioning:** This strategy assumes that the "10" ratings achieved by the Leading Edge and IBM models are inaccurate perceptions; that in actuality the Merton Mini is at least their equal in both areas. Here again, a point-by-point comparison might effectively prove this equality.

- **Stressing neglected attributes:** Research might show that an overlooked feature of the Merton Mini—its unusually rugged construction, which permits it to be used on hazardous construction engineering projects— would be considered its most important attribute if only engineers were aware of it.

- **Altering importance weights:** The rugged construction of the Merton Mini, which permits it to be used in hazardous situations, might persuade engineers to reevaluate the weight assigned to this attribute (previously 0.2), so it now becomes the most important attribute, with a weight of 0.5.

- **Shifting buyer's ideals:** This strategy implies use of a highly persuasive "cosmic statement" to shift buyer focus away from attributes to a generalized, often vague, ideal. For example, it is the kind of strategy political candidates occasionally use to replace mundane concerns of today with a glittering vision of tomorrow. In support of the Mini, this strategy might focus on an idealized version of a macho "Merton Man" using his Mini in dramatic engineering situations.

YOU SHOULD REMEMBER

Five product-related concepts explain four decision models used by buyers to evaluate alternative choice-set products during the fourth stage of the buyer decision process: (1) *attributes,* or product features that relate to buyer needs; (2) *salient attributes,* or attributes most likely to come to mind when the product is named; (3) *brand image,* or the sum of buyer perceptions of each attribute; (4) *utility function,* or extent to which buyer satisfaction will vary with changes in attribute levels; and (5) the *ideal product,* which embodies the optimum utility level for each attribute. The four decision models deriving from these concepts also focus on product attributes: (1) the *expectancy value model* buyer assigns values and weights to each attribute, and chooses the product with the highest score; (2) the *conjunctive model* buyer insists on a set of minimum attribute levels in product choices; (3) the *disjunctive model* buyer focuses on a high utility for a single attribute; and (4) the *lexicographic model* buyer focuses on salient attributes in making product choices. An understanding of how these models apply in different situations can suggest a variety of strategic options for improving product positions in choice sets, including (1) real repositioning; (2) psychological re-positioning; (3) competitive depositioning; (4) stressing neglected attributes; (5) altering importance weights; and (6) shifting buyer ideals.

DECISION TO PURCHASE

The model in Figure 8–6 depicts the relationship between the alternative-evaluation stage just examined and the critical purchase-decision stage. Assume

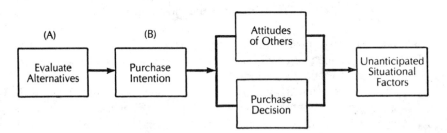

Figure 8–6. Purchase Decision Model.

that, thanks to an effective "psychological repositioning" promotional strategy, the Merton Mini attains top ranking in the engineer's choice set (A), so that he and his target market associates now express an intention to purchase the Mini (B). At this point, two variables—attitudes of others and unanticipated situational factors—can still intervene to prevent the actual purchase of the Mini. (The impact of these factors was documented in a study which showed that, of 100 people stating an intention to purchase a specific dishwasher brand, only 44 actually purchased a dishwasher and, of this total, only 30 purchased the brand named.)

- **Attitudes of others:** The impact of this variable depends on the intensity of the negative attitude, and the consumer's motivation to comply. For example, the purchasing agent at the engineer's firm might strongly recommend a less expensive alternative to the Merton Mini, but the engineer's felt need for the Mini might be strong enough to overcome this recommendation.

- **Unanticipated situational factors:** Heavily influencing buyer risk-reduction routines, such as postponing the decision, gathering additional information, or settling on a safe name brand, is the degree of perceived risk that the product will not perform as expected or will reduce the buyer's self-esteem. The high cost, high visibility, and relative importance of the Mini made it highly susceptible to these risks.

POST-PURCHASE BEHAVIOR

Even assuming the buyer does purchase the product, the decision-making process still is not finished: This final stage of the process focuses on the psychological responses of buyers to their purchase decisions. An understanding of these post-purchase responses is important to marketing managers because they strongly influence the likelihood that buyers will repurchase products or encourage others to purchase or not purchase the product. These issues can be effectively addressed in promotion campaigns directed toward people who have already purchased the product, based on an understanding of the buyer's psychological response to the purchase and subsequent reactions:

Psychological response: According to Festinger[1], all purchase decisions produce some degree of **dissonance**, which measures the gap between buyer expectations and product performance. For example, largely because of the time, effort, and expense he put into procuring his Mini, the engineer can be assumed to have high expectations for its performance, and will likely perceive that it is not performing up to these expectations. This dissatisfaction, or **cognitive dissonance**, will likely lead to "coping" behavior, such as another search for information to reinforce the purchase decision. Alternatively, the buyer might react to this dissonance by actually magnifying the gap between expectation and performance, and begin to criticize the product to friends and associates.

Post-purchase reactions: A satisfied customer is much more likely to recommend and repurchase the product; a dissatisfied customer is more likely to return the product or reduce dissonance by seeking confirming information. These reactions can be either public or private: public reactions might include legal action seeking redress directly from the firm, or com-

---

1. Leon Festinger, *A Theory of Cognitive Dissonance* (Stanford, CA: Stanford University Press, 1957), p. 260.

plaints to private or government agencies; private reactions could include an individual's boycott of the product, or warning friends against its use.

To anticipate and address these post-purchase reactions, Merton devised a promotional strategy directed toward segments of each target market which had already purchased the Mini. For example, every engineer who had purchased a Mini received a congratulatory telegram reinforcing the wisdom of the decision, and noting "the satisfaction your associates have already experienced with the Merton Mini's strength, speed, and reliability."

Comments from customers, both satisfied and dissatisfied, were also solicited by the consumer division's marketing research department and followed up in various ways. Customer service representatives contacted dissatisfied customers and made every effort to eliminate the causes of dissatisfaction. The customer's complaints, in turn, were fed into the MIS database for analysis in designing future Mini offerings.

Favorable comments were also recycled through the MIS database and used in publicity and testimonial promotional campaigns both to persuade prospective buyers and to reassure existing buyers. Reassuring promotional messages were also incorporated into comprehensive instruction booklets.

YOU SHOULD REMEMBER

During the fourth stage of the buyer decision process, attitudes of others and unanticipated situational factors—such as the perception of performance, financial, or social risk—can intervene to encourage postponement of the purchase, the gathering of additional information to reinforce the purchase decision, and similar risk-aversion activities. Assuming the fourth stage results in a favorable purchase decision, marketing managers must still concern themselves with fifth-stage post-purchase behavior, particularly with relatively expensive, highly visible products. Of particular concern is cognitive dissonance, or the perceived difference between actual and expected product performance. In response to this dissonance, buyers frequently seek supportive information or denigrate the product. Alternatively, satisfaction with product performance can result in favorable word-of-mouth endorsements and the likelihood of re-purchase. To stimulate favorable post-purchase responses, marketing managers frequently devote the same kind of attention to promotion campaigns among buyers as to those among prospects.

KNOW THE CONCEPTS
DO YOU KNOW THE BASICS?

1. Describe how a single television commercial for a reducing salon addresses people in all five stages of the buyer's decision-making process.

2. How would you describe the following buying situations, and why?

   • Attracted by the cover story, you purchase a copy of *TV Guide* at a supermarket checkout counter.

   • In its first year on the American market, you consider the purchase of a Yugo automobile.

   • You plan your itinerary for your first trip abroad.

3. Give an example of a product offering designed to reduce (a) performance risk; (b) financial risk; (c) physical risk; (d) psychological risk; (e) social risk; (f) time-loss risk.

4. Describe how four different sources might have assumed four different roles in a corporate decision to retain an accounting firm to conduct a financial management seminar for senior managers.

5. What is the significance of the roles assumed by the sources in question 4, above, to the accounting firm partner in charge of promoting the financial management seminar?

6. Show how both commercial and personal information might have been used during the information-search stage leading to the purchase of a new family automobile.

7. Which alternative-evaluation model would be most appropriate in the following situations?
   a. NASA is searching for a new prime contractor to build a new, more reliable space shuttle.
   b. The city of Houston is asking for bids on a contract to haul garbage.
   c. The college you attend must have a second-to-none mathematics department and be within easy commuting distance to Chicago.
   d. No matter what the reviewers say, you buy all of Bruce Springsteen's records and attend all of Jane Fonda's movies.

8. How might the Greek government, concerned about declining tourist revenues resulting from bad publicity over terrorist highjackings in Athens Airport, make simultaneous use of the following positioning strategies to counteract the negative influence of the publicity and persuade American tourists to visit Greece: shifting buyer's ideals; psychological repositioning; real repositioning.

9. Which positioning strategies were illustrated by the following appeals during various presidential election campaigns?

> Bush, 1992: The issues are character and trust
> Mondale, 1984: If elected, I'm going to raise taxes
> Reagan, 1984: Get government off our backs
> Johnson, 1972: The Great Society
> Nixon, 1972: Peace with dignity

TERMS FOR STUDY

active information search
awareness set
behavior
brand image
buyer
choice set
cognitive dissonance
commercial sources
competitive depositioning
conjunctive model
convenience goods
decider
disjunctive model
dissonance
evoked set
expectancy value model
extensive problem solving
financial risk
ideal product
impulse decision

influencer
initiator
limited problem solving
low involvement products
performance risk
personal sources
physical risk
post-purchase behavior
problem recognition
product attributes
psychological repositioning
psychological risk
real repositioning
routinized problem solving
salient attributes
social risk
some search
shopping goods
specialty goods
utility function

ANSWERS
KNOW THE BASICS

1. The commercial might (a) stimulate *problem recognition* by pointing out health risks associated with excess weight; (b) assist in an *information search* by providing specifics on how the salon painlessly reduces excess weight; (c) help the buyer *evaluate alternatives* by comparing its painless approach to other weight-loss approaches; (d) reduce the impact of perceived risk on the *purchase decision* by presenting a testimonial from a respected spokesperson; (e) reduce post-purchase dissonance by reassuring people who have already enrolled in the salon program.

2. Suggested problem-solving situations for each example:

- The *TV Guide* purchase: routinized problem-solving; a low-cost, low-risk, low-involvement convenience good

- The contemplated Yugo purchase: limited problem-solving; an unfamiliar brand in a familiar "shopping good" product class

- The first trip abroad: extensive problem-solving; an unfamiliar brand in an unfamiliar product class

3. (a) performance risk: the reliable Volkswagen, the Diehard battery; (b) financial risk: Irving Trust's "personal banker"; (c) physical risk: gentle Philip's milk of magnesia ("MOM"); (d) psychological risk: burglar alarms; (e) social risk: Amy Vanderbilt's "Etiquette" reference; (f) time-loss risk: bank by telephone.

4. The firm's training director might have initiated the decision, influenced by requests from senior managers for such a course; the firm's president decided to spend the money for the course, and the first class of managers taking the course were the users.

5. To do an effective job of marketing the financial management seminar, the partner should consider which individuals, assuming which roles, will contribute to a favorable decision, and how each can be effectively motivated. For example, the partner might persuade potential users of the course to influence an initiator, who might, in turn, persuade a decider to contract with the accounting firm to conduct the course.

6. Commercial information might have included a television commercial which activated the problem-recognition stage, and dealer literature that assisted in the information-search stage. Personal information might have included disparaging comments about the condition of the original family car from an embarrassed older daughter, and a recommendation for the new model from a friendly neighbor.

7. a. *NASA's search:* the expectancy value model; a number of attributes (such as engineering expertise, financial capability), each given an "importance weight," will be evaluated for a number of firms in selecting the prime contractor.

   b. *Houston's search:* the conjunctive model, emphasizing low attribute levels; by law, the hauler selected must submit the lowest bid from among firms that meet minimum standards.

   c. *College search:* the disjunctive model, emphasizing high attribute levels (if two prospective colleges have equally fine math departments, you will go to the one closest to Chicago).

   d. *Springsteen's records and Fonda's movies:* The lexicographic model emphasizing a single *salient* attribute (in this case, the personalities of the performances).

8. In its "come home" campaign, the Greek tourist bureau employed the following positioning strategies in the following ways:

   • *Shifting buyer's ideals:* The "come home" campaign theme was an idealistic emotional appeal reminding Americans that Greece, as the birthplace of democracy, was also their spiritual home and should be visited.

   • *Psychological repositioning:* Campaign literature attempted to change perceptions of Athens airport as unsafe by attempting to show, statistically, that it was actually as safe as, or safer than most other large world airports.

   • *Real repositioning:* In spite of its actual excellent safety record, the campaign stressed that measures would be taken to make the airport even safer.

9. Bush Appeal: A generally unsuccessful attempt to shift buyer's ideals
   Mondale Appeal: A generally unsuccessful attempt to alter importance weights
   Reagan Appeal: A generally successful attempt to shift buyers' ideals
   Johnson Appeal: Another generally successful attempt to shift buyers' ideals
   Nixon Appeal: A successful attempt to psychologically reposition an issue.

9

ORGANIZA-
TIONAL MARKETS
AND BUYING
BEHAVIOR

KEY TERMS

organizational buying the decision-making process by which formal organizations establish the need for purchased products and services and identify, evaluate, and choose from among alternative brands and suppliers

organizational market marketplace made up of producers, trade industries, governments, and institutions

producers components of the organizational market who acquire products and services that enter into the production of other products and services that are sold, rented, or otherwise supplied to others (also called **industrial market**)

suppliers individuals and organizations that provide resources needed by a company and its competitors to produce goods and services

trade industries components of the industrial market comprising wholesalers and retailers who purchase goods and services to resell or rent to others at a profit

---

In Chapters 7 and 8, we examined components and characteristics of the consumer market, which consists of all individuals and households that buy or otherwise acquire goods and services for personal consumption. In this chapter, we examine another large market aggregate: the *organizational market*. This market consists of all individuals and organizations that acquire goods and services to

1. produce other products
2. resell or rent at a profit
3. carry out governmental functions
4. provide institutional services

We will examine these organizational market components in the same way we examined consumer markets in the previous two chapters, focusing on factors that motivate and shape buyer behavior; buyers' decision-making practices, and how marketing managers relate marketing mix strategies to industrial market dynamics.

For illustrative purposes we will refer to the industrial products division of the Merton Electronics Company, which manufactures and markets products and product systems to industrial firms like IBM and Apple. While primarily interested in industrial market demand patterns, the marketing manager for Merton's industrial division is also concerned with demand patterns in the consumer market, which largely shape industrial market demand patterns. Similarly, the manager of Merton's consumer products division is interested in developments in segments of the industrial market, such as the wholesalers and retailers who will distribute consumer division products to consumer market members.

COMPONENTS OF THE ORGANIZATIONAL MARKET

Table 9-1 categorizes components of the organizational market in terms of (1) the major functions performed; (2) the Standard Industrial Classification (SIC) code numbers assigned to industries engaged in these functional activities; and (3) the relative size of each industry as a whole and in terms of its individual members. We will use these categories to define the nature and scope of the organizational markets.

Categorized by function, the organizational market consists of production, trade, and government aggregates. (A fourth component, the institutional market, will be examined as a separate entity in Chapter 12.)

INDUSTRIAL PRODUCER MARKET

This market consists of all individuals and organizations that acquire goods and services that are used, directly or indirectly, in the production of other products and services which are sold, rented, or otherwise supplied to others. Included are manufacturing firms; farmers and other resource industries; construction contractors; and providers of such services as transportation, public utilities, finance, insurance, and real estate. This market is the largest and most diverse organizational market aggregate, comprising more than 14 million or-

Table 9-1. Organizational Market Categories

Functional Category	SIC Category	Size Categories No. of organizations	Size Categories No. of employees	Employees per Organization
INDUSTRIAL PRODUCERS				
Agriculture, forestry, fishing	01–09	3,486,000	3,571,000	1
Mining	10–14	181,000	1,028,000	6
Construction	15–17	1,412,000	5,756,000	4
Manufacturing	20–39	569,000	20,286,000	36
Transportation, utilities	40–49	570,000	6,552,000	11
Finance, Insurance, Real estate	60–67	2,179,000	6,270,000	3
Services	70–89	4,777,000	30,090,000	6
TOTAL		13,174,000	73,553,000	6
TRADE INDUSTRIES				
Wholesalers	50–51	383,000	4,120,000	11
Retailers	52–59	1,855,000	16,638,000	9
TOTAL		2,238,000	20,758,000	9
GOVERNMENTS				
Federal	91–97	1	2,862,000	
State		50	3,747,000	
Local		82,290	9,324,000	
TOTAL		82,341	15,933,000	
OVERALL TOTALS		15,494,341	110,244,000	8

Source: *Statistical Abstract of the United States* (Washington, D.C.: U.S. Government Printing Office, 1984).

ganizations. These organizations purchase more than $3 trillion worth of goods and services each year, as compared to the $2 trillion dollars in personal-consumption expenditures by the 240 million members of the consumer market. In terms of value added by manufacturing—or the difference between the price charged by manufacturers and the cost of their inputs—the industrial-producer component of the organizational market contributes about $900 billion.

TRADE INDUSTRIES MARKET

This market consists of retailers and wholesalers who purchase products to resell or rent to others at a profit. Sometimes these resale products are finished goods (like automobiles or appliances) which are marketed to consumers; in other instances, some processing or repackaging may take place, as when lumber dealers process car loads of lumber to the quantity and size specifications of individual customers. Like the producer market, the reseller market is huge: its 396,000 wholesalers and 1,923,000 retailers purchase more than $2 trillion worth of goods and services a year. Thus, when combined with the producer market, the total buying power of these two market aggregates ($5 trillion) is about two and a half times the total buying power of the entire consumer market.

Many more dollars and items are involved in producer and trade markets than in consumer markets because these markets involve many more transactions. To illustrate, Figure 9-1 shows the transactions involved in producing and selling a single Merton Mini.

RAW MATERIAL PROCESSOR	MERTON CONSUMER PRODUCTS DIV.	WHOLESALER	RETAILER	CONSUMER
BUYS: Copper, plastics, silicon Equipment Labor Energy	BUYS: Wire Plastic forms chip circuits Equipment Labor Energy	BUYS: Personal computers Space Equipment Labor Energy	BUYS: Personal computers Space Equipment Labor Energy	BUYS: Personal computer
SELLS: Wire, plastic forms etc.	SELLS: Personal computers	SELLS: Personal computers	SELLS: Personal computers	

Figure 9–1. Organizational market transactions in producing one product

SIC CATEGORIES DEFINE INDUSTRIES AND TRADES

The federal government's Standard Industrial Classification (SIC) system, which precisely defines individual industries and trades within the total organizational market, is an invaluable asset to industrial marketing managers in planning and controlling marketing plans. Under the SIC system, two-digit code numbers are assigned to each of 11 broad industry categories (see column 2, Table 9-1): Merton's industrial division falls within the category of "Electrical machinery, equipment and supplies," which is assigned the code number "36." That category is part of the broad "manufacturing" industry, whose two-digit codes range from 20 to 39.

Within each industry classification, sub-industries are further identified and defined with a third code digit. For example, within the "36" SIC category, the addition of the third digit "7" (367) more precisely defines the industry as "electronic components." For certain industries, four, five, and even seven-digit SIC codes are assigned. The SIC code number "3679," for example, identifies firms that manufacture electronics products primarily marketed to the appliance and computer industries.

The *Standard Industrial Classification Manual*, also published by the government, further defines each coded industry in terms of the products or services it produces and the processes and products used in these production activities. Other information on SIC-coded industries, such as their size and sales potential characteristics, is available from a diversity of government publications (such as the *Census of Manufacturers* and *Census of Retailing and Wholesaling*) and from trade associations, business publications, state industrial directories, and private firms like Dun & Bradstreet, which also use the SIC code to organize and present information on industrial trends and developments.

The SIC code system, through the vast amount of information it gathers, organizes, and presents, offers industrial marketing managers clearly identified, defined, and pre-segmented markets. The marketing manager for Merton's industrial division would have ready access to extensive information about the five three-digit industries that generate more than 80 percent of the division's sales and profits. This information is summarized in Table 9-2.

Table 9–2. SIC Analysis of five key industries

(1) Code	(2) Industry	(3) No. of Employees	(4) Payrolls (000)	(5) Total Reporting Units	(6) No. of Reporting Units by Employee Class		
					8-49	58-99	100 +
361	Electric distribution products	6820	12,841	30	16	5	9
364	Lighting and wiring devices	5840	11,178	41	32	3	6
365	Radio, television equipment	1078	2,000	15	10	1	4
366	Communication equipment	669	1,090	10	7	2	1
367	Electronic components	7302	11,560	61	41	10	10

This summarized information, derived from a useful Labor Department publication called *County Business Patterns*, enables the marketing manager to know how many employees are in each industry in a single state in Merton's territory, as well as how much they get paid (columns 3 and 4). These are useful measures of the relative size and buying power of each industry. The final two columns in the table also provide useful information on the degree of concentration in each industry. For example, there are relatively few small firms in the "361" industry (where nine of 30 firms each employ more than 100 employees), and many more such firms in the "364" industry, where only six of 41 firms employ more than 100 employees.

This readily accessible information from *County Business Patterns* can then be supplemented with more detailed information from Merton's own sales records and from other government publications, trade journals, and associations serving the "36" industry. The marketing manager can then develop, implement, and control comprehensive marketing plans based on the needs and characteristics of industries within the entire target market. (In Chapter 11, we will illustrate how SIC data is used to develop sales potential data to start the strategic planning process.)

A marketing plan based on data in Table 9–2 would direct sales people to the most profitable firms in the most profitable industries in the most efficient manner, while coordinating all other elements of the marketing mix (price, promotion, product specifications) to meet buyer needs in these targeted industries.

In the remainder of this chapter, we will examine the characteristics of the industrial producer, trade, and governmental segments comprising the organizational market, with emphasis on how industrial marketing managers can relate their product offerings to market needs.

YOU SHOULD REMEMBER

The organizational market consists primarily of three large market aggregates: (1) the industrial producer market, comprising individuals and organizations that acquire goods and services used in the production of other goods and services; (2) the trade industry, comprising retailers and wholesalers that resell products to others at a profit; and (3) the government market, comprising local, state, and federal governments. Because many more transactions are involved in the industrial market than in the consumer market, more than twice as many dollars are also involved. The Standard Industrial Classification (SIC) system identifies all industries and subindustries encompassed by the industrial and trade markets. Code numbers (up to seven digits long) identify each industry in terms of the products manufactured, the processes involved, and/or the functions performed. The SIC system, supplemented by information from private and governmental sources, is very useful to marketing managers for measuring market potential and devising marketing plans for relating offerings to needs.

INDUSTRIAL MARKETS

The organizational market differs significantly from the consumer market in terms of the products purchased, the demand patterns, and the purchasing practices.

PRODUCT CATEGORIES

Merton's industrial division sold a variety of products and systems to the Emco Corporation, a large manufacturer of home appliances. Those products could be classified into the four broad categories of products purchased in industrial markets: expense items, capital items, maintenance/repair/operating (MRO) items, and original equipment items for manufacture (OEM items).

Expense items are short-lived goods and services which are charged off against revenues as they are used, usually in the year of purchase. Examples include supplies used in operations such as paper clips and machine lubricants.

Capital items are long-lived business assets—such as mainframe computers or large production machines—that are depreciated over time by charging a portion of the asset's cost as a deduction against the company's annual revenue in determining net income. Business managers are usually slow to purchase capital items, which can become expensive liabilities during economic downturns. To reduce this risk, they will frequently lease machines and equipment, thereby eliminating the problems associated with capital products (high initial outlay, long-range liability potential) and gaining the advantages of expense items (more capital available for productive investments, state-of-the-art products, tax advantages, and continued service from suppliers like Merton). For companies like Merton, the advantages of leasing their products include a larger market (since more firms can now afford Merton products) and higher net profits.

Merton sold and leased both expense and capital items to Emco. Merton custom-engineered and sold an entire computerized production system—a capital item—which Emco used in manufacturing its consumer appliances. Emco also leased three electronically activated robots from Merton to supplement this production system and purchased expense item floppy disks used to activate the production system and robots. These products purchased or leased by Emco from Merton could also be categorized as MRO and OEM products:

MRO items are products that fall into one of three categories: (1) maintenance products (paint, nails, brooms, etc.); (2) repair products (parts needed to repair equipment); and (3) operating products (components and systems used to operate Emco's production line, for example).

OEM items are products used as **original equipment** in products manufactured by Emco. For example, Merton Moonshot chip circuits were used as original equipment in microwave ovens manufactured by Emco.

These two categories overlap, and the same product used in an MRO application can also be used in an OEM application—for example, a Merton Moonshot chip circuit can be used in Emco's microwave oven and in the robots and the production line used to manufacture the microwaves.

YOU SHOULD REMEMBER

Products and services purchased in industrial markets can be categorized as (1) short-lived expense items charged off against revenues; or (2) long-lived capital items depreciated over time. Many customers *lease* capital items (trucks, large computers) to minimize problems associated with such products (high initial cost, long-run liability risk, etc.) and gain benefits of expense items (tax advantages, more funds available for more productive investments, etc.). Products purchased by industrial customers can also be categorized as MRO—used for maintenance, repair or operations—or OEM, used as original equipment in products manufactured. Depending on how it is used a product may fall into either category.

DEMAND PATTERNS

Demand patterns among firms in industrial markets differ from those in consumer markets. Industrial demand patterns are more concentrated, more direct, more dependent on demand patterns in other markets, more elastic initially and inelastic in the short run, and more likely to be dependent on reciprocal arrangements.

Concentrated demand: Industrial market demand is much more concentrated (1) geographically, with about half of all manufacturing plants concentrated in eight states; (2) by industry, with specific industries, such as steel or electronics, concentrated where natural or human resources are most available; and (3) by purchasing practices, with most purchasing offices for large manufacturers concentrated in large metropolitan areas. Demand concentration is also displayed in a disproportionate relationship between size and productivity: for example, in 1990, only four percent of 400,000 manufacturing plants employed 57 percent of all production employees, and generated 63 percent of all value added by manufacture. Two consequences of this high degree of concentration are of particular significance to Merton's industrial division marketing manager: (1) It is easier to communicate with customers and prospects, most of whom are located in a handful of offices in Palo Alto, California, New York, and Boston, and (2) It is just as easy for Merton's competitors to contact these customers and prospects.

Direct purchasing: Industrial buyers are more likely to purchase products directly from manufacturers, and in larger quantities, than are consumers. This is particularly true for products that are complex and expensive.

Derived demand: Demand for industrial products derives largely from demand for final consumer goods. For example, if consumers do not buy the appliances Emco manufactures, Emco will not buy the Merton chip circuits used as original equipment in these appliances.

Fluctuating demand: A small change in consumer demand can initiate a large change in industrial demand. Assume that demand for Emco's popular microwave ovens exceeds the firm's capacity to produce them. Emco must then build a large new plant to handle this small excess demand and the anticipated future demand. Thus, Emco's demand for Merton's electronic components will increase dramatically to meet the needs of this large new production capability (not the relatively small increase in sales volume). Conversely, Emco's sales of microwaves might drop only five percent, but as a result, Emco might cut back its chip circuit purchases by 100 percent, selling microwave ovens from inventory until market conditions improve. The disproportionate change in industrial demand caused by changes in consumer demand illustrates the **accelerator principle.**

Inelastic/elastic demand: Industrial demand is inelastic to the extent that demand for many industrial products is not influenced by short-run price changes. For example, assume Emco contracts to purchase 100,000 Merton Moonchips at a cost of $1 per chip, and streams them into the production of its microwave ovens. If the price of the Moonchip then drops to 90 cents apiece, Emco will not purchase additional quantities because it does not need them, and because the cost of storing them would exceed the small savings. Nor is Emco likely to renegotiate its contract with Merton if one of Merton's competitors comes in with this 90-cent-per-chip price; it would be too disruptive to change suppliers in midstream. Of course, if the competitor's price were appreciably less, to the point where product sales, reflecting this lower cost, would appreciably increase, Emco might change suppliers.

Industrial demand can also be extremely elastic during the early negotiating stage of the purchasing process, in that many sellers, like Merton, are actively competing for the same contract.

Joint demand: Frequently, demand for some industrial products is related to demand for other industrial products. For example, if Emco has delivery problems with other components used in its microwave ovens, the firm will have to cut back on its purchases of Merton Moonchips.

Reciprocal arrangements: Frequently, industrial buyers will select as suppliers firms that also purchase their products. For example, Merton's use of Emco appliances in all its employee lounges and lunchrooms was consideration in Emco's selection of Merton as a prime supplier. However, both the Federal Trade Commission (FTC) and the Justice Department forbid reciprocity arrangements that unfairly shut out competition. If a competitor can prove that a reciprocity arrangement overrode considerations of price, quality, and service, the arrangement could be voided.

YOU SHOULD REMEMBER

Key demand pattern characteristics that distinguish industrial markets from consumer markets include (1) greater concentration geographically (with most manufacturing done in ten states), by individual industry (which tends to be located close to resources), by purchasing office (frequently centralized in large urban areas), and by size (with a relatively small proportion of larger firms responsible for a large proportion of production and purchases); (2) greater likelihood that products will be purchased directly from manufacturers; (3) demand derived largely from demand in consumer markets served by industrial markets, and (4) the tendency of demand to fluctuate dramatically with changes in consumer market demand patterns (the *acceleration principle*). During the early stages of the purchasing process, demand tends to be *elastic*, as many suppliers compete for contracts; once contracts are signed, how-

> ever, demand tends to become *inelastic*. Reciprocity arrangements that restrain free trade are prohibited by the FTC and the Justice Department.

INDUSTRIAL BUYING PROCESS

Largely because of the high costs, risks, and opportunities associated with the industrial buying function, it is frequently viewed as an important profit center, where the investment in goods and services purchased can be managed and controlled to improve the firm's profits and competitive posture. With this emphasis on profitability, many modern purchasing departments have evolved along lines similar to those of marketing departments, integrating many functions—such as traffic, production scheduling, warehousing, and inventory control—not traditionally associated with core procurement functions. This growth in size and importance is often reflected in a new title for the traditional purchasing agent: he or she is now frequently referred to as a "materials manager."

This broadened perception of the purchasing function as an integrated, professionalized profit center, combined with the application of modern management techniques and controls in implementing this function, can spell opportunity for marketing managers who understand and can relate to these trends.

To illustrate, we will examine the sale of a single Merton product—an electronic production timing system (EPTS) developed for Emco's production line—in terms of the organizational structures and purchasing procedures Merton's salesperson had to face, and what she had to do and know to deal effectively with them.

• *"BUYING CENTER" CONCEPT*

The increased complexity and professionalism of the purchasing function has led to the development of the buying center concept. This is defined as "all individuals and groups that participate in the purchase decision process because they share common risks and goals arising from buying decisions." Membership in buying centers varies with the cost and complexity associated with buying situations, or "buyclass" categories. These are generally classified as straight-rebuy, modified-rebuy, and new-task situations.

• *"BUYCLASS" CATEGORIES*

- **Straight-rebuy** situations involve purchases of a routine, repetitive nature, such as office supplies or inexpensive plant maintenance items. Such products require no modifications and are generally purchased on a regular basis from suppliers on the customer's "list."

- **Modified-rebuy** situations are essentially straight-rebuy situations which have been taken out of this category by a change in price or specification.

For example, the inexpensive floppy disks Merton had been selling to Emco as straight-rebuy products became modified-rebuy products when a competitor offered Emco a disk with greater capacity at a smaller cost.

- **New-task** situations involve products never purchased before, thus entailing a higher degree of risk and cost than is associated with straight- or modified-rebuy situations. New task situations involve a larger number of participants and a greater need for product information, which focuses on product specifications; price limits; delivery, service, and payment terms; order quantities; and acceptability standards for vendors.

Understanding how Merton's products were perceived in terms of these buyclass categories helped Merton's salesperson recognize competitive threats and opportunities and do a more creative job of serving Emco's needs in a mutually profitable manner. She was continually on the lookout for situations where:

- competitors were trying to transform straight-rebuy situations involving Merton products into modified-rebuy situations involving their products.

- she could reverse the process and turn competitive straight-rebuy situations into Merton's modified-rebuy situations.

- she could create new-task situations involving Merton products and systems. This was what happened when she developed a proposal for using Merton components in the complex, expensive, electronic timing system she eventually sold to Emco.

Classifying product procurement situations into these buyclass categories also makes it easier for Emco's buying center to bring appropriate resources to bear in specific procurement situations. For example, a straight-rebuy situation might require no input at all from buying center members beyond preparing a purchase order, while a complex new-task situation might require input from all buying center members.

• *ROLES OF BUYING CENTER MEMBERS*

Understanding and responding to buyclass situations also requires an understanding of the various roles assumed by buying center members as they also respond to these situations. For example, in preparing her presentation in behalf of the electronic production timing system, the Merton salesperson had to deal with:

- a **gatekeeper** who controls the information flow; in this case, a chief engineer who first assessed her concept and decided whether, and in what form, it warranted further consideration

- two **influentials** in the form of master mechanics who were quite enthusiastic about installation of the new system and helped develop specifications for the system

- a **decider** in the form of a vice-president of manufacturing who made the final decision whether the system would be purchased, and from which supplier

- a **buyer** with whom the salesperson had to negotiate the details of the transaction

- the **user** in the form of the production manager who would operate the EPTS system and who identified the need for it in the first place

In the case of simple, inexpensive products in a straight-rebuy category, major influences motivating favorable purchase decisions are usually personal in nature, often based on friendship and social relations between buyer and seller. As products become more complex and costly, however, industrial salespeople must deal with more people assuming more roles, and with more customer concerns in a variety of areas. Typical economic concerns, for example, focus on cost/benefit relationships, product and supplier reliability, product guarantees and warrantees. Environmental concerns focus on the likelihood of materials shortages, competitive advantages, and technological obsolescence. Organizational concerns focus on the compatibility of products with the firm's existing systems, policies, and procedures.

YOU SHOULD REMEMBER

The modern perception of the procurement function as a profit center which integrates a diversity of functions (such as purchasing, inventory control, and production scheduling) has led to the creation of *buying centers* in which all individuals sharing common risks and goals arising from buying decisions participate in making these decisions. To facilitate the proper allocation of buying-center resources in making these decisions, producer-customers categorize buying situations as (1) straight-rebuy situations involving the routine, repetitive purchase of inexpensive items; (2) modified-rebuy situations involving a change in specifications for straight-rebuy items, and (3) new-task situations, typically involving the purchase of expensive new products or systems from new suppliers. As situations move from straight rebuy to new task, more members of the buying center become involved in the decision-making process, assuming such roles as *gatekeepers, influencers, deciders, users* and *buyers*. Understanding buyclass situations, and roles people assume in the purchase decision process, can also help industrial salespeople focus their resources and develop strategies for transforming straight-rebuy into modified-rebuy situations, and identifying mutually profitable new-task situations. To implement these selling strategies the marketing manager must also understand the motives of various buying team members, which might be purely social in straight-rebuy situations but can be influenced by economic, environmental, and organizational considerations in new-task situations.

• "BUYPHASE" ACTIVITIES

In addition to classifying product procurement situations into buyclasses, modern materials management departments also classify procurement activities into "buyphases" which they relate to each buyclass situation. Table 9-3 outlines, for example, the buyphase activities at Emco that were typically assigned to each buyclass situation to provide guidelines for covering each situation efficiently and productively. Here, for example, is how buyphase activities were involved in the purchase of the Merton computerized production timing system:

Table 9–3. Buyphase activities related to buyclass situations

STAGES OF THE BUYING PROCESS (BUYPHASES)	BUYING SITUATIONS (BUYCLASSES)		
	New task	Modified rebuy	Straight rebuy
1. Problem recognition	Yes	Maybe	No
2. General need description	Yes	Maybe	No
3. Product specification	Yes	Yes	Yes
4. Supplier search	Yes	Maybe	No
5. Proposal solicitation	Yes	Maybe	No
6. Supplier selection	Yes	Maybe	No
7. Order routine specification	Yes	Maybe	No
8. Performance review	Yes	Yes	Yes

Source: Adapted from Patrick J. Robinson, Charles W. Faris, and Yocam Wind, *Industrial Buying and Creative Marketing* (Boston: Allyn & Bacon, 1967), p. 14.

1. **Problem recognition:** During this initial stage, internal stimuli (such as a machinery breakdown or poor service from a supplier), often supplemented by external stimuli (such as a salesperson's call), alert buying center personnel to a problem requiring new specifications and, possibly, new suppliers. At Emco, production line slowdowns, quality-control problems, and late shipments of finished products alerted members of the buying center to the problem of inefficient production systems and procedures.

2. **General need description:** During this second buyphase stage, members of the buying center cooperated to develop performance standards to be achieved by the production line, including the amount of downtime, the percentage of products rejected, and the production cost per unit.

3. **Product specification:** During this third buyphase stage, "value analysis" techniques were used by a team of buying center members to study com-

ponents of the existing production line system to see if any could be redesigned or standardized to achieve agreed-upon productivity goals.

4. **Supplier search**: During this buyphase stage, the buying center team undertook to identify appropriate suppliers by first establishing standards (for example, technical expertise in production systems), then locating suppliers that met these standards through such sources as yellow page listings and supplier associations. Subsequent interviews with supplier representatives—including the Merton salesperson—indicated which should be dropped from consideration.

5. **Proposal solicitation**: Suppliers selected for consideration were invited to submit formal proposals, based on which six suppliers were selected to make presentations before the buying center team.

6. **Supplier selection**: During this buyphase stage, the four selected suppliers were systematically evaluated against desired attributes, through a **vendor analysis** process, to further narrow down the list. Table 9-4 shows the rating scale matrix used to conduct this analysis, and how Merton arrived at its high 3.6 score.

7. **Order routine specification**: The purchasing agent on the Emco buying center team now wrote the final order for the two suppliers—Merton included—selected to engineer and build Emco's new production system. Covered in this order were technical specifications for system components, expected completion times, costs, and warranties.

8. **Performance review**: This final buyphase stage encompassed procedures for monitoring the performance of the two suppliers to assure compliance

Table 9–4. Vendor analysis rating scale evaluation of performance of Merton's industrial division

ATTRIBUTES	RATING SCALE				
	Unacceptable (0)	Poor (1)	Fair (2)	Good (3)	Excellent (4)
Technical and production capabilities					x
Financial strength				x	
Product reliability					x
Delivery reliability				x	
Service capability					x

$4 + 3 + 4 + 3 + 4 = 18$

Average score:
$18/5 = 3.6$

with the contract. Essentially, their performance was evaluated against the same criteria used during the "supplier selection" stage to review their proposals.

As noted previously in Table 9-3, the number of buyphase stages involved varies with the buyclass situation, with only product specification (stage 3) and performance review (stage 8) typically involved in a straight-rebuy situation. An effective industrial salesperson can recognize, and often create, buy phase stages, and become actively involved in each stage. For example, during the buyphase stages leading up to Emco's purchase of the EPTS, the salesperson helped the buying center team recognize and describe the problem (stages 1 and 2), design the system to solve the problem (stage 3), and establish standards for supplier acceptability (stage 4). During stage five, she prepared a proposal which was as much a sales document as a technical document, and helped assure Merton's selection during stage 6. In effect, she was working as a member of Emco's buying center team, helping to define and solve problems and ensuring that the specifications drawn up would include Merton products.

The EPTS analysis also illustrates the **system buying** trend, whereby firms like Emco find it more profitable to purchase an entire "turnkey operation" system from one or two vendors, rather than purchase and combine the system components themselves. For progressive vendor firms like Merton, systems buying represents an opportunity to set up systems selling programs to promote groups of interlocking products. In so doing, they effectively create many more profitable modified-rebuy and new-task situations to help win and hold accounts.

YOU SHOULD REMEMBER

In addition to understanding how to create *buyclass* opportunities by understanding how the roles and motives of buying center members differ from straight-rebuy to new-task situations, salespeople calling on producer customers can create sales opportunities by participating in the stages of the *buyphase* process. Thus, they can help customers recognize problems (stage one), describe products needed to solve these problems (stage two), establish product and supplier specifications (stages three and four), submit proposals (stage five), and assist in supplier selection, order routine, and vendor evaluation (stages six through eight). Participation as an effective member of the customer's buying center team involves an understanding of vendor and value analysis procedures, an ability to negotiate effectively, and a recognition of which stages of the process are most applicable in different situations.

RESELLER, GOVERNMENT, AND FARM MARKETS

Although buying policies and practices in the three other large components of the organizational market are similar, in many respects, to those in the industrial producer market, there are also significant differences. These differences, and the reasons for them, should be taken into account by industrial marketing managers planning marketing programs to attract members of the reseller, government, and farm markets.

RESELLERS

Significant differences in purchasing practices between industrial producers and wholesaler and retailer resellers derive from the fact that the latter are primarily purchasing products to sell or rent to others, not to be used up in producing products. In effect, they are acting as purchasing agents for their customers, and creating time, place, and possession utilities in the process.

For marketing managers, this difference means that their marketing campaigns should stress how their reseller customers can make more profit by reselling the producer's products, or cut costs by reselling their other products more efficiently. The Merton Mini personal computer, for example, used both of these appeals: it was promoted, first, as a profitable, fast-selling product to resell and, second, as an efficient device for handling the reseller's paperwork.

Beyond this difference in basic appeal, however, reseller purchasing processes and procedures are conceptually quite similar to those of producers. Similar to producer buying centers, for example, are reseller buying committees, whose members assume the same roles as buying center counterparts (gatekeepers, influencers, users, buyers), although their titles are different. For example, a supermarket buying committee might be headed by a merchandise manager responsible for developing brand assortments, and the buying committee for a large department store chain would include a "resident buyer"—an independent buying agent who works in central markets for several retailer and wholesaler accounts. In a small store, the owner might assume all the roles and titles.

Resellers, like producers, also categorize procurement situations into buyclasses and buyphases to help buying committee members make better, more profitable purchasing decisions. Three types of reseller buyclass situations of interest to Merton's salespeople included (1) **new-item situations**, where Merton had an opportunity to sell its products for resale on a "yes/no" basis; (2) **best-vendor situations**, where Merton presented its offerings to a reseller customer as a potential supplier, sometimes agreeing to manufacture products that the reseller would sell under its own private label name; and (3) **better-terms situations**, where a reseller customer pressed Merton for better arrangements in such areas as volume discounts, credit extension, and promotional assistance.

In understanding and dealing with these situations, Merton salespeople also had to understand the reseller's buying decision-making process, and how this process applied in different buyclass situations. For example, what problems faced by reseller customers triggered the search for new products, or sales aids, and how could the salesperson help a prospective reseller customer recognize and define these problems? Also, what standards did the prospective reseller customer apply to vendors and their products to solve these problems? According to a study by the A. C. Nielsen Company, the most important criteria motivating a decision to accept a new product include, in order of priority, (1) evidence of customer acceptance; (2) advertising/promotion assistance; (3) introductory terms and allowances; and (4) the reason the product was developed.

We will cover reseller problems and practices in more specific detail in Chapters 14 and 15.

GOVERNMENTS

The huge government component of the organizational market comprises all federal, state, and local governments which, in 1990, comprised more than 82,000 buying units that purchased $892 billion in goods and services. The federal government was responsible for purchasing more than 40 percent of this total.

From the perspective of the industrial marketing manager, the fact that governments must respond to the will of the electorate has a number of significant implications. To ensure public review, many products are purchased through a mandatory bidding procedure, and governments often are required to accept the lowest bid. Contracts for products not easily described, or without effective competition, can be negotiated directly but, in any case, the ability to write clear specifications and precisely identify costs is important to marketing managers interested in serving the government market. Also important is an understanding of the environmental, organizational, and interpersonal factors that influence government buying decisions. These are generally similar to those in the producer segment, except that government buying decisions are more likely to be influenced by non-economic criteria such as the needs of depressed industries and areas, or the mandates of policies favoring small businesses or combating racial, sex, or age discrimination. A tolerance for the considerable paperwork involved in dealing with the complex bureaucracies characterizing government purchasing practices is also helpful.

FARMERS

The farm market in the United States resembles the industrial producer market in two ways of significance to marketing managers. First, a high cash income gives farmers, as a group, considerable purchasing power. Second, it is a highly centralized market. Less than four percent of the population live on farms, which since 1945 have decreased in number from six million to about two million, while increasing in size from an average of 200 acres to more than 400 acres. As a consequence, fewer than half the farmers in this country produce more than 90 percent of farm output.

Beyond these similarities, the farm market differs significantly from other components of the organizational market with respect to buying motivations, which are much closer to those of the consumer market. For example, many farmers are unwilling to shop around for the lowest price, preferring the convenience of local dealers for farm implements or feed.

YOU SHOULD REMEMBER

The reseller component of the organizational market is similar to the producer component in that profits are a major motivator in buying decisions, although these profits derive primarily from products sold to others, not produced for resale by others. In planning marketing programs attractive to retailers, marketing managers should think in terms of the product needs of the reseller's customers, and look for ways to help the reseller serve customers more efficiently at less cost. An understanding of different buying situations (new item, best vendor, better terms) and of the reseller buying process will also help the marketing manager tailor offerings to customer needs. The huge governmental market, while generally similar to reseller and producer markets in terms of buying motives and structures, differs from both in its emphasis on bidding procedures (with the associated red tape), and deemphasis of purely economic buying motives. Also, because government purchasing budgets are dependent on the will of the electorate, they are frequently less stable and predictable than are other organizational market segments. Finally, the farm market represents substantial purchasing power for marketing managers interested in attracting this segment. Like the producer market, it is a highly concentrated market in terms of the location of large "agribusiness" farms and the disproportionate purchasing power of the larger farms. Frequently, however, buying motives are closer to those of the consumer than the industrial markets.

KNOW THE CONCEPTS
DO YOU KNOW THE BASICS?

1. Discuss the differences between organizational and consumer markets with respect to the number of transactions and the dollars and products involved in these transactions.

2. Discuss the differences between the industrial producer and consumer markets with respect to the number of buyers and geographic concentration.

3. Define "derived demand" and the "acceleration principle" in terms of the operations of a local pizzeria.

4. Using the same pizzeria example, explain the statement that demand patterns in producer organizational markets tend to be inelastic in the short run.

5. Still referring to the pizzeria example, illustrate "fluctuating" and "joint" demand characterizing producer markets.

6. Describe the conditions under which a decision by an airline to purchase a new airplane from Boeing aircraft could be (1) a straight-rebuy situation; (2) a modified-rebuy situation; (3) a new-task situation.

7. Assuming the airplane procurement situation in question 6 qualifies as a new-task situation, speculate on how considerations in each of the following environmental areas might influence a decision to cancel the contract: (a) the economic outlook; (b) the cost of money; (c) supply conditions; (d) technological change; (e) political and regulatory developments; (f) competitive developments.

8. According to an article in the *AACSB Bulletin* by Betsy Gelb ("The College of Business: An Industrial Marketer"), a typical college of business administration is an industrial marketer marketing its products (i.e., students) in the same way, say, that Merton markets its Moonchip circuits to the electronics industry. Assuming this is so, describe how the buyphases characterizing the decision-making process in organizational markets might be involved in a college recruiting trip by the personnel partner in the tax practice of a large public accounting firm.

9. According to an article in the June 22, 1987 issue of *Fortune* ("Leasing is on the Move"), growth rates for leasing range between 10 percent and 15 percent. Explain this growth rate in terms of the following situation: Executone, Incorporated—a large nationwide interconnect company competing with the likes of AT&T and Sprint in the telecommunications market—receives a very attractive offer from its automobile rental firm to purchase the 500 automobiles it presently leases for its sales fleet.

Speculate on why this firm made this offer—and why Executone turned it down.

10. In terms of roles assumed by participants in the industrial purchasing decision process, speculate on how the decision to reject the leasing company's offer (question 9, above) was made.

TERMS FOR STUDY

accelerator principle	new item situation
best vendor situation	new task situation
better terms	OEM items
buyclasses	order routine specifications
buying center	organizational market
buyphases	performance review
capital items	problem recognition
concentrated demand	producer market
decider	product specification
derived demand	profit center
direct purchasing	proposal solicitation
expense items	reciprocal arrangements
fluctuating demand	reseller market
gatekeeper	standard industrial classification (SIC)
government market	straight rebuy
influentials	supplier search
joint demand	systems buying
leasing	trade industries
modified rebuy	turnkey operations
MRO items	users

ANSWERS
KNOW THE BASICS

1. Because industrial producer and trade organizational markets are inter-mediaries between the producers of raw materials and the ultimate consumers who purchase the products made from these raw materials, there are many more transactions, products, and dollars involved in organizational than in consumer markets. For example, the process of making a single pair of shoes for a consumer involves multiple transactions among hide tanners, shoe manufacturers, wholesalers, and retailers involving a

diversity of products and services. Reflecting all these transactions, aggregate purchasing power among these industrial producer and trade organizational markets is more than three times that of consumer markets, and this huge figure almost doubles when governmental and institutional components of the organizational market are considered.

2. The producer market has many fewer buyers than the consumer market; in 1990, for example, there were only 14 million manufacturing firms as compared to 240 million consumers. Also, the industrial market is much more concentrated geographically, with ten states accounting for 57 percent of annual shipments.

3. The pizzeria's demand for products which are used to make pizzas is derived from the demand for pizzas by ultimate consumers. If consumer demand declines, so will derived demand. When the pizzeria no longer has the capacity to serve its market, and must enlarge its premises to serve the overflow, its purchases will quickly accelerate beyond its immediate needs. For example, it might have to construct a new wing, and purchase a new oven, in anticipation of future growth in business.

4. At the beginning of each year, the proprietor of the pizzeria contracts for certain quantities of products and services (for example, flour to make the pizzas, an accountant to audit the books) to cover anticipated annual needs. This results in economies of scale and eliminates problems associated with uncertain supply sources (which might necessitate closing down the pizzeria). Thus, unless a competitive price for any of these pre-purchased products is unusually attractive, resulting in increased sales and profits, the proprietor is unlikely to go to the disruptive bother of canceling existing contracts.

5. Because demand for pizzas derives from the willingness and ability of consumers to purchase them, it will tend to fluctuate as environmental factors (the new competitor in town, a sudden societal aversion to fattening foods) affect this derived willingness and ability. Joint demand means that the demand for one product will be affected by the availability of another product with which it is used; for example, the pizza maker needs both mozzarella cheese and tomato paste, jointly, to make the pizzas.

6. The purchase of the aircraft could be a straight rebuy if the specifications don't change; a modified-rebuy if specification changes are relatively minor—for example, different microwave ovens to heat passenger meals; and new-task if major specification changes are called in, such as a new form of propulsion.

7. (a) The economic outlook: people are traveling less by air due to concern over terrorist highjackings; (b) the cost of money: interest rates on the money the airline will have to borrow to purchase the airplane are expected to decline further in the near future; (c) supply conditions: Boeing is taking longer than anticipated to get the new plane properly

"debugged"; (d) technological change: Lockheed has an airplane to go into production shortly which will render obsolete the features of the Boeing airplane that first attracted Virgin Airways; (e) political and regulatory developments: a new tax law will have the effect of reducing business air travel by disallowing many of the deductions involved in entertainment; (f) competitive developments: stiff competition from other airlines competing for the "no-fringe" flyer is reducing the airline's cash flow.

8. Sample analysis of buyphase activities:

Problem recognition: Turnover in the tax accounting practice of the accounting firm has severely depleted its personnel, to the point where morale is suffering and clients are complaining.

General need description: An analysis of the present and prospective workload of the tax practice, as compared to the present and future size of the practice if present turnover rate continues, indicates that 50 new hires per year will be required in each of the next three years; half of these people will come from college graduating classes.

Product specifications: A sample criterion is that new hires in the tax practice must have graduated from an accredited program within the top ten percent of their class.

Supplier search: A number of colleges are contacted and evaluated to identify those whose students meet the "product specifications."

Proposal solicitation: Prospective graduates of selected colleges visited by the personnel partner submit resumes, from which the partner selects between five and ten students at each college for follow-up interviews.

Supplier selection: Based on interview results, the partner selects 50 prospects to receive job offers.

Order routines: Terms of employment (starting salaries, working conditions, benefits, etc.) are negotiated with the 30 prospects who accept the offers.

Performance review: A continuing evaluation program rates both the people hired and the colleges that provided them.

9. Why did the leasing firm make the offer? Probably to increase its cash flow, possibly with the idea of investing in a fleet of late-model automobiles to replace those it is offering Executone. The firm can afford to offer Executone a deep discount because the new automobiles, still under the manufacturer's warranty, will generate a much higher return than the cars offered to Executone. Why does Executone turn down the offer? Because the benefits to it through leasing more than offset the proposed price savings. Among other things, Executone, by leasing, (1) has its working

capital freed for more productive investments; (2) proves, and improves, its credit rating; (3) is freed of the risk of obsolescence; and (4) receives tax benefits (leasing costs are fully deductible).

10. A gatekeeper, in the form of the materials manager who first received the proposal, evaluated it and submitted it for further consideration. The sales manager, whose salesmen would use the automobiles, was influential in requesting that the deal be turned down ("I don't want the sales force to get involved in the automobile maintenance business"); the financial vice-president was the decider who made a cost/benefit analysis and decided to overrule the sales manager. The sales people who would use the purchased automobiles had little to say about the decision.

10 MARKET SEGMENTATION, TARGETING, AND POSITIONING

KEY TERMS

market actual or potential buyers of a product

market positioning finding a market niche which emphasizes product strengths in relation to competitive weaknesses

market targeting choosing a segmentation strategy most consistent with competitive strengths and marketplace realities

mass marketing selecting and developing a single offering for an entire market (also called **undifferentiated marketing**)

product differentiated marketing selecting and developing two or more offerings, each with different features and benefits, to meet the needs of a single market segment (also called **concentrated marketing**)

segmentation bases geographic, demographic, psychographic, and behavioristic criteria used to identify and define market segments

target marketing selecting and developing a number of offerings to meet the needs of a number of specific market segments (also called **differentiated marketing**)

MARKETS DEFINED

In the previous three chapters, we examined (1) the variables that motivate and shape buying behavior among members of the consumer and organizational markets; (2) decision-making processes and procedures whereby these market members arrive at buying decisions; and (3) marketing strategies and tactics for motivating and shaping favorable buying decisions.

In this chapter, we examine a systematic approach for segmenting and defining markets so marketing managers can do a more efficient, productive job of moving market members toward favorable buying decisions. This approach uses demographic, geographic, psychographic, and behavioristic variables to identify and define groups of people with similar needs and characteristics called target markets. We also show how these target markets can be effectively penetrated, and products effectively positioned in each.

Originally, a market was defined as a physical place where buyers and sellers came together to exchange goods and services. This definition is as true for today's supermarket as it was for the early centralized and decentralized markets described in Chapter 1.

From an economist's perspective, a market is defined as groups of buyers and sellers that execute transactions involving anything of value: labor, commodities, talent, money, stocks and bonds, etc. Economists focus on the structure and function of such markets and on the effect of all these transactions on the economy and society at large. In this text, we define markets from the perspective of marketing managers, as groups of actual or potential buyers of a product. For illustrative examples, we will refer to the Friendship Camp case introduced in Chapter 7. We will assume that the original Friendship Camp has already been positioned into a group of "Lifestyle Camps," with offerings for a diversity of market segments on most echelons of the socioeconomic spectrum.

MARKET SEGMENT CHARACTERISTICS

As actual or potential buyers of the services offered by each Lifestyle Camp, members of each of these market segments have in common certain characteristics summarized by the acronym "MAD": sufficient *money* to afford these services, *authority* to purchase them, and the *desire* to use them. An "R" may be added to the MAD acronym (MADR), indicating that the *response* of all members of the market to the offering will be reasonably homogeneous. For example, a group of people with the money, authority, and desire to attend the Lifestyle Culture Camp would really constitute two markets if part of this group responded to a promotional appeal to learn about the finer things in life and the rest to an appeal to meet and mingle with people interested in these finer things.

In the remainder of this chapter, we will discuss basic segmentation concepts, and examine procedures and guidelines for identifying and defining these MADR market segments, devising appropriate strategies for penetrating these market segments, and positioning products to best competitive advantage.

BASIC SEGMENTATION CONCEPTS
SEGMENTATION STRATEGIES

Essential to any segmentation strategy are decisions defining how many market segments will be encompassed by the firm's marketing program, and how boundaries for these segments will be established. At one extreme, the marketing manager might elect to consider all actual or prospective customers as comprising a single market, and design a single offering to satisfy needs in this single market. At the other extreme, the marketing manager might consider each customer a unique, discrete target market in itself, and devise distinctive offerings to appeal to each. An example of this is the large airframe manufacturers (Lockheed, Boeing) serving a relatively small number of large airlines (American, United, TWA, etc.).

Along this spectrum from total to individual market segments, three segmentation strategies can be identified: mass marketing, product differentiated marketing, and target marketing.

- The *mass marketing* strategy, with one offering for all customers. Example: Coca Cola, AT&T. Major advantage: "mass market" economies of scale resulting from mass production and mass marketing efficiencies. Major drawback: "cherry picker" competitors, with offerings attractive to subsegments of the mass market, can effectively undercut the mass marketing strategy.

- The *product differentiated* marketing strategy offers two or more products, each with different features, to the same target market. Example: Hewlett Packard's strategy of offering a broad diversity of computer products to the science/engineering target market. Main advantage: greater brand loyalty among members of the targeted market. Main disadvantage: "All eggs in one basket" philosophy means firm is totally dependent on conditions in single market.

- The *target-marketing* strategy selects and develops offerings tailored to the wants and needs of specific target market segments. For most products sold in consumer markets, this approach helps identify marketing opportunities more effectively than does the mass marketing approach, and avoids dependence on the single market that characterizes the product-differentiated strategy. However, as the number of market segments served increases (each with its own offering), total costs increase while economies of scale decline. For example, it cost a lot less to run the single "Friendship Camp" than to run all the "Lifestyle" camps that emerged from it.

YOU SHOULD REMEMBER

Markets can be viewed as (1) physical places where people meet to exchange goods or services; (2) groups of buyers and sellers who execute transactions involving anything of value; or, from a marketing perspective, (3) actual or potential groups of buyers. In identifying needs of market members and developing marketing mix offerings to satisfy these needs, marketing managers typically begin with one of three possible strategies for segmenting markets into groups of "MADR" people with the money, authority, and desire to respond favorably, and similarly, to their offerings. These include (1) a *mass-marketing* (or undifferentiated) strategy of developing a single offering for all market members; (2) a *product-differentiated* (or concentrated) strategy of designing two or more offerings for a single target market segment; or (3) a *target-marketing* (or differentiated) strategy of developing several offerings for several target market segments. As segmentation strategies move from mass to targeted, competitive pressures and economies of scale lessen.

SEGMENTATION CRITERIA

The main determinant of which segmentation strategy to choose—mass, product differentiated, or target marketing—is primarily the nature of the market or markets the firm proposes to serve.

Thus, if all submarkets for an offering are similar in terms of MADR criteria, the marketing manager might be best advised to combine them all into a single market aggregate, and adopt either a product-differentiated or a mass-marketing strategy. Alternately, if unique segments can be identified that will produce greater profit served individually than collectively, a target marketing segmentation strategy is probably called for.

The key, then, is to identify the optimum number of market segments beyond which overall profits will begin to decline. This analysis of marginal utility can be aided by applying five criteria that define a potentially profitable market segment:

1. substantial   4. operational

2. homogeneous within   5. accessible

3. heterogeneous with respect to other segments

To illustrate these criteria, consider the characteristics of the student market segment attending the Lifestyle academic camp. These characteristics also apply to other segment members attending other Lifestyle Camps (culture, ethnic, career, retirement, etc.).

First, this segment is substantial enough to justify the expense of creating a camp to serve its needs. Second, its members are homogeneous with respect to the MADR criteria which combine to define them as a market segment: they can afford to attend, have the authority and desire to attend, and will respond in a similar manner to the same offering. However, these market members are sufficiently different from members of other Lifestyle market segments (i.e., heterogeneous) to justify treatment as a discrete entity (for example, they are much younger than members of the retirement camp target market). Fourth, all members of this segment can be reached by the camp's offering (accessible) and, finally, the segment is operational to the extent that the characteristics of its members that predispose them to want to attend the camp can be measured and used to help develop the camp's unique offering.

Note that these five segmentation criteria can be viewed as either qualifying or determining in nature—an important distinction when they are actually applied to devise a segmentation strategy. Qualifying criteria are the same for all market segments: for example, all the Lifestyle target markets are sufficiently substantial and accessible to justify developing offerings to meet their needs. Also, the needs of all these target market members can be measured and used to develop these offerings, so each segment meets the operational criteria to qualify as a segment. However, each segment also possesses characteristics that distinguish it from the other segments (i.e., homogeneous within, heterogeneous without), and these two characteristics will determine how its offering will also be distinguished from those for other segments.

YOU SHOULD REMEMBER

A useful market segment typically displays five characteristics: it is sufficiently *substantial*; its members are *homogeneous* with respect to MADR criteria, and *heterogeneous* with respect to MADR characteristics of other segments; the segment is *operational* in the sense that these MADR characteristics can be measured and related to marketing mix components; and segment members are *accessible* to marketing mix offerings. The main consideration governing the number of segments encompassed in a target marketing segmentation strategy is profitability; the number of segments should not extend beyond the point where profits would begin to decline. Segmentation criteria can be viewed as either *qualifying* or *determining* in nature; qualifying criteria (size, accessibility, operationability) are common to all segments; determining criteria (homogeneity, heterogeneity) differ from one segment to the next, and determine differences in offerings.

SEGMENTATION BASES

Larger market aggregates may be subdivided into smaller target market segments on the basis of geographic, demographic, psychographic, and behavioristic characteristics.

• *GEOGRAPHIC BASES*

These focus on the location of target market members and the distinguishing characteristics associated with each location. Marketing managers can focus offerings on a single area, a few areas, or many areas, depending on such considerations as the size of each geographic market and the cost of serving it. If more than one area is selected, offerings may be tailored to different needs among these areas. For example, the offering for the Lifestyle culture camp recognized the different cultural interests of attendees from southern and northern states.

• *DEMOGRAPHIC BASES*

These refer to such state-of-being criteria as age, sex, family size, family life cycle, income, occupation, and nationality. All can be used to identify and define profitable target market segments, and develop offerings attractive to each segment.

Age: baby food, the retirement camp

Sex: cosmetics, magazines

Family size: packaged soup, mini-vans

Family life cycle: dog food; baby, adult aspirin

Income: luxury automobile, no-frills products

Occupation: work shoes, the Executive Learning Institute (ELI)

Nationality: ethnic foods and movies

• *PSYCHOGRAPHIC BASES*

These are the bases that have a direct influence on buyer behavior. They include social class, personality, and lifestyle, as measured by a diversity of tests, such as the AIO test (page 168). For example, members of the Lifestyle culture camp target market were found to closely match the profile of the "emulators" group identified by Arnold Mitchell in his VALS (values and lifestyles)[1] typology, which classifies the American public into nine lifestyle groups. Emulators (who represent ten percent of the population) are "ambitious, competitive and ostentatious," and strive to move ahead by emulating the richer and more successful. They tend to be hard working, less conservative, and fairly successful, but less satisfied with life.

---

1. Arnold Mitchell, *The Nine American Lifestyles* (New York: Macmillan, 1983).

• *BEHAVIORISTIC BASES*

These bases define target market groups in terms of how market members behave, as consumers, toward the seller's offering: how frequently they use it, how loyal they are toward it, what benefits they seek from it, and so on. The marketing manager frequently begins with these behavioristic variables in segmenting a market, first identifying and defining groups that display them, then relating offerings to the needs of these groups.

Here is how this process was carried out in relating Lifestyle Camp offerings to behavioristic variables:

Occasions: Market segments can be identified in terms of the occasions when its members get the idea to actually buy or use the product. For example, the researchers identified peak vacation weeks when people would be most likely to attend summer camp, and geared promotional campaigns to coincide with these periods.

Benefits sought: A usually effective base for behavior segmentation focuses on the benefits to which market segments will respond favorably. Not only do these desired benefits help identify determining dimensions of the segment, but they can influence the development of all marketing mix components. For example, the Lifestyle Camp researchers discovered, surprisingly, that the main benefit sought by career camp enrollees was not better career opportunities, but the opportunity to meet and mingle with members of the opposite sex with similar career and other interests and values. This benefit became an important aspect of the camp's features and promotion.

User status: Frequently, market segments can be defined in terms of the extent to which segment members make use of the product. Lifestyle Camp researchers developed profiles of people who were not interested in any of the camps (non-users), people who had attended a camp once and never returned (ex-users), and people who attended camp year after year (regular users). Analysis of these profiles provided insights into the size and characteristics of new prospective target market segments, and suggested ways to attract more members from new and existing segments. For example, non- and ex-users' responses that traditional camp features (swimming, boating, backpacking, etc.) were missing from Lifestyle camps triggered the development of an "adventure" Lifestyle Camp to attract members of this large group.

Usage rate: Many products sold in consumer and industrial markets can be defined in terms of the relatively small percent of the population that purchases a disproportionate amount of that product. Figure 10-1 shows this relationship among consumers of two products, beer and colas. Note the significant buying pattern differences between these two products: an extremely small proportion of the entire population are heavy beer drinkers—16 percent—but they consume a disproportionately large amount of the product—88 percent. A marketing manager would find it worthwhile to focus the offering on this numerically small market, which is responsible for almost all sales volume.

A much larger percentage of the population are heavy cola drinkers—39 percent—who consume a disproportionately large portion of the product. Here, the

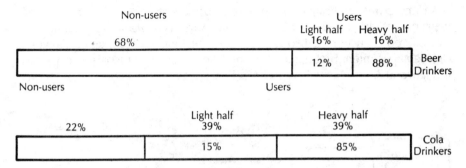

Figure 10–1. Comparative usage rates: beer and cola drinkers.

marketing effort would be less targeted than with beer market consumers. Lifestyle Camp marketing management attempted to identify among camp enrollees the extreme usage rate relationships that would produce marketing economies and efficiencies associated with targeted campaigns. They discovered that the usage rate pattern for the retirement camp reflected that of cola drinkers. Camp enrollments were derived from a much larger proportion of the population than was the case with the culture camp, where a relatively small proportion of potential users made the most use of camp services.

Loyalty status: This behavioristic measure carries the "user status" analysis a step further by profiling degrees of loyalty, and resulting usage patterns, of Lifestyle Camp enrollees. For example, the following profiles of camp attendees were used to position, reposition, and promote the camps:

- **Hard core loyals** returned to the same Lifestyle Camps again and again.

- **Soft core loyals** sampled a diversity of camps within, and outside of, the Lifestyle complex of camps.

- **Switchers** showed no loyalty to any camp, attending whichever camp offered the best deal in price or other incentives.

- **Shifting loyals** shifted their hard-core loyalty from one camp to another.

• *BUYER READINESS*

At any point, actual and prospective buyers may be in different stages of readiness to purchase Lifestyle Camp services. Some, for example, might be completely unaware of the Lifestyle Camp concept; others may be aware, but not especially interested in it; still others may be informed, others interested, others desiring to buy camp services. Segmenting markets in terms of these buyer-readiness stages can provide useful clues for positioning and promoting products. For example, during its formative years, most prospective buyers of Lifestyle Camp services were either unaware of the camp's existence or were not especially interested in it.

An interesting application of the buyer-readiness stage as a determining segmentation criterion is the CAPP (Continuing Advertising Planning Program) service offered clients of the Leo Burnett advertising agency. For example, a typical CAPP analysis might profile the buyer-readiness stages for a typical client shown in Figure 10-2.

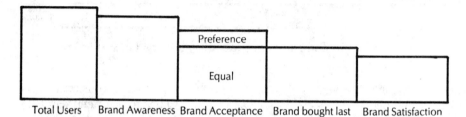

Figure 10–2. Continuing Advertising Planning Program (CAPP) Analysis.

According to this analysis, a large proportion of total users of the product category (cola drinks, for example) are aware of the client's brand. Similarly, a large proportion of this total accept the brand, although only a small proportion prefer it to other brands. The last two categories, "brand bought last" and "brand satisfaction," show that a relatively large proportion of the "brand acceptance" group actually purchased the brand the last time they bought a cola product, and that, of this total, almost all were satisfied with their purchase. A profile like this suggests a diversity of marketing and advertising strategies, such as improving brand distribution to increase the size of the "brand bought last" category, or improving promotional appeals to increase the size of the "preference" category.

• EVALUATING SEGMENTATION BASES

In general, demographic and geographic base criteria are not as useful as psychographic or behavioristic variables in devising appealing offerings. For example, knowledge of a woman's motives for purchasing a particular brand of perfume or of the benefits she expects from this purchase, would be considerably more useful in positioning and promoting this perfume than the demographic fact of her gender or the geographic fact that she lives in Houston. Frequently, however, psychographic and behavioristic criteria can be associated with demographic or geographic criteria; for example, music preferences might be associated with different age or location groups. Eventually, all segmentation strategies must be linked to demographic or geographic criteria, if only to determine whether segment members have sufficient money or accessibility to qualify as target markets.

YOU SHOULD REMEMBER

Bases for identifying and defining market segments with the five desired segment criteria (substantial, homogeneous within, heterogenous without, operational, accessible) can be grouped into four categories: (1) *geographic* bases which often define regional product preferences; (2) *demographic* bases such as age, sex, and income, which can also often determine product needs; (3) *psychographic* bases such as personality and social class, and (4) *behavioristic* bases such as benefits sought, usage rate, and buyer-readiness stage. In addition to determining product choices, psychographic and behavioristic criteria are also useful in designing offerings. Eventually, however, all segmentation strategies must be linked to demographic and geographic criteria, if only to assure that segment members can afford the product, as well as to indicate where and how they can be reached.

DEFINING MARKET SEGMENTS

We will now demonstrate a procedure for identifying and defining worthwhile market segments. We will focus on the segmentation analyses undertaken by the Lifestyle Camp marketing team to identify, define, and cultivate market segments for the career camp.

• SELECT PRODUCT/MARKET AREA

The product offered by the career camp, and the market area to which the product would be offered, were both covered in the firm's mission statement:

> ...to create an environment in which mature, motivated men and women can examine, compare, and learn about different career paths, and choose a path most consistent with self-fulfillment goals.

• IDENTIFY NEEDS OF POTENTIAL CUSTOMERS

In developing a list of all needs of potential customers in this product/market area, the Lifestyle Camp researchers conducted in-depth interviews among members of the two groups most likely to enroll: (1) college graduates seeking entry-level positions in different career fields, and (2) dissatisfied business practitioners and professionals looking to change career paths. Within each of these groups, there were also significant differences that suggested they might be subdivided further. The entry-level group was composed of students from graduate and undergraduate institutions, and the practitioners were mainly from middle and senior management levels. There were also significant differences between the groups; the student group had many more women members than the practitioner group, for example. Also, while both groups had certain basic core needs (acceptance, achievement, sociability), and needs related to the camp's mission (industry outlook information, networking opportunities, etc.), other needs were peculiar to each group. Thus, for example, many members of the entry-level group expressed needs for sensuous experiences and relaxed play that rarely appeared in responses from the practitioner group.

• MATCH NEEDS WITH MARKET SEGMENT CHARACTERISTICS

It was apparent from questionnaire responses that more than one clearly defined market segment was being served by the career camp offering, and that different marketing mix offerings should be considered to meet the needs of these segments. To pin down these segments, and develop prospective offerings to meet segment member needs, it was necessary to match identified needs with the demographic, geographic, psychographic, and behavioristic characteristics of people exhibiting these needs. For example, members of the entry-level group generally displayed different age, education, sex, income, loyalty status, and buyer-readiness characteristics than practitioner group members.

• PROFILE EACH SEGMENT

At this point in the segmentation groups of people with similar needs had been defined in terms of the segmentation criteria common to each group. Many of these criteria were common to all the groups (qualifying) and many peculiar to each group (determining). Now, in profiling each group, emphasis was placed on determining criteria, as illustrated in these profiles of entry level and practitioner groups:

> *Entry level:* The experientials: Seeking intense personal experiences and emotions . . . action and interaction important . . . politically, socially liberal . . . independent and self-reliant . . . fairly happy lives . . . appreciate nature, seek spiritual meaning, concerned with environmental issues.

> *Practitioners:* The confuseds: In transition between various life and career stages . . . outlook generally cautious and conservative . . . orientation toward safety and security generally makes them less interested in an adventurous, experimental lifestyle, or in external issues of interest to the "experiential" group.

CHOOSING A SEGMENTATION STRATEGY

After identifying and defining possible market segments for the career camp, the marketing team faced the crucial question of whether it would be profitable to develop a specific career camp to meet the peculiar needs of each identified segment. Research indicated that each segment—entry level and practitioner—displayed all the MADR characteristics of a legitimate segment, but would two camps be cost-effective?

To answer this important question, the team referred to a matrix (Figure 10-3) which relates segmentation strategies to product/market characteristics. Relat-

PRODUCT/MARKET CHARACTERISTICS	SEGMENTATION STRATEGY OPTIONS		
	Undifferentiated	Concentrated	Differentiated
Company resources	Sufficient	Limited	Sufficient
Product homogeneity	Homogeneous (e.g., steel)	Capable of being differentiated	Capable of being differentiated
Product life cycle stage	Introductory stage	Introductory stage	Mature stage
Market homogeneity	If buyers have same MAD-R characteristics	Buyer groups have different MAD-R characteristics	Buyer groups have different MAD-R characteristics
Competitive strategies		Competitors practice undifferentiated strategies	Competitors practice undifferentiated strategies

Figure 10–3. Segmentation strategies related to product/market characteristics.

ing this matrix to study findings, the team decided that a differentiated strategy of designing a distinct marketing mix for each identified segment was justified: company resources could afford it; the camp was no longer in the introductory stage of the product life cycle; both the camp and its market were unique (i.e., homogeneous) as compared to other, competitive situations, and most competitors had opted for undifferentiated strategies of attempting to appeal to many market segments.

CHOOSING A SEGMENTATION STRATEGY IN THE ORGANIZATIONAL MARKET

Many of the same bases used to segment consumer markets can be used to segment producer and reseller components of organizational markets, especially geographic bases and such behavioral bases as benefits sought, user status, usage rate, loyalty status, readiness stage, and attitudes. In addition, industrial markets can be effectively segmented by end user and size.

Frequently, as with consumer segmentation strategies, bases can be combined, as illustrated in the Figure 10-4 flowchart showing segment options for promotion of the Merton Moonshot chip circuit. Three large potential markets included (1) resellers who sold the chips in make-your-own-stereo kits; (2) manufacturing

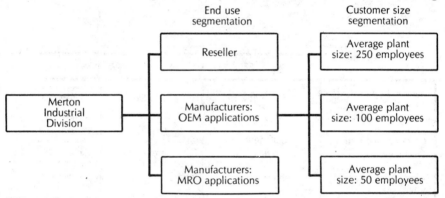

Figure 10–4. Segmenting the industrial market with "end user" and "customer size" segmentation.

firms that used the chips as original equipment in products they manufactured; and (3) manufacturing firms that used the chips in maintenance/repair/operating applications. In terms of "customer size," however, there was no question as to the most lucrative market to focus on, since plants using the Moonshot chip for OEM applications were more than twice as large as the next largest category. Subsequent analyses identified specific industries with the greatest demand for the chips, the benefits desired, and the readiness stages among different industries.

MARKET POSITIONING: FIND A SAFE NICHE

The final decision in the target marketing process, once the market for the product has been segmented and a segmentation strategy decided upon, is to decide what positions the product can most profitably occupy in each selected segment.

The concept of a position is an extension of the brand image concept, defined in Chapter 8 as "a set of perceptions, favorable or unfavorable, about each product attribute ..." In brief, a product's position is its brand image with respect to competing products—the way the product is competitively defined by consumers on important attributes.

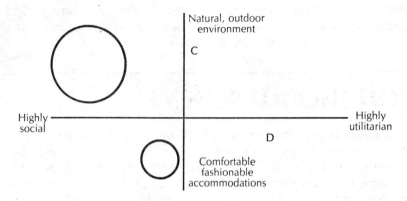

Figure 10–5. Perceptual map helps determine positioning strategies.

The perceptual map in Figure 10-5 illustrates an approach for deciding on a productive product positioning strategy. This map assumes two major attributes of concern to consumers in selecting a career camp: (1) the camp's basic orientation, which can range from highly social, offering opportunities to meet and mingle with like-minded people, to highly functional, with a single-minded focus on experiencing new career options, and (2) the camp's living accommodations, which can range from a natural, outdoor environment to comfortable, modern accommodations.

This perceptual map also assumes that competitors are already positioned in two of the four quadrants, with the size of the "balloon" indicating the relative size of the segment. One competitor is a socially oriented organization of the "Club Med" type, the other is a camp offering both social opportunities and fashionable accommodations similar to the ELI concept.

Here are some guidelines to help the Lifestyle research team decide whether to position the entry level camp in an unoccupied quadrant or next to one of the two competing camps.

The camp should position itself in an unoccupied quadrant if:

- there are a sufficient number of buyers to justify the position

- the position is technically feasible (i.e., Lifestyle management has the expertise to create the desired environment) and economically feasible (it can afford to)

The camp should position itself next to a competitor if:

- the above conditions for positioning itself in an empty quadrant prevail
- the camp can be made superior to the competitor's offering
- the position is consistent with the camp's mission

Given these conditions and limitations, especially Lifestyle's limited finances and the excellent reputations of the two competitors, the Lifestyle group decided to position the two career camps in empty quadrants—the entry level camp at point "C," and the practitioner camp at point "D."

YOU SHOULD REMEMBER

To apply segmentation criteria to identify and define worthwhile market segments, begin with the firm's mission statement, then list all the needs of prospective customers in the product/market area covered, then form actual segments by tying these needs to demographic, geographic, psychographic, and behavioristic bases. Finally, profile each segment in terms of its salient characteristics and needs. The decision whether to adopt a differentiated, undifferentiated, or targeted strategy for entering the market segment(s) depends on company resources, the life cycle stage of the product, the strategies competitors have adopted, the uniqueness of the product, and market homogeneity. Market positioning strategies derive from a researched understanding of competitive positions and the firm's abilities to match these strategies. In general, if the firm has the resources and expertise to create a superior product that is consistent with its mission, it should position itself against competitive offerings; otherwise, it should position itself away from competitors by stressing attributes they do not display. Choosing segmentation strategies for firms serving organizational markets is similar to the process of choosing such strategies for consumer markets; geographic and behavioristic criteria are essentially the same, additional size and end-user criteria may also be used.

KNOW THE CONCEPTS
DO YOU KNOW THE BASICS?

1. Describe how a brokerage firm fits the three definitions of a market in this chapter.

2. In terms of the four MAD characteristics that combine to define a market, why would neither of the following groups of high school graduates qualify as a market for a rigorous education at the Massachusetts Institute of Technology (MIT):

	SAT SCORE	AVAILABILITY OF FUNDS	INTEREST IN ATTENDING MIT	INTEREST IN ENROLLING ELSEWHERE
Group A	High	High	Low	High
Group B	High	Low	High	Low
Group C	Low	High	High	Low

3. How would you label the strategies (i.e., mass marketing, product differentiated, target marketing) defined by the following product/market situations?

   • The Kellogg Company positions its traditional corn flakes to appeal to the "economy" segment of adult cereal consumers and its line of high-fiber bran cereals to appeal to more affluent consumers.

   • Mothercare Stores specialize in maternity wear

   • *TV Guide* has the largest circulation of any magazine in its class

   • The original Model-T Ford was available in "any color you wish as long as it's black"

4. In terms of the five criteria for defining a market, speculate on why an Italian restaurant that goes into business in New York's "Little Italy" just as quickly goes out of business.

5. Describe how segmentation bases (geographic, demographic, psychographic, behavioristic) might have been used to identify and define markets and develop marketing mix offerings for these products:

   • Rolls Royce automobiles

   • General Electric "Power Saver" air conditioners

   • Johnny Walker Scotch whiskey

6. Describe how geographic, psychographic, and behavioristic criteria might have been used to develop the basic offering for a $5,000-per-person New Year's Eve party featuring a Concorde flight to Paris for a gourmet meal.

7. Explain the difference between qualifying and determining dimensions in terms of the selection of a spouse.

8. Describe conditions under which it would be worthwhile for a new delicatessen to start operations in a town that already has two delicatessens.

9. Identify the significant differences in segmentation approach between consumer and industrial markets.

TERMS FOR STUDY

behavioristic bases	perceptual map
benefits segmentation	positioning
brand image	product differentiated marketing
buyer readiness stage	psychographic bases
determining criteria	qualifying criteria
end user segmentation	segmentation bases
geographic bases	segmentation criteria
hard core loyals	segmentation strategies
heterogeneous segments	shifting loyals
homogeneous segment	size segmentation
loyalty status	soft core loyals
MADR	switchers
market	target marketing
mass marketing	usage rate
occasions segmentation	user status
operational	

ANSWERS
KNOW THE BASICS

1. The brokerage firm can be perceived as (1) a physical place where customers come to purchase stocks and bonds; (2) an economic entity comprising both buyers and sellers of stocks and bonds; (3) a buyer of products (e.g., computers, office supplies) required to run the brokerage business.

2.

	SAT SCORE	AVAILABILITY OF FUNDS	INTEREST IN ATTENDING MIT	INTEREST IN ENROLLING ELSEWHERE	Market members lack
Group A	High	High	Low	High	response, desire
Group B	High	Low	High	Low	money
Group C	Low	High	High	Low	authority

3. • Kellogg Company: targeted marketing

   • Mothercare stores: product differentiated (or concentrated) marketing

   • *TV Guide:* mass (or undifferentiated) marketing

   • Model T: mass marketing

4. Speculative reasons for the failure of the Italian restaurant: (1) the market was not sufficiently large, since most residents of Little Italy did not consider Italian food an attraction or felt they could get superior meals in their own homes; (2) the market was not operational to the extent that it was difficult to measure the attitudes of market members, especially those that might be potentially embarrassing (such as the admission that they are tired of Italian food); (3) the offering was not perceived as sufficiently heterogeneous with respect to the many other Italian restaurants in Little Italy; (4) since the offering was not perceived as different or heterogeneous, a homogeneous target market group that perceived it as different could not be identified; (5) the restaurant, located on an obscure street in the center of Little Italy, was generally inaccessible to its real homogeneous target market: tourist visitors to Little Italy.

5. Demographic criteria might be used to develop income and occupational profiles of typical Rolls Royce buyers; psychographic criteria, in the form of Attitude-Interest-Opinion, might be used to develop Lifestyle profiles; and behavioristic criteria might be used to profile prospective customers in terms of the benefits they desire and their buyer readiness stage. The same criteria could be applied to define market segments and marketing mix components for Johnny Walker Scotch. In addition to the above criteria, geographic base criteria would also be applied to define the market and offering for the General Electric air conditioner.

6. The relatively small, select target market group that could afford to attend this event—or would even want to—would have behavioristic characteristics (such as benefits desired, user status), psychographic characteristics (attitudes and interests), and demographic characteristics (such as age, income, family life cycle) which could be used in developing the offering. For example, the cost of the party (price) would derive from income segmentation; the product itself (such as the Concorde flight and the menu at the French restaurant) from Attitude-Interest-Opinion psychographic segmentation; and the promotion campaign from segmentation of psychographic variables such as attitudes, motives, and perceptions. A media strategy for effectively delivering this message would also require an understanding of where party market members live through geographic segmentation.

7. Qualifying dimensions are the same for a prospective spouse as for any other prospect, and would include such demographic features as the sex of the prospective spouse. Determining dimensions distinguish the pro-

spective spouse from other prospects on the basis of such characteristics as political attitudes or religious beliefs.

8. The following conditions might justify this decision: (1) there is a sufficient number of people in the town to use the services of all the delis; (2) the new deli has the technical and economic expertise to operate profitably; (3) the new deli can position itself so it is viewed as superior to its competitors in certain attribute areas.

9. In segmenting industrial markets, greater emphasis is placed on geographic and behavioristic segmentation than on demographic and psychographic segmentation. Segmentation bases more likely to be used in segmenting industrial markets include the type of industry, the company size, and the end-use of the products.

11

MEASURING MARKET AND SALES POTENTIAL

KEY TERMS

judgmental forecasts forecasts based on the judgment of people or groups presumed to have a superior knowledge of sales or market potential

market demand total volume purchased in a specified geographic area by a specified customer group in a specified time period under a specified marketing program

market forecast expected level of market demand resulting from a planned level of marketing expenditure

market potential limit approached by market demand as marketing expenditure approaches infinity in a given marketing environment

market share one company's percentage share of total sales in a given market

quantitative forecasts forecasts based on measurements of numerical quantities which are multiplied, totalled, correlated and/or projected

sales potential company's expected share of market as marketing expenditures increase in relation to competition

sales response function likely sales volume during a specified period associated with different levels of marketing effort

In Chapter 10, we examined strategies for (1) defining and prioritizing market segments; (2) effectively penetrating high-potential target market segments, and (3) effectively positioning products to competitive advantage in these segments.

Now, in this chapter, we will examine approaches and techniques for determining potential sales volume in market segments of interest to market managers. For illustrative examples, we will refer again to both the industrial and consumer products divisions of the Merton Company. As background, we will discuss

1. the relationship between marketing efforts and demand levels which forecasts attempt to project

2. the role of effective sales and market forecasts in the marketing planning effort

3. considerations involved in planning a forecasting strategy

FUNCTIONS OF FORECASTS

FORECASTS MEASURE RELATIONSHIPS BETWEEN MARKETING EFFORTS AND DEMAND LEVELS

To understand the importance of reasonably reliable forecasts to marketing managers requires, first, an understanding of the nature and purposes of the forecasting process, as illustrated in the model depicted in Figure 11-1.

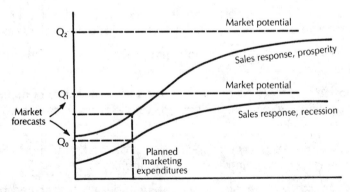

Figure 11–1. Sales responses as a function of planned expenditures: prosperous and recessionary environments.

On this model, the horizontal axis shows different possible levels of industry marketing expenditure in a given time period, and the vertical axis shows demand levels associated with each expenditure level. Point Q_0, the *market minimum*, represents sales volume that would result without any industry marketing expenditures. For example, in the personal computer industry, word-of-mouth promotion alone would result in the sale of *some* computers like the Mini. Greater marketing expenditures would yield more sales, and push the sales response curve closer to the market potential line, which represents, in dollars or units, what all prospective customers *could* purchase of these products. The distance between the market minimum (Q_0) and market potential (Q_2) shows the overall *marketing sensitivity of demand*. If the distance is great, the market is capable of great growth (i.e., it's highly expandable), and will be much more likely to respond to marketing expenditures than if the distance is small. The market for an innovative new product like the Merton Mini would probably be highly expandable; the market for a staid old product like the opera would probably not have much expandability left, and hence would not respond appreciably to increases in marketing expenditures.

Line Q_1 on this model shows how market potential declines during a recession; also shown: the change in the sales response line consistent with this decline.

FORECASTS HELP MARKETING MANAGERS PLAN AND ACHIEVE MARKETING GOALS

The above exhibit, which depicts the relationship among market potential, planned marketing expenditures, and the sales response curve in different market environments, also highlights the value of market forecasts to marketing managers.

Specifically, a reliable forecast can be perceived as the first important step in the marketing planning process, providing information on the nature and potential of market segments, and how sales and share of market outcomes are likely to change with changes in marketing expenditures. This information helps the marketing manager

1. establish realistic marketing objectives

2. allocate resources to achieve these objectives

3. monitor performance against budgeted expectations

Thus, reliable forecasts help marketing managers budget dollars to individual product marketing plans consistent with the sales and profit potential of the markets for these products. Poor forecasts, on the other hand, can result in overstocked inventories, such as faced U.S. automobile manufacturers in the mid-eighties, or lost sales and good will as a result of being out of stock, such as faced the manufacturer of the Cabbage Patch doll in the early eighties. Either outcome can have disastrous consequences.

YOU SHOULD REMEMBER

Forecasts of sales and market potential quantify the extent to which changes in marketing effort will produce changes in sales response in different product markets and market environments (for example, a new product introduced into an expandable growth market). In so doing, reliable forecasts are an important starting point for the marketing planning effort, providing marketing managers with insights into how much should be budgeted for marketing plans, and what kinds of sales and share-of-market objectives can be achieved with these expenditures. Sales forecast figures also represent a yardstick against which marketing performance can be evaluated. Marketing plans based on poor forecasts can produce potentially disastrous results like overstocks or out-of-stocks.

MEASURING POTENTIAL
SEVERAL DIMENSIONS

As shown in Figure 11-2, market and sales potential can be measured along a number of dimensions.

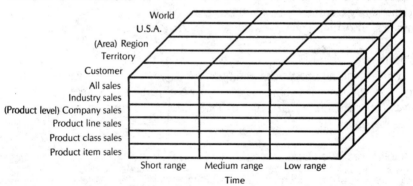

Figure 11–2. Product/Space/Time dimensions identify 90 categories.

Along the *area dimension*, for example, the marketing manager of Merton's industrial division might be interested in measuring the sales potential of a single customer (such as the Emco Corporation that purchases Merton Moonchips for the appliances it produces), or all the customers in a given territory or region. Then, as the basis for deciding if Merton should market its Moonchips to other areas, the marketing manager might develop forecasts for the country and the world.

Along the *product level dimension*, the marketing manager will want to know what the demand is for Moonchips (product item), for all the diverse chip circuits Merton makes and markets (product class), or for all the diverse electronic components manufactured in the industrial division. At higher corporate levels, managers will want an overall forecast for sales of *all* Merton products from both the industrial and consumer divisions, so they can effectively allocate company resources to achieve these results.

These managers will also want to know how Merton is doing in relation to its competition, so industry sales will also be forecast. For reasons we will discuss next, these managers will also want to know how Merton's sales, and sales in the entire electronic products industry, are doing as compared to all sales of all products in this country, so this forecast will also be made.

Along the *time level dimension*, any of these product/space level forecasts might be made for a short-range period (up to one year); a medium-range period (one to three years); or a long-range period (more than three years).

THE THREE-STEP APPROACH

Although marketing managers are typically most interested in measuring short-range potential by product classes in target market territories, these figures become more meaningful when compared to forecasted figures for the national economy as a whole, and the firm's industry as one component of the national economy.

To illustrate the usefulness of these three forecast levels—national, industry, company—assume a situation in which the Merton Mini proves itself a commercial success, and attracts many other competitors with similar offerings. Also assume that, in a given year, Merton projects a ten percent increase in sales. If this increase is considerably less than increases competitors are forecasting (the industry forecast), it might result in a loss of market share for Merton, and suggest that the marketing plan be modified. Alternately, Merton's forecast might indicate much better expected performance than the industry as a whole. The point is, the significance of Merton's annual forecast can best be understood, and acted on, in a broader context of general economic and industry forecasts.

Generally, national economic forecasts are available from so many sources listed in Chapter 5—including government publications, industry associations, trade magazines, banks, and private research organizations—that marketing research managers can usually find a single forecast, or combination of forecasts, that have worked well in the past to forecast future trends and developments.

Many of the same organizations that produce national economic forecasts, including banks, trade associations, business and government publications, also prepare sales forecasts for specific industries. Unfortunately, these forecasts are frequently made for broad industrial categories—steel, housing, electronics, for example—and aren't as useful to marketing managers until broken down more specifically into submarket categories, like the "portable personal computer" or "chip circuit" markets. This is when marketing management looks to its own forecasting tools and techniques to generate valid, reliable, useful forecasts.

FORECASTS RELY ON JUDGMENT, NUMBERS, OR BOTH

In general, approaches for forecasting industry and company sales potential can be categorized as either judgmental or quantitative in nature. Judgmental techniques rely on the judgment of people presumed to have a special knowledge of the impact of different variables on sales; salesmen, for example, or prospective customers, would presumably have a first-hand knowledge of how customers and markets will respond to a firm's products, and the environmental factors influencing these responses.

Quantitative techniques rely primarily on sales volume and other numbers (such as disposable income and gross national product) generated in the past and presumed to have predictive value into the future. In the specific quantitative techniques we will shortly discuss, these figures are typically added or multiplied, and/or projected into the future, and/or related to other figures in developing sales forecasts. For example, if aggregate past sales for Merton Minis were ten million dollars last year, and disposable income, with which these sales figures have correlated closely in the past, is expected to increase by ten percent next year, then Mini sales for next year might be projected at $10,100,000 ($10,000,000 × 10 percent, plus 10 percent). Use of quantitative techniques assumes that numbers on past sales experience exist, which obviously wouldn't be the situation with a totally new product like the first Mini version. Such numbers become more useful and reliable as more sales experience accumulates and significant trends and developments begin to emerge, such as, say, a consistent, predictable relationship between variables like sales and disposable income.

In planning sales forecasts, the marketing research manager must first make two important, interrelated determinations: (1) what purpose(s) will the forecast(s) serve, and (2) which specific forecasting techniques, or combinations of techniques, will be used to serve these purposes?

YOU SHOULD REMEMBER

Sales and marketing forecasts can be conducted to encompass at least 90 possible combinations of area, space, and time attributes (such as a long range forecast of sales for a product line in a regional territory). For planning purposes, marketing managers typically develop product/market sales forecasts in the broader context of industry forecasts, and forecasts for the economy as a whole. Thus, marketing plans account for the broad range of environmental and competitive influences implicit in national and industry forecasts. Although forecast information on the economy as a whole is readily available from a diversity of secondary sources, such as government reports and business magazines, marketing research managers typically have to develop forecast information from primary sources for product/market and, frequently, industry forecasts. Methods used to develop these forecasts are broadly categorized as quantitative and judgmental. Two important questions to be answered in planning a sales or market forecast strategy: what purposes will the forecast serve? and which forecasting techniques should we use?

PURPOSE OF FORECASTS

To answer this first key question, it frequently helps to perceive the firm's markets in terms of attributes discussed in Chapter 10 as defining potential and existing markets. Among these criteria: *money, authority* and *desire* to purchase the product, and *access* to the product. Figure 11-3 shows how these attributes might be used to define potential and existing markets for the Merton Mini, and how this definition might influence forecasting strategies of the marketing research manager of Merton's consumer products division.

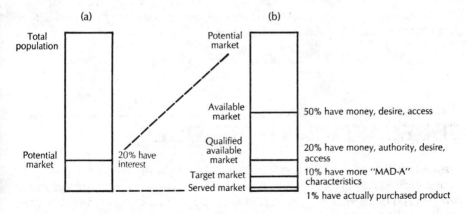

Figure 11–3. Divisions of potential market in terms of money/authority/desire/access characteristics.

Figure 11-3a depicts two key market dimensions:

1. the *total population*, of all people everywhere, who might conceivably have use for a portable personal computer

2. the *potential market* for the Merton Mini, consisting of people who Merton management is interested in selling to, now or in the future. Perhaps, for example, Merton isn't interested in selling to people who aren't in certain businesses or professions.

Figure 11-3b begins with the 20 percent of the total market (from Figure 11-3a) that represents the potential market for Merton Minis, and further defines and delimits this market. Thus, of all the people who could potentially use the Mini, only 50 percent constitute its *available* market, comprising people who are interested in, and have access to, a portable personal computer, and can afford it. However, Merton management is only interested, initially at least, in certain target markets—for example, they have developed Mini models for the engineering and accounting professions—so its *qualified available market* would comprise only members of these professions who have desire, income and access to Merton Minis. The target market, or that ten percent of the total market Merton decides to pursue, might only comprise one or two industries that Merton has targeted initially as representing the highest per capita potential, while the *penetrated* market would comprise the one percent of the target market that has actually purchased Merton Minis.

Viewing markets in terms of these categories is a useful starting point for planning marketing and forecasting strategies. For example, it might show Merton management that its target market isn't being effectively penetrated, and trigger initiatives, such as an intensive advertising campaign, for converting target market members to members of the served market. Dividing the market into these categories might also indicate when, where, and how Merton can expand its market. For example, Merton might decide to change its entire marketing mix offering to attract more members of the available market.

FORECASTING TECHNIQUES

Purposes which sales and marketing forecasts serve in the marketing planning process are an important determinant of which techniques, or mix of techniques, will be used in implementing a forecasting strategy. For example, market forecasts might begin with definitions of the large potential market, using secondary source data, then narrow down to estimate sales potential in the available market, using such primary source data as sales force estimates or buyer expectations.

If product demand is highly stable and predictable, then the forecast might consist of a simple projection of past sales into the future. For example, in Merton's industrial division, sales forecasts for certain products sold to defense subcontractors were based on adding a five percent inflation factor to last year's sales to get this year's anticipated sales.

As market behavior becomes less predictable, however, more diverse and complex forecasting methods are called for. With new products, where there is little or no past sales history to project into the future, these methods will usually be of the "judgmental" variety, relying on attitudes and opinions of people assumed to have a special understanding of future market trends and developments. Judgmental methods are also heavily relied on in situations where a product with a past sales history finds itself in a new environment (as when the success of the Mertin Mini attracted many new competitors), or appreciably alters its marketing mix.

Regardless of the extent to which quantitative and judgmental techniques are used in developing industry and company sales forecasts, they are usually used in such a way that results from one technique validate results from other techniques. For example, if projections of past sales experience indicated a ten percent sales increase (quantitative), but the collective judgment of the firm's sales force indicated a ten percent sales decline (judgmental), one, or perhaps both, forecasts would be suspect, and other forecasts, using other methods, would be incorporated into the final forecast.

YOU SHOULD REMEMBER

A useful way to understand the purposes a specific company forecast strategy serves is to define the firm's market in terms of *interest, income, access* and *authority* criteria with respect to the firm's offering. Thus, for example, members of the *potential* market would at least have some interest in the offering, while members of the available market would also have access to the offering, and sufficient income to afford it. The specific segment of the market being measured (potential, available, served, etc.) will help define specific forecasting approaches and techniques used, with primary source judgmental and quantitative techniques used more frequently as markets get smaller and more product specific. Other determinants of the number and "mix" of quantitative and judgmental techniques used: stability and predictability of industry and company sales, and the availability of historical sales data from which to build projections into the future.

In the remainder of this chapter, we will examine quantitative and judgmental techniques most used, and often combined, to forecast sales and market potential. We will continue to use the industrial and consumer products divisions of the Merton company for illustrative examples.

QUANTITATIVE TECHNIQUES

To illustrate quantitative techniques, we will examine strategies employed by researchers in Merton's consumer and industrial products divisions to develop "big picture" forecasts of industry and area market potential and then to forecast product sales in specific areas.

• *CONSUMER DIVISION FORECASTING STRATEGIES*

The Consumer Division forecasting strategy began with a correlation analysis to develop data or overall market potential for personal computers in Merton's trading area, then used market factor index, chain ratio and total market demand approaches to convert market potential figures into figures representing sales potential for the Merton Mini and other consumer division products. We assume that these products have been on the market for at least five years, permitting sufficient sales data to have accumulated to employ quantitative techniques.

> • *Correlation analysis* This technique makes use of regression analyses to measure the degree of association (correlation) between potential sales of a product and a market factor which has closely paralleled sales of this product in the past. Ideally, this "market factor" is a measurement of economic activity, called a *leading series,* which changes in the same direction but ahead of product sales being measured. For example, historical experience showed Merton researchers that consumer disposable income correlated closely with personal computer sales in the past, and had been projected into the future in previous years with unusual accuracy by a number of private and government economists. For the year for which Merton was interested in forecasting sales, the consensus among these forecasters was that disposable income would increase by ten percent. Since total personal computer sales in Merton's trading area had been $100 million the previous year, they projected total personal computer sales at $100,100,000 for the upcoming year.

Two major limitations of correlation analyses:

1. it requires a lengthy sales history to develop relationships—at least 20 quarters of sales records

2. it is an expensive, time consuming approach, invariably requiring a computer and often beyond the skill of marketing people

• The *market factor index* technique was used as a check on the correlation analysis to develop forecast data on overall personal computer sales potential in Merton's trading area. In Merton's past experience, the *buying power index* formula, published each year by *Sales and Marketing Management* magazine in its *Survey of Buying Power,* had accurately reflected sales of personal computers in Merton's trading area. This formula is based on three weighted factors: the area's share of the nation's disposable personal income (*yi*), retail sales (*ri*), and population (*pi*). Hence, the formula for buying power (*Bi*):

$$Bi = .5yi + .3ri + .2pi$$

In Merton's trading area, the respective *yi, ri* and *pi* shares of national totals were .06, .08 and .07; hence, this area could account for .068 of total potential national demand for personal computers. Since a number of sources—including the association of electronics products manufacturers and two computer industry trade magazines—had forecast national personal computer sales of about $1.7 billion, area sales, assuming the accuracy of the .068 share figure, would be about $116 million, or reasonably close to the $110 million figures deriving from the correlation analysis.

• The *Chain ratio* technique involves multiplying a base number, such as total number of buyers in the market, by various "qualifying" percentages which refine this base number to reflect the specific characteristics of submarkets under study. For example, in Merton's trading area, researchers estimated a total of 50,000 engineers with interest in, and access to, personal computer purchases—the potential market. Of this total, however, only forty percent were estimated to have the disposable income to afford a personal computer, and only 10 percent of that total were employed in engineering fields for which the Merton Mini was designed. Thus, Merton's qualified available market comprised only 2000 engineers (50,000 × .40 × .10).

• The *Total Market Demand* approach builds up to a total market demand figure (Q) by multiplying total number of buyers (n) by the quantity (q) purchased by the average buyer, and the price (p) of an average unit. Thus, starting with the "2000 engineers" figure emerging from the chain ratio calculation, and assuming one in five of these engineers would purchase a Mini at an average cost of $2000, Merton estimated its sales potential to be $800,000 (Q = 2000 × .20 × $2000).

• *INDUSTRIAL DIVISION FORECASTING STRATEGIES*

In Merton's industrial division, where market and sales potential figures tended to be more stable and predictable than in the consumer division, the two most commonly used forecasting techniques were the *market buildup* approach and *time series analyses.*

- The *market buildup* approach involved "building up" to total potential figures for an entire trading area by adding together potential figures for specific industries in this area. Here, SIC categories, discussed in Chapter 9, proved useful to categorize individual target market industries for further study. For example, here is how Merton researchers arrived at total potential figures for the Merton Moonchip in two target industries—the SIC 3621 and the SIC 3628 industries—which used Moonchips as original equipment in products each manufactured:

(1) SIC Code	(2) # Employees	(3) # Firms	(4) Potential sales per employee	(5) Market Potential
3621	50,000	500	$200	$10,000,000
3628	50,000	5000	$ 60	$ 3,000,000

This analysis shows that, in industry 3621, a relatively small number of firms (500) employs a total of 50,000 employees, while in 3628—which might comprise many small "job shop" suppliers for the 3621 industry—5000 firms employ 50,000 employees, or an average of ten per firm. After checking its own past sales records and other primary and secondary information sources (including interviews with buyers in a sample of firms in each industry), Merton researchers concluded that, in industry 3621, the average firm would purchase $200 worth of chip circuits for each employee (column 4), while in 3628, firms would purchase $60 worth of chips for each employee. Market potential figures resulted from multiplying columns (2) and (4); *sales* potential figures resulted from estimates of how much of this potential Merton could reasonably expect to generate. In the 3621 industry, for example, research indicated that Merton would sell one out of every four chip circuits purchased; hence, sales potential in this industry was estimated at $2,500,000.

- *Time series analysis:* This approach assumes that changes in sales levels in past periods (i.e., the time series) can be used as a basis for predicting sales in the future. For many of Merton's industrial market products, basic trends underlying sales changes were relatively stable, so this approach had excellent predictive value. In general, these trends comprised four components:

1. A long-term *trend* (T) reflecting an underlying pattern of sales growth or decline, found by fitting a straight or curved line through past sales.

2. An intermediate-term *cycle* (C), reflecting cyclic changes in economic or competitive activity, depicted by wavelike changes on the trend line.

3. A *season* component (S) reflecting any recurrent weekly, monthly, or quarterly changes in the sales pattern.

4. An *erratic events* (E) component, reflecting unexpected events (strikes, floods, fads, etc.) which might influence sales.

Here is an example of how Merton forecasters used time series trend analysis to forecast sales of a customized chip circuit used as original equipment in the toy industry. The forecasters were specifically interested in sales for the first quarter of the upcoming year.

> First, since the long-term trend line (T) indicated a ten percent sales increase, they projected $500,000 in additional sales to this year's sales of $5 million, or $5,500,000. In addition, the cycle line (C) indicated that the economy would enter a boom period, with a five percent increase in growth, so another $275,000 was added, or $5,775,000. In the toy industry, however, more original equipment components were purchased during the first period, with a seasonal index (S) of 1.9, in preparation for the Christmas season period, when most sales took place. Thus, first period sales were estimated at $2,743,125 (i.e., $5,775,000/4 = $1,443,750 × 1.9 = $2,743,125). After this forecast was prepared, Merton management discovered that one of the toys in which the chip would be used—a talking koala bear—would be the "fad" toy of the year (E), so the forecast was given another five percent boost to $2,880,281.

YOU SHOULD REMEMBER

Quantitative forecasting techniques, which derive forecasts by adding, multiplying, or correlating numbers, either build-up to aggregate totals of area or industry market demand, or start with these aggregate totals and break them down into more focused forecasts for individual products or submarkets. Examples of these techniques include (1) correlation analyses, which use one set of data to forecast another set of highly correlated data; (2) the market factor index method, which uses a formula incorporating factors predictive of sales volume to derive a market index figure; (3) the chain ratio method, which multiplies a base number by various qualifying percentages to derive forecasts; (4) the total market demand technique, which multiplies number of buyers by expected number of purchases, and cost per buyer, to derive forecast figures; (5) the market buildup approach, which totals estimated sales figures for individual products or market segments to derive forecast figures; and (6) time series projections, which project past sales trends into future periods.

JUDGMENTAL TECHNIQUES

Groups whose judgment is typically solicited in preparing judgmental forecasts include experts, sales people, and customers. Here is how each group might have been used to compile a sales forecast for the Merton Mini during the third year following the product's introduction, when a certain amount of data on past sales had already accumulated.

- *Survey of expert opinion:* This approach relies on the opinion of various people with presumed knowledge of different variables affecting sales. Merton's own executives, with their "big picture" understanding of various macroenvironmental influences, might constitute one such group; another might be a trade association of computer manufacturers, or publications serving this field, which gather and disseminate statistics from many sources, including manufacturers, sellers, and government researchers.

    In developing such expert information from Merton executives, the marketing research manager used the "Delphi" technique, whereby estimates of future sales are sent back to the people who originally submitted these estimates until a consensus figure emerges. For example, the first estimate ranged from a predicted sales decline of six percent to a predicted increase of 12 percent. After summaries of these estimates, and the rationale supporting each, were submitted and considered two more times, a consensus figure projecting a four percent sales increase finally emerged.

- *Composite sales force opinion:* Similar to the survey of expert opinion, this approach bases sales forecasts on the opinion of salespeople. Logically, sales people, closer to happenings in the marketplace, should be able to provide reliable estimates, although it is frequently argued that they lack a "big picture" overview of factors affecting sales, and the relative impact of these factors. It is also argued that sales people might have incentives to provide low estimates (for example, to be assigned a realistic quota) or, conversely, that the optimistic nature of the sales personality might encourage unrealistically high estimates.

- *Survey of buyer intentions:* Typically, a firm will retain an independent marketing research firm to conduct these surveys, to avoid bias and potential embarrassment if the survey is associated with the firm itself. A typical survey instrument used in these probes, the *purchase probability scale,* uses rating scale probabilities of from .00 (no chance) through .50 (fair chance) to 1.00 (for certain) to measure purchase intentions. Using this technique, Merton researchers uncovered a much higher degree of intent to purchase Merton Minis among chain store buyers than had been indicated by expert or sales force opinion surveys.

    Among the many research organizations that publish forecasts of buyer purchase intentions, the Survey Research Center of the University of Michigan, with its consumer sentiment measure, is probably the best-known.

YOU SHOULD REMEMBER

Typical judgmental forecasting techniques used to estimate future sales and market potential include the survey of expert opinion, the composite sales force opinion, and the survey of buyer intentions. When sufficient historical sales data isn't available to make use of quantitative methods, these techniques are all that are typically available to researchers in forecasting trends. Even when this historical data is available, judgment techniques are usually used to supplement and validate quantitative techniques, especially in the less stable consumer market environment.

KNOW THE CONCEPTS
DO YOU KNOW THE BASICS?

1. Explain the relationships among demand levels, marketing expenditures, and marketing forecasts.

2. How does a reliable sales forecast assist in the marketing planning effort?

3. Assume the following conditions occur before the Christmas buying season: (1) a local department store underestimates demand for a popular toy; (2) a local shoe store overestimates demand for a well-advertised tennis sneaker. Identify two costs associated with each situation that could adversely influence short and long-range profits for each store.

4. In terms of the space-product-time context in which market forecasts are made, how would you define the following forecasting situations facing the chairman of a large political party who would like to know:

   • How the party in general will do in the next decade in attracting voters

   • How the party's presidential candidate will fare in the next election, two year's hence

   • How the party's slate of senatorial candidates will fare in this year's election

   • Whether one of the party's "star" candidates will upset the incumbent in the year's Pennsylvania gubernatorial election

5. A large automobile manufacturer forecasts an increase in sales revenues of six percent next year. In terms of economic and industrial forecast

contexts in which this forecast will be evaluated, speculate on why this product forecast was considered to be such depressing news by the company's president and marketing manager.

6. Describe the difference between the potential market, the qualified available market, the target market and the penetrated market for professional education courses put on by the Executive Learning Institute (the case company introduced in Chapter 2).

7. Assume that the Executive Learning Institute's forecast of enrollments among members of its target market for next year is considerably below expectations. Describe a marketing planning strategy ELI's marketing manager might undertake with respect to its qualified available market, and its available market, to increase enrollments to desired levels. Why would reliable forecasts be important in justifying these strategies?

8. When Coca Cola introduced its Cherry Coke line, would it be more appropriate to use judgmental or quantitative techniques to forecast demand for this product during its first two years? Which specific judgmental techniques might be most appropriate, and why?

9. A large manufacturer of golf clubs is planning to expand its market into territories where at least two million dollars in sales potential justifies the marketing effort and expense involved. Using, respectively, the market factor index technique, the chain ratio technique, and the total market demand technique to develop each forecast, which of the following territories would qualify?

- *Territory A* has .03 percent of national income, .04 percent of national retail sales, and .05 percent of national population. Last year, national sales of this manufacturer's golf clubs totalled $50,000,000.

- *Territory B* has 200,000 golfers, of which 70% will actually buy golf clubs at least once during their lifetimes. On average, one in twenty of this total will buy a set of the manufacturer's clubs in a typical year, paying, on average, $300.

- *Territory C* has 5000 golfers who will purchase a new set of the manufacturer's golf clubs at least once during a lifetime, at average intervals of once every ten years. Being a more affluent group than residents of territory B, each will pay an average of $400 for his or her clubs.

10. Why would it probably not be wise to rely only on the single forecasting technique for each market mentioned in question 9?

11. Assume Merton is attempting to estimate potential for its Moonchip in a new territory, and has the following facts and figures to go on based on its experience with the Moonchip in other territories: 50 percent of its Moonchip sales are in the SIC 3661 industry (telephone/telegraph equipment), and the SIC 3662 industry (radio and TV equipment). SIC 3661,

with a total of 1500 employees in firms served by Merton, purchased $75,000 worth of Moonchips; SIC 3662, with 2000 employees in served firms, purchased $200,000 worth. In the new territory, SIC 3661 firms employ 1200, SIC 3662 firms 1000. What do you estimate the sales potential for Moonchips to be in the new territory?

TERMS FOR STUDY

available market
buying power index
chain ratio method
company sales potential
correlation analysis
Delphi method
expandable demand
forecasting
leading indicator
market buildup method
market factor index method
market forecast
market potential
market share

market test method
marketing sensitivity of demand
penetrated market
potential market
primary demand
qualified available market
sales force survey
sales forecast
sales response function
Survey of Buying Power
survey of expert opinion
time series projection
total market demand

ANSWERS
KNOW THE BASICS

1. The amount a firm spends in marketing a product will determine the extent to which market potential is transformed into sales dollars for this product. At one extreme, some sales will probably result with no expenditures at all; at the other extreme, a point will be reached beyond which each additional dollar invested in marketing effort will produce less than a dollar's return in sales. Between these extremes, valid and reliable sales forecasts indicate the extent to which sales, in units or dollars, will increase with incremental increases in marketing expenditures.

2. A sales forecast indicates the amount of sales (i.e., the sales response) that a firm can expect to generate in a given product market given a planned level of marketing expenditure. This forecast also indicates the amount of sales, stated as shares of market, that competitors will generate in this product market. Strategic marketing planning involves, essentially, identifying marketing opportunities and projecting goals and plans that will make productive use of the firm's resources to achieve these opportunities against the efforts of competitors to do the same thing. Thus, an

effective sales forecast is basic to the marketing planning effort in that it helps define the opportunity (the sales response), the competitive share of market, and the planned level of expenditure needed to achieve the opportunity.

3. Costs associated with underestimated demand include the cost of lost sales—and the profits to be made on these sales—and the possible cost of future lost sales resulting from a loss of customer good will. Costs associated with overestimated demand include the cost of carrying excess inventory (which, over the course of a year, will usually wipe out all profits on the product stocked) and the cost, later, of reducing the price of inventory to get it off the shelves.

4.

	Space	Product	Time
The party in general	country	company	long range
The presidential candidate	country	item	medium range
The slate of candidates	country	class	short range
The "star" candidate	territory	item	short range

5. In terms of the overall economic forecast, a 6% increase in sales revenues might actually represent a projected decline in automobiles sold if, for instance, price increases, or the combined total of inflation and sales tax increases, exceeded 6%. In terms of an industry forecast, the 6% increase in revenues could represent a significant loss of market share if sales of the industry as a whole were expected to increase by, say, 10%.

6. The potential market would comprise all consumers with some level of interest in attending ELI courses. The qualified potential market would supplement this interest with sufficient income and qualifications to attend these courses (thus completing the "MAD" acronym: money, authority, and desire). In addition, members of the qualified potential market would also have access to ELI courses. The target market is the portion of the qualified available market ELI decides to pursue, and the penetrated market is that portion of the target market who have actually attended ELI courses.

7. If ELI determines that potential enrollments for next year will fall below expectations, it might attempt to do a more effective job of penetrating its target market, thereby increasing its share of this market vis a vis its competitors. Additionally, it might attempt to increase the size of its target market—or add other target markets to this market—by broadening its qualification criteria. For example, instead of just accounting professionals, banking and insurance professionals might also qualify to enroll. Either strategy—focusing on the target market or the qualified available market—must be justified in terms of a forecasted understanding of the size

of each market, competitive conditions in each market, and the extent to which marketing expenditure increases will increase sales response.

8. Judgmental techniques would probably be more appropriate since, as a new product, Cherry Coke wouldn't generate sufficient sales data during its first two years to effectively apply correlation or time series forecasting techniques. The judgmental approaches that would probably be most appropriate would include (1) a survey of buyer intentions conducted among bottlers or supermarket chains; (2) composite of sales force opinion, since Coca Cola has a large sales force; and (3) a survey of expert opinion among Coca Cola executives who have had experience with other Coca Cola product introductions (Classic Coke, Diet Coke, etc.).

9. Territory A will not be cultivated, as yet:
.5 × .03 + .3 × .04 + .2 × .05 = .037, multiplied by $50,000,000 national sales = $1,850,000 (under the $2,000,000 cutoff).
Territory B will be cultivated:

200,000 golfers
× .70 will buy new clubs
_____
140,000
.05 (one in twenty) will buy manufacturer's clubs
_____
7000 golfers × $300 per golfer = $2,100,000 sales

Territory C will not be cultivated:
40,000 golfers will purchase a new set of clubs
.10 once every ten years
_____
4,000 golfers, spending, on average, $400 apiece, for $1,600,000

10. Because any single forecast technique, whether judgmental or quantitative, makes certain assumptions which may or may not hold in a given situation, distortion results when they don't hold. For example, two of the techniques illustrated above assume buyers will purchase golf clubs at certain predictable intervals, but other environmental factors (such as the effect of special promotions or competitor initiatives) might change these intervals in a given year. When a diversity of forecasting techniques go into building a forecast, these biasing factors tend to be accounted for and appropriately discounted. For example, a survey of expert opinion would probably indicate the effect of other factors on purchase intent. In addition, to the extent that marketing planning must account for a diversity of environmental factors—such as competitive initiatives and economic projections—a diversity of forecasting techniques will be required.

11. Answer: $320,000
Calculations: $50 per employee in the 3661 industry; $100 per employee in the 3662 industry; therefore, in the new territory, with employment of 1200 and 1000, respectively, in these industries, total sales forecasted will be $160,000; however, this is only half of Merton's anticipated sales in this territory, ergo: $320,000.

12

PRODUCT MANAGEMENT: DESIGN AND DEVELOPMENT STRATEGIES

KEY TERMS

industrial goods products used in the production of other products that are sold, rented, or otherwise supplied to others

new product a product that is perceived as new by potential customers; can be an original product, a product improvement, a product modification, or a new brand of an existing product

product a bundle of need-satisfying physical, service or symbolic attributes offered to the market for attention, use or consumption

services intangible, perishable, variable, interactive activities offered for sale to satisfy needs in consumer and organizational markets

To this point, we have focused on the marketing management process, with emphasis on how marketing managers identify and define target markets, and plan strategies for fulfilling market needs. Now we will focus on the elements of the marketing mix offering through which needs are fulfilled.

Specifically, this is the first of eight chapters that deals with the four components of the marketing mix:

- *products* offered in consumer or organizational markets

- the *place* where these products are offered, and the means of getting them there

• the *price* paid for these products

• *promotion* programs which support efforts to market products.

We start with the product component of the marketing mix for two reasons. First, it is the most important thing a firm has to offer—its reason for being. Second, all the other elements of the marketing mix derive logically from how the product, and its market, are defined. For example, an understanding of how product benefits satisfy defined needs in a defined market segment helps determine where this product should be distributed, and how it can most effectively be promoted.

Then, after we define products from a number of perspectives useful in devising product marketing strategies, we examine the steps in the new product development sequence, from initial idea generation to final commercialization. Policy decisions pertaining to branding, labelling, packaging and servicing products are examined in Chapter 13.

Our source of illustrative examples in these two chapters will be the Executive Learning Institute (ELI) case, introduced in Chapter 2. Recall that ELI emerged in response to deteriorating market prospects for Roper College, after adverse environmental influences forced enrollments and funding well below profitable levels. In this context, ELI represented a diversification strategy involving new programs targeted to the potentially highly profitable new "business professional" market segment.

> Now, eight years have passed since ELI's highly successful first year, when it just offered programs to accounting executives in its New Jersey headquarters campus. Since then, its programs have expanded to encompass many additional segments of the business/professional market, as well as new strategies for delivering and promoting these programs, including videotaped lectures and on-site courses, and franchise affiliations with motel chains to conduct ELI courses. A key element in ELI's success, in addition to its commitment to well-integrated organization, planning and control systems, is its commitment to an aggressive program for developing and nurturing new products.

PRODUCTS DEFINED: BUNDLES OF SATISFACTIONS

In this chapter, we will categorize and define products from the perspective of the marketing manager, in terms of how product attributes, uses, and buyer responses influence marketing mix decisions.

In the broadest sense, **products** are defined as anything offered to markets for attention, use, or consumption that is capable of satisfying needs. The satisfaction can derive from a tangible product, like a bar of soap, or from a service, like a good haircut, or from a symbolic idea, like a political slogan. From the marketing manager's perspective, they are all products in that they can all be marketed to provide need-fulfilling satisfactions.

Figure 12-1 shows how a marketing manager might view these possibilities along a broad spectrum from totally tangible "pure goods" at one extreme to totally intangible "pure services" at the other.

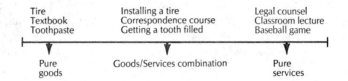

Figure 12–1. The goods-services spectrum.

In the modern concept of "product," this spectrum can be extended to include intangible psychic satisfactions provided by people (such as an attractive political candidate), ideas (such as a religious belief), places (a beautiful park) or organizations (a concerned employer).

Note that most goods situated along this spectrum represent some combination of "goods" and "services." A tire, for example, is a pure good, although its total purchase price may or may not also include the service of installing and balancing it.

The ELI case illustrates products along this spectrum. At the "goods" extreme are textbooks used in class; at the "services" extreme are professor's lectures. A course comprising videotaped lectures would be a good (the videotape cassette) combined with a service (the lecture).

In addition to being defined in terms of their location on this goods-services spectrum, products can be defined in terms of the depth of attributes each exhibits at any point on this spectrum. On the uppermost level, for example, is the *generic* product, which is generally defined in terms of such intrinsic attributes as quality level, features, price, styling, color, brand and packaging. Tangible generic products which are normally consumed in one or a few uses, such as a candy bar or a bar of soap, are called *nondurable* goods; tangible generic products that normally survive many uses, such as a refrigerator or drill press, are called *durable* goods; *services* are activities, benefits, or satisfactions offered for sale, such as a haircut or a Spring tune up.

Next, a level down, is the **core product,** defined in terms of benefits it offers or problems it solves. For example, an ELI videocassette course, objectively defined as a videocassette disk with supplementary textbooks and workbooks, would be defined, in its "core" sense, as a convenient way to improve the productivity of executives. To the extent that successful marketing managers sell benefits, not features, they generally focus on core products in developing product market strategies.

Then, another level down, is the extended, or augmented, product, which includes all additional product attributes, including the level of service offered, guarantees, and brand name associations. A key decision facing marketing managers in designing and managing products is determining how, and how far, to augment the product. Frequently, this decision involves first examining the buyer's total consumption system, or the way the buyer performs all tasks associated with use of the product, including where, when, and how it is purchased. For example, ELI's videocassette courses were augmented with classroom sessions when research showed this was an important part of participants' expectations.

YOU SHOULD REMEMBER

Products are broadly defined as "bundles of satisfactions"—from highly tangible goods like tires or textbooks, through less tangible combinations of goods and services, like a haircut, to highly intangible symbolic values embodied in people and philosophies. Wherever a product exists on this tangible/intangible spectrum, it can be further defined in terms of the depth of attributes associated with it. At the uppermost level is the generic product, defined in terms of such attributes as price, features, and quality; then, a level down, the "core" product is defined from the consumer's perspective in terms of benefits; finally, the next level down, the "augmented" product is defined in terms of expanded attributes like guarantees and follow-up services offered. Defining products broadly and in depth helps marketing managers evolve productive product marketing strategies. For example, these definitions help determine what core product values and augmented attributes will appeal most to target market prospects.

PRODUCTS DEFINED IN TERMS OF CONSUMER/INDUSTRIAL BUYERS

Another way to define products that is useful in developing product marketing strategies is in terms of buyers in consumer and industrial markets.

Tables 12 -1 and 12 -2 summarize classes and categories of products purchased in each market, buying behaviors displayed with respect to these products by consumer and industrial buyers, and marketing mix implications of interest to marketing managers.

Table 12.1: Consumer Products: Buyer Behavior and Marketing Mix Attributes

Consumer Product Classifications	Examples	Buying Behavior	Marketing Mix Attributes			
			Product	Price	Place	Promotion
CONVENIENCE Inexpensive habit or impulse purchases; little service or selling costs • Staples • Impulse • Emergency	food, drug items TV Guide, candy bar umbrellas	Purchases often planned in store, based on "best buys" Fast, unplanned purchases; based on strong felt need Purchased when need great; little shopping done	Branding, packaging, labeling important to encourage impulse purchases, inform buyers	Low unit price for staples, impulse goods; higher for emergency goods	Carried by many outlets; impulse goods in highly conspicuous locations, near checkout counters; emergency items often carried as "fill in" items	mass market advertising main element in promotion mix
SHOPPING Products perceived as worth time and effort to compare with competition • Homogeneous (perceived basically the same) • Heterogeneous (perceived as different)	certain sizes, types of refrigerators, TV sets; relatively expensive supermarket items (coffee, butter), furniture, cameras, clothing	Looks for lowest price Compare on basis of preconceived quality standards, features	Extended product attributes (installation, credit, follow-up, delivery, services) developed; wide assortments needed to satisfy individual tastes	Usually cost more than convenience goods	Location convenience stressed	Homogeneous products stress extended product features (service, quality); Heterogeneous competitive features, benefits. Personal selling key part of mix
SPECIALTY Perceived as worth a special trip	Mercedes automobiles, Gucci boots, Cabbage Patch dolls	Buyer wants a specific product; no comparison required; will expend considerable time and effort to acquire	Brand identification important, also extended product attributes like service, packaging; product line extension decisions important	Unique product characteristics, brand name associations permit high price	Location of outlets, rather than number, most important	Stresses unique product attributes and associations; Advertising appeals and media decisions reflect product image; personal selling important
UNSOUGHT Customers don't want product, or are unaware they can purchase it	New unsought: compact disk players, smoke detectors Known unsought: life insurance, encyclopedias	Need exists, but buyer not motivated to satisfy it No product search	Extended product attributes (service, guarantees) important	Must be competitive to overcome buyer resistance, but high enough to cover selling costs	Unsought status requires many outlets, often in-house presentations	Require strong emphasis on all elements of promotion mix, especially advanced personal selling methods; Benefits rather than features emphasized

Table 12.2: Industrial Products: Buyer Behavior and Marketing Mix Attributes

Industrial Product Classifications	Examples	Buying Behavior	Product	Marketing Mix Attributes			
				Price	Place	Promotion
INSTALLATIONS Long-lived capital goods depreciated over time	Buildings (used); Buildings (new); Fixed equipment customized standardized	Motives primarily economic (return on investment); multiple, high-level buying influences; negotiation with vendors important	Purchase expense and risk often makes leasing more attractive than buying; form of product doesn't change; very low consumption rate	High per-unit price; demand tends to be inelastic, especially during economic upswings with attractive ROI; otherwise, competition on bid basis	Usually purchased directly from manufacturer	Indirect promotion (advertising, publicity) much less important than personal selling; can be focused in centralized market, but to meet needs of individual buyer
ACCESSORY EQUIPMENT Short-lived items that don't become part of finished product	Tools, equipment for production, office activities (portable drills, typewriters, etc.)	Many more potential customers, but fewer buying center influences than for installations; smaller order size	More standardized than installations; leasing attractive in some target markets; engineering services less important	Medium per-unit price; demand tends to become more elastic as equipment becomes more standardized	Market geographically dispersed, so use more middlemen	More use of indirect promotion (especially sales promotion)
RAW MATERIALS Unprocessed expense items that enter production process	Natural and nurtured resources (crude oil, iron ore, lumber); also farm products	Low-level decision making; supply continuity, cost efficiency key motives; prefer sorted, graded products; may encourage contract purchasing to control supply	Perishable, seasonal, not expandable in short run	Often depends on supply, which is difficult to adjust to demand; generally inelastic for industry, elastic for individual firms	Constant demand, seasonal production mean emphasis on storage, transportation, grading; dispersed producers, centralized buyers mean large, centralized distributors vertical integration	Products difficult to differentiate, so direct selling important component of promotion mix
COMPONENTS Expense items that require more processing than raw materials; also enter production process	Parts (finished or nearly finished, ready for assembly); tires, small motors; Materials (need further processing) wire, yarn, iron	Modified rebuy or new task situation if components are important, expensive; straight rebuy for standards; economic needs (price, availability, quality, important); usually many back-up sources	Highly rapid consumption puts emphasis on service and continuity	Industry demand derived and basically inelastic, but elastic for individual firms, with price a key factor in mix; unit price low	Many suppliers create competitive market conditions	OEM, and after markets, especially attractive
SUPPLIES MRO items; don't become part of final product	Paint, nails, brooms, nuts, paper clips, lubricating oils	Require backup sources; usually straight rebuy, with few buying influences, little shopping; may negotiate contracts to create straight rebuy situation; reciprocity often expected	Branding important to make buying easier; packaging for easy storage; rapid consumption puts emphasis on reliability; should offer full line	Unit prices very low; highly elastic demand in short run	Many suppliers create competitive conditions	Media advertising, sales promotion support direct selling efforts
SERVICES • Maintenance and repair • Business advisory	Painting, machinery repair, janitorial; Management consulting, accounting	Frequently purchased on contract or retainer basis, often handled internally	Brand associations, product quality, service	Demand often inelastic if unique product; otherwise, wide range of prices possible through negotiation	Difficult to expand distribution; importance of location varies with amount of customer contact	Personal selling dominant for highly personalized service; referrals important; advertising more important as becomes less personal

CONSUMER PRODUCTS

Note that, in consumer product markets, products are defined in terms of the buying behavior of shoppers. Thus, convenience goods are purchased often, quickly, and with little comparison or effort. Shopping goods involve product comparisons on such bases as quality, price, style and suitability. Specialty goods possess unique attributes for which a significant group of buyers is willing to make a special effort. These shopping characteristics, in turn, determine marketing mix emphasis for each product type. For example, the often impulsive nature of convenience goods purchases puts stress on the "place" element to make sure these products are widely available and highly visible, while the "brand insistence" status of specialty goods places emphasis on promoting the product brand name.

INDUSTRIAL PRODUCTS

From the marketing manager's perspective, industrial products are typically categorized in terms of how they are used in productive processes, and defined in terms of the behavior of people who purchase them. As noted in Chapter 10, this buying behavior differs appreciably from buying behavior in consumer markets. For example, demand for industrial products typically derives from demand for consumer products, is more inelastic, fluctuates more, and is characterized by more concentrated buying by more people to more demanding standards. Just as consumer buying situations were categorized as "convenience," "shopping" and "specialty," in terms of buyer behavior, industrial buying situations are categorized as "straight rebuy," "modified rebuy," and "new task" in terms of buyer behavior. These categories are discussed in Chapter 10.

Certain kinds of industrial goods, such as raw materials and components, become a part of the finished product, while others, such as installations and supplies, become part of the "maintenance, repair and operating" activities involved in getting other products produced.

Buyer behavior toward industrial products, and the use made of these products, largely determine marketing mix responses toward different product categories. For example, expensive installations, depreciated over time, typically require high-level expenditure authorization and participation by groups of buying influentials from the firm's buying center. To reach these influentials, emphasis is usually placed on the personal selling element of the promotion "P." and the service element of the product "P." On the other hand, with less expensive products, purchased routinely in "straight rebuy" situations, initial emphasis is likely to be on price, especially for products hard to differentiate.

SEGMENTATION IMPLICATIONS

Categorizing and defining consumer and industrial products in terms of uses and buyer behavior is an excellent basis for segmenting markets, as well as for determining marketing mix emphasis. For example, the marketing manager for a large insurance company can define market segments in terms of demographic and behavioral characteristics deriving from its "unsought" status: what age, income, and attitude characteristics do people have in common that makes this product unsought? Similarly, market segment profiles can be derived from an understanding of characteristics of people who perceive products as "shopping," or "specialty," or "new task," or "straight rebuy," etc. Then, marketing mix strategies can be devised to attract each defined segment. In devising these segmentation and marketing mix strategies, however, the marketing manager should be aware that the same product can be viewed in different categories by different customer groups. For example, a package of Merton computer floppy disks sold in consumer markets might be perceived as a convenience good by members of the computer "hacker" segment, and as a shopping good by members of the new owner segment. In the industrial market, the same package of disks might be used in activating a production line in a "maintenance, repair, operating" application, or be an accessory to the product the firm manufactures in an "OEM" original equipment application.

YOU SHOULD REMEMBER

Consumer and industrial products and services are categorized and defined in terms that will help develop marketing mix strategies. Thus, consumer products are defined in terms of consumer buying behavior toward them as "convenience," "shopping," "specialty" and "unsought" goods. These definitions, in turn, help define such marketing mix strategies as a "place" emphasis to make convenience goods quickly accessible, or a "price" emphasis to maintain the image of a specialty good.

Industrial products are categorized in terms of how they are used in the production process, and buyer purchasing habits toward them, which are largely conditioned by the derived, inelastic, fluctuating, concentrated nature of demand patterns in industrial markets. Components and raw materials become part of the finished product, and installations, supplies services and accessories become part of the MRD environment in which products get manufactured. Buyer response toward industrial products, categorized as straight rebuy, modified rebuy, or new task, helps define marketing mix emphasis for these products. For example, a product perceived as a "straight rebuy" would require much less direct selling, but more emphasis on price, than an installation purchased in a new task situation. In relating marketing mix strategies to product categories in consumer or industrial markets, marketing managers should recognize that the same product can be perceived in different categories in different situations.

CHARACTERISTICS OF SERVICES DEFINE APPLICATIONS AND MARKETING STRATEGY

To this point in our discussion, our focus has primarily been on tangible products sold in consumer and industrial markets; however, statistics show that service businesses, combining both tangible and intangible attributes, are not only the fastest growing segment of the economy (See Figure 12-2), but the largest as well, employing 75 percent of the total workforce in 1990 and generating 70 percent of total gross national product. Nine out of ten jobs created during the 80s were in the service sector, with data processing, management consulting, and engineering/architectural services among the fastest growing fields.

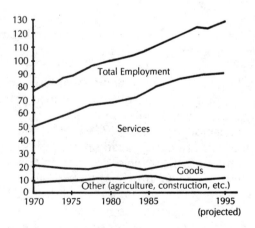

Source: U.S. Department of Labor, Bureau of Labor
Statistics

Figure 12-2. Growth of service employment in the U.S. (1970–1995).

WHY SERVICES GROW SO FAST

The reasons for the remarkably rapid growth of the U.S. to the world's first service economy can be traced to practically all the macroenvironmental factors discussed in Chapter 3, including new technologies and the increasing complexity of tangible products requiring service; smaller families, more disposable income, and more leisure time to make use of services; and more women in the work force to both provide and require services.

HOW SERVICES ARE CLASSIFIED

Services can be classified and defined in a diversity of ways. The *Fortune* magazine classification categorizes services according to industries represented by the 500 largest service firms. Figure 12-3 shows the largest companies in each of the seven industry categories in *Fortune's* "Service 500."

COMMERCIAL BANKING	DIVERSIFIED FINANCIAL	LIFE INSURANCE	TRANSPORTA- TION	UTILITIES	DIVERSIFIED SERVICES
Citicorp	Federal National Mortgage Assn.	Prudential	Allegis	GTE	Super Value Stores
Chase Manhattan	American Express	Metropolitan	United Parcel	Bell South	Fleming Companies

Figure 12-3. Top service firms in each of *Fortune's* "Service 500" categories.

Services can also be classified in terms of types of customers served, with service firms like Benton & Bowles (advertising) and Peat Marwick (accounting) serving the organizational market, and service firms like Lawn Doctor and Home Box Office serving the consumer market.

Still another way to classify service firms is in terms of the extent to which the service combines tangible with intangible elements. For example, a visit to a doctor's office might have about 5 percent goods content—say, the stethoscope used to listen to heartbeats—and 95 percent nongoods—say, the feeling of satisfaction resulting from the knowledge that you're in great shape. A janitorial service, at the other extreme, might be 90 percent goods content—mops, pails, etc.—and only 10 percent nongoods: a clean workplace. Services with a relatively high goods content are also often classified as "equipment based," while less tangible, nongoods-type services are classified as "people based." These categories can be further broken down as shown in Figure 12-4.

SERVICES ARE MORE INTANGIBLE, INSEPARABLE, VARIABLE AND PERISHABLE

From the perspective of the marketing manager interested in segmenting markets and devising marketing mixes for services, perhaps the most productive way

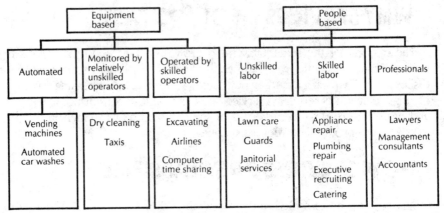

Source: Adopted from Dan Thomas, "Strategy is Different in Service Businesses" *Harvard Business Review,* July–August 1978 p. 161

Figure 12–4. Types of service businesses.

to classify and define services is in terms of key attributes which differentiate services like a computer repair service from tangible products, like computers. Table 12-3 highlights these differences, and shows how they influence marketing mix service strategies.

As a concrete illustration of how these attributes of services might influence marketing planning, consider some of the problems faced in marketing ELI's "people based" educational service in the first year of its existence. Because this service was perishable, the classrooms had to be filled to profitable levels—they couldn't be kept in inventory; because they were intangible, there was no way to assure enrollees of any benefits from taking the courses as could be assured, say, from a pair of glasses or an electric light bulb. And because the service was variable, benefits would vary from course to course. Labor intensity was another problem, making it difficult to cut costs and raise profits through economies of scale and learning curve efficiencies.

Largely as a means of overcoming these service related drawbacks, a strong component of ELI's new product development program focused on developing tangible new products. The systematic approach used to conceive, develop, and commercialize ELI's new products is discussed next.

YOU SHOULD REMEMBER

Services, which combine both tangible and intangible attributes, are the largest and fastest-growing segment of the economy, employing 76 percent of the workforce in 1990. Key reasons for this growth:

new technologies, more disposable income, more women in the work force. Services are classified in a variety of ways. The *Fortune 500* list classifies them in terms of major service industries; others classify them by types of customers (mainly, organizational and consumer customers), or extent to which they combine tangible with intangible elements (equipment-based services, like airlines, tend to have more tangible "goods" content, while people-based services like doctors and accountants have more pure service content). In terms of devising marketing mix strategies for services, a useful way to define services is in terms of how they differ from more tangible products. For example, a highly "people based" service, like an accounting service, would be more intangible, inseperable, variable, perishable and labor intensive than its more tangible product counterparts, and have legal and ethical associations which would all have to be addressed in marketing programs for this service.

NEW PRODUCTS

From the perspective of the marketing manager, a new product can be anything management believes to be new, usually categorized as a major innovation, a minor innovation, or a modification.

- *A major innovation* is a product that has never been sold by any other organization, such as the first videocassette recorder.

- *A minor innovation* is a product not previously sold by the company, but by other companies. Most of the new courses ELI added to its curriculum as it developed programs attractive to new market segments fell into this category.

- *A modification* is any adjustment of a product's tangible features (style, color, etc.), any product improvement, or a brand change. Improving ELI's accommodations would qualify as a modification.

A study of new products by the Booz, Allen & Hamilton consulting firm indicates that 70 percent of new products brought to market by American companies are product modifications, 20 percent minor innovations, and 10 percent major innovations. This study also showed that major innovations get greater support from top management.

Another way to view new products is suggested in this Booz, Allen & Hamilton study. According to this study new products can be categorized as new-to-the-world products (such as cellular telephones), new product lines that allow entry into new markets, additions to existing lines, improvements of existing products, and new products brought on by cost reduction measures or

Table 12.3: Services: Characteristics and Marketing Mix Attributes

Service Characteristics	As Compared to More Tangible Products	Examples	Marketing Mix Attributes			
			Product	Price	Place	Promotion
Intangibility	More difficult to taste, feel, see or otherwise sample before using	Quality of a haircut, audit, or advertising campaign	Build, sustain quality image and track record; tangible symbols in brand names (Merrill Lynch's bull)	Strong track record, quality image can justify high price; some services are indirect pricing to avoid issue (e.g., travel agency commissions)	Tangible aspects of service environment stressed (in-flight meals, magazines in dentist's office etc.)	"Image" advertising, spokesperson testimonials, free trials, referrals, and personal selling important to document expected benefits
Inseparability	More difficult to separate from person or image of seller	Psychiatrists, doctors, lawyers	Brand name associations with seller image (H&R Block)	Highly personal service fees often negotiated (accountants, real estate brokers); Strong seller image; often commands high fees	Channel opportunities restricted for highly personal services, encouraging direct-run operations (Jacoby and Myers) or franchises (H&R Block, McDonalds)	Promotion focuses on quality of service personnel (Club Med associates, reliable airline pilots), often using service personnel as spokespersons (H&R Block, bank presidents)
Variability • in use	Number of users more likely to change from time to time	Resort seasons, rush hour train schedules	Often incorporate tangible equipment (e.g. automatic teller machines) to spread usage to off periods	Wide range of negotiated prices possible	Important that service have supplies when needed	Media schedules must conform to service use periods; promotion encourages off peak use
• in quality	Quality of use experience more likely to change from time to time	Boring baseball games, 2-hour flight delay	Work to achieve, maintain high quality levels; often modify to relate to new needs	Must often price higher in peak seasons to recoup off-peak costs	Location can enhance "quality" image (Saks Fifth Avenue)	Emphasizes quality experiences (an exciting world series)
Perishability	Must often be consumed while being produced; difficult to keep in inventory	Physical examination, television air time	Customize service to meet needs of customer at time of use (Burger King, hamburger)	Emphasis on a variety of pricing incentives (seasonal, cash, quantity discounts, etc.) to insure commitment to use	Service must be made efficiently accessible to customer when needed	Promotes special incentives to commit to service use (e.g., tangible rewards for buying airline, magazine subscriptions)
Labor intensity	Services are generally more dependent on quality, ability of personnel; difficult to achieve economy of scale, learning curve benefits	Physical examination, ocean cruise, income tax preparation	Important to select, motivate and train service personnel for high productivity	Tends to push up price for services, since labor is typically the highest cost component	Service must be located for convenient access by staff members	Service employees encouraged to play active role in selling service, are often used in promotion (e.g., Avon Lady, Lawn Doctor)
Legal, ethical barriers	Higher standards mandated and policed by service industry itself and/or government regulatory bodies	American Association of Advertising Agencies, Securities and Exchange Commission, utility regulatory boards	High codes of ethical behavior, especially for personal services (drug tests for police, review panels for doctors)	Concern for legislative response often important in determining prices (e.g., medical services); Some service prices (utilities) determined by regulatory bodies	Personalized merchandising services (door-to-door, direct mail selling) frequently subject to fraud and subsequent legal constraints	In regulated services, tends to be defensive in nature, anticipating regulatory curbs (e.g., a politician's apology) advertising even considered unethical in some fields (law, physicians)

by repositioning existing products. Figure 12-5 defines these categories in terms of newness to market or company, and percent of all new product introductions represented by each category.

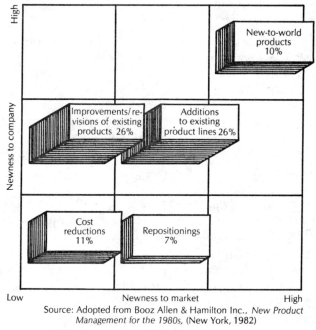

Source: Adopted from Booz Allen & Hamilton Inc., *New Product Management for the 1980s,* (New York, 1982)

Figure 12–5. New product categories.

Regardless of how categorized, many firms consider the continuing, systematic development of new products critical to growth and profitability in competitive markets. These firms find new products an invaluable means of achieving a diversity of corporate objectives, such as matching competitors, completing a product line, meeting sales growth objectives and utilizing excess capacity.

Other firms shun new product development, assuming, instead, a "follow the leader" stance in relation to new product pathfinder firms like IBM, GE, 3M and Gillette. Reasons cited for their reluctance: fragmented markets, meaning lower sales and profits from smaller segments; a shortage of new product opportunities brought on by a shortage of important new technologies on the magnitude of computers or xerography; much shorter life spans for the relatively small number of successful new products; the extreme, accelerating costliness of new product development; and the general lack of capital to meet this cost.

ORGANIZING FOR NEW PRODUCT DEVELOPMENT

ELI's commitment to a continuing program of new product development assumed that these threats were outweighed by potential opportunities; that one huge success could make up for a dozen failures. This commitment also recog-

nized the importance of properly organizing the new product development function for optimum creativity and productivity. Among the possible structures
management considered were brand manager, new product department, new
product committee, and venture team structures.

- Under a *brand manager* (also called product manager) approach, a single
  manager would assume responsibility for determining objectives, defining
  target markets, and devising marketing mix strategies for a single product
  or product line. Typically, in interfacing with other internal and external
  groups, such as sales forces or advertising agencies, brand managers have
  little line authority to enforce decisions. With all these responsibilities for
  a full range of marketing functions, brand managers typically have little
  time for new product development, which was one of the reasons ELI
  management rejected this structure.

- A *new product department*, comprising a group of specialists involved in
  all aspects of new product development—research, finance, production,
  marketing, etc.—was also rejected as being too elaborate for ELI's needs.

- A *new product committee*, comprising top managers from various key
  functional areas—including ELI's treasurer, the marketing research manager, the dean of faculty and the marketing manager—would meet periodically to consider and screen new product ideas, then return to their
  regular positions. Advantages of this approach include top management
  involvement and expertise in the process, and fast approval of ideas
  deemed worthwhile. Disadvantages include the consumption of valuable
  executive time, and a tendency for managers to put departmental interests
  first.

- *Venture teams*, although conceptually similar to new product committees
  in that they bring together managers from many functional areas to develop new product concepts, differ from these committees in two significant respects: first, they are considered temporary, although the life of a
  venture team can extend for years, until a new product is fully developed
  and commercialized; second, venture teams have authority to actually plan
  and carry out new product ventures, independent of other functional
  departments. Indeed, in some organizations, the venture team becomes
  a division which serves as the nucleus for a new company.

After considering each of these structural options, ELI management decided to
combine both the new product committee and the venture team structures in
an integrated system whereby new product committees, meeting regularly, would
assist in developing ad hoc venture teams meeting to focus energies on products
deemed worthwhile by committee members.

WHY NEW PRODUCT VENTURES FAIL

Along with the formalized structure of the new product development process came a formal approach for generating, evaluating and implementing new product ideas. Based on new product research conducted by the Booz, Allen & Hamilton consulting firm, this approach encompassed eight steps, ranging from idea generation to ultimate commercialization of the product that survives the intervening steps. Guiding the deliberations of new product committee members were general statistics on the likelihood of new product success, and major reasons for new product failures:

- According to a recent study by Booz, Allen & Hamilton, companies are now able to turn one of seven ideas for products into successful new products, as compared to one in 58 ideas in 1968. A successful new product is defined as one which meets projected sales and profit objectives; a new product entry that achieves profits short of projected goals is defined as a relative failure, and an absolute failure doesn't even regain production and marketing costs. One recent study of 700 firms showed that 33 percent of commercialized new products never return a profit; indicates the failure rate to be 20 percent for industrial products, 15–20 percent for services, and 40 percent for consumer products.

- *Why new products fail*: The same Conference Board study that found failure rates as high as 40 percent for new products also found some major reasons for these failures, listed in the following order of priority:

Cause of Failure	Companies reporting failure (%)
Inadequate market analysis, such as failing to define market, or overestimating its size	45
Product problems or defects	29
Lack of effective marketing effort, such as ineffective positioning, poor pricing or promotion strategies	25
Higher costs than anticipated	19
Competitor strength or reaction	17

YOU SHOULD REMEMBER

From management's perspective, a new product can be a major innovation, never ever produced anywhere, a minor innovation, never produced by the firm, or a modification to a product already marketed. Most new products introduced into U.S. markets (70%) are product modifications, with 20% minor innovations and 10% major innovations. New products are important to many firms for a diversity of reasons, including meeting sales and profit objectives, matching the competition, completing a product line, and/or utilizing excess capacity. In spite of these benefits, many firms shun new product development, citing high costs, lack of capital, smaller segmented markets, and a shortage of new product ideas as key reasons. Firms that are committed to new product development usually organize this function in one or more of four ways: brand managers, new product departments, new product committees, or venture teams. Stressing the importance of effective new product organizations and procedures are statistics which show that only 2% of new product concepts ever reach the commercialization stage, and only 65% of commercialized products ever return a profit. Major causes of new product failures: inadequate market analysis; product defects; lack of effective marketing effort.

HOW NEW PRODUCTS GET DEVELOPED

There are eight steps in the new product development process. In examining these steps we will focus on the role of each in helping ELI create, consider and commercialize a family of videotape-based courses called "Great Professors" (GP) courses.

• *IDEA GENERATION*

A continuous idea process at ELI encompassed both sources of new product ideas, and methods for generating these ideas.

- *Idea sources:* Table 12-4 shows major sources of new ideas for both consumer and industrial products. At ELI, information from these sources was systematically gathered and organized into the firm's MIS database (discussed in Chapter 5), with market-related sources kept separate from lab-related sources. For example, in developing the videotaped line of courses, a survey of participant needs (market-related source), and lab-related secondary source data pertaining to videocassette technology, both helped to spark the idea generation process.

Table 12.4: Sources of New Product Ideas

Source	Industrial Products (%)	Consumer Products (%)	Total (%)
Research & development	24.3	13.9	20.8
Internal other than research and development	36.2	31.6	34.6
User suggestions, complaints	15.8	12.7	14.7
Formal research user needs	10.5	17.7	13.0
Analysis competitor products	27.0	38.0	30.7
Analysis published information	7.9	11.4	9.1
Suggestions from suppliers	12.5	3.8	9.5

Source: Leigh Lawton & David Parasuraman, "So You Want Your New Product Planning To Be Productive" *Business Horizons* (December 1980)

- *Idea generation:* Supplementing ELI's systematic procedures for gathering new product idea source data were techniques for transforming these data into new product concepts. Two of these techniques—product analysis and brainstorming—were used in generating the videotaped courses concept. Product analysis involved a systematic assessment of a diversity of competitive electronic education programs to identify key features and benefits that produced marketplace success—and failure.

During the brainstorming session, committee members were brought together to generate ideas in a free wheeling environment in which criticism of ideas was discouraged, and participants were encouraged to "piggyback" on the ideas of others. All ideas, no matter how outlandish, were recorded, with the full realization that few would emerge from the next stage of the process.

• IDEA SCREENING

The purpose of this second step of the process was to reduce ideas generated during the first step to the few worth further consideration. In so doing, committee members aimed to avoid "drop" errors, whereby a product with real potential gets dropped from consideration (as, for example, both IBM and Kodak dropped the Xerox copy technology), and "go" errors, whereby the firm decides to go with a product that later fails (the Edsel, for example).

Basic to ELI's screening process was a checklist, covering general product characteristics, marketing characteristics, and production characteristics, with a rating scale and weights associated with each criteria item. New product concepts were assessed against criteria in each category to determine if they were consistent with ELI's goals and resources, and were likely to succeed. When this concept was applied to the "Great Professors" concept, it scored 33.4 (Figure 12-6), well within the range of a "good" chance of success. In addition to pro-

Product Addition Criteria	Relative Weight	No	2	3	4	5	6	7	8	9	Yes	Rating
A. Economic criteria: product has relatively	.3	1	2	3	4	5	6	7	8	9	10	
1. Low investment level	.3						X					1.8
2. Low risk level	.3						X					1.8
3. High profit potential	.3									X		2.7
4. Positive influence on existing lines	.3				X							1.2
5. High patentability potential	.3			X								.9
B. Marketing criteria: product has relatively	.5										Total	8.4
1. Strong appeal to present segments	.5									X		4.5
2. Low probability of competitive response	.5								X			4.0
3. Large, growing market potential	.5										X	5.0
4. Promotable attributes	.5										X	5.0
5. Good distribution channels	.5				X							2.0
C. Product criteria: product has relatively	.2										Total	20.5
1. Lengthy product life cycle	.2									X		1.8
2. Good fit with production capabilities	.2						X					1.2
3. Easily produced features	.2			X								.6
4. Few service problems	.2							X				1.4

Rating Scale: 13-22 = Poor   28-38 = Good   Grand Total 33.4
23-27 = Fair   39-48 = Excellent

Figure 12–6. Product screening weighted rating checklist.

viding this quantitative index of success, this checklist also points out areas where actions can be taken to improve success chances. For example, improving distribution for the GP courses (B5) would move the product closer to an "excellent" chance of success.

After the GP concept was written up on a standard form, containing largely speculative data on its market, competition, development costs and profit return, it moved on to the next step in the process.

• CONCEPT DEVELOPMENT AND TESTING

This third step of the new product development process aimed to further develop product ideas into product *concepts* defined in terms meaningful to consumers. The general approach used was to develop the initial idea into alternative product concepts, and evaluate the relative attractiveness of each concept by presenting an elaborated version of each, with descriptive copy and pictures, to consumers who responded to questions like:

Does this product meet a real need?

Does it offer significant benefits over competitive offerings?

How would you improve it? What should it cost?

What is the likelihood that you would buy it? (Definitely? probably? probably not? definitely not?)

At ELI, this step produced two concepts, in particular, that seemed to offer promise: the first, a totally self-contained videotape/correspondence course for middle managers not qualified to take courses at ELI campuses, and the second, tentatively called the "Great Professors" (GP) course, a videotape course for senior executives who *were* qualified to take these courses, but couldn't for logistical or other reasons. These courses combined videotaped lectures by prestigious professors, conference call telephone meetings, and one long weekend on an ELI campus.

• *MARKETING STRATEGY DEVELOPMENT*

If a product survives to this step of the new product development process, it has been developed and tested to the point where a marketing strategy can be formulated. The statement elaborating this strategy, which is the model for the marketing plan formulated later, typically includes 3 sections, each containing the following information for the "Great Professor" Line of courses for senior executives:

1. *The product, the market for the product, and the competitive environment in which it will be launched.* The objective product was described (taped lectures, telephone conferencing, intensive weekend session, etc.), along with augmented features and core product benefits (convenience, higher productivity, etc.). Also described: present and future target markets (starting with executives in the financial services field), competitive offerings, and GP's position with respect to this competition, with emphasis on the quality of the "great professor" faculty, and state-of-the-art courses.

2. *Planned marketing mix strategy in support of the product launch:* For the GP line, this section focused on many of the product decisions discussed in Chapter 13, such as brand name strategy and level of service offered. Also covered: (1) the rationale for its prestige pricing strategy ($4000 per course), and discounts from this price; (2) the GP distribution strategy (primarily through direct marketing and affiliated campuses); and (3) the nature of the promotional program supporting the marketing effort, with emphasis on promotional appeals, media channels for delivering messages to target market members, and the promotional mix of advertising, publicity, sales promotion and direct selling (covered in Chapters 18 and 19).

3. *Long range marketing mix strategies, and sales/profit projections:* This section, covering the first five years of the GP line, explained how marketing mix elements would change as new market segments and courses were added, the cost of these changes in emphasis, and the results in sales and profits. This section anticipated that GP profits would increase dramatically as the innovative program achieved a strong leadership position in the

market, with competition constrained by the limited supply of raw materials, i.e., Great Professors.

• *BUSINESS ANALYSIS*

During this step of the new product development process, many of the optimistic assumptions and projections of previous steps were exposed to the harsh light of economic analysis. Key questions addressed: What size investment will be required to launch and sustain this product? At what future rate will sales, costs and profits grow? Will anticipated return on investment be sufficient to justify this investment over other, less risky, alternatives? What will be the effect of the growth of GP profits on other existing ELI products, such as on-campus and in-house courses?

In addressing these and related questions, ELI financial people made use of breakeven, cash flow, and return on investment analyses. For example, a breakeven analysis (Figure 12-7) showed that, with 200 GP courses sold by May (after a January product launch), total revenues (at $4000 per course) would be $800,000. This would just cover total costs incurred to that point, including $500,000 in fixed startup costs (for example, fees to the "great professors", regardless of whether or not a single course was sold), and $300,000 in variable costs that increased as sales increased (for example, royalties paid to the great professors based on sales of the courses). Then, between May and December, profits would accumulate dramatically as sales revenues increased at a much faster rate than costs, reaching $400,000 at the end of the year.

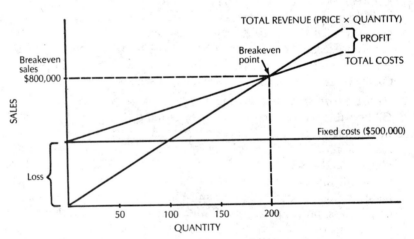

Figure 12–7. Breakeven analysis.

Profits accumulated in the first year were then projected into future years, using a discounted cash flow (or present value) analysis which discounted future profits back to their present value, under the likely assumption that the effects of inflation and interest rates would make dollars earned in the future worth less than present dollars.

Then, present and future return on investment was estimated by dividing present and future profit dollars by the manufacturing and marketing costs required to produce these profit dollars. These figures showed a probable overall return on investment, at the end of a five year period, of 1100 percent—considerably higher than any other alternative investment anyone could think of.

• *PRODUCT DEVELOPMENT*

During previous steps of the new product development process, the GP line had undergone a series of changes, from a word picture, to "paper prototype" drawings, to an actual mockup of the course, with sample taped lectures and workbooks.

During this step of the process, ELI's research and development department was charged with the job of developing prototypes of the course that would embody all the attributes of the final product and could be used to determine if the GP line was commercially, as well as economically, feasible. The cost of this step exceeded the combined cost of the other steps, but produced prototypes which could be tested functionally, under laboratory conditions, and in simulated market conditions, to get feedback from prospective buying influences (such as people with an economic, technical and user involvement in the product) in a number of key areas. For example, could the product be improved? How? Were promotional claims believable, and persuasive? Was the price consistent with value received? How did this product compare with competitive offerings?

• *TEST MARKETING*

This step of the process involves introducing the product offering in a "real life" environment, such as two test market cities, and then measuring the relative impact of various marketing mix combinations under experimental conditions described in Chapter 5. As is frequently the case with relatively expensive, innovative products like the GP line, this step of the process is omitted, usually for reasons of cost and competition.

- *Cost:* A large quantity of complete GP courses would have to be manufactured and marketed in test markets for a sufficiently long period of time to develop reliable data on satisfaction and repeat purchases—an extremely expensive undertaking which would be increased by the cost of manipulating each marketing mix variable.

- *Competition:* Frequently, test markets offer competitors the opportunity to steal a worthwhile concept and beat the tester to market, or to "jam" the test, and distort test results, by manipulating their own marketing mixes. For example, an ELI competitor might offer prospective purchasers of GP courses a half-price opportunity to purchase their courses.

Given these possibilities, plus the extensive testing that had already been done on the GP line, ELI management decided to move right to the commercialization step.

• *COMMERCIALIZATION*

The final step of the new product development process is invariably the costliest, involving outlays for full-scale production and marketing capabilities which sometimes exceed $100 million in commercial markets.

To protect this investment, and improve launch success odds, ELI focused its attentions in four key decision areas: where, at whom, when and how to launch the GP product line.

Where to launch: To save budget dollars and work out possible "bugs" in the product and marketing program, a "market rollout" strategy was planned involving, successively, local, regional, and national product line introductions over a five year period. In effect, the local initial launch was a substitute for a test market launch.

At whom to launch: The initial target market comprised executives in banks, brokerage firms, and other companies comprising the financial services industry. Later, as the rollout campaign progressed, marketing mix offerings would be developed to attract executives in other target markets.

When to launch: The launch was timed for February, when executives would have less competing attractions to completing GP assignments.

How to launch: The two major concerns here included: how much to spend for the GP launch, and how to allocate these funds among the four components of the marketing mix.

In addressing the first concern, the ELI marketing team used an "objective and task" approach whereby desired launch sales objectives were first projected, then specific tasks required to achieve these objectives (such as marketing research and advertising), and the cost of each, was estimated. The sum of these estimates became the launch budget, with sufficient funds remaining to sustain the product into successive years. (Other approaches for estimating budgeted costs are covered in Chapter 17.)

In addressing the second concern, pertaining to how budgeted dollars would be allocated among marketing mix elements in the short and long range, the ELI marketing team referred to Product Life Cycle model guidelines for products similar to the GP line. This model, which indicates how relative expenditures for marketing mix elements change as products enter their introduction, growth, maturity and decline stages, will be examined in Chapter 13.

YOU SHOULD REMEMBER

The eight steps of the new product development process include (1) idea generation, during which new product ideas from internal and external sources, organized in marketing information systems, generate product ideas during "brainstorming" and other group creativity sessions; (2) idea screening, during which ideas generated during step 1 are assessed against checklists for conformity to company objectives and resources; (3) concept development and testing, during which ideas surviving the screening stage are elaborated into product concepts in terms meaningful to consumers; (4) marketing strategy development, during which a comprehensive marketing strategy, encompassing the product, its market, and long- and short-range marketing strategies for bringing them together is developed; (5) business analysis, during which long- and short-range sales, cost, and profit projections are subject to financial and economic scrutiny; (6) product development, during which product prototypes are developed containing all the attributes of the final product; (7) test marketing, during which product prototypes are marketed in "real life" environments to test the effect of various marketing mixes; and (8) commercialization, during which the product is introduced into consumer markets after who, where, when and how issues are addressed.

KNOW THE CONCEPTS
DO YOU KNOW THE BASICS?

1. Describe conditions under which a videocassette recorder (VCR) could be (1) a convenience good; (2) a shopping good; (3) a specialty good; (4) an unsought good.

2. What would be the VCR manufacturer's likely policy with respect to number of retail outlets if its product fell into each of these categories (i.e., convenience, shopping, specialty)?

3. Assume the reason you rented the VCR was to watch a videotape cassette borrowed from a friend entitled "Jack Nicklaus on Golf." Describe this videotape as (1) a generic product; (2) a core product; (3) an extended product.

4. Provide an example of how one of the definitions of a VCR in question one, above, might be used by a marketing manager to (1) select a target market; (2) develop a marketing mix to attract members of this target market.

5. Describe how five different classifications of industrial products might have been used in the production of the Jack Nicklaus cassette. Give examples of each.

6. In terms of characteristics of services that differentiate them from tangible products, why do TV stations offer remarkably high discounts for sponsors who purchase commercial prime time well before the regular broadcasting season begins?

7. Match up the service in column "A" with the environmental influence in column "B" which was probably most responsible for its growth.

Column A	Column B
time shares	more leisure time
fast food restaurants	more disposable income
automatic banking	flight to the suburbs
nursing homes	new technologies
housecleaning services	franchise distribution
Lawn Doctor	more working women
country clubs	longer lifespans

8. Referring to the brewing industry, give an example of a new product in each of the three categories used to define new products.

9. Speculate on why seven out of ten new products introduced into consumer markets are product modifications.

10. Could the eight stages of the new product development process be applied as effectively in generating, developing, and commercializing ideas for new services or, at the extreme end of the tangibility spectrum, ideas for new ideas?

11. Using the Product idea rating scale, below, speculate on the following new product successes. Specifically, for each success, indicate the criteria categories (it might be just one or two for each) where scores were sufficiently high to overcome smaller scores in other criteria areas. The Mustang automobile; Tasters Choice Freeze Dried Coffee (vs. Maxim); the Compaq Computer (an IBM clone); *USA Today*; Pampers disposable diapers; Kodak Disc camera; Jarvic artificial heart; Classic Coke; Polaroid Land camera.

	A Relative Weight	B Product Idea Rating										Overall Rating A×B
		1	2	3	4	5	6	7	8	9	10	
A. Economic criteria: product has relatively	.3											
1. Low level of investment	.3											
2. Low risk level	.3											
3. High profit potential	.3											
4. Positive influence on existing products	.3											
5. High patentability potential	.3											
B. Marketing criteria: product has relatively	.5											
1. Strong appeal to present segments	.5											
2. Low probability of competitive response	.5											
3. Large, and growing, market potential	.5											
4. Promotable attributes	.5											
5. Good distribution outlets	.5											
C. Product criteria: product has relatively	.2											
1. Lengthy product life cycle	.2											
2. Good fit with production capabilities	.2											
3. Good differential possibility	.2											
4. Easily produced features	.2											

Figure 12-8.

TOTAL:

12. Now, match the following product failures in column A with the reason in column B that best explains it.

Column A

1. The Edsel is perceived as an ugly car with no clear-cut image, introduced when smaller automobiles were beginning to emerge.

2. Heinz Great American Soups fail to compete against Campbell's Soups. Heinz later sues Campbell's for jamming its test marketing attempts.

3. Dowgard antifreeze fails in its efforts against Prestone.

4. Susan B. Anthony dollars

5. Laker Airlines

6. "New" coca cola

7. Johnson and Johnson disposable diapers (vs. Pampers)

8. McDonald's McRib sandwiches

Column B

1. Inadequate market analysis

2. Product problems or defects

3. Lack of effective marketing effort

4. Higher costs than anticipated

5. Competitive responses

TERMS FOR STUDY

accessory equipment	impulse goods
augmented product	industrial goods
capital items	installations
commercialization	maintenance/repair/operating
components	market testing
concept development	natural products
concept testing	new product
consumer goods	operating supplies
convenience goods	product
core product	raw materials
drop error	services
emergency goods	shopping goods
generic product	specialty goods
go error	staples
idea generation	supplier
idea screening	unsought goods

ANSWERS
KNOW THE BASICS

1. The VCR could be (1) a convenience good if it were just being rented for an evening to show a movie; (2) a shopping good if the customer were searching for the "best buy," in terms of quality and price, during Presidents' Day sales; (3) a specialty good if the consumer had his or her mind made up to purchase only one VCR brand, and was willing to make a trip to the only store in town that sold this brand; (4) when it was first introduced into consumer markets, the VCR was an unknown, hence an unsought product.

2. As a convenience good, the VCR would be distributed through many outlets, since consumers, not expecting to search for them, would purchase, or rent, the VCR at the most convenient location. As a shopping good, the VCR would be sold at fewer outlets, because consumers would expect to travel to more than one outlet to compare prices and features. As a specialty good, the VCR would be sold in only one outlet in a given area, recognizing that customers who insisted on this model would be willing to travel to this outlet to get it.

3. As a generic product, the videotape cassette would be described in terms of such intrinsic qualities as its price, quality level, and features; for example, it costs $89.00, has a high degree of durability and fidelity, and features Jack Nicklaus explaining how to use each golf club in the bag. As a *core* product, the cassette would be defined in terms of the satisfactions its use will bring to the user; for example, the joy of cutting a few strokes off a golf handicap. The augmented product would be defined in terms of additional attributes possessed by the product beyond its objective and core attributes, such as the prestige of the Jack Nicklaus name, or a money-back guarantee of satisfaction (if not a lower handicap).

4. For example, a group of people who would rather rent, than purchase, a VCR (i.e., a convenience good) might be defined in terms of significant geographic, psychographic, demographic and behavioristic criteria they have in common. They might tend to reside in areas of economic depression; have positive attitudes toward certain types of motion pictures; tend to cluster, statistically, in certain age and income groups; and be "brand loyal" toward a VCR outlet that also carries a large list of movie titles.

   Based on this profile of the target market for its "convenient" VCRs, the marketing manager could develop, position, and promote a sturdy, stripped-down VCR model (the product), at a price to meet target market needs—assuming, of course, that the target market possessed, collectively, "MADR" (money, authority, desire, response) characteristics to justify this effort.

5. The factory in which the cassettes are manufactured, and the production line on which the cassettes are processed to completion are long-lived *installations* which would be depreciated over time. The tools used by workers on the production line (such as glue guns and drills) to assemble the cassettes are examples of *accessory equipment*. The plastic material which is processed into the final product is an example of a nurtured *raw material*; the actual videotape, made elsewhere and installed in the plastic cassette housing is an example of a *component*; and the oil used to lubricate the production line machinery is an example of *supplies*.

6. The fact that services are *perishable* means that the commercial broadcast time can't be kept in inventory, and if sponsorship money isn't forthcoming for each time slot, it will be lost; the fact that services are variable means that the sponsor is as likely, perhaps likelier, to purchase a loser than a winner of the "Cosby Show" stripe. And the fact that benefits of services are largely intangible means that even if the sponsor purchases a winner, it would be difficult to attribute any specific dollar-and-cents benefits to this fact. Taken together, these characteristics create a strong incentive to get the service sold, even at bargain basement rates.

7.

Column A	Column B

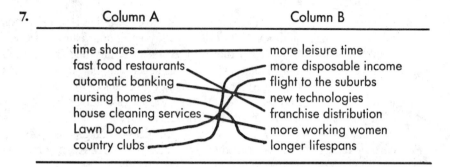

Column A:
time shares
fast food restaurants
automatic banking
nursing homes
house cleaning services
Lawn Doctor
country clubs

Column B:
more leisure time
more disposable income
flight to the suburbs
new technologies
franchise distribution
more working women
longer lifespans

8. When Gablinger's marketed the first low calorie beer they produced a major innovation—a product never sold before. When Budweiser introduced its light beer—after Miller had proved it to be a commercially feasible product concept—it was introducing a minor innovation, a product never sold before by Budweiser. When Miller distributed its beers in 7-ounce bottles, it produced a product modification—a change in a product already marketed.

9. As noted earlier in this text (especially in the Chapter 2 discussion of marketing planning options), diversification marketing strategies that entail changes in both markets and products tend to be much riskier than either market development strategies, which involve existing products sold in new segments, or product development strategies, which involve new products sold to existing segments. And penetration strategies, involving existing products more aggressively marketed in existing segments, are usually the least risky of all strategic options. In this context, major and minor innovations are more likely to represent higher risk diversification or product/market development strategies than product modifications, which are usually part of penetration strategies. Safer product modification strategies also make sense in terms of trends which work against new product success, such as higher developmental costs; a shortage of capital; smaller, less profitable, segmented markets; and a shortage of dramatic new technologies that spawn new product ideas. In spite of these adverse circumstances, many firms, such as Proctor and Gamble and 3M, are committed to developing major and minor innovations, recognizing that "higher risk" also often implies the possibility of much higher rewards.

10. Quite easily. To illustrate, envision a situation where a group of politicians meet to hammer out a platform for their candidate (the "product" supported by the ideas in the platform). Ideas would be generated during a brainstorming session; screened for consistency with the larger party platform; developed and tested among a sample of the electorate; transformed into a marketing strategy, including media advertising, publicity, and speak-

ing engagements; subjected to cost/benefit economic scrutiny, during the business analysis stage, to determine if the expected votes are worth the expense; then further developed, test marketed, and finally commercialized during the last three steps of the process.

11. Here is one possible analysis of rating scale strengths of each successful product launch, although others are possible:

Column A	Column B
Taster's Choice	large market potential high profit potential strong differential
Mustang Auto	large market potential good fit with product line strong appeal to present segments
Compaq Computer	low competitive responses probability large market potential high profit potential
USA Today	large market potential low repetitive response good distribution outlets
Pampers	good fit with production capabilities strong differential large market potential
Kodak Disc Camera	fit with production capabilities strong differential large market potential
Jarvic Artificial Heart	high profit potential patent protection appeal to current segments
Classic Coke	fit with production capabilities fit with product line large market potential
Polaroid Land Camera	patentability protection high profit potential large, growing market potential

12. Although all the column B reasons might apply, to some degree, to column A failures, the following matchups seem most prominent.

Column A	Column B
1. The Edsel	Inadequate market analysis
2. Great American Soups	
3. Dowgard antifreeze	Product problems or defects
4. Susan B. Anthony	
5. Laker Airlines	Lack of effective marketing effort
6. "New" Coca Cola	
7. J & J disposable diapers	Higher costs than anticipated
8. McDonald's McRib sandwiches	
	Competitive responses

13

PRODUCT MANAGEMENT: PLANNING FOR PROFITS

KEY TERMS

brand name term, symbol, design or combination thereof that identifies and differentiates a seller's products

product life cycle (PLC) stages of development and decline through which a successful product typically moves. Each stage suggests changes in competitive challenges and marketing mix responses to these challenges

product line a group of products related to each other by marketing, technical or end-use considerations

product mix the total of all products in all the seller's product lines

---

In Chapter 12, we began our discussion of the four elements of the marketing mix by defining categories and characteristics of products and services, and illustrating a systematic approach for creating, evaluating and commercializing new product concepts.

In this chapter, we will continue our discussion of the product component of the marketing mix with an examination of decisions calculated to help achieve and maintain profitability in product markets. These decisions pertain to product lines, mixes, brands, quality, service, packaging and labeling. We will also examine how the product life cycle (PLC) model helps anticipate changes in the competitive environment, and suggests appropriate marketing mix responses to these changes.

For illustrative examples, we will continue examining ELI product lines that emerged from the eight-step new product development process illustrated in Chapter 12, particularly the Videotape Assisted Management Training Programs called "VAMP."

PRODUCT LINE DECISIONS: ADDING, STRETCHING, FILLING, FEATURING

A **product line** consists of related products with similar technical features, or markets, or end-use applications. ELI's product lines, for example, comprised programs of courses given (1) on ELI's main and affiliated campuses (the campus line), (2) on client premises (the in-house line), and (3) through VAMP videotapes, supplemented with other course materials. Taken together, all the products comprising these lines constituted ELI's **product mix**.

Product line decisions facing ELI's marketing manager during all stages of each line's life cycle included product line length, stretching, filling, and featuring.

- *Product line length* decisions pertain to the number of products included in the line. Generally, products are added to a line as long as they contribute to profits, are consistent with the firm's mission, and don't cannibalize sales and profits of existing products.

- *Product line stretching* decisions refer to products added to an existing product line to attract less profitable markets (downward stretch), more profitable markets (upward stretch), or both (two-way stretch).

- *Product line filling* decisions focus on plugging gaps in an existing line, usually to gain additional sales or profits, utilize excess capacity, or respond to competitive initiatives or dealer requests.

- *Product line featuring* decisions pertain to products featured in promotional campaigns. Sometimes products at the low, inexpensive end of the line will be featured to build traffic for other products in the line; sometimes products at the high end will be featured to enhance the prestige of the entire line.

ELI's course on personal financial planning illustrates these concepts; it was introduced into its VAMP line to meet competitive offerings (line filling) and, in the process, attracted profitable new market segments (line stretching). As a profitable new addition to the VAMP line, this course was featured in ELI's promotional campaigns for this line.

PRODUCT MIX DECISIONS: HOW WIDE, DEEP, CONSISTENT

In addition to decisions affecting the success of individual product lines, ELI marketing management also faced decisions involving its product mix, comprising all products in ELI's lines. These decisions pertain primarily to mix width, depth and consistency.

- *Mix width decisions* refer to how many different lines the firm carries. At ELI, mix width decisions were similar to line length decisions; that is, before an additional line, such as the VAMP line, was added to the mix, it was evaluated in terms of profit potential and consistency with ELI's mission and existing product lines. For example, ELI marketing management realized that the VAMP line of videotaped courses would probably attract prospective enrollees from its other lines; however, they decided that VAMP's profit potential more than offset this drawback.

- *Mix depth decisions* pertain to total number of products in each product line. A deep mix can satisfy the needs of many different customer groups for the same product, maximize shelf space, ward off competitors, cover a wide range of prices, and sustain dealer support. For example, the VAMP line encompassed a range of products from relatively inexpensive training courses, with videotaped lectures only, to elaborate courses featuring videotapes augmented by personal telephone conversations with professors, weekend seminars at ELI campuses, and computer assisted "electronic libraries." This diversity of offerings within the VAMP line made it easy for ELI to satisfy needs of many segments in depth, and made it difficult for competitive producers of management training courses to position products against ELI weaknesses. Figure 13-1 summarizes product mix depth/width alternatives.

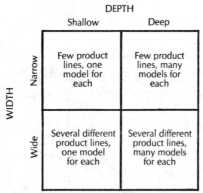

Figure 13–1. Product mix depth/width alternatives.

• *Mix consistency decisions* focus on how closely related the firm's product lines are in terms of common end uses, distribution outlets, price ranges, and markets served. A highly consistent mix, with product lines similar in most of these areas, allows firms to concentrate production and marketing efforts, and achieve economies in the process. A consistent mix also helps create a strong image and solid relations with retailers and wholesalers. On the other hand, too consistent a mix can stifle a firm's growth and leave it vulnerable to competitive threats that wouldn't exist if it had a cushion of diversified lines to fall back on. Although ELI's lines differed appreciably as to price range, they all had identical end-uses — executive education —and served essentially the same market; hence, management could anticipate both advantages and disadvantages of highly consistent mixes.

YOU SHOULD REMEMBER

Product lines comprise related groups of products with similar technical features, markets, or end-use applications; **product mixes** comprise the totality of a firm's product lines. Product line decisions focus on adding products to lines, stretching product lines to include more or less profitable market segments; filling product lines to match competitive offerings; and determining which products in product lines to feature. Key considerations in all these decision areas; product profitability, consistency with the firm's mission and existing products in the line. Product mix decisions focus on width, depth and consistency of the mix, with highly consistent mixes creating a strong image and solid channel relations, while increasing vulnerability to environmental threats.

PRODUCT BRAND DECISIONS: DEFINITIONS, PROCEDURES, BENEFITS, CHARACTERISTICS

A **brand** is a name, term, sign, symbol, design, or combination thereof that identifies and helps to differentiate and control the products of a single seller, like Proctor and Gamble, or a group of sellers, such as the American Association of Manufacturers.

A **brand name** is that part of the brand that can be spoken; the Prudential Insurance Company, for example. A **brand mark** is that part of the brand that can be recognized—the entire design—but is not utterable; for example, the Rock of Gilbralter mark of the Prudential Insurance Company. A **trademark** is a brand name or mark that is given legal protection; for example, the Xerox trademark can only be legally used by the Xerox Corporation. A copyright is the legal protection given literary, musical or artistic work so they can only be published or sold by the copyright holder.

BRAND SPONSORSHIP DECISIONS

One of three brand sponsorship options is available to sellers: a manufacturer's brand, a private brand, or a generic brand. A *manufacturer's*, or national, brand, is assigned by the manufacturer of the product, such as Hellman's mayonnaise. A *private,* or dealer, brand, is assigned by the wholesaler or retailer of a product, such as Ann Page brand mayonnaise (A&P). Under the *generic brand* option, certain staple goods and pharmaceuticals are plainly marked with no identification. Dealers see generic, or "no frills," brands as a way to increase profits by saving on advertising, packaging, and other costs associated with manufacturer and private brands.

Frequently, a seller opts for more than one branding strategy; for example, the Whirlpool Corporation manufactures products under its own brand name (Whirlpool dishwashers, for example) and under Sears' private brand name (the Kenmore line).

Competition for supermarket shelf space between manufacturer's brands and private brands, called the "battle of the brands," is a fast-growing trend that is especially troubling to manufacturers, who must frequently make unwanted concessions to dealers for desired shelf space.

BRANDING BENEFITS BUYERS, SELLERS, SOCIETY

To understand how branding benefits buyers, sellers and society at large, assume a mother regularly purchases a particular brand of toothpaste for her family because she perceives that it offers unique cavity protection. From her viewpoint, the brand name makes it easy for her to identify and shop for this toothpaste, and for new products the producer might introduce. In that the producer has put its reputation on the line with its brand name, it also helps to ensure a consistent level of product quality. From the seller's viewpoint, the strength of the brand name, and its associations of quality and unique product values, makes it easier to control product pricing and promotion. By actively promoting the brand name, the seller can build a strong corporate image for all its product lines, attract a loyal, profitable group of target customers, and successfully introduce new products under the brand name. Branding can also help sellers segment markets; the toothpaste producer, for example, can offer different formulations of its toothpaste, under different brand names, to attract different benefit-seeking segments.

Branding also benefits society at large. If a product achieves success under its promoted, protected brand name, other firms will be encouraged to improve on this success. Thus, branding stimulates innovation and continuing product improvement, in addition to making shopping more efficient and maintaining product quality.

CRITICISMS OF BRANDING

Critics of branding claim abuses arise when the competition branding stimulates is carried too far. Frequently, they maintain, true product innovation is replaced by trivial or imaginary differentiation, especially for essentially homogeneous goods, like detergents or aspirin. Sometimes, critics claim, imaginary differentiation, such as the status associated with a prestige automobile, can lead to higher-than-necessary prices, and encourage status and class consciousness.

IMPORTANCE OF BRANDING DECISIONS

Given the importance of branding, many firms implement formal procedures for arriving at productive brand decisions. At ELI, for example, branding decisions were made by the new product committee, often with the same consideration given to generating and testing new product concepts. These branding decisions pertained to brand name strategies, brand quality levels, and level of customer service associated with ELI brands.

BRAND NAME STRATEGIES

The following four brand name strategies were considered by committee members in devising brand names for lines of VAMP training programs:

- *An individual brand name strategy*, with a brand name applied to each product in the line, and the company name deemphasized. Example: Proctor & Gamble's detergent brands, including Tide, Bold and Cheer. Advantages: Brands can be targeted to specific markets; failure of one brand doesn't endanger others; and more individual brands can mean more shelf space.

- *Separate family names for different categories of products.* Example: Sears' strategy of having a family brand name for appliances (Kenmore) and another family brand name for tools (Craftsman). Advantages: Easier to implement a brand extension strategy of launching new or modified products under a successful brand name; less expenditure for research to identify effective brand names; and less cost for promoting brand-name recognition, preference.

- *A blanket family brand for all products.* Examples: General Electric, Heinz 57 product lines. Generally the same benefits as for the separate-family-names strategy examined above.

- *A company brand name combined with an individual product name.* Example: Kellogg's Raisin Bran, Kellogg's Rice Krispies. Advantages : Easier to launch new products under company brand, while targeting markets under individual brand names.

Deciding which of these brand name strategies, or combinations thereof, to implement depends on product/market conditions in which products are introduced and commercialized. For example, if a firm's product mix lends itself to segmentation, an individual name brand strategy might be most appropriate; if a firm sells all its products to a single segment, a blanket family name for all products might be more appropriate. However, if a firm's product lines differ dramatically, such as Swift and Company with its Premium brand hams and Vigoro fertilizer, a family brand name may not be able to stretch far enough, and a combination family/individual brand name strategy might be most appropriate. For its purposes, ELI marketing management decided on such a strategy for all the lines in its mix, combining the "ELI" family name with individual brand names to identify individual lines within the VAMP product mix.

FINDING SPECIFIC BRAND NAMES

At ELI, the following five-step process was used to arrive at an effective individual brand name to use with the ELI family name for a line of VAMP courses targeted to senior executives.

- *Establish brand name criteria:* The main criterion used by committee members to assess product names was compatibility with the product's image and its marketing mix; that is, the name should reflect the prestige, and high price, of these executive courses, and lend itself to product promotions. Beyond that, the brand name selected should be distinctive; suggest something about product features or benefits; be relatively easy to recognize, recall and pronounce; be easily translated into foreign languages; and be applicable to other products added to the line.

- *Create a list of potential brand names*: Primary sources for brand names include names of products already in the mix, the name a dealer gives the product under a private name policy, a name licensed from a firm that holds the trademark on it, or any of a variety of original names, including initials (IBM, ABC), invented names (Kleenex, Kodak), numbers (Century 21), mythological characters (Atlas tires), personal names (Lipton), geographical names (New England Bell), dictionary names (Sunbeam Appliances), foreign names (Nestle), and word combinations (Head and Shoulders). Using these sources, committee members came up with 120 possible brand names for the new VAMP executive line, including VAMP.

- *Screen the list to select those most appropriate for further testing*: At ELI, this involved matching the 120 names selected in step two with step one criteria, and retaining the 10 names that best fit the criteria.

- *Obtain consumer reactions to the remaining names*: This step involved informal surveys and focus group interviews with ELI staff, faculty, and executives taking ELI courses. Five names remained after this evaluation.

- *Conduct a trademark search:* Be sure the remaining names can be registered and legally protected. Under the federal Lanham Act of 1946, any aspect of a product or its package may be registered as a trademark if the feature is nonfunctional. (A functional feature, such as the VAMP videocassette, may be patent protected for 17 years.) Assuming the trademark adheres just to the product, its package or its label; doesn't imply characteristics the product doesn't possess; is not confusingly similar to other trademarks; and is used in interstate commerce, a trademark protects exclusive use of the brand name as long as the product is marketed. One exception is if a brand name becomes generic public property by becoming too popular, as happened to brand names like aspirin, cellophane and linoleum, and is threatening to happen to brand names like Xerox and Kleenex. One approach to prevent brand names from going generic is to constantly advertise the brand as the exclusive property of the firm, as Xerox does; another is to link the product brand name to the company name, as Eastman Kodak does.

At the conclusion of this five-step process, ELI emerged with the "Great Professor" brand name for courses in its VAMP line targeted to senior executives. Later, it would use the same process to arrive at the brand name "Great Careers" for a much less expensive line of VAMP courses targeted to the middle management market.

YOU SHOULD REMEMBER

A **brand name** or **brand mark,** legally protected through trademarks and copyrights, identifies and differentiates a seller's products, and helps control pricing and promotion strategies. Effectively promoting a brand name can build a strong seller image, attract loyal, profitable customers, help segment markets, and ease the introduction of new products. It can also assure a consistent level of product quality, stimulate innovation that improves products, and enhance shopping efficiency. Critics of branding claim it fosters trivial or imaginary product differentiation which can encourage product proliferation, overpriced products, and false social values. Branding decisions involve deciding a brand name strategy, with possibilities including individual brand names, separate family brand names and/or family and individual brand name combinations.

DETERMINING BRAND QUALITY

Defined in terms of user perceptions, and applicable to national, private and generic brands, quality is the rated ability of the brand to perform its functions through such objective and subjective attributes as durability, safety, reliability, appearance, ease of operation, and assurance of service.

Sellers have three brand quality option strategies available: (1) to continually upgrade quality; (2) to maintain the existing quality level; or (3) to reduce quality, usually in response to rising costs or the expectation of higher profits.

• *WEBER'S LAW*

In general, if quality is raised, sellers hope buyers will recognize the change; if quality is lowered, they hope buyers won't notice. A useful way to determine how much to raise, or lower, brand quality is to apply Weber's Law, which maintains that K, or the just-noticeable-difference (jnd), is a constant that varies over the senses and can be determined as follows:

$$K = \Delta I/I$$

...where ΔI equals the smallest increase in stimulus intensity that will be perceived as different from the existing intensity, and I equals the existing stimulus intensity.

For example, if ELI could improve the visual resolution of its videotaped courses by 11 percent, would it be worth the additional expenditure in research and development, and the more expensive technology? Possibly, if the K, or jnd, of the average viewer were, say, 8 percent, in which case:

$$K = 11/100, \text{ or } 11 \text{ percent, or three points over the } jnd.$$

On the other hand, if the downside jnd is 10 percent, then a decrease in the quality of visual resolution up to this point won't be noticed.

Weber's Law is applicable in many other marketing situations, such as in determining how much to raise or lower a price, or whether people will notice changes in color or noise intensity in promotional campaigns.

For ELI, however, there was little likelihood that the quality of any of its product lines would be lowered, especially in light of a growing body of research indicating that more people are willing to pay more for better quality in merchandise. Indeed, for products where quality differences are difficult to perceive—like automobiles—price is often regarded as a surrogate for quality. Japan's dedication to quality, for example, has been its major weapon in dominating many world markets.

This trend toward greater emphasis in quality in products is summarized in Figure 13-2, which indicates that, while superior quality increases profitability only slightly over high quality, low quality hurts profits substantially, and profits increase appreciably between "average" and "high" quality levels. However, circumstances can change these conclusions; for example, if all competitors deliver high quality, lowering product quality to offer a lower price might be a quick path to profits.

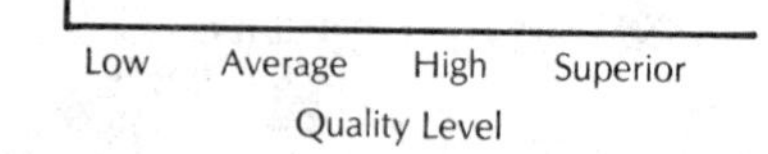

Figure 13–2. Relationship between quality levels and profitability.

PROVIDING CUSTOMER SERVICE

Along with product quality, the quality of customer service is assuming increasing importance as a competitive tool, and many firms have established customer service departments to address customer needs and complaints, and formal procedures for arriving at decisions pertaining to (1) services included in the service mix, and (2) level of service to offer.

Both of these questions can be addressed by systematically analyzing customer needs, competitive offerings, and company resources pertaining to services. At ELI, for example, a survey of customer service needs indicated the following to be the three service attributes most desired by prospective customers for GP courses: good warranty coverage, low service price, and extension of credit. Similarly, this survey indicated the following to be the least important service attributes: replacement guarantee, convenient service locations, and fast deliveries.

Then, having identified most and least important service attributes, ELI conducted surveys to determine (1) the level of service customer firms were presently receiving from firms competing with ELI in this market, and (2) what level of service ELI could afford to offer.

Service mix and service level decisions then were based on data from these surveys. For example, although "good warranty coverage" was the most desired service attribute, none of ELI's competitors offered the level desired by customers, so ELI designed a warranty slightly superior to that offered by its major competitor.

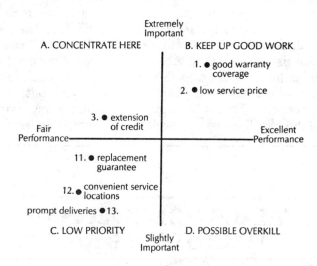

Figure 13–3. Approach for measuring and controlling service effectiveness.

Figure 13-3 shows the approach used by ELI to monitor its service mix. The vertical dimension on this exhibit ranks these attributes from "extremely important" to "slightly important," the horizontal axis rates how effectively the service needs of buyers of the GP course are met. Note, for example, that the first two most important service attributes—good warranty coverage and low service price—are positioned in the "excellent performance" quadrant, where the mandate is to "keep up the good work." The third important attribute—credit extension—is positioned in the "fair performance" quadrant, where the mandate is to "concentrate here." The three least important attributes are also positioned in the fair performance quadrant, but this didn't overly concern ELI marketing management since this was a low priority area.

YOU SHOULD REMEMBER

Brand quality decisions focus on subjective and objective product attributes like durability, safety, appearance and ease of operation. Research indicates that, of three quality options available to sellers—to raise, maintain or reduce quality—the most profitable strategy is to opt for high instead of average quality levels. Weber's Law offers a formula for deciding the extent to which quality—and many other marketing mix elements—should be increased or lowered. The key element of this formula is the "just noticeable difference," beyond which people will notice a change in marketing stimuli. Customer service decisions typically center about which services to include in the mix, and the level of service offered. The general approach for addressing both of these issues is to arrive at a realistic compromise between what customers expect, what competitors offer, and what the firm can afford. A systematic approach for monitoring the effectiveness of brand service decisions involves assessing service offerings in terms of the relative importance of each, and the effectiveness with which the firm provides each.

PRODUCT PACKAGING DECISIONS RESPOND TO CUSTOMER NEEDS, MARKETING MIXES

As with decisions relating to product branding, quality and service, product packaging decisions can strongly influence customer responses to the product, and all marketing mix elements supporting the product.

Given this potent influence of packaging decisions, many firms focus considerable attention on arriving at packaging decisions that will best further marketing and marketing mix objectives. At ELI, for example, packaging decisions emerged from a systematic process of relating packaging objectives to ELI marketing objectives. Thus, consideration of the following packaging objectives produced a package design for the Great Professors line.

- *Contain and protect the product*: Actually, a product's package is usually three separate packages:

    the immediate container for the product, called the primary package the package containing the primary package, called the secondary package

the package used to transport and store a number of secondary packages, called the shipping package

As related to the first packaging objective of containing and protecting the product, the three packages combine to maintain the product in its original form and protect it through the stages of the distribution process, from initial shipment to final reception, preventing breakage, spoilage, contamination, and ensuring a reasonable shelf life.

A variety of materials are available to contain and protect products, including paperboard, plastic, metal, glass, styrofoam and cellophane.

- *Encourage product use:* Jumbo detergent packages and 6-packs of soda are examples of package designs that encourage greater use of the product, as do packaging features that make it easier to use the product, such as boil-in bags and flip-top beer cans.

- *Communication:* Package design can facilitate communication on two levels: the *information level,* by identifying the brand and providing in-gredients and directions, and the *promotional level*, by differentiating the product from competing products, presenting a sales message extolling product features and benefits. The promotional function is particularly important for products that lend themselves to impulse or self-service purchase, and in light of the fact that it is the last message the buyer sees before making a purchase, and serves as a constant promotional reminder after the purchase. Key packaging decisions in this area: How can package size, color, and shape be tailored to the promotional message? Where should instructions appear on the package? What informational message and promotional "image" should the package convey? Will promotional inserts be required?

- *New Product Planning:* A new package design can reinforce the image of a product as new (such as the "Cup-A-Soup" package in which indi-vidual serving soup mixes were introduced), or can be, in itself, what is "new" in the product (such as shipping packages that dispense beer a can at a time). Typical concerns pertaining to this objective: what size, color, shapes, and other visual and written messages can best be used to communicate "newness"? Will a family packaging policy, with every pack-age similar to others (Campbell Soup, for example), make it difficult to implement this objective?

- *Channel Cooperation:* Package design can help address needs of whole-salers, retailers and other channel members by making it easier for them to handle, store and display products; mark prices and control inventory; and ensure a reasonably long shelf life. In the food industry, the Universal

Product Code (UPC), a series of lines imprinted directly on the package, allows electronic scanners to read the type of product and its price, and enter this information in the cash register, speeding up inventory control and the checkout process. Optical Character Recognition (OCR) codes, used in department stores, perform essentially the same functions, but can be read by both people and machines.

Key concerns in developing packages that take dealer needs into account: Are there traditional packing practices expected by dealers? What are competitors' packaging practices?

PACKAGING DECISION TRADEOFFS

In relating packaging objectives to product market and marketing mix objectives, the ELI marketing team realized that a number of tradeoffs would be necessary in devising a package design most appropriate for the GP line of courses. For example, materials selected to contain and protect the product might interfere with other packaging objectives, such as encouraging product use, as when customers face the frustration of trying to open shrink wrapped packages. Or, a feature designed to encourage product use might discourage efficient handling and storage: this is what happened in the case of the new easy-pour plastic containers for motor oil, which occupied considerably more storage space than the traditional metal can they replaced.

TYPICAL CRITICISMS OF PACKAGING

In addition to these tradeoffs, the ELI marketing team also considered typical criticisms of packaging, which usually derive from the potentially adverse environmental impact of certain kinds of packages, and increasing costs to consumers of unfunctional package features. For example, throwaway bottles, which contribute to environmental pollution, also use three times as much energy to produce as returnable bottles—a cost usually passed on to the consumer. Responding to public pressures, many sellers package products in biodegradable containers, and a number of states have laws requiring consumers to pay a deposit on beverage containers.

HOW LABELING DECISIONS SUPPLEMENT PACKAGING DECISIONS

The main function of a label on a package is to provide information about the packaged product, or about the seller of the product. The label may be printed as a part of the package itself, or on a tag affixed to the product.

Labeling decisions typically involve three basic kinds of labels:

Grade labels that announce product quality with letters (Grade A), numbers (#1), or conditions ("prime")

Informative labels, which focus on the care, use and preparation of the product ("keep away from heat or direct sunlight")

Descriptive labels that explain important characteristics and benefits

In general, labeling decisions supplement packaging decisions in helping to encourage product use, promote communication, market segmentation and new product planning. Labels also play an important role in responding to social and legal considerations. *Open dating* indicates the expected shelf life of the product to avoid spoilage. *Nutritional labels* disclose amounts of nutrients and calories in processed foods. *Unit pricing* allows customers to compare values among competing products by stating these prices in terms of basic units, like ounces or pounds.

YOU SHOULD REMEMBER

Product packaging decisions can strongly influence customer response to the product, and all marketing mix elements supporting the product. An effective approach for developing an effective packaging strategy is to relate packaging objectives to market needs and marketing objectives. Thus, such packaging objectives as containing/protecting the product, encouraging product use, communicating information and promotion, and helping achieve new product success and channel cooperation can all be reflected in the package design, after necessary tradeoffs have been considered. Criticisms of packaging addressed by bottling bills and other legislative and corporate initiatives include environmental hazards, a proliferation of unnecessary packages, and excessive consumer costs. Labeling decisions supplement packaging decisions by communicating information, helping to segment markets, and assisting in new product planning. Labeling strategies have responded to social and economic pressures through open dating, nutritional labels, and unit pricing.

The GP Course Package

After applying objectives, considerations and guidelines pertaining to packaging and labeling decisions, the ELI marketing team designed this package for the various components of each Great Professors course:

The primary package contained a series of videotaped lectures on a particular subject, combined with a workbook and a textbook, all shrink-wrapped in a plastic covering. Then, between this shrink-wrapped primary package and the

Figure 13–4. Package for Great Professors course.

cardboard secondary package, small polyester pellets acted as a protective buffer. Twenty-four secondary packages were included in each shipping package.

The photograph on the front of the primary package depicted, from a student's perspective, a professor delivering a lecture at ELI's main campus, with modern training facilities and accommodations prominently featured. The back of the package depicted the same lecture from the professor's perspective, with informal, comfortable accommodations, and interested, involved executive participants prominently featured.

PRODUCT LIFE CYCLE (PLC)

At the time ELI marketing management decided to commercialize its Great Professors and Great Careers lines of videotaped executive training courses, it also committed the firm to a number of changes, over time, in marketing emphasis, as sales, profits, customers and competitors also changed. Assisting ELI management in anticipating and implementing these changes was the Product Life Cycle model (Figure 13-5), which was popularized by Theodore Levitt .

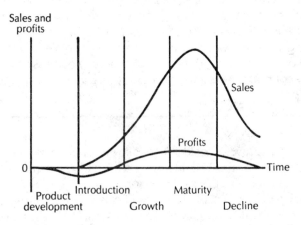

Figure 13–5. Sales and profits over stages of Product Life Cycle.

According to the Product Life Cycle (PLC) model, products introduced into commercial markets tend to go through four sequential stages—introduction, growth, maturity, and decline—with each stage posing competitive threats and opportunities that marketing managers must respond to in maintaining product profitability.

Typical threats, opportunities and responses characterizing each stage of the PLC are listed in Figure 13-6. Before discussing how these characteristics might have influenced ELI's Great Professor's Course through its life-cycle odyssey, we will first discuss some characteristics and constraints of the PLC.

	Stage in Life Cycle			
Characteristics	Introduction	Growth	Maturity	Decline
Marketing objective	Attract innovators and opinion leaders to new product	Expand distribution and product line	Maintain differential advantage	(a) Cut back (b) revive (c) terminate
Industry sales	Increasing	Rapidly increasing	Stable	Decreasing
Competition	None or small	Some	Many	Few
Industry profits	Negative	Increasing	Decreasing	Decreasing
Profit margins	Low	High	Decreasing	Decreasing
Customers	Innovators	Affluent mass market	Mass market	Laggards
Product mix	One basic model	Expanding line	Full product line	Best sellers
Distribution	Depends on product	Expanding number of outlets	Expanding number of outlets	Decreasing number of outlets
Pricing	Depends on product	Greater range of prices	Full line of prices	Selected prices
Promotion	Informative	Persuasive	Competitive	Informative

Figure 13–6. Threats, opportunities and marketing mix responses characterizing each PLC stage.

CHARACTERISTICS OF THE PLC
• *DIFFERENT LENGTHS*

Depending on such considerations as cost, sophistication of technology, level of user benefit, and marketing effort expended, PLC length can vary dramatically. For example, costly, complex technology kept color television in the introductory stage for more than a decade. At the other extreme, a number of simple, inexpensive, aggressively marketed fad products, like pet rocks, hula hoops and Cabbage Patch Dolls, traversed all the stages of their cycles in fewer than three years.

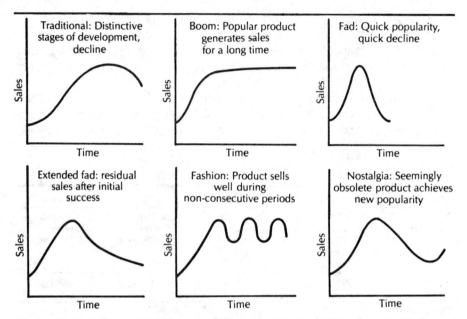

Figure 13–7. Different PLC patterns based on different product-market situations.

• *DIFFERENT SHAPES*

Figure 13-7 shows six different PLC patterns characterizing different product/market situations, including traditional, boom, fad, extended fad, fashion, nostalgia and bust situations. Note that each of these shapes is largely contingent on customer response to the product.

• *RELATION TO DIFFUSION PROCESS*

In Chapter 7, we examined the adoption process, which focuses on the size and sociopsychological characteristics of different groups that adopt new products

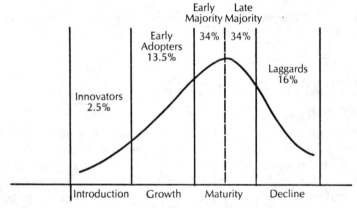

Figure 13–8. Adopter group stages help define PLC stages. From Everett M. Rogers, *Diffusion of Innovation* (New York: Free Press, 1962).

over time. Figure 13-8, which superimposes adopter group stages over the PLC stages, will help explain the product/market environment, and marketing mix responses, during each PLC stage.

USES AND LIMITATIONS OF PLC

By helping to define competitive environments during various PLC stages, and suggesting marketing mix responses to these environments, the PLC is useful as a planning framework for entire product lines and mixes, as well as for individual products. For example, at any given time, ELI's marketing manager could super-impose PLCs for all ELI products on each other to determine which products were in each stage of the cycle. If, say, most are in the decline stage, then strategic initiatives are suggested to, perhaps, introduce new lines to counterbalance these decliners, or reposition some of them in the "growth" or "maturity" stage.

Typical strategies appropriate to various PLC stages are discussed after we exa-mine environment and responses characterizing each stage. In using the PLC to plan strategic responses, however, it is well to remember PLC limitations. First, PLC length, shape, and even stages entered into by products is determined by product type and a diversity of external factors that are difficult to predict, such as the inflation rate, legislation, changing consumer lifestyles, and extent of com-petitive response. In addition to the difficulty of anticipating when the next PLC stage will appear, or the shape it will assume, it is often difficult to accurately judge what stage the product is in at present. For example, a product may appear to attain maturity when it has actually only reached temporary plateaus in the growth stage.

TYPICAL PLC STAGES

With these uses and limitations in mind, then, here are brief summaries of typical situations and responses during each PLC stage which influenced planning for ELI's GP line, and its entire product mix:

- *Introduction:* The main objective of this stage is to build sales for the product, frequently at the cost of profits. Although competition is lim-ited—or, in the case of a major innovation, non-existent—profit margins are low because:
  - the initial market, largely comprising risk-taking innovators, isn't as large as subsequent markets will be
  - production and marketing costs, on a per-unit basis, are usually higher than they will be during other PLC stages, reflecting the high costs of gaining momentum

  Because costs are so high, usually only one model of the product is sold during this stage. For a convenience item, like a new magazine, distri-bution is extensive; for an expensive shopping or specialty item, like ELI's in-house courses, it is usually selective or exclusive. Depending largely on product type, the product may have a high status price or a low mass market price. Promotion generally aims to make prospects aware of the product, and inform them of its features and benefits—persuasive competitive promotion comes later. Product trial is encouraged through coupons and samples, such as ELI's invitation to attend a sample lecture.

- *Growth:* The main marketing objective during this stage is to expand distribution and range of product alternatives. Primary demand for the product class increases rapidly as more firms enter a highly attractive market with substantial untapped potential. Unit profits increase because members of the large early adopter segment are willing to pay higher prices for the still-limited quantity of products available. To accommodate the needs of this fast-growing market, modified versions of the product are offered (such as the GP course with the electronic library). Additionally, distribution is expanded, price ranges are offered, and mass promotion becomes more persuasive, focusing on competitive features and benefits.

- *Maturity:* This stage is characterized by intense competition, and sales stabilize as the market becomes saturated with firms eager to capitalize on still sizeable demand. Main marketing objective of the firm: to maintain its differential advantage, and profits associated with this advantage, through more product models and features, lower prices, more service options, and more innovative promotion. As discounting becomes popular, total industry and unit profits begin to decline. As early and late majority segment members are attracted, the average-income mass market now makes its purchases. A full product line is made available, sold through many outlets at many prices.

- *Decline:* Demand decreases during this stage because customers are fewer, and other products more attractive. Sellers now face three alternatives: (1) cut back on marketing programs, reducing the number of products marketed, outlets sold through and promotion used; (2) revive the product by repositioning, repackaging or otherwise remarketing it; or (3) terminate the product. As industry sales decline, the product mix concentrates more on the best selling products, most productive distributors, and most effective pricing and promotion strategies.

HOW THE PLC HELPS DEVISE MARKETING STRATEGIES

By providing an overview of competitive environments during various product life stages, the PLC also suggests marketing mix strategies appropriate to each stage for product mixes, lines, and individual products. For example, if products in the firm's mix are situated primarily in the highly competitive growth stage, line stretching and filling decisions, discussed earlier, might be indicated to meet these competitive threats. Mix width, depth and consistency decisions might also be made largely in response to competitive environments indicated by the PLC, with products added or modified during growth periods, and pruned and narrowed during periods of decline.

For individual products comprising the line, three strategies in particular are appropriate for later PLC stages, as competition becomes more intense, and markets and profits decline:

- *Repositioning Strategies* involve use of advertising and promotion campaigns to create changed consumer perceptions of the product. For example, when ELI attempted to change its "blue chip, senior executives only" image to accommodate its line of less expensive courses for middle managers and even supervisors, it engaged in a repositioning strategy. The danger of such a strategy—brought home to ELI management when senior executive enrollments declined precipitously—is the possibility of confusing, and losing, the firm's main "mission" market.

- *Product Life Extension Strategies* entail one or more of the following tactical options: new uses for product; new product features or benefits; new classes of customers for present product; increased product usage; and/ or a changed marketing strategy. Actually, ELI's entire line of videotaped courses represented a product life extension strategy in terms of the declining situation facing its original campus course line of executive training courses: through this VAMP line, it aimed to attract new customers, with new products and an entirely new marketing strategy.

- *Product Deletion Strategies* involve removing products from the line when they are no longer profitable. The three major deletion strategy options include:

  - a *continuation strategy* of doing what had been done until the product is dropped

  - a *milking strategy* of cutting back marketing expenses to maintain profits by cutting costs in the product's declining stage

  - a *concentrated* strategy of aiming all marketing efforts at the strongest market segment, and phasing out all others

The danger implicit in milking and concentrated deletion strategies is that they will be applied prematurely, or without regard to the impact of deletion on the rest of the line. Possibly, for example, the promotion program, not the product, is responsible for disappointing sales, or deletion of a poorly selling product will lose customers, and profits, for other products in the line, or force these other products to assume overhead costs previously assumed by the dropped line.

YOU SHOULD REMEMBER

The **Product Life Cycle** (PLC)—which traces the life of products through introduction, growth, maturity and decline stages—helps identify and define competitive climates in each stage, and suggest marketing mix strategic responses to these climates. However, before applying the PLC, marketing managers should recognize its characteristics and limitations. For example, depending on such considerations as consumer interest and technological complexity, lengths and shapes of PLCs differ appreciably across products and markets. Furthermore, these lengths and shapes are difficult to predict, because they are influenced by a diversity of environmental factors. In using PLCs, it often helps to superimpose buyer adoption stages over the lifestyle stages, to understand the size and nature of markets in each stage, and to superimpose individual product life cycles over each other to identify stages which tend to be occupied by entire product lines, or the product mix. Mix, line and individual strategies appropriate to specific PLC stages include mix width and depth strategies, line filling, featuring, modification and extension strategies, and individual product strategies pertaining to product repositioning, product life extension, and product deletion. All these strategic options, however, should be considered in the context of PLC constraints. For example, the consequences of deletion decisions, and the possibility that the product isn't ready to be deleted, should be evaluated before implementing such a strategy.

KNOW THE CONCEPTS
DO YOU KNOW THE BASICS?

1. In his article, "Leveraged Lifestyles," Thomas O'Donnell comments on a powerful new trend, predominant among members of the 25–45 age group segment, to "lease life styles." In general, members of this group save very little from high earnings, preferring to invest these earnings in a broad diversity of products designed to help "build life experiences," including boats, airplanes, recreational vehicles, home computers, vacation supplies, hot tubs, and sporty automobiles. Part of the rationale is economic: for example, the monthly $520 lease payment for a $47,000 Porsche is less than monthly payments if the car were purchased without a down payment. One significant statistic illustrating this leveraged

lifestyle approach: at the end of 1990, over 60 percent of automobiles marketed in the United States were leased, as against only 10 percent in 1975.

Assume you set up a leasing firm to exploit this trend. Briefly describe, with specific examples, how and why you might have occasion to implement the following product line strategies during a typical year: product line filling; a two-way stretch; product line featuring to (1) build traffic; (2) enhance the prestige of the entire line.

2. A mutual fund, comprising a portfolio of investment instruments (stocks, bonds, etc.), can be viewed as a product line, in that the instruments it contains can be grouped in terms of similar features, similar markets and/or similar end use applications. For example, a fund consisting entirely of relatively safe government bonds, marketed to retirees, might meet all these criteria.

Assume your brokerage firm markets only such "safe" funds, which offer fairly predictable dividends, but little growth potential.

- Appraise the risks and benefits of this mix in terms of mix consistency concepts.

- Under what conditions would you consider adding a high risk, high reward growth fund, comprising stocks in "new frontier" technology companies, to your mix?

3. In his article in the *New York Times* ("Advice for Detroit's Humbled Giant"), John Holusha cites the following reasons for the poor showing of General Motors automobiles: "G.M. has consistently produced more cars than the American Public wanted to buy"; ". . . despite the billions that have gone into design, look-alike styling has made it difficult for buyers to differentiate between Oldsmobile and Cadillac, and sales of both have declined"; "When it lowered G.M.'s credit rating recently, Standard & Poor noted that the company 'no longer dominates . . . having lost both styling and quality leadership . . .'"

Based on this account, describe how mix width and mix depth decisions might be instrumental in reversing the sagging fortunes of G.M.'s product lines.

4. What do the following "prestige" brand names have in common in terms of (1) benefits to the branding firms; (2) benefits to the prospective buyer; (3) benefits to society? What criticism might the practice of branding these products attract? Baileys Irish Cream; Brooks Brothers clothes; Rolex watches; Finlandia Vodka.

5. Using a jar of mayonnaise as an illustrative example, distinguish between manufacturers, individual, and generic brand names.

6. In terms of criteria for effective brand names, analyze and assess the expensive name change from Bank Americard to VISA.

7. Give examples of automobile names derived from the following sources: geographic; foreign; word combinations; mythical; personal; invented; numbers; initials.

8. Describe how Weber's Law might have been employed with respect to all components of the marketing mix (i.e., product, price, place, promotion) for a new service that purchases unsold space on airlines and ocean liners at sizeable discounts, then sells them to the traveling public as a discount from the retail price that still permits the firm to make a profit. Travel agencies will receive a commission for distributing the tickets, which will be promoted primarily through advertisements in the Travel Sections of Sunday newspapers.

9. Describe services the following firms would probably include in their service mix: (1) a savings bank; (2) a sporting goods store.

10. What do the following excerpts from an article in the March 1, 1987 *New York Times* ("Detroit Wages a Warranty War") say about the importance of product quality?

   > "In a measure of consumer satisfaction with automobile performance conducted by the J. D. Power firm, Japanese companies averaged 134 on an index where the overall average was 100, while the American automobile industry stood at 90..." "In another attempt to cope with its reputation for building low-quality cars, last month General Motors doubled the length of its warranty period..." "With all three (American Big Three) manufacturers offering extended warranties, analysts said any additional marketing clout had been cancelled out..."

11. According to the *European Journal of Marketing*, Canadian buyers of industrial equipment ranked these service elements in the following order of importance: (1) delivery reliability, (2) prompt quotations, (3) technical advice, (4) discounts, (5) after-sales service, (6) sales representation, (7) ease of contact, (8) replacement guarantee. Given these priorities, what advice would you, as a consultant, give an industrial distributor serving Canadian buyers whose service level profile looks like this:

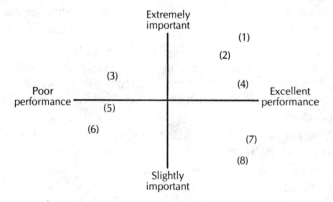

12. Describe two typical packaging objectives performed by each of the following packages:

    • wine in pop-top cans

    • L'eggs Pantyhose in egg-shaped package

    • A shipping carton that converts into a compartmentalized display rack for eight bulbs

    • WP-40 rust inhibitor available in 8 or 12 ounce cans and 55 gallon drums

13. In terms of typical criticisms of packaging, comment on the following packages:

    • Evian moisturizer consists of 5 ounces of natural spring water in an aerosol spray bottle costing $5.50

    • A customer receives his insurance policy in an expensive leather folder

    • Soda sold in aluminum cans

14. Identify the following items taken from a bottle of grapefruit juice and a carton of milk: ACME Lowfat Milk; Grade A; 2% milkfat; No sugar or preservatives added; calories 120, protein 8 grams; sell by May 18.

15. Since it is extremely difficult to specify, in advance, the length of a product life cycle for a specific product, or even to identify the precise location of the product on the life cycle curve, why are marketing managers interested in the PLC concept?

16. Discuss the nature and role of promotional expenditures at each stage of the product life cycle for the new compact audio disks with remarkable fidelity characteristics.

17. Describe PLC curves for the following products: (1) Johnson's baby shampoo is repositioned as a product for adults; (2) convertible automobiles, popular in the 40's and 50's, reappear in the 80's; (3) Gary Hart's aspirations nosedive in scandal; (4) fast food chains introduce salad bars; (5) miniskirts make a reappearance.

TERMS FOR STUDY

battle of the brands	line length
brand	line stretching
brand extension	manufacturer's brand
brand mark	milking strategy
brand name	mix consistency
concentrated strategy	mix depth
continuation	mix width
copyright	nostalgia product
decline stage	nutritional labeling
deletion strategies	open dating
descriptive labels	packaging
diffusion process	private brand
fad product	product life cycle
family name	product life extension
fashion product	product line
generic brand	product mix
grade labels	quality
growth stage	repositioning
individual brand name	service
introduction stage	service level
just noticeable difference	service mix
labeling	trademark
line featuring	unit pricing
line filling	Weber's Law

ANSWERS
KNOW THE BASICS

1. *Product line filling:* You take on a new product—for example, videocassette cameras—to match a successful competitive offering. *Two way stretch:* you might stretch a product line to attract members of more and less affluent market segments; for example, luxury limousines at the high end, economy subcompacts at the low end; *Product line featuring:* to build traffic for the entire line of leased autos, you might promote a special on the economy subcompacts; to enhance the prestige of the entire line, you might feature a luxury limousine.

2. Benefits of this highly consistent product mix include the ability to (1) concentrate promotion in a relatively narrow area; (2) build a strong company image; (3) attract loyal market members attracted to this well-

promoted product area; (4) introduce new products under the umbrella of this well-promoted image of a consistent mix. Major risks implicit in this strategy: highly vulnerable to (1) environmental influences (for example, a sharp decline in interest rates might make the safe funds highly unattractive); (2) competitive initiatives (for example, if the economy improves while interest rates decline, existing customers might be attracted away from your income fund to growth stock funds).

Three key conditions under which you might consider adding a high-risk growth fund to your line of conservative income funds: the new fund would be (1) consistent with your mission; (2) profitable; (3) consistent with existing funds. For example, if such an addition would attract customers of your existing funds (i. e., cannibalize these funds), and conflict with your mission of providing safe investments for retirees, it wouldn't meet these criteria.

3. Mix width decisions might be instrumental in addressing G.M.'s problem of "lookalike styling" and loss of "quality leadership" by adding lines to its mix which address these perceptual problems; (in fact, this is what G.M. did in affiliating with Japanese automobile manufacturers under licensing arrangements designed to jointly manufacture and market automobiles with the "quality" Japanese imprimateur); mix *depth* decisions might be illustrated by adding automobiles to existing lines (for example, the Chevrolet, Oldsmobile and Cadillac product lines) with sufficiently distinctive styling to differentiate automobiles in each line from those in other lines.

4. In terms of benefits to the branding firms, the listed prestige brand names, effectively promoted over the years, will attract a loyal clientele of customers who associate the brand with attractive benefits, and make it easier for these firms to introduce new products with these brand names. From the buyer's benefit, the name symbolizes product values each desires, assures a desired level of quality, and simplifies the shopping process; each buyer simply specifies the product by its name. From society's perspective, greater shopping efficiency is assured to the extent that many shoppers find it easier to specify these products; also, presumably, society will benefit from the innovation and competition generated as other firms attempt to emulate the success and profitability of these blue chip products.

The main criticism of the practice of branding these products—and effectively promoting these brands—might focus on the possibility that competition, instead of being encouraged, might be stifled by the dominating strength of the brand name. Another criticism: people might pay for the "psychic satisfaction" of displaying the brand, which might be considerably more than the product is objectively worth, and encourage class conscious social values which some claim are reprehensible in a democracy.

5. Hellman's mayonnaise, produced by the Best Foods Corporation (the manufacturer), would be an example of a national, or manufacturer's, brand; Ann Page mayonnaise, produced by one company but branded by A&P, a large retailer chain, would be an example of an individual, or private, brand. The unbranded, or "no frills" jar of mayonnaise on the supermarket shelf, which costs less to the consumer (but is usually more profitable for the seller), would be an example of a generic brand.

6. As compared to its original "Bank Americard" brand name, the "VISA" brand is distinctive; short, easy to pronounce, recognize and remember; suggests something about product benefits (i.e., a "visa" to the exciting lifestyle portrayed in its commercials); and doesn't have negative connotations in foreign languages. Since changing its name to VISA, the card has surpassed MasterCard as the most widely used credit card.

7. Geographic: Yugo; Foreign: Mitsubishi; Word combinations: Volkswagen; Mythical: Mercury; Personal: Ford; Invented: Jeep; Numbers: V-8; Initials: BMW.

8. Product: The routes chosen for travel discounts would have to be perceived as sufficiently attractive; Place: The discount offered travel agents would have to be perceived as sufficiently large; Price: The discount offered prospective customers would have to be sufficiently large to attract target market members; Promotion: The size of newspaper ads would have to be sufficiently large to attract the attention of prospective customers.

9. A savings bank might offer drive-in teller service, electronic banking, consultant services for investing money, and service hours keyed to customer needs; a sporting goods store might also offer hours keyed to customer needs, and sales clerks who could advise on golf and other athletic equipment.

10. Taken together, these excerpts dramatize the importance of quality—or the perception of quality—as a purchase incentive, particularly for complex, expensive products like automobiles where breakdowns can prove extremely costly. These excerpts suggest that quality is the single most important reason for the dominance of Japanese automobiles in the smaller car market segment, and that American car manufacturers are prepared to make extreme financial sacrifices to regain the quality image required to compete effectively.

11. This service profile indicates that the firm's customers are not served well by the firm's outside sales force, with generally poor performance ratings for "technical advice," "after-sales service," and "sales representation." Once the order is placed, however, customers are well served, with high ratings for "reliability," "prompt quotations," and "discounts." Indeed, the customers might be *too* well served, perhaps to compensate for the lack of effective salesmen, since the relatively unimportant attributes "ease of

contact" and "replacement guarantee" are also highly regarded. According to this analysis, the firm should probably work harder on training its salesmen to do a more creative, conscientious job of selling its products, while perhaps achieving savings by cutting back on its guarantees.

12. The following analysis lists major packaging objectives for each package; actually, an argument could be made that each package design, to some extent, furthers all the objectives:

OBJECTIVES

PRODUCT	CONTAIN/ PROTECT	ENCOUR- AGE USE	COMMUNI- CATE	PLAN NEW PRODUCTS	CHANNEL COOPERATION
wine in pop-top cans		X		X	
L'eggs pantyhose			X		X
convertible shipping carton	X		X		X
rust inhibitor containers		X		X	X

13. *Evian moisturizer:* Major criticism of this package would probably be its cost, which considerably exceeds the cost of the product it contains, and, critics would claim, unnecessarily increases the price of this product.

The insurance folder: Major criticism, again, would be unnecessary cost and, probably, use of scarce resources.

The aluminum cans: Major criticism would probably focus on unnecessary cost and pollution, as compared, for example, to returnable deposit bottles. Forty percent of total solid waste is made up of packaging material, which includes many beer and soda cans that litter the countryside. Disposing of this solid waste represents a sizeable consumption of labor and energy; aluminum cans themselves represent a sizeable diversion of a scarce resource: aluminum.

14. Following are the various functions of labels illustrated by the excerpts from milk and grapefruit juice labels: *identification* (Acme Lowfat Milk); *grading* (Grade A); *description* (No sugar or preservatives added); *nutritional labeling* (calories 120, protein 8 grams); *open dating* (sell by May 18).

15. Used by itself, without reference to the overall environment in which products are introduced and marketed, the product life cycle (PLC) can actually be worse than useless. However, marketing managers typically use the PLC with other analytical tools and techniques to identify and define competitive environments (such as the BCG and GE models discussed in Chapter 4), and to focus human judgment (such as the Delphi technique discussed in Chapter 11). Used with these analytical aids, PLCs are extremely valuable for three related reasons: first, they include many environmental variables—economic, competitive, and market-related—

in their predictive and explanatory revelations; second, they are based on the experience of many products over many years, which enhance their validity and reliability; and, third, they are broadly applicable to both products, or entire product lines or product mixes, in identifying the shape of curves before products are introduced, or suggesting strategies to be followed during, and prior to, each life cycle stage.

16. During the introductory stage of the products' life cycle, advertising and publicity would perform an essentially pioneering role, attempting to make innovator and early adopter groups aware of, and informed about, the new product, and building primary demand for the products' class. Sales promotion would also be stressed to encourage early trial, and personal selling to get distributors interested. During the growth stage, with competition much more aggressive, focus would be on building selective demand for the product itself, rather than for the product class; advertising and publicity continues to be important, but sales promotion is reduced because fewer incentives to buy the product class are required. During the maturity stage, when competition increases appreciably, sales promotion becomes important again in the promotion mix; firms that have achieved a leadership position engage in reminder advertising; others, high aggressive persuasive advertising; during the final, decline stage, reminder advertising continues to prevail; publicity and sales promotion is downgraded or eliminated, and salesmen give the product minimum attention.

17. The following PLC curves best fit these situations:

- *Repositioning Johnson's baby shampoo:* A traditional curve that has been extended (usually done during the maturity or decline stage), often by finding new customers for the product, or getting present customers to use more of the product.

- *Convertible autos reappear:* A revival or nostalgia curve

- *Gary Hart:* Fad curve: quick popularity and sudden decline

- *Miniskirts reappear:* seasonal or fashion; product sells well during nonconsecutive time periods.

14
DISTRIBUTION: PLACING PRODUCTS IN MARKETS

KEY TERMS

distribution channel all individuals or organizations involved in the process of moving products from producer to consumer

distribution planning systematic decision-making involved in planning and implementing programs to physically move products from producer to consumer. It includes channel selection and control.

physical distribution the broad range of activities involved in the efficient, profitable movement of materials and final goods from points of origin to points of use to meet customer needs. It includes the transportation forms used, inventory levels and warehouse facilities, and locations of plants, warehouses, and other channel intermediaries.

In the preceding two chapters, we examined the first component of the marketing mix: product. We saw how defining a product's characteristics can help in devising marketing strategies, and how new products are created, evaluated, and commercialized. Then we discussed how decisions affecting product characteristics help achieve profitability.

What is gained in making wise product decisions, however, can be lost if equal care is not devoted to questions of place; specifically, where the product will be offered and how to get it there. These decisions are heavily influenced by the type of product being marketed, the competitive environment in which it is marketed, company policies and resources, and consumer needs. These place decisions, in turn, influence decisions pertaining to pricing and promoting the product.

CHANNEL FUNCTIONS, CHARACTERISTICS HELP DETERMINE CHANNEL STRATEGY

In this chapter, we will discuss a variety of distribution channels: their functions, advantages, and organization, as well as considerations and constraints involved in establishing a channel strategy.

For illustrative examples, we will refer again to the Merton case, focusing on problems and processes involved in developing efficient distribution networks for the firm's line of Mini personal computers. As background, we will begin with the following situation, which faced the marketing manager for Merton's new Consumer Products division, well before any of the division's products were actually commercialized:

> Merton's Consumer Products Division has problems to solve regarding place-ment of their product, or *distribution*. In Chapter 4, the analysis of business strengths on the Strategic Business Planning Grid showed that "geography" represented a weakness Merton would have to address if the Mini were to succeed. A distribution network would have to be created where none had previously existed.
>
> Questions of price would have to wait for distribution decisions to be ironed out: an expensive, complex distribution network would add to the price of the Mini; cutting operational costs here would result in a lower price. Promotion would also be affected; for example, distributors would have to be persuaded to carry the Mini product line, and ultimate customers made aware of how and where the product could be purchased. Previously unforeseen problems in distribution could cause plans for the product itself to be mod-ified.

KEY DISTRIBUTION DECISIONS: WHAT KIND, HOW MANY CHANNELS

In planning a distribution network for the Mini line, Merton's marketing manager will have to decide first whether or not to use intermediaries at all. If she does decide to set up a distribution network, she has more decisions to make regarding the types and organization of intermediaries (retailers or wholesalers, for ex-ample). She must also consider elements of physical distribution to ensure that the product moves efficiently and profitably from Merton to the customer. Finally, these decisions must be reviewed in terms of tomorrow's selling environment. Once in place, distribution networks are costly to change.

How many channel levels? (Usually zero to three)	What functions should channel members perform? (Research, promotion, contact, matching, physical distribution, financing)	How should distribution flows be managed? (Physical title, payment, information promotion flows)	How should distribution network be structured (Vertical, horizontal, multilevel systems)	How should physical distribution be managed to efficiently and profitably move products? (Order processing, transportation, inventory management, warehousing)

Figure 14–1. Key decisions in setting up a distribution system.

Figure 14-1 shows the route of the marketing manager's analysis, from the initial decision whether or not to use marketing intermediaries, through decisions regarding types and organization of marketing channels, to decisions regarding the physical distribution of the product.

DISTRIBUTION CHANNELS: BRINGING PRODUCTS TO MARKET

Distribution channels are defined as the individuals and organizations, also called intermediaries, used to get products from producers to consumers. Channels can vary in length (number of intermediaries used), depending on the functions the manufacturer needs to have performed, and the feasibility of delegating these functions to others.

Figure 14-2 illustrates four different types of marketing channels.

- A zero-level channel, or direct marketing channel, involves only the producer and the consumer. At Merton, this could take the form of sales staff calling on and selling directly to the customer.

- A one-level channel contains one intermediary. In Merton's industrial division, a broker or sales agent would fulfill this function. In the consumer market, Merton would sell the Mini to a retailer who would then sell to the public.

- A two-level channel, for Merton, would involve a wholesaler who would then sell to retailers, who then sell to the final consumer.

- A three-level channel contains three intermediaries, typically adding a jobber between the wholesaler and retailer. This channel is used when wholesalers cannot properly service retailers on their own.

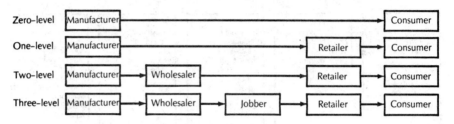

Figure 14–2. Control problems increase as number of levels increase.

Using more than three marketing intermediaries is possible but infrequent because of the loss of control the manufacturer suffers when it relies on too many individuals or organizations to market its product.

At first, the marketing manager considered the possibility of setting up a zero-level channel, where Merton itself would act as the retailer, or where salespeople would call directly on the public. Perhaps Merton could save the costs of intermediaries, and thus increase profits. In order for this strategy to be successful, a number of considerations had to be addressed.

- *Initial investment.* Merton would need cash to set up the retail outlets or the sales force. However, the Mini's production was going to be subsidized by income generated by industrial division products, and no profit return was expected on the Mini for at least two years. Extra cash would be hard to find.

- *Practicality.* For convenience, customers often like to buy related items in the same place. Offering different products also helps achieve economies of scale needed to support direct marketing operations. The original plan for the Consumer Products division, however, called for the Mini to be the only product sold for two years, when it was expected to generate enough revenue to finance other products. The only new products planned before then were a few directly related to the Mini, which were intended to enhance its marketability, not necessarily to make a profit. The product plan, therefore, did not fit in with the practical aspect of a zero-level channel.

- *Opportunity cost.* Even if Merton had the needed cash, it might be better off investing it differently. If the money used to increase production resulted in a 15 percent return, it would be a wiser investment than to use those funds for retail outlets that resulted in a 10 percent return.

- *Efficiency.* Because Merton had no distribution network in the consumer market, it would have to establish contacts, hire specialized staff, and develop efficient ways to move its product without the benefit of prior experience. Could Merton, which had mainly concentrated on manufacturing, achieve the efficiency of other marketing intermediaries? Perhaps these intermediaries, because of their greater efficiency, could sell more product than Merton could on its own, and thus generate a higher profit return on the Mini.

Taking these considerations into account, the marketing manager decided that the Mini could not be distributed by Merton alone; a one-, two-, or three-level channel would be needed.

HOW CHANNEL FUNCTIONS INFLUENCE CHANNEL CHOICE

Having decided on a multilevel channel strategy, the marketing manager now considered the following functions that could be performed by channel intermediaries, and how these functions would influence Consumer Division marketing programs. The extent to which Merton could perform these functions itself would influence its choice of intermediaries:

- *Research.* Although Merton did conduct initial research on the potential viability of the Mini, ongoing research with customers and potential customers would be difficult to maintain.

- *Promotion.* In the past, Merton's promotional efforts had been limited to the industrial market, but the marketing manager anticipated the creation of an in-house advertising agency to advertise Consumer Division products. However, if retailers were used, they would run local promotions.

- *Contact.* Merton, traditionally oriented toward the industrial market, was ill-equipped to find customers in the consumer market that retailers could find.

- *Matching.* Using feedback from intermediaries, Merton could modify pricing, packaging, or product features in order to meet consumer needs. Further, where Merton might not possess the flexibility or opportunity for personal contact to negotiate with customers, an intermediary would.

- *Physical distribution.* Merton had the means to physically move computer parts to industry; however, the company did not have the facilities to move consumer division products to the thousands of individual customers who would purchase them.

- *Financing.* Assuming the risks of financing the Mini from beginning to end could result in higher profits—if it sold well. If it didn't, Merton could become cash poor and lose what is needed to keep the Mini alive for the expected profitless years. Better to sell to an intermediary and share the risk.

HOW CHANNEL FLOWS INFLUENCE CHANNEL CHOICE

Next, the marketing manager assessed various channel level strategies in terms of the necessity and complexity of the channel flows of goods, ownership, payment, information, and promotional materials, illustrated in Figure 14-3. Each channel member always deals with the intermediary adjacent to it up and down the chain.

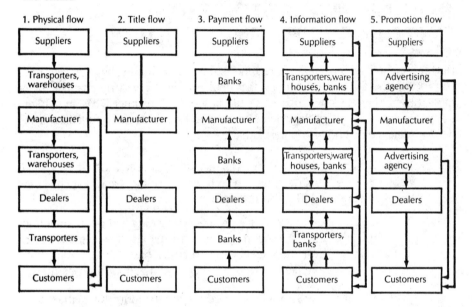

Figure 14–3. Marketing flows emphasize complexity of channels.

- *Physical flow.* The supplier ships parts to the manufacturer, which are then made into computers and further delivered down the line.

- *Title flow.* Merton buys parts, then sells computers; thus, ownership passes from the supplier to Merton, then to the dealer, then to the consumer. Sometimes the manufacturer assumes the risk of resale by offering merchandise on consignment, delaying payment from the dealer—and passage of ownership—until the product is resold.

- *Payment flow.* This is a "backwards" flow, where money passes from customer to intermediary to manufacturer to supplier, to pay for goods delivered.

- *Information flow.* Perhaps the most complex arrangement, for if products are to succeed, each link on the chain must adjust according to information provided by other channel members.

• *Promotion flow*. Merton will receive promotional materials from suppliers for parts it needs; it may then promote itself to dealers it hopes will carry the Mini, who may further promote the Mini to customers.

Trying to balance Merton's need for help in distributing the Mini with a practical desire to limit the complexity of the system, the marketing manager decided that a two-level channel, involving wholesalers and retailers, would best serve the goals for the Mini. Now, how to organize the system? Various options, discussed next, were available.

YOU SHOULD REMEMBER

Following up decisions as to the number of intermediaries to include in a distribution channel, distribution planners face decisions pertaining to functions and flows implemented by channel intermediaries. As to functions performed, an efficient wholesaler or retailer can provide ongoing research on market characteristics and potential; attract prospective customers through promotion programs; contact these customers and match the manufacturers products to their needs; buy, store and deliver products for customers; and assume financing risks. In the process of performing these functions, flows are created among manufacturers, intermediaries, and consumers, including a physical flow of goods, a title flow of ownership, a promotion flow to help sell products, an information flow of useful feedback, and a "backwards" payment flow of money from customer to intermediary to manufacturer.

VMS STRUCTURES AID CHANNEL COOPERATION

The whole marketing system's success depends on how well members interact to get the job done. But each member is dissimilar from the others, and has only its own immediate best interests in mind: performing its function efficiently and profitably. Although each channel member benefits individually when the whole system works well, competitive pressures often prevent individual members from behaving to benefit the group.

Knowing that cooperation is a desirable but difficult objective to achieve, what can the manufacturer do to foster it? Many companies employ vertical marketing systems to enhance cooperation. In these arrangements, the producer, wholesaler, and retailer behave as a unified system and conflict is thereby kept to a minimum.

Various types of "VMS"s are possible.

- A *Corporate VMS* combines successive stages of production and distribution under single ownership. For example, Sears, a retailer, has equity in many manufacturers that supply its products, while Sherwin-Williams, a manufacturer, owns more than 2000 retail outlets. Merton's marketing manager chose to reject this type of VMS for the same reasons it chose to use marketing intermediaries in the first place: lack of ready cash. The firm couldn't afford to buy or invest in intermediaries because it needed all its assets for the production of the Mini and the maintenance of its industrial line.

- A *Contractual VMS* comprises independent channel members that join together for mutual benefit. In the producer-wholesaler-retailer model, there are three combinations possible:

  - *Producer-wholesaler.* This may take the form of a franchise operation, where the manufacturer licenses the wholesaler to distribute its product. Coca Cola, for example, licenses bottlers to process its syrup concentrate into soda and then to sell it to independent retailers.

  - *Producer-retailer.* This, too, usually consists of a franchising operation, where the producer gives the retailer the right to sell its product in return for the retailer's meeting producer-imposed conditions. The automobile industry, with its system of dealerships, is an example of this type of VMS. Service industries, too, often use this approach; restaurant and motel chains are often made up of individually licensed and owned retail operations.

    Producer-wholesaler and producer-retailer systems help producers maintain control over channels without investing precious cash resources to own them. In order for a franchise to be successful, however, the product has to be sufficiently attractive so that others will want to invest in it. The Merton marketing manager liked the idea of a franchise operation, but doubted that it would be feasible until the product had proven successful in the marketplace.

  - *Retailer-wholesaler.* These systems are split into those controlled by the retailer, and those controlled by the wholesaler. In wholesaler-sponsored voluntary chains, independent retailers are encouraged to band together to order large quantities from the wholesaler, who passes on price and policy advantages otherwise available only to large chains. The producer and wholesaler benefit from the larger orders and the retailer benefits from the lower price. Perhaps when the Merton marketing manager evaluates wholesalers, she can look for one that encourages this type of cooperation.

    Retailer-controlled systems are called cooperatives, in which retailers join together to create their own wholesaling operation. Co-op members buy from the jointly-owned wholesaler, and share in the profits it generates. Merton could seek to have the Mini carried by one of these wholesalers, which would increase its chances of being ordered by the retail co-op members, thereby increasing sales.

- An *Administered VMS* is based on the size and power of one of the channel members. IBM, for example, could command greater cooperation and support from resellers than could a newcomer like Merton. The Mini, which had no market presence, could only be a victim of this type of VMS.

Because Merton's competitors employed VMSs to enhance cooperation and overall channel performance, the marketing manager knew that Merton also had to attempt to achieve this goal. But the Mini's newness (and therefore, weakness) make an administered VMS unlikely, and Merton's unwillingness to invest in a corporate VMS prohibited that possibility. Only contractual VMSs were workable. And since producer-retailer or producer-wholesaler franchises depended upon attracting franchise investors by offering an already strong product, which the Mini was not, the marketing manager was left with only two ways to enhance cooperation through VMSs: through using wholesalers or retailers participating in co-ops or chains.

ALTERNATIVES TO VMSs: HORIZONTAL, MULTI-CHANNEL SYSTEMS

Other sources of cooperation besides VMSs exist as well, however. In horizontal marketing systems, different companies on the same channel level combine to use channels on other levels. For example, Merton could look for a company with a strong system of wholesalers and retailers already in place, for which the Mini might be a complementary product. A company specializing in business computer systems, but not personal computers, might be a good choice. It would then be mutually beneficial for Merton to team up with such a company. Merton would not have to invest in creating a channel to achieve an efficient organization, and the second company could offer its customers variety without investing in a product they otherwise had no interest in.

Finally, Merton could employ a multichannel marketing system, in which increased sales are achieved through diversifying on one channel level. For instance, Merton could choose a retailer who sells to businesses through office supply stores, and to consumers through electronics specialty stores. In this way, the Mini could reach two separate markets but Merton would have to oversee only one intermediary.

It seemed then, that Merton was at the mercy of the wholesalers and retailers in choosing a channel strategy. Rather than make a firm decision about channel organization now, the marketing manager decided to postpone a decision until she had thoroughly investigated these two types of intermediaries.

YOU SHOULD REMEMBER

As a practical matter, self-interest and competitive pressures on channel members frequently prevent them from interacting and cooperating for the welfare of the entire system. Knowing that cooperation is a desirable but difficult objective to achieve has led to the formation of Vertical Marketing Systems (VMSs), which integrate intermediaries under various arrangements to enhance cooperation. Among the arrangements: (1) a corporate VMS, with successive stages of production and distribution under single ownership (i.e., Sears); (2) a contractual VMS, featuring contractual mandates to cooperate among producers and wholesalers (Coca Cola), or producers and retailers (McDonalds), or retailers and wholesalers (IGA, consumer co-ops); or (3) an administered VMS, based on the size and power of one of the members (IBM, McKessen Robbins). In addition to vertical marketing systems, manufacturers can also structure channels along horizontal lines in which firms affiliate with other firms on the same level to expand distribution systems, or multichannel systems in which manufacturers diversify in selecting channels to cover different markets.

PHYSICAL DISTRIBUTION: GETTING PRODUCTS TO CUSTOMERS

At this point, the marketing manager had addressed important distribution planning questions pertaining to number of channels to comprise the Merton Consumer Division distribution system, number of levels—or intermediaries—to comprise each system, specific functions to be performed by each group of channel intermediaries, and the nature of the "flows" that would be generated within each channel. Based on considerations and criteria to be discussed in Chapter 15, she had also decided which specific kinds of intermediaries, performing which functions, would best meet Merton's needs, and which structural arrangements were best calculated to engender cooperation among all channel members.

Now, she turned her attentions to the last, and, in many ways, the most critical area of concern in planning efficient, productive distribution systems: *physical distribution*, or the process of getting products from Merton, the manufacturer, to final customers effectively and profitably.

It is imperative that customer needs be met; if a product isn't available when and where the customer needs it, there will be no sale. On the other hand, the cost of order processing, warehousing, carrying inventory, and transporting goods, if not controlled, can wipe out profits.

These four separate functions make up an interdependent system. The marketing manager keeps this possibility of savings through efficient integration in mind as she considers the four elements of physical distribution.

ORDER PROCESSING

Merton's challenge here is to find a way to get orders processed and filled quickly and accurately. Fortunately, a computerized system is already in place in Merton's industrial division that can be expanded to encompass the needs of the Consumer Products division in processing orders from channel intermediaries. Upon receipt of an order, the system is programmed to (1) determine customer credit standing and product availability, (2) issue a shipping order and bill, (3) note the decrease in inventory, and (4) order new stock.

In integrating Merton's order processing system with systems of wholesalers and retailers in its distribution channel, the marketing manager planned to subsidize, where necessary, computerized systems initiated by *electronic point of sale* (EPOS) terminals. Resembling cash registers and installed in Consumer Division retail and wholesale outlets connected to Merton's EPOS terminal, the system would record each retail sale and automatically send an order to the supplier when inventory fell below levels determined through inventory control procedures.

In planning this integrated order processing system—which, in turn, was integrated with other elements of the physical distribution system—the marketing manager was particularly cognizant of the tradeoff between cost (EPOS was quite expensive) and the value of order processing timeliness and accuracy.

WAREHOUSING

If demand for goods always matched production, there would be no need to store goods. Naturally, this is not the case, so manufacturers must warehouse product, though this incurs additional costs. Merton must determine the level of product availability it wants to achieve. Will the Mini be distributed nationwide? Are particular areas targeted to produce higher sales than others? If so, Merton may consider stocking the Mini in multiple locations. They could use their private warehouses, already operating to serve the industrial market, or rent space in public warehouses. The marketing manager decides to use a combination of the two. Though the order processing function has been computerized, Merton's warehouses remain relatively inefficient. Because availability is so important with a new, innovative product, it will be worth the extra cost in important target markets to rent space in a public warehouse with an efficient, computerized system for moving goods. In areas of less anticipated potential for the Mini, cutting costs by using the Merton warehouses is justified.

INVENTORY

Though the marketing manager would like to be able to respond 100 per cent to customer demand for the Mini, she knows that this would mean carrying an excessive (and expensive) level of inventory. Each item carried in stock represents interest, production, and storage expense, and is threatened with damage or obsolescence. On the other hand, carrying insufficient levels of stock could decrease profits; some customers might wait until the merchandise is available, but others will switch to another manufacturer's product, and may then continue their patronage. The challenge, once more, is to balance costs with potential profits.

Three formulas were of particular value in helping the marketing manager—and managers of wholesalers and retailer intermediaries in Merton's distribution channel—meet this goal of balancing costs and profits. The first formula (for determining the point at which to reorder merchandise for inventory) assures that there is sufficient merchandise in inventory to meet most customer needs while waiting for ordered inventory to arrive:

• *THE REORDER POINT FORMULA*

The reorder point formula, as used in the following example, accounts for the time it takes for stock to arrive (lead time), the rate at which the Mini is expected to sell (usage rate), and the amount of stock needed to cover unanticipated delays:

Order lead time	Usage rate	Safety stock	Reorder point
6 days	× 2 items per day +	5 items =	17 items

Thus, when stock level reaches 17 Minis, it will be time to reorder.

• *THE EOQ FORMULA*

The next formula shows the quantity of stock to order when the reorder point is reached. As quantities ordered increase, economies of scale lower the cost of ordering each individual item. For example, one purchase order, costing $20 to process, can be used to order one or one thousand Minis; obviously, if 1000 are ordered for inventory, ordering costs per unit are quite low. However, each item ordered carries costs for interest, storage, insurance, taxes, and risk of obsolescence, so if 1000 Minis were, indeed, ordered for inventory, carrying costs would far exceed ordering cost savings.

The marketing manager prepared a graph of these two functions: how purchasing cost per item declined, while carrying costs per item increased. (See

Figure 14-4.) The point at which the two curves intersect represents the quantity of stock to be ordered that will minimize combined ordering and carrying costs. The formula for finding this economic order point is:

$$EOQ = \sqrt{2\ SO/iP}$$

Where: S = annual quantity sold in units, O = cost of placing an order, i = carrying cost, as a percent of selling price, and P = dollar price per unit.

For example, assume the following figures for a distributor of Merton Minis: S is 500, O is $20, i is 20 percent, and P (the price of each Mini) is $1000. Plugging these figures into the EOQ formula produces a figure of 10; that is, the distributor should reorder 10 Minis each time the reorder point of 17 Minis (determined by the first formula) is reached. Since annual quantity sold is 500, 50 orders will be placed over the course of the year.

• *THE AVERAGE INVENTORY FORMULA*

The third formula employed by Merton and its distributors used data from the first two formulas to determine average inventory, or the average amount of Minis in inventory at any given time. This formula is:

$AI = OQ/2 + ss$, or the amount of inventory ordered each time *(OQ)* (from the EOQ formula), divided by 2, and added to the safety stock (from formula #1). Thus, assuming Merton's distributor wants to maintain a safety stock of 5, average inventory would be 10 (10/2 + 5). Average inventory is especially useful as a basis of comparison with inventory management procedures of other distributors.

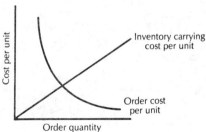

Figure 14–4. EOQ is point at which ordering and carrying costs intersect.

TRANSPORTATION

Transportation incurs the highest costs of all the physical distribution functions. Of course, savings are possible by using slower, less reliable, or less careful carriers; but customer satisfaction will be affected, along with sales. The marketing manager considers these factors in examining rail, water, truck, pipeline, and air transport.

Railroads. Responsible for more than 1/3 of all freight shipped, railroads specialize in transporting large, heavy shipments over long distances. For shipments of a carload or more, they are comparatively inexpensive; and they provide a fair degree of speed and reliability. Rail service is a good choice for shipments of lumber, coal, and agricultural products.

Water. Transport by ships and barges is the second most popular mode. It is fairly cheap, but very slow and unreliable due to its dependence on the weather. And since ships may go only where there is water, its delivery areas are limited.

Truck. Because trucks can go anywhere, while trains must follow the rails and ships the waterways, they are the transportation of choice where flexibility is at a premium. Truck transportation is also fast and dependable, but because limited by their size to smaller quantities, not as economical as rail or water.

Pipeline. The Alaska Natural Gas Transportation System (or the "Alaska Pipeline") is perhaps the best-known example of this type of transportation. When finished, it will transport 2.4 billion cubic feet of natural gas per day to the continental U.S. There are no stops or alternate routes and only fluid products (gases, liquids, or semi-liquids) can be transported. Once in place, however, pipelines provide cheap, reliable transportation.

Air. Where speed is a priority, air transportation is ideal. It is the most expensive of all, and fairly undependable because of constantly changing air schedules. Use of air transport may remove the need for extra warehouses because of its ability to span long distances quickly.

All things considered, the marketing manager decides to use trucks to transport the Mini. Though rail would be cheaper, she fears damage will be higher in the large carloads. Besides, the warehouses she has chosen are not directly on rail lines, and there would be an extra cost for transport from the train to the warehouse. And because the Mini is entering a volatile market, trucking's flexibility will allow the Mini to be quickly shipped to areas of high demand. Although air service would be even quicker, the added cost does not justify this particular benefit for the Mini.

YOU SHOULD REMEMBER

The physical distribution (PD) function, which represents both a large cost area and a significant competitive variable, comprises order processing, warehousing, inventory control, and transportation subfunctions. Most decisions involved in setting up an integrated PD system, or individual subfunctions comprising this system, involve tradeoffs between costs and such PD aspects as availability, timeliness, and quality. In deciding on these tradeoffs, marketing managers recognize that, in an integrated system, weaknesses in one area impact on the others; for example, slow, inefficient transportation can nullify benefits of efficient order processing of inventory control systems. They also recognize goals and options in each subfunction area: (1) in order processing, to fill orders quickly and accurately, (2) in transportation, to utilize the best mode, or modes, of delivery from among such options as railroads, motor carriers, pipelines, waterways and air, (3) in inventory management, to balance such inventory costs as capital investment, warehousing, and risk, which rise with inventory levels, with costs of lost sales, lost discounts, and illwill, which increase as inventory levels decline, and (4) in warehousing, to make efficient decisions pertaining to how many warehouses are needed, where they should be located, whether they should be public or private, and what materials handling equipment should be used to fill orders quickly and efficiently and minimize theft and damage.

KNOW THE CONCEPTS
DO YOU KNOW THE BASICS?

1. How many channel levels are used in generating transactions between the following firms and target market members: Sears; Tupperware; Foodtown supermarkets?

2. Using the Tupperware situation in question one as an example, and thinking in terms of key considerations involved in deciding number of channel levels, why do you suppose management selected a zero-level channel in preference over multilevel channels? (*Note*: Your answer should also apply to other zero-level channel users like Fuller Brush and Avon Home Products.)

3. It is frequently fashionable among legislative groups and social critics to blame distribution channels for high prices paid by consumers for products. Typically, their arguments view channel intermediaries as unproductive leeches, sucking profits and increasing costs at each level between producer and consumer. In recent years, for example, congressional investigators blamed the high cost of many farm-belt end-products—such as a loaf of bread—on distribution channel leechery. If these do-nothing middlemen could just somehow be eliminated, the argument continues, these costs would be passed on to consumers in the form of lower prices. Evaluate this argument.

4. An article entitled "IBM's 84 Retail Stores are Acquired by NYNEX" (*The New York Times*, April 23, 1986, pp. D1, D2) announced that IBM had sold all 84 of its company-owned product centers, located in almost every

major American city, and had decided to distribute its products only through "independent channel members and company sales personnel." Your assignment: in terms of functions performed by intermediaries, speculate on the reasons for IBM's change of mind.

5. In the 1970s, 180 distributors handled about half of all pharmaceutical products, with manufacturers distributing the rest directly. By the late 80s, 106 distributors handled 65 percent, with McKesson and Robbins far and away the largest distributor. Explain, in terms of channel "flows," how this trend toward larger wholesalers, and less direct distribution, might have come about.

6. Speculate on how specific types of VMSs might have mitigated the following instances of channel conflict and recommend the specific type of VCR most appropriate in each situation:

   • An article in the *Wall Street Journal* of June 17, 1986 ("Coca Cola to Buy Bottling Operations from Beatrice Companies for About $1 Billion") reports tension between Coca Cola and 300 independent wholesalers that distribute about 80 percent of its soda products. Among other things, the bottlers believed Coca Cola was less interested in the U.S. than overseas markets, and many resented the fact that all bottlers had been given the "same commercials," which they considered "inappropriate for their market."

   • An article in the March, 1985 issue of *Progressive Grocer* ("UPL Update: Shape Up That Symbol") reports that Pathmark and Safeway supermarket chains may drop suppliers that don't redesign UPC symbols to make them more legible.

7. Describe what kinds of channel structures (vertical, horizontal, multichannel) are implicit in the following product/market situation:

   • Sherwin Williams, the world's largest paint producer, distributes paint through more than 1600 company-owned and independent paint stores, mass merchandisers, wholesale distributors and, for some industrial markets, direct selling.

8. What types of vertical marketing systems (VMSs) are implicit in the following product/market situations:

   • In the automobile industry, after 1900, increasing automobile travel created demands for nationwide distribution of gasoline, oil, and tires.

   • One-fifth of all retail grocery sales in the United States are generated by groups of retailers who set up wholesale operations to compete more effectively with the chains.

   • Magnavox obtains aggressive promotional support from its retailers because of the strong reputation of its brand.

- Hartmax markets its brands of men's clothing through a company-owned network of 259 stores.

- McKesson and Robbins has established a large voluntary retail drug chain with a common store name and similar inventory.

9. Distinguish between intermediaries and facilitating agencies (see "flow" diagram, Figure 14-3, for examples of both) in terms of the basic role of each in moving products from producer to consumer.

10. Which mode of transportation do you judge would be most appropriate for the following products, and why:

  - kegs of beer for a fraternity party
  - the late Dutchess of Windsor's jewelry collection, auctioned off in New York
  - oil from Prudhoe Bay, Alaska

11. Here are three inventory management problems, the first involving reorder points, the second economic order quantities, and the third average inventory size.
    Reorder point: Assuming a distributor of consumer electronics products sells, on average, 5 computer modems a day, and desires a safety stock of 20 modems, and realizes it will require, on average, 20 days for an order of modems to arrive from the manufacturer, how many modems will remain in inventory when a reorder is placed?
    Economic order quantity: Assume that annual demand for the modems is 1000 units, ordering cost per unit is $25, and inventory carrying costs are 25% of the $100 selling price of each modem. What is the amount to be ordered when the reorder point (above) is reached? How many orders would be placed each year?
    Average inventory size: Given the facts and figures in the two problems, above, what is this firm's average inventory of modems?

TERMS FOR STUDY

administered VMS	information flow
carrying costs	intermediaries
channel functions	inventory control
channels	lead time
contractual VMS	multichannel systems
corporate VMS	one-level channel
distribution channels	opportunity costs
economic order quantity	order processing
horizontal systems	payment flow

physical distribution	three-level channel
physical flow	title flow
producer–retailer VMS	transportation
producer–wholesaler VMS	two-level channel
promotion flow	usage rate
reorder point	vertical marketing systems
retailing	warehousing
retailer–wholesaler VMS	wholesaling
safety stock	zero-level channel

ANSWERS
KNOW THE BASICS

1. Sears, as a large retail chain purchasing from producers for resale to customers, uses a one-level channel (MRC); Tupperware, as a manufacturer of home plastic products sold to consumers by its own sales force, uses a zero-level channel (MC); Foodtown, a large retail chain selling a broad diversity of food and nonfood products to consumers, uses at least three channel levels (MWRC) in getting products to consumers. If wholesalers use food brokers, more than three levels would be involved (MBWRC).

2. Tupperware's decision to employ a zero-level channel was probably justified in terms of organizational goals and resources, and the fact that the nature of the firm's products and markets lent themselves to a zero-level approach. For example, the firm (like Fuller and Avon) manufactures a broad diversity of products, thus assuring the customer choice utility offered by retail firms for manufacturers with less diverse product lines. Also, because there is such a huge market for Tupperware products—practically every household in the country—the company can capitalize on economies of scale also usually facilitated by multilevel channels. Given these conditions, Tupperware management, which had the resources to recruit, train, and manage a national sales force, decided its return on investment in this sales force, which included discounts and commissions it would otherwise have to pay distributors, made it the best "opportunity cost" of all the channel alternatives. An additional benefit: the degree of control a zero-level channel gives Tupperware. They can hire, train, motivate, and control salespeople to their specifications, and know they are only selling Tupperware products.

3. Most, practically all, investigations of "lecherous middlemen" by legislative and other investigatory bodies arrive at the conclusion that the distribution function is at worst a necessary evil and at best a necessary good, but

always necessary. Indeed, in Marxist states, where provision for the distribution function was generally ignored in centralized planning, this function has had to invent itself. In general, what most critics seem to overlook in their assessments is the value of three "utilities" provided by distributors that, singly or collectively, frequently equate to the single form utility contributed by manufacturers: time, place, and utility. Thus, for example, if you purchase a digital watch battery in a Foodtown supermarket, the fact that you got the *proper* battery, in a convenient location, when you needed it, are all utilities contributed by the distribution system, as against the single form utility contributed by production. Actually, an efficient distribution channel with a number of intermediaries usually reduces the costs we pay for products, as evidenced by a comparison of prices for similar products in economies with strong, mature distribution networks and those with weak, or nonexistent, distribution systems.

4. A distribution network with a broad range of electronic product lines supplementing its IBM line, and serving a broad diversity of consumer and organizational target markets—such as the Computerland and Prodigy networks—would have a larger base of prospective customers to contact, and a broader base of products to match to the needs of these prospects. Additionally, this deeper product/market base would provide the base for more useful marketing research feedback, and a more productive response to promotional efforts supporting IBM's product line. Finally, this independent distribution network would be better able to move IBM's products to customers—physical distribution—since this is their essential business, just as making electronic business machines is IBM's essential business. Another plus: IBM is now sharing much of the financial risk with distributors—such as the risk of no-pay customers or another PC jr. debacle—not assuming this risk solely by itself.

5. Just as mass marketing can create manufacturing "economies of scale" for producers, so can it create distribution "economies of scale" for wholesalers, which tend to foster centralization and much more efficient flows among channel intermediaries. For example, McKesson, in performing the information flow, provides suppliers with tailor-made reports showing detailed sales, inventory, and marketing research data, including best-shelf placement for pharmaceutical products, and major illnesses and allergies requiring medical (and pharmaceutical) attention. Using this information and its sizable resources, McKesson is also better positioned to promote and sell its suppliers' products (promotion flow), and to make sure proper assortments and quantities of pharmaceutical products are stocked and transported throughout the channel (physical distribution). With all these distributional values available—plus the steady predictable sales volume represented, and risk reduction that results when distributors take title to and pay for merchandise ("title flow" and "payment flow"), it is probably understandable that the trend is away from direct selling, at least in this field.

6. In both these instances, channel conflict could have been largely mitigated through administered VCRs, in which Coca Cola and the supermarket chains could dictate, through their power and prestige among other channel members on their level, terms of behavior for the "uncooperative" channel members. Also, in both instances, channel conflict could be practically eliminated under corporate or contractual VCRs. In the first instance, the uncooperative members would be an owned, integrated component of the corporate family, and not likely to work against corporate interests; in the second instance, such uncooperative behavior could possibly be contractually mandated against.

   Realistically, however, none of these VCR options might be possible. Each field—soft drinks and supermarkets—is simply too competitive for one firm to assume a position of preeminent administrative leadership; corporate VCRs, in these diverse, burgeoning fields, would probably be prohibitively expensive if they were expected to compete successfully with the independents; and there probably aren't sufficient incentives to persuade these independents to contractually sacrifice their independence.

7. Sherwin Williams: company owned outlets would be an example of a corporate vertical marketing system. When paired with independent paint stores, it is also an example of multichannel distribution. It is also an example of horizontal integration to the extent that Sherwin Williams purchased other paint companies and now uses their channels in addition to its own.

8. *Automobile industry*: franchising contractual systems
   Retailer groups: retail cooperative contractual systems
   Magnavox: administered system
   Hartmax: corporate system
   McKesson and Robbins: Wholesaler-sponsored chain (a corporate system)

9. Facilitating agencies, such as advertising agencies, banks, and transportation companies, perform specialized functions to aid the flow of products; they do not generally get involved in "place" decisions as these decisions relate to overall marketing strategy.

10. *Kegs of beer*: by truck, because it requires flexibility in delivery, and is probably traveling a short distance
    Dutchess of Windsor's jewelry: by air, because it is high in value, low in bulk
    Prudhoe Bay oil: by pipeline, because it isn't solid and must move a long distance

11. Reorder point:

Order lead time		Usage rate		Safety stock		Reorder point
20	×	5	+	20	=	120

Economic order quantity

$$EOQ = \sqrt{\frac{2(1000)(25)}{(.25)(100)}} = \sqrt{500} = 22$$

Average inventory
$AI = {}^{OQ}\!/_2 + ss$
$\qquad 22.5 + 20 = 43$

15
RETAILERS AND WHOLESALERS

In Chapter 14, we examined the systematic distribution planning process whereby marketing managers arrive at decisions pertaining to number of channel intermediaries, channel functions and flows, structures for assuring cooperation among channel intermediaries, and components of efficient, integrated physical distribution systems.

Now, in this chapter, we examine characteristics and components of two key channel intermediaries selling in consumer and organizational markets: wholesalers and retailers. Evidence of the importance of these intermediaries emerges from their statistical profiles; in 1990, more than 450,000 wholesalers had annual sales of more than $2 trillion, while 2 million retail stores had sales of more than $1.6 trillion.

RETAILERS AND WHOLESALERS

Both retailers and wholesalers help get the producer's product to market; wholesalers buy merchandise from manufacturers and sell to retailers, who then sell to the final consumer. Each has different functions and modes of operation that we will examine in this chapter.

Retailers perform activities directed toward selling goods or services to the final consumer for personal use. Most stores are retailers. As such, they perform distinct functions.

- *Buying* products and offering them for sale. Each retailer makes individual decisions about the assortment of products to be offered.

- *Handling* merchandise: storing, pricing, and displaying products.

- *Informing* customers via promotional materials and sales staff; informing other channel members of market research results.

- *Selling* products. This function includes providing customer services to help close transactions. Services include credit, return and delivery policies, convenient hours and locations, and helpful store personnel.

Wholesalers buy or handle goods or services for later resale to retailers, business, or other wholesalers. They form the link between manufacturers and retailers. Though they perform much the same functions as retailers, they perform them in quite different ways.

- *Buying*. Wholesalers buy from many manufacturers and handle a large assortment of products. Because they buy in large quantities, they can pass bulk-rate savings on to their customers. This saves the retailer the time and effort of shopping around for the particular variety of merchandise it wishes to offer. Wholesalers often share business risks with the manufacturer by taking title to goods and bearing the cost of damaged, deteriorated or unwanted goods.

- *Handling*. Wholesalers warehouse inventories of goods, assuring their availability when needed and reducing the need for retailers and manufacturers to bear inventory costs. They provide transportation more efficiently than manufacturers because they are frequently closer to their retail customers and because they have more effective systems in place.

- *Informing*. Wholesalers' sales forces contact retail customers that manufacturers could never otherwise hope to reach. Similarly, the wholesaler can inform the manufacturer of trends in the market, through its contact with many different retailers.

- *Selling*. By granting credit, providing information about products, keeping adequate stock, transporting efficiently, and pricing competitively, wholesalers are able to complete transactions with retailers.

The functions retailers and wholesalers perform are summerized in Table 15-1.

Table: 15.1: Functions performed by retailers and wholesalers

	BUYING	HANDLING	INFORMING	SELLING
RETAILERS	from wholesaler; assortment and quantity depend on individual store	storing, pricing, displaying	advertising directed at final consumer; market research directed at manufacturer and wholesaler	to final consumer, offering convenient hours, helpful sales staff, credit and pricing policies
WHOLESALERS	from many manufacturers, buy large assortments and quantities; assume risk of ownership from manufacturers	warehousing, transporting, pricing	promotional efforts aimed at retailers; reporting market trends to manufacturer	to retailer; offering efficient delivery, adequate product assortment, credit and pricing policies

YOU SHOULD REMEMBER

Wholesalers buy products from manufacturers for later resale to retailers, organizational buyers, or other wholesalers. Retailers buy products from wholesalers for later resale to final consumers for personal use. In the process of meeting customer needs, both retailers and wholesalers make decisions pertaining to buying and handling merchandise, informing customers and suppliers, and selling products. However, they make these decisions in different ways, based on different needs of their different target markets.

RETAILERS AND WHOLESALERS DEFINED BY SERVICES OFFERED

Just as retailers and wholesalers differ in the ways in which they carry out marketing functions, there are individual types of retailers and wholesalers that operate to achieve different marketing goals.

TYPES OF RETAILER

To stay in business, retailers must offer certain price, service, convenience, or product assortment features to the customer while simultaneously keeping costs down. The features each retailer stresses, and those it dispenses with, will determine the nature of the retail operation.

The following are the predominant types of retailers in business today, and descriptions of the mix of features each employs to implement its marketing strategy.

- *Convenience store.* As its name suggests, this type of retailer sells "convenience." Offering long hours and locations close to residential areas, convenience stores cater to "emergency" purchases. Thus, prices are higher, selection is limited, and the stores are basically self-service, meaning customers choose their purchases with little or no help from store personnel. 7-Eleven is an example of this type of retailer.

- *Specialty store.* Product depth, rather than width, is emphasized in specialty stores. That is, this type of retailer will carry a narrow product line (such as donuts) but offer many different kinds (jelly, powdered, chocolate, etc.). Hours and location must be convenient enough to draw some impulse shoppers, but by and large, the greater depth of product offerings provides the main draw. Consequently, prices are relatively high. Because the merchandise offered is frequently of a complex nature (stereo equipment, for example), or because customers preferring small specialty stores also prefer good service, these retailers are often classified as full-service, meaning the customer receives assistance in all phases of evaluating and choosing merchandise. Specialty stores are often clustered together to form shopping malls.

- *Department stores.* A high degree of product assortment characterizes these retailers. Because they need to serve large numbers of customers to turn over their large inventory, department stores are placed in centralized locations and offer convenient hours. Pricing varies according to store image; high overhead, full-service department stores will charge more than their limited-service, limited-atmosphere counterparts.

- *Supermarkets.* In the 1930s, price-conscious post-depression consumers patronized the first supermarkets. Offering low prices, centralized locations, convenient hours, and a wide selection of groceries, meat, and produce, these retailers depend on high sales volume to operate profitably. The earliest supermarkets pioneered a concept still used in supermarkets as well as in other retail stores today: self-service.

- *Superstores.* Superstores combine the product assortment of a supermarket with that of a department, or sometimes specialty, store. It was one step to ask people to give up the butcher, the baker, and the grocer for a supermarket. This next step makes it possible to shop for books, cameras, appliances, and to purchase services, such as dry cleaning or fast food, where one also shops for food. Superstores are usually similar to supermarkets in terms of hours, location, and amount of service provided. However, because nonfood items have higher profit margins than food items, yet apparently can be sold right along with lower margin food items, superstores are gaining in popularity as a retail option.

- *Discount store.* This type of retail operation features consistently low prices on brand name goods as its chief attraction. Therefore, location need not be optimal, store facilities can be "no-frills," and customer services can be minimal. Discount stores usually offer wide product assortments. Recently, the distinction between department stores and discount stores has blurred as some discounters have sought to upgrade their image. Taking their place are "specialty" discounters, selling, for example, only appliances or furniture. All discounters rely on high sales volume for profits.

- *Catalog showroom.* These retailers offer even less service than the discounters; customers often must wait in line to examine or pick up merchandise, credit and return policies are limited, location is sometimes inconvenient, and facilities are spare. Catalog showrooms offer deep discounts on high-ticket, name-brand goods, and for the consumer who has a particular product in mind to purchase, the lower prices offset the lack of service and convenience.

  A discussion of retailing would not be complete without mentioning nonstore retailers. Examples include service businesses; vending machines; mail, telephone, and television retailing; and door-to-door retailing.

- *Service businesses.* For movie theatres, banks, taxi companies, hospitals, and health clubs, to name a few, the "product" is a service. Marketing strategies and ways of doing business vary greatly between and within individual service industries.

- *Vending machines* represent the ultimate in self-service. Recently, they have been enlisted in the service industry, i.e., automatic teller and video game machines.

- *Direct marketing.* Examples of this retailing form are mail order catalogs, direct response advertising, direct mail, telemarketing, and television shopping. Because they offer convenience, these types of selling are increasing in popularity.

- *Direct selling.* This type of retailing involves personal contact with customers in their homes, and is also known as door-to-door selling. Home sales parties, popularized by Tupperware, are also classified with this type of retailing.

Table 15-2 summarizes features of different kinds of retailers.

	CONVENIENCE STORE	SPECIALTY STORE	DEPARTMENT STORE	SUPERMARKET	SUPERSTORE	CATALOG SHOWROOM	DISCOUNT STORE
PRICE (High-low)							
LOCATION (convenient inconvenient)							
DEGREE OF SERVICE (high-low)							
HOURS (long-short)							
PRODUCT ASSORTMENT (wide-limited)							

YOU SHOULD REMEMBER

The nature of a retail outlet, including product lines featured, store location and amenities, and prices charged, depends mainly on customer needs served by this store. Thus, convenience stores offer long hours, convenient locations, assortments of "emergency" products, and higher prices. Specialty stores offer convenient hours and locations, relatively high prices, and full service; department stores, the same values as specialty stores, with much wider product assortments; supermarkets, the same general values as department stores, with broader lines of food products and a self-service stress. Superstores feature product assortments of department stores, specialty stores, and supermarkets combined. Discount stores, like "no frills" department stores, feature consistently low prices, low-rent locations, and minimal cost. Catalog showrooms are discount stores where customers wait to examine or pick up merchandise. In addition to these store retailers, a diversity of nonstore retailers, including service businesses, vending machines, direct marketing and direct selling specialists offer products and services related to needs of specific target market groups.

TYPES OF WHOLESALER: MERCHANT, MANUFACTURER, AGENTS, BROKERS

There are three principal types of wholesalers: merchant wholesalers, agents/ brokers, and manufacturer wholesalers.

- *Merchant wholesalers.* These are independently owned operations that buy and take possession of goods for future resale. They represent the largest group of wholesalers, accounting for more then 50% of all sales. This group is further divided into full-service and limited-service wholesalers.

  Full-service wholesalers maintain inventory, provide credit, make deliveries, offer research, management, and promotional assistance, and further service their customers with sales personnel. This model is common in the pharmaceutical, grocery, and hardware industries.

  The two types of full-service wholesalers each serve different markets. Wholesaler merchants sell principally to retailers, and vary greatly in the assortment of products they carry. Industrial distributors, on the other hand, sell to manufacturers, and typically supply equipment, parts, or maintenance and repair supplies.

  Limited-service wholesalers buy merchandise, but may not maintain an inventory. A drop shipper takes an order, finds a company to fill it, takes title of the merchandise, and arranges for its delivery directly to the customer. Cash-and-carry wholesalers provide no credit or delivery. "Fill-in" items (such as auto parts) or perishable goods (such as fish) are often handled this way. Truck wholesalers carry semiperishable merchandise (bread or milk, for example), and simultaneously sell and deliver along a regular sales route. Mail-order wholesalers maintain no sales force, relying on catalogs to get attention for their products, which retailers may order and receive by mail. Rack jobbers set up displays (on racks or shelves) of their merchandise in stores. They totally maintain the stock and displays, and collect money only on what has been sold.

- *Brokers and agents.* This form of wholesaling does not involve ownership of goods, and limits the amount of service offered. Brokers are employed as needed to bring buyers and sellers to terms. Though paid by the seller, they are useful to both because of their knowledge of market conditions and their ability to negotiate. Real estate brokers typify this group.

  Agents are permanent, independent sales people who represent either the buyer or the seller. They may represent more than one manufacturer. An agent's independence is an advantage to the manufacturer since it removes the need for investing in a sales force. There are several different types of agents.

Manufacturers' agents represent two or more firms carrying complementary, noncompeting items. By selling many different products, these agents can make it economically feasible to cover geographically scattered markets. Small manufacturers may have only one product represented by agents; this product would get wider exposure by being grouped with others. Manufacturers' agents work on commission, do not offer credit, carry limited inventory, and have little say over pricing and promotional policies.

Selling agents, though also independent, handle a manufacturer's entire product line. This, too, saves the manufacturer from maintaining a sales force. The selling agent negotiates terms of pricing, delivery, and credit and may perform many other wholesaler functions, with the exception of taking ownership of goods. Selling agents are prevalent among small manufacturers.

Purchasing agents work for the buyer, choosing and often warehousing and shipping suitable merchandise to the retail outlets it serves.

Commission merchants are common in agriculture. They take goods on consignment, sell them, and keep a portion of the proceeds as a commission.

- *Manufacturer wholesalers.* This wholesaler type is owned and operated by manufacturers themselves. Typical of large companies for whom sales volume justifies such an investment, these operations consist of sales branches, which warehouse and sell goods, and sales offices, which are limited to arranging for merchandise distribution.

YOU SHOULD REMEMBER

Differences among wholesalers derive primarily from differences in services—such as risk assumption, credit extension, and physical distribution—provided for their producer suppliers and retailer customers. Merchant wholesalers, accounting for more than 50 percent of all sales, are independently owned corporations that buy and take possession of goods for future resale; this group is further categorized in terms of services offered, ranging from full-service wholesalers who provide ownership, storage, sales, credit and research assistance to suppliers, retailers, and organizational customers, to limited service drop shippers who arrange sales, take title to merchandise, but do little more. Other forms of merchant wholesalers, offering differing degrees of service, include cash and carry wholesalers, truck wholesalers, mail order wholesalers, and rack jobbers. Brokers and agents, who do not take possession of goods, function to bring buyers and sellers together. Agents assume a more independent, permanent role and represent sellers only, while brokers, though paid by the seller, represent both buyers and sellers. Agents are further classified as manufacturers' agents and selling agents, with the latter handling a manufacturer's entire product line. Purchasing agents work for buyers, choosing and often warehousing merchandise. Commission merchants are common in agriculture. Manufacturer wholesalers, the third major category, consist primarily of sales branches that warehouse and sell goods that are owned and operated by the manufacturers themselves.

RETAILER AND WHOLESALER MARKETING STRATEGIES

Retailer and wholesaler intermediaries can also be compared by examining the choices each makes in target market selection and marketing mix emphasis.

- *Target market selection.* For both retailer and wholesaler, all other decisions regarding products, prices, promotion, and distribution follow this initial decision. Both attempt to narrow prospective markets to the most profitable segments.

  Using such demographic data as age, income, and geographic location of profitable prospect groups, retailers tailor product offerings, prices, store location, and store atmosphere to attract these groups.

  Wholesalers use retailer characteristics to determine target markets. Will they serve large or small retailers? Variety stores or specialty stores? Those in need, or not in need, of quick delivery? Answers to these questions determine the nature of wholesalers' operations.

- *Product.* Retailers consider many factors when deciding on product assortment. Should a wide variety be stocked? Or only a few product lines, but many products within those lines? Should high-quality or lower-priced goods be emphasized? Further, intangibles such as service and the atmosphere in which products are presented must be considered. Customers of high quality merchandise expect high quality service, and likely wouldn't shop in a self-service store.

  Wholesalers, on the other hand, are always expected to carry a large assortment of goods, to meet retailers' immediate needs. Since wholesalers generally pay for the goods they stock, however, carrying a large inventory is expensive. Further, retailers' desire for services such as credit and delivery must also be considered. Each wholesaler must find a balance between serving the customer and maintaining profitability.

- *Price*. For retailers, price decisions are contingent upon product decisions. A high-quality product line will naturally require high pricing; a strategy that rests on quick turnover of stock points to lower pricing. Similarly, high overhead resulting from liberal customer services and the cost of providing "atmosphere" will raise prices. Still, the key to profitability is buying intelligently, with an understanding of the price that can reasonably be charged for the goods. Retailers often employ creative pricing policies, where under-priced items draw customers, who then also buy more profitable products. Or products are overpriced initially, because a percentage of the stock will sell at that price, and it is likely that markdowns will have to be made later regardless of initial price (for example, as seasons change in the fashion business).

  Though wholesalers need not consider as many variables, they too operate under the "buy low, sell high" law of profitability. However, if wholesalers can find appropriate merchandise at low prices, the price break may be passed on to the retailers to encourage volume buying or to attract new customers. Again, a balance between cost, price, and profit must be reached.

- *Promotion*. Retailers vary greatly in the types and degree of promotion they use to attract customers. A funeral home would never advertise on television that its prices were "insane," and an out-of-the-way discount store would never rely on word-of-mouth advertising. As with the other marketing decisions we have discussed, target market determines the nature of promotional strategy.

  Wholesalers, on the other hand, advertise very little. Because image counts less, and because wholesalers perform a straightforward service, there is less need for descriptive advertising. Some wholesalers do employ sales forces, however, and may find it wise to promote themselves to retailers in other ways as well.

- *Place*. Because this is an important consideration in attracting customers, retailers pay a great deal of attention to location. A number of options are possible. An isolated store may be fine for a discount store or a catalog showroom, where price advantages will impel customers to drive out of their way to shop. Specialty stores and service businesses may choose to locate in an unplanned central business district, where there is heavy foot traffic. In neighborhood or regional shopping centers (shopping malls), a planned mix of stores benefits all retailers located there.

  Wholesalers mimic low-end retailers in their choice of location. For them, a functional building in a low-rent, low-tax area is ideal. The only real considerations are geographical proximity to manufacturers, retailers, or major connecting highways. Any money spent on improving facilities is usually directed at increasing efficiency, such as by computerizing or automating warehouses.

FUTURE TRENDS IN RETAILING AND WHOLESALING

The retail industry is constantly evolving. Innovative retailers discover ways to cut costs and thus offer lower prices, effectively competing with established businesses that aren't as "hungry." But as the "wheel of retailing" concept explains, soon these new operations upgrade their product lines and offer more services. Because costs are higher, prices rise and the retailer now serves a different target market. The wheel is completed when a new, innovative retailer cuts costs and attracts the customers the other retailer left behind. Retailers must constantly be aware of rapid changes in demographics and lifestyles in order to compete effectively.

Wholesalers are in danger of becoming obsolete. Retailers and manufacturers would like to be able to do without the additional expense of a wholesaler. Their future success depends on their ability to move product to markets more efficiently and cheaply than manufacturers and retailers can.

YOU SHOULD REMEMBER

Differences among retailers and wholesalers can also be identified in terms of different strategic marketing decisions made by each intermediary concerning target markets and marketing mix offerings attractive to target markets. Concerning target markets, retailers rely mainly on demographic data—customer age, income level, location, etc.—to identify worthwhile segments and decide on store location and atmosphere, products and product prices, and promotional strategy to attract segment members. Wholesalers, in turn, use these characteristics of retailers to identify worthwhile retailer characteristics and define such operating characteristics as depth and width of product line and services offered to retailer customers.

KNOW THE CONCEPTS
DO YOU KNOW THE BASICS?

The first three questions, below, are based on the following facts and figures pertaining to the Tandy Corporation's Radio Shack distribution system:

The Tandy corporation manufactures more than 1000 electronic and computer products, stores merchandise in regional warehouses, ships via trucks, and sells its products in more than 9000 Radio Shack retail stores. Six thousand of these retail stores are company owned, 3000 are privately owned franchisees. Thirty-two company-owned factories are also integrated into the distribution system, making, assembling, and packaging products that account for 55% of the firm's $3 billion annual sales.

On the retail level, each of approximately 7500 Radio Shack stores carries a full line averaging more than 2700 products, from telephones to security systems. Other Radio Shack stores have specialized their product mixes to meet target market needs, including stores specializing in consumer computer product lines, advanced microcomputer applications for business/professional target markets, and business telecommunications systems.

Backing up this entire corporate vertical marketing system are extensive service facilities.

1. In terms of decisions retailers make pertaining to the establishment of target markets and marketing mix offerings attractive to these target markets, speculate on why and how Tandy might have decided to set up its retail distributors of business telecommunications systems.

2. Describe and discuss differences between retailers and wholesalers in terms of activities each would perform in the following functional areas: buying, informing, selling.

3. How would decisions made on the manufacturer level of Tandy's distribution system differ from those made on the wholesaler level in developing marketing plans?

4. Why do wholesalers have aggregate sales (over $2 trillion) higher than aggregate retailer sales (over $1.4 trillion)?

5. How do efficient wholesalers help manufacturers and retailers operate more productively and profitably?

6. Why might a manufacturer of industrial solvents want to replace agents with merchant wholesalers?

7. Match the product/market situation in column A, below, with the column B intermediary most appropriate to the situation. Justify your selection.

A	B
A small (10–20 employees) manufacturer of marine fittings for yachts seeks to penetrate a new market: police and other municipal boats.	Selling agent
You receive a patent on your new invention—an industrial vacuum cleaner that tests better than any models currently on the market.	Brokers
General Motors, Proctor and Gamble, and Continental Baking discover there are no preexisting wholesaler channels for their products in Brazil.	Manufacturers' agent
You want to sell your house.	Manufacturer wholesaler

8. Which type of retailer would be most appropriate in the following product/market situations?

   • Gucci introduces its latest line of handbags.

   • Panasonic introduces a new food processor in time for the Christmas shopping season.

   • Coca Cola plans to sell its new soft drink on college campuses.

   • Heinz introduces a new bar-b-q sauce.

9. In each of the above product/market situations, which of the following marketing mix elements would be emphasized?

	Convenient Location	Low Price	High Price	Mass Promotion	Product features	Store Atmosphere	Service Stress
Gucci							
Panasonic food processor							
Coca Cola							
Heinz sauce							

TERMS FOR STUDY

agents
brokers
cash-and-carry wholesalers
catalog showroom
commission merchants
convenience store
department store
direct marketing
direct selling
discount store
drop shipper
full-service wholesalers
handling
industrial distributors
limited-service wholesalers
mail-order wholesalers

manufacturers' agent
manufacturers' wholesaler
merchant wholesaler
nonstore retailer
purchasing agent
rack jobbers
retailer
sales branches
selling agent
specialty store
supermarket
superstore
truck wholesalers
vending machines
wheel of retailing
wholesalers

ANSWERS
KNOW THE BASICS

1. Demographic data pertaining to the location and nature of business firms most likely to require business telephone systems (industry? sales volume? applications for phone systems? types of systems required?) was gathered, analyzed, and used as the basis for decisions pertaining to such marketing mix variables as lines of telecommunications products handled, price ranges, supplementary services offered (such as extended warrantees and extension of credit), store location and ambiance, and message/media characteristics of promotional materials. All of these marketing mix variables could differ among retail store groups based on target market characteristics.

2.

	Tandy retailers	Tandy wholesalers
B U Y I N G	Retailers would order from wholesalers to meet needs of consumer and organizational end users.	Tandy-owned wholesalers would order product assortments from Tandy producers to meet needs of Tandy retailers; independent wholesalers would order a large assortment of products from Tandy and other manufacturers.
I N F O R M I N G	Retailers would keep other channel intermediaries informed of changing marketplace needs and competitive responses to these needs; customers and prospects would be kept informed, via marketing communication programs, of Tandy offerings to meet their needs.	Tandy wholesalers would gather and organize data from retailers and other sources (including their sales people) to provide Tandy and other suppliers with data and information on marketplace trends, threats, and opportunities. They would also keep retailers informed on price, product, promotion, and market applications information, mainly through sales people calling on them.
S E L L I N G	Would make major use of media promotion (newspaper advertising, direct mail) and catalogs prepared at central headquarters to attract prospects to stores.	Much greater emphasis on direct selling, rather than media advertising, in persuading retailers to take on Tandy lines, or help them sell these products.

3. At the manufacturer level, decisions pertaining to markets served and marketing mix offerings would probably be based on deeper and broader information sources than decisions made by wholesalers, and relate to much broader, deeper objectives. For example, manufacturer level objectives would account for a broad diversity of target markets and uncontrollable social, economic, competitive, and technological threats and opportunities, as compared to the limited thrust of wholesaler or retailer concerns. In addition to feedback from its channel intermediaries, Tandy's manufacturer-level MIS would gather demographic, psychographic, and behavioristic decision information from a broad diversity of other sources, including government reports, marketing research specialists, consultants, and commercial data sources like Nielsen and SAMI.

4. The reason wholesaler intermediaries generate much more sales volume than retailer level intermediaries can be explained in terms of multiple transactions that take place on the wholesale, but not the retail, level. For example, a single product can go from the producer to an agent to a merchant wholesaler to another merchant wholesaler before finally being purchased for resale by a retailer.

5. An efficient wholesaler can help a manufacturer operate more productively and profitably in a variety of ways. For example, it can integrate its physical distribution functions—notably, order processing, inventory management, and materials handling—with those of the manufacturer to keep products

moving smoothly through the channel to ultimate customers, generating profit dollars and customer goodwill in the process. In addition to performing the physical distribution functions it performs best—so manufacturers can focus on production activities they do best—the wholesaler also generates sales and profit dollars for manufacturers by finding and meeting the needs of many more customers than manufacturers could find by themselves, and assuming much of the risk of financing sales to these customers. In a nutshell, wholesalers are the best possible customers for manufacturers, usually buying products in large, economical, predictable quantities, and paying their bills when due.

The wholesaler can also help retailers function more profitably and productively in many of the ways it helps manufacturers: by providing information, assuming credit risks, and helping them target their marketing efforts more effectively. In addition, wholesaler-sponsored chains help groups of independent retailers compete more efficiently with larger chains like A & P and Shoprite.

6. Particularly for manufacturers interested in building a territory for a new or generally unknown product or product line, agents offer manufacturers strong distribution benefits. For example, since agents only receive commissions when they sell something, supplier expenses are kept low, and agents have a strong incentive to push the supplier's product—their livelihood. However, once product lines are established to the point where merchant wholesalers are willing to take them on, these wholesalers offer a number of benefits not provided by agents, of importance in fully developing markets and profit potential. For example, merchant wholesalers assume risk of product obsolescence by taking title to merchandise, reducing storage and transportation costs by keeping products in inventory and delivering them to buyers, and assuming financial risk inherent in extending credit—all functions not generally performed by agents.

7. (1) The small manufacturer of marine fittings would probably not have sufficient sales volume nor potential to attract the services of a merchant wholesaler, nor sufficient resources to set up its own manufacturer-wholesaler VMS. Since this firm needs to penetrate a new market, however, it probably needs broad marketing capability in identifying, defining, and attracting target market segments that selling agents, who market a manufacturer's entire line, are in business to provide. (2) The case of the patented industrial vacuum cleaner is similar, except that, as a single product, it probably wouldn't attract even the professional interest of a selling agent, but might be accepted by a manufacturer's agent, who would sell it along with other, similar products in his or her line. (3) The fact that these firms simply couldn't find preexisting wholesaler facilities in Brazil points to the need to set up their own manufacturer-wholesaler channels (which they did), since they certainly have the expertise and resources to do so. (4) Selling your home, unless done directly (zero channel), is probably best

handled through brokers who, by definition, are wholesalers who bring buyers and sellers together, representing both in the process.

8. Gucci boots: *specialty store*, featuring product depth, full service
   Panasonic: *discount store*, featuring no-frills and wide assortments
   Coca Cola: *vending machines*
   Heinz sauce: *supermarkets*

9.

	Convenient Location	Low Price	High Price	Mass Promotion	Product Features	Store Atmosphere	Service Stress
Gucci boots	X		X		X	X	X
Panasonic		X		X	X		
Coca Cola	X			X			
Heinz	X	X		X	X		

16
ESTABLISHING PRICING OBJECTIVES AND POLICIES

KEY TERMS

price exchange value of a product from perspective of both buyer and seller

price elasticity of demand sensitivity of buyers to price changes in terms of products purchased

price planning systematic decision-making process for establishing pricing objectives, policies, strategies, and tactics

pricing objectives goals or targets that management tries to reach through pricing policies, structures, and strategies

pricing policies general guidelines, based on an understanding of price objectives and both internal and external influences on pricing decisions, intended for use in devising effective price strategies and tactics in specific situations

pricing strategies framework within which initial price ranges and planned tactical price movements through time are defined in terms of price objectives and policies

In this chapter, we continue our examination of product/place/price/promotion marketing mix elements with an examination of the price component of the mix.

We will continue to refer to the Merton Case, focusing on decisions involved in pricing two products: (1) the innovative Merton Mini personal computer, which compresses features and benefits of stationary desktop computers in a portable attache case model, and (ረ) the imitative Merton modem used as an optional accessory to communicate between the Mini and other computers.

Specifically, these two products will provide examples to illustrate the price-planning process whereby marketing managers arrive at pricing objectives, policies, strategies, and tactics.

An example from the Merton Case illustrates key relationships among these four pricing concepts. In Merton's industrial division, an entrenched pricing *objective* mandated that all new products developed for Merton's customized industrial timing devices line must return a profit on investment (ROI) of at least 15 percent over their life cycles. This objective, in turn, helped define a set of pricing *policy* guidelines that mandated cost-plus pricing strategies in establishing and modifying prices for these timing devices over their life cycles. Each of these strategies, in turn, focused on adding a desired profit to computed costs in defining initial price ranges and price changes over time. Specific price changes—such as a price increase to maintain profits during the decline stage of the product life cycle—are examples of pricing tactics.

In this chapter, we first discuss the importance of price in terms of its impact on sales, profits, markets, and other marketing mix elements, then we examine the first two stages of the price-planning process: establishing pricing objectives and pricing policies through the systematic analysis of data on products, markets, competitors, and other "uncontrollables." In Chapter 17, we examine the process whereby objectives and policies are translated into pricing strategies and tactics.

PRICES INFLUENCE SALES, PROFITS, OTHER MARKETING MIX ELEMENTS

Two surveys among marketing executives—the first in the early 1960s, the second in the late 1980s—highlight the rising importance of pricing among marketing mix elements. In the earlier study, pricing ranked sixth in importance among twelve marketing factors, behind product planning, marketing research, sales management, advertising and customer services. In the latter survey, pricing was cited as the most critical of all the factors.

Among the reasons for the increased importance of pricing in the marketing scheme of things were rising costs and prices during the 70s and 80s, increasing buyer sophistication, certain product shortages, and deregulation of communications, banking, transportation, and other industries.

All of these reasons relate to three important roles of the pricing function: its role in generating sales, profits, and marketing mix values.

To illustrate these roles, we will make some assumptions about the price of the Merton Mini, and consumer responses to this price.

Assume, first, that Merton prices the Mini considerably above the cost of actually making and marketing each computer. Say that Merton's costs are $1000 for each computer, and the firm decides to price each at $2000. Also assume that most consumers perceive the combination of values comprising the Mini to be worth $1100, so sales are disappointing until Merton lowers its $2000 price closer to this $1100 market price.

Now assume a different scenario. In an effort to quickly penetrate the portable minicomputer market, Merton prices the Mini at a level below its costs, say at $700 per unit. The firm anticipates that this price will generate economies of scale (i.e., lower procurement, production and marketing costs associated with mass production efficiencies and experience), and a strong market leadership position, which will permit it to reduce costs, increase prices, and dramatically generate profits in the long term. At this lower price, however, prospective customers perceive the Mini to be a cheap substitute for a "real" personal computer, rather than the technological marvel it is perceived to be at the $1100 price. Realizing its miscalculation, Merton raises the Mini's price up toward the $1100 level and discovers, to its corporate delight, that sales remain stable, or actually increase, with each incremental price increase. This is the pattern of the "Giffon Good," typically a luxury product whose sales and profits increase with price increases.

If a product's price can have a potent influence on consumer perceptions and the sales volume produced by these perceptions, however, its influence on profits can be dramatic. To illustrate, consider one of the price increases that Merton discovers it can make without adversely affecting sales volume, say, from $1100 to $1200. Note that this 9 percent price increase (100/1100) levers a 100 percent increase in profits—from $100 to $200.

HOW PRICES SUPPORT MARKETING MIX ELEMENTS

Since a product's price, which can refer to both monetary and nonmonetary exchanges of goods and services, represents the value placed on all the tangible and intangible variables comprising the product, such as store location, product features, and selling effectiveness, price planning is invariably done in conjunction with product, place, and promotion planning. In the Mini's case, for example, special price discounts were offered to dealers to encourage them to carry the Mini line; differences in quality among products in the Mini line were reflected in different prices; and selection of appeals and media for promoting the Mini reflected the Mini's price-quality relationship. Thus, just as price can effectively enhance sales and profits, it can also enhance the effectiveness of marketing mix elements in achieving marketing goals. Further enhancing the price element's effectiveness in marketing planning is its unique flexibility. Unlike the product, distribution channels, and promotion campaigns, prices can be raised or lowered within hours.

This relationship among price, marketing objectives, and other marketing mix elements will become clearer as we examine the approach used by Merton's marketing manager to arrive at profitable price policies and strategies for Merton products and product lines.

YOU SHOULD REMEMBER

Price, which can be changed on short notice, is the most flexible of the marketing mix elements. It is also the only marketing mix element that generates revenues—the other three elements all generate costs. Its importance in the marketing mix derives from its influence on consumer perceptions of the product, which translate into sales volume and profits. In addition to its role in enhancing perceptions, sales, and profits, price also supports all other marketing mix elements. For example, a proper price can influence distributors to carry and push a product line (place), support a prestige or discount product image (promotion), and dictate product components or characteristics, as in "no-frills" products priced beneath the market.

WHEN PRICING IS VIEWED AS A MARKETING FUNCTION

Early on, when she was involved in structuring and staffing Merton's new Consumer Products Division, the marketing manager persuaded Merton's senior management to view pricing as a marketing function to be handled by marketing people. This view was in contrast to Merton's traditional cost-plus perception of pricing as essentially an accounting function.

The marketing perception of pricing is typical of large, multiline firms oriented toward consumer markets, where product managers play a key role in deciding such things as price levels, degree of price flexibility, discounts and allowances offered to distributors, and price modifications over the course of a product's life cycle. In other situations, where cost is a more important consideration than competition or consumer response, pricing is handled by accounting or financial people rather than by marketing people. For example, large public utilities set prices almost solely to achieve targeted profit returns acceptable to regulatory boards. In many firms, pricing is viewed as a function in itself, and pricing departments are given the organizational importance of, say, a marketing or materials management department. At U.S. Elevator, for example, top management now allows marketing people to price only jobs under $100,000. All other pricing assignments are handled by estimating groups in a pricing department at headquarters.

At Merton, however, pricing for Consumer Division products was preeminently a marketing function, to avoid the following failures that the marketing manager had experienced in situations where pricing was not so perceived: failure to (1) relate prices to the needs and perceptions of target market members; (2) properly integrate prices with other marketing mix elements; or (3) modify pricing policies and prices to match changing competitive environments, or different product life cycle stages.

NONPRICE COMPETITION SHIFTS DEMAND CURVES

Viewing pricing as a marketing function also recognized the paradoxical point that, as much as possible, the marketing manager planned to engage Consumer Division products in *non*price rather than price competition, as illustrated in Figure 16-1.

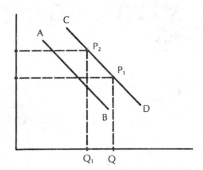

Figure 16–1. Nonprice competition shifts consumer demand curve to the right.

Line AB in Figure 16-1 shows a demand curve characterizing price competition, which sellers attempt to move up or down by changing prices. In nonprice competition, sellers attempt to shift product demand curves to the right (line CD) by creating distinctive products and services that are perceived by customers as unique in terms of such variables as promotion, packaging, delivery, availability, and customer service. Thus, at points p^2 and p^1, higher quantities of the product are sold than in a price competition situation.

YOU SHOULD REMEMBER

In large, consumer-oriented, multiline firms, pricing is viewed as a marketing function, with product managers and other marketing managers involved in deciding price levels and modifications, distributor discounts and allowances, and degree of price flexibility. Viewing pricing as a marketing function helps relate prices to consumer perceptions, changing competitive environments, and other marketing mix elements. In situations where consumer and competitor responses are not major considerations, as when large utilities determine prices, devising pricing policies and strategies is viewed as a financial or accounting function, or as a separate function in itself. Perceived in a consumer-oriented context, a key role of the marketing manager is to avoid price competition by differentiating products so that greater quantities are sold at the same price. Nonprice competition, then, is defined in terms of moving demand curves to the right.

ESTABLISHING PRICING OBJECTIVES AND POLICIES

Following is the systematic approach used by the marketing manager to exploit advantages of nonprice competition. This approach begins by establishing pricing objectives, then it examines the impact of internal and external factors affecting prices, and concludes with pricing policies and strategies designed to achieve pricing objectives.

1. *Establish pricing objectives*: Typically, pricing policies and strategies are established, or modified, to help achieve one or more of the following objectives:

   - *Target return objectives*, used by both middlemen and manufacturers, specifies a percentage dollar return on either sales or investment. For example, retailers and wholesalers set a percentage markup on sales large enough to cover anticipated operating costs plus a desired profit for the year. On average, wholesalers earn about 2 percent on net sales, department stores about 3 to 4 percent on net sales. Target return on investment (ROI) pricing refers to the practice of setting price at a level that achieves a specified after-tax percentage return on invested capital. Common ROI targets are typically between 10 and 30 percent after taxes, with lower returns usually set to discourage competition, higher returns when little competition is expected.

In large companies, a target return on investment objective simplifies measuring and controlling the performance of many divisions and departments, all of which use capital. It can also simplify the pricing process: over time, many firms learn that their investments have earned a certain average rate of return, which becomes the target rate desired for new product introductions.

This emphasis on profit return, however, often deemphasizes other important factors affecting pricing decisions, and is often cited as a reason for the lackluster competitive performance of American firms vis a vis offshore firms willing to sacrifice short-term profits for larger profits in the long run.

- *Market share leadership* goals usually forego initial profits for larger, long-range profits by pricing products below the market to achieve a strong market leadership position. In this entrenched leadership position, firms benefit from mass market economies of scale, while competitors—Pepsi vs. Coke or Goodrich vs. Goodyear—are forced to play a more expensive game of catch-up. Leader firms are also better positioned to increase prices, later, to make up for early low prices.

- *Product quality leadership* objectives typically require a high introductory price to create and connotate product quality to target market members. Customer perceptions are a key consideration in achieving this objective. If the product's prestige image drops below its high price, sales and profits will also drop.

   Other objectives that pricing strategies and tactics can help achieve include (1) helping to sell other products: for example, a supermarket's low price for hamburger attracts customers who pay higher prices for other products; (2) simple survival: for example, an airline's "Super Saver" rates ensure a sufficiently large number of passengers and dollars to at least pay for fuel and flight personnel salaries, while not producing profits.

2. *Understand competitive costs*: Since all marketing-oriented pricing policies and strategies assume that prices will be pegged above, below, or at competitive price levels for products and product lines, an understanding of competitive prices is a necessary early step in the price-planning process.

   In the case of an innovative product like the Mini, which has no competition during the introductory stage of its product life cycle, information on competitive prices must be envisioned. Various surveys among prospective customers conducted during business analysis and product development stages of the new product development process (described in Chapter 13) can provide useful clues as to the value consumers place on a product. Supplementing these surveys, Merton's marketing manager also made use of the substitute method, involving careful analysis of products similar to the innovative product being introduced. Since few products are entirely new, this method can also provide estimates of upper and lower levels of sales associated with different price levels.

In the case of an imitative product like the Merton modem, for which many competitive products already exist, a diversity of methods can be employed to determine the range and average of competitive prices, including analysis of competitive price lists, comparison shopping, and surveys of buyers of competing products.

3. *Understand demand behavior.* Basic to an understanding of pricing policies and strategies best calculated to achieve pricing objectives is an understanding of how consumers perceive products, as shown in demand curve behavior. If, for example, prospective customers perceived the Mini to be both unique and necessary, then the marketing manager might adopt a strategy of pricing the Mini well in excess of what it actually costs to make and market the product. Alternately, if the Mini is perceived as "just another personal computer," such a pricing strategy could spell financial disaster.

In attempting to document consumer perceptions of product values, the marketing manager developed the demand schedules shown in Figure 16-2 depicting relationships between price and demand for both the Mini and the modem.

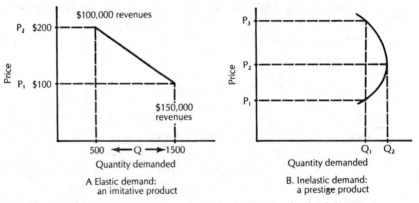

Figure 16-2. Elastic and inelastic demand schedules.

In the case of the modem (Figure 16-2a), demand followed an *elastic* pattern, whereby quantity demanded (Q) increased sufficiently to increase total revenue if price was decreased (p^1), and vice versa if the price was increased (p^2). This is typically the situation for a product perceived as having many substitutes, and not considered a necessity.

In the case of the Mini (Figure 16-2b), however, a different demand curve emerged, in which the demand schedule, instead of sloping downward in either a straight or curved line, sloped upward from (p^1, Q^1), through (p^2, Q^2), to point (p^3, Q^1). Thus, at point (p^2, Q^2), demand for the product actually increases, even though the Mini's price has also increased. Even at point (p^3, Q^1), where price is three times as high as at point (p^1, Q^1), demand is still at least as strong as at point (p^1, Q^1). Inelastic demand situations like this, where price changes have little effect on quantities demanded, characterize products that have few substitutes, for which buyers do not readily notice a higher price, or find such a price justified. A. doctor's bill, for example, might fit these criteria. From the marketing manager's perspective, such a desirable demand pattern offers high profit potential through higher prices without declining sales.

YOU SHOULD REMEMBER

A systematic approach for establishing pricing policies and strategies in competitive, consumer-oriented markets begins with the establishment of pricing objectives that will help achieve broader marketing and corporate objectives. Among objectives that pricing can help achieve are the following: target return objectives, also used by wholesalers and retailers, which specify dollar return on sales or investment and often simplify the pricing process and market share leadership objectives, which typically mandate lower prices to gain larger market share and higher long-range economies and profits. Other objectives are maintaining a quality product image, selling other products in the line, and simple survival. Except for target return objectives, all these pricing objectives focus on consumer perceptions and competitive responses as well as costs. After pricing objectives are established, the price planning process develops data on competitive price levels, which is related to the final prices that will be set. The third step in the price-planning process involves identifying consumer perceptions of price, and demand patterns deriving from these perceptions. Marketing managers engaged in nonprice competition generally work for inelastic demand patterns, where products are perceived as both necessary and unique.

---

4. *Understand cost behavior.* Earlier in her analysis, the marketing manager had estimated competitive prices to be faced by the Mini and the modem; now, to determine the profit consequences of prices pegged above, below, or at these competitive price levels, she undertook an analysis of the *types* of costs involved in making and marketing these products, and how these costs could be expected to behave under different conditions of demand. These changing demand conditions would result from changing economic climates and product life cycle stages.

In her analysis, the marketing manager considered the behavior of the following kinds of costs:

- *Fixed costs (FC)*, such as rent, taxes, and executive salaries, that remain constant regardless of how many Minis are produced.

- *Average fixed costs (AFC)* are total fixed costs divided by the number of units produced. The more Minis produced, the less AFC per Mini. For example, if it costs $1,000,000 in fixed costs to set up production for the Mini, and 10,000 Minis are produced, each would be allocated an average of $100 in fixed costs.

- A *variable cost (VC)* is a cost directly related to production; when production stops, so do these costs. Material costs or sales commissions are examples of variable costs, which can be controlled in the short run simply by changing the level of production.

- *Average variable cost (AVC)* is total variable cost divided by the number of units produced. Usually high for the first few units produced, AVC decreases as production increases owing to various economies of scale. For example, after a time, production workers would learn to make more Minis per hour, and salesmen could sell more in a given day. Eventually, however, a point was reached when AVC increased as Merton's existing facilities reached capacity and expensive new facilities were required.

- *Total cost (TC)* is the sum of total fixed and variable costs for a specific quantity produced.

- *Average total cost (ATC)* is total cost (TC) divided by number of units produced.

- *Marginal cost* is the cost of producing each additional unit, and suggests the minimum extra revenue that should be generated by each additional unit. It is usually equal to the variable cost of producing the last unit.

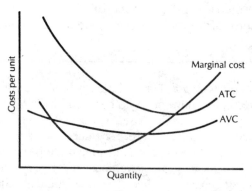

Figure 16–3. How unit costs change as quantity increases.

The interrelationships among these costs is graphically displayed in Figure 16-3, which shows how these costs change with changes in quantities produced. Note that all three costs drop over the quantity output range, then begin to rise at different quantity levels. Also note that marginal cost per unit begins to rise at a lower level of output than average variable cost, then intersects AVC and ATC curves from below at their low points, then rises rapidly (the fact that AVC and ATC are averaged over many units keeps their rise gradual; marginal cost, the same as variable cost per unit, rises rapidly because it is assigned to a single unit). For pricing purposes, the marginal cost per unit is the most important cost, since this is the extra cost extra revenues must cover. Thus, the rule for maximizing profits: the firm should produce that level of output where marginal cost is just less or equal to marginal revenue. All units produced up to this point have been profitable, and these accumulated profits represent the most the company can make on the product.

Another important cost consideration for establishing prices over the long-range product life cycle is that although (as indicated in Figure 16-3) cost curves arc upward in the short range, these arcs tend to arc upward at lower levels in the long range, as shown in Figure 16-4. Thus, long range cost curves generally curve downward.

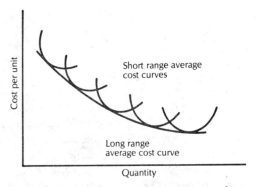

Figure 16–4. Long range cost curves curve downward.

Using costs alone as a basis for setting prices is usually appropriate in situations where extraneous marketing conditions—such as competitive prices and consumer responses to price—are not key concerns. Even in highly competitive marketing environments, however, where a diversity of internal and external influences affect demand patterns, an understanding of the nature and behavior of costs associated with making and marketing products at different price and demand levels is important not only for establishing initial prices, but for modifying prices over the product life cycle. Here, for example, is an excerpt from a schedule the marketing manager prepared in order to pull together data she had developed on estimated demand and cost behavior patterns for the innovative Mini. It shows that at a $1200 price, expected initial volume in a single target market would be 4800 Minis, while at a slightly lower price of $1000, an expected 5000 Minis will be sold. Note that, after all costs are subtracted from expected revenues, each price produces a sizeable first year loss, a fact that (in Chapter 17) assumes considerable significance in devising a pricing strategy for the Mini.

a. Price	$1200	$1000
b. Expected volume	4800	5000
c. Channel discount (30%)	$ 360	$ 300
d. Net price (1–3)	$ 840	$ 700
e. Fixed cost per unit	$ 100	$ 90
f. Variable CPU	$ 290	$ 290
g. Semi-variable CPU	$ 620	$ 600
h. Total CPU (5+6+7)	$ 1010	$ 980
i. Total revenue (2 x 4)	$4,000,000	$3,500,000
j. Total costs (2 x 8)	$4,848,000	$4,100,000
k. Total income	($848.000)	($1,400,000)

5. *Understand the impact of economic and public policy influences.* To this point in her analysis, the marketing manager had accounted for the following factors that would combine to help define pricing policies and strategies for consumer division products and product lines: company objectives that pricing policies and strategies can help achieve; competitive prices faced by new imitative or innovative products; consumer demand patterns at different price levels; and anticipated cost behaviors at different output levels.

At this point, all that remained in preparing the documentation required to devise goal-oriented pricing strategies was a consideration of the impact of the economic and legal environments on pricing decisions. For example, competition from other domestic or offshore manufacturers could quickly change a pricing strategy, or factors like inflation, increasing interest rates, or legal constraints could change assumptions on which prices were based.

In Chapter 3, we examined the nature of four economic climates in which products compete for market share: climates of monopoly, oligopoly, monopolistic competition, and pure competition. We also examined the influence of each of these climates on markets and marketing mix elements—including the price element. In Chapter 17, each of these climates will be matched with product life cycle stages as a frame of reference for examining various cost, demand, and competition-based pricing strategies appropriate to each climate and stage.

As to legal aspects of pricing, the marketing manager considered how laws and regulations in the following areas would influence prices to both ultimate and intermediate customers over the course of product life cycles.

- *Price fixing*, in collusion with competitors, is illegal in itself, except when price agreements are carried out under the supervision of a government agency, such as in the regulated transportation industries, or recent price support legislation favoring the domestic automobile industry.

- *Resale price maintenance*, whereby a manufacturer requires dealers to charge a specified retail price, is also illegal. However, manufacturers can suggest such retail prices. Although a manufacturer cannot refuse to sell to, or otherwise punish, a dealer who ignores this suggested retail price, the manufacturer can refuse to sell to a dealer for reasons not related to the dealer's independent pricing action.

- *Price discrimination*, or offering different prices to buyers at the same trade level (for example, all retailers of electronic components in the same sales volume category), is illegal under the Robinson-Patman Act unless the seller (Merton, for example) can prove its costs are different when selling to different retailers; for example, one retailer might purchase in larger quantities than another, and earn a larger discount. Different prices might also be offered to distributors in similar trade categories to "meet competition," providing this price discrimination is "temporary, localized, and defensive."

- *Minimum pricing* legislation mandates that sellers may not sell below cost with an intent to destroy competition. In more than half the states, minimum pricing laws require retailers and wholesalers to mark up their prices by a certain minimum percent over their cost of merchandise plus transportation, in order to protect small merchants from larger merchants who might sell below cost to attract customers.

- *Price increases* are legally regulated only for public utilities; otherwise, companies are free to increase their prices to any level except in times of price controls.

- *Deceptive pricing*, more common in selling consumer than business goods, is covered by FTC guidelines that forbid, among other things: (1) a claim that a price has been reduced from a former level, unless the original price was offered on a regular, reasonable basis; (2) an unverified claim that a firm's price is lower than the price offered by other outlets in the same trading area; (3) a suggested list price advertised as a reference point for a product that has not actually been sold at that price; (4) bargain offers such as "free," "two-for-one," and "buy one, get one free," if the terms of the offer are not disclosed at the beginning of the presentation or advertisement, or the quality of the product is reduced, or the price increased, to create the impression of savings.

YOU SHOULD REMEMBER

Understanding the interactions among fixed, variable and marginal costs helps understand the extent to which different prices, at different levels of demand, will influence profits. Average fixed and variable costs tend to decline over time as they are allocated to more units, and manufacturing/marketing experience accumulates. Eventually, however, they increase, as capacity limits are reached and new facilities are required. At this point, average fixed and variable costs slowly rise, moderated by the number of units to which they are allocated; marginal costs rise quickly, since they are assigned to the single unit produced last. Long-run costs, like short-run costs, also trend downward over time. Although costs are important in determining short- and long-run profitability of prices pegged at different levels, they are never properly used as the sole criterion for pegging prices in competitive markets, where competitive responses and consumer perceptions must also be accounted for. Legal constraints on prices pertain to price fixing, resale price maintenance, price discrimination, minimum pricing, price increases, and deceptive pricing.

KNOW THE CONCEPTS
DO YOU KNOW THE BASICS?

1. A four-part exercise with all 4 parts based on the assumption that you are going into business for the summer selling submarine sandwiches from a roadside stand.

a) Using the formula $S = P \times U$ (sales volume = price × number of units sold), what is your sales volume if you sell 1000 submarines during the summer at a cost of $2 per sub?

b) Using the formula $NP = S - CGS - E$ (net profit = sales volume − cost of goods sold − expenses), how much profit will you make if the ingredients in each sandwich cost $1, and your total expenses for the season (primarily, expenses involved in selling and delivering the subs) totalled $500?

c) Assume there was such a demand for your subs that you discovered you could increase the price of each to $2.20 without losing sales. By what percentage would your net profits have increased if this had been your price throughout the season?

d) Using the formula $ROA = \dfrac{NP}{assets}$ (i.e., profit return on assets = net profit divided by the total of inventory, fixed assets, accounts receivable, and cash), what was your return on assets for the summer assuming that it cost you $150 to construct your roadside stand, and at any given point in time you had an average inventory of $50 worth of unsold submarines and sandwich makings? Since you didn't extend credit, and spent your profits as soon as you earned them, there were no "accounts receivable" and "cash" categories in your asset base. Given these facts and figures, what was your profit return on assets for the summer? What would this percentage have been if you sold your subs at the $2.20 price all summer?

2. What do the four exercises above say about the role of price in influencing consumer perceptions, sales, profits, and other marketing mix elements?

3. Describe how the following campaigns illustrate either price competition or nonprice competition:

• Miller Light's "tastes better, less filling" campaign featuring retired superstar athletes

• Schweppe's tonic campaign, featuring, as its spokesman, the worldly, urbane "Schweppesman," Commander Whitehead

• Alamo Rent-A-Car's advertised $39 weekly rates in Florida

4. Discuss how the following excerpts from an advertisement in the *New York Times* for the Trump Parc Condominium residence integrate the elements of the marketing mix, and the role of price in this mix:

"Trump Parc . . . A significant contemporary renaissance . . . no element of modern ease, comfort, and convenience is overlooked . . . to your right and left the sophisticated ambiance of Central Park South . . . from serene pied-a-terres (amazingly priced from under $200,000) to spectacular penthouses . . . even the unusual staffing of Trump Parc . . . recall civilities seldom encountered today . . . ."

5. Briefly discuss how the following product failures illustrate reasons for pricing failures noted in this chapter:

- Among low cost motel chains, the La Quinta chain, which stresses its "value discount" approach, grows much faster than the Motel 6 chain, which emphasizes its spartan, no-frills amenities (pay television, plastic cups, etc.).

- Sales of G.M. automobiles suffer because of consumer perceptions of stylistic sameness among Buick, Oldsmobile, and Cadillac lines.

- Some traditional airlines (Eastern, Braniff) go out of business while others (United, Delta) compete effectively in a deregulated environment.

6. Draw demand schedules for the following product-market situations:

- Virgin Atlantic provides basic air travel with no extra services at the lowest possible price, makes $3.5 million in pretax profits the first year.

- Charles Schwab makes the promotional claim: "We give you more quality services than any other discount broker."

- Haagen-Dazs ice cream, at $9 per half gallon, costs three times as much as standard brand Sealtest, six times as much as the discount house brand.

7. Define the following costs involved in printing a newspaper:

- the cost of renting the printing plant
- the cost of extra paper and die purchased to print an "Extra" edition of the newspaper
- the cost of producing the last newspaper comprising the "Extra" edition
- the sum of all costs divided by the number of newspapers produced

8. Explain why, in the exercise 7 example, profits are highest, then begin to decline, at the point when marginal revenue just equals marginal cost.

9. In terms of elasticity concepts, explain why digital watches, which sold for more than $2000 in the early 1970s, can now be purchased for as little as $10.

10. Identify, on the matrix below, the major pricing issues illustrated by the following pricing situations.

	Price Fixing	Resale Price Discrimination	Minimum Pricing	Deceptive Pricing
1. A shoe store calls its normal retail prices "factory" prices				
2. A large plumbing supply house lowers its price below its cost to put a small competitor out of business				
3. A large photographic supplies manufacturer threatens to remove its advertising subsidy to a retailer that sells beneath the manufacturer's suggested resale.				
4. Members of an association of power transmission distributors agree to maintain identical prices in their shared territory.				

TERMS FOR STUDY

average fixed costs
average total costs
average variable costs
competitive prices
cost curves
current profit maximization
deceptive pricing
demand curves
economies of scale
experience curve
fixed costs
imitative products
innovative products
marginal cost
marginal revenue
market share leadership objectives
minimum pricing
nonmonetary exchange

nonprice competition
prestige goods
price
price discrimination
price elasticity
price fixing
price inelasticity
pricing objectives
pricing policies
pricing strategies
pricing tactics
profit leverage
resale price maintenance
substitute method
survival objectives
target return objectives
total cost
variable costs

ANSWERS
KNOW THE BASICS

1. a) $S = P \times U$; $2000 = 2×1000
   b) $NP = S - CGS - E = $500 = $2000 - $1000 - 500
   c) $NP = S - CGS - E = $700 = $2200 - $1000 - 500

   $$= \frac{200}{500} = 40\%$$

   d) $ROA = \dfrac{NP}{\text{assets}} = \dfrac{700}{200} = 350\%$

2. The fact that the price of the subs could be raised without lowering sales shows that customers perceived product values to be worth more than the $2.00 price you charged for each sub. This perception of the subs' price-quality relationship was sufficient to generate sales for your entire output. However, while price can influence sales, its impact on profits can be dramatic, as shown by the 40 percent profit increase when price was increased by 10 percent. Continued high demand at this higher price reflects consumer perceptions of all marketing mix elements comprising the sub, including its flavor (product), the location of your stand (location), and how you advertise your subs (promotion).

3. *Miller Light:* illustrates nonprice competition by promoting values and associations that justify a higher price.

 Schweppes' tonic: illustrates nonprice competition by promoting an association between the product and a desired lifestyle that justifies a higher price.

 Alamo Rent-A-Car: illustrates price competition; no product claims (cleaner cars, faster service) other than price are made.

4. Product and place elements are stressed in descriptions of condominium apartments and the exclusive Central Park South address. Promotion is stressed through the effectiveness of the promotional appeal to upper class values, and the selection of a medium—*The New York Times* magazine—directed to this group. The price mention effectively integrates and highlights these perceived values.

5. Although each pricing situation, to some extent, might illustrate all the pricing failures noted in this chapter, the following failures seem most prominently associated with each:

   - *La Quinta vs. Motel 6:* Improper integration of price with other marketing mix elements. Specifically, its product is probably perceived as *too* spartan, and its promotion is probably misdirected in stressing these "no frills" accommodations rather than (as La Quinta does) stressing values it has in common with higher-priced motel chains.

   - *G.M. auto sales slump:* Failure to relate prices to the needs and perceptions of specific target markets—in this case, the huge target markets that consider distinctive automobile styling an important value.

   - *Traditional airlines compete against economy airlines:* Inability to match changing competitive environments as effectively as some airlines that changed aspects of their marketing mix (for example, offering competitive supersaver rates or frequent-flier bonuses) to compete effectively.

6. Virgin Atlantic and Charles Schwab brokerage: Highly elastic; Haagen-Daz ice cream: Highly inelastic.

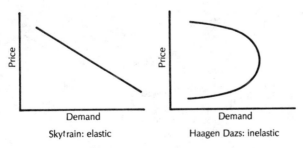

Skytrain: elastic   Haagen Dazs: inelastic

7. rental cost: a fixed cost
   extra paper and dye: a variable cost
   cost of the last newspaper: marginal cost
   all costs divided by numbers produced: average cost

8. As long as marginal revenue (or the additional sales volume produced by each additional newspaper run-off) exceeds marginal cost (or the cost of producing this newspaper), each newspaper will add to profits. Profits will be greatest where marginal revenue and cost are equal, because it will be the total of profit on all the individual newspapers produced to this point. After this point, profits begin to decline because it costs more to produce each one than either is generating in revenues.

9. During the introductory stage of the life cycle for digital watches, they were perceived by at least one market segment as unique and necessary—both conditions for an inelastic demand pattern. Thus, members of this segment willingly paid $2000 for each watch. Now, in the maturity (or perhaps decline) stage of the digital watches' product life cycle, where many producers are producing many digital watches and digital watch substitutes, its unique novelty value has long since worn off, and it is in a highly elastic environment, where slight price increases deter sales increases and vice versa.

10. the shoe store: deceptive pricing
    the plumbing supplies wholesaler: minimum pricing
    the photographic supplies manufacturer: resale price discrimination
    the association members: price fixing

17
PRICING STRATEGIES AND TACTICS

In Chapter 16, we examined major considerations and constraints involved in arriving at realistic, profit-oriented pricing policies. These policies, in turn, help to define and guide pricing strategies and tactics calculated to help achieve a diversity of possible pricing objectives pertaining to sales, profits, stability, or product image.

Now, in this chapter, we will examine a variety of price strategies most commonly employed in consumer and industrial markets: *cost-based strategies*, which determine prices by adding a predetermined profit to computed costs; *demand-based strategies*, which link prices to consumer preferences and channel needs; *competition-based strategies*, which stress competitors' prices, over demand or cost considerations; *product mix* pricing strategies, which deal with products in groups, rather than individually; and *product change* pricing strategies, which focus on strategies for raising or lowering prices.

As a format for examining these strategies, we will follow the two products introduced in Chapter 16—the Merton Mini and the Merton modem—through their life cycle stages, illustrating pricing strategies appropriate to each stage and focusing on the Mini. For the Mini, these strategies are cost-based during the introductory stage, when demand is strong and competition weak; then, through competitive, maturity, and decline stages, they become more oriented toward consumer demand patterns and competitive intitiatives.

Each stage of the Mini's life cycle also roughly coincides with one of the economic climates examined in Chapter 3: first, a monopoly during the introductory stage, then, through the next three stages, climates of oligopoly, monopolistic competition, and pure competition. Thus, we will examine pricing strategies in the context of individual product life cycles and economic climates broadly influencing products and markets.

One important point as background for our examination of pricing strategies is that titles given to these strategies, while suggestive, are not exclusive. Thus, cost-based suggests an emphasis on cost, but doesn't preclude some consideration of demand or competitive considerations. Similarly, demand and competition-based strategies do not exclude other factors that influence pricing strategies.

INTRODUCTORY STAGE PRICING: A MONOPOLISTIC CLIMATE

During the introductory stage of its product life cycle, the Mini, as a unique, patent-protected product, found itself in a monopolistic economic climate in which the marketing manager, in theory, could set the Mini's price as high as the market would bear.

Other considerations, however, suggested a low introductory price; perhaps even lower than the cost of producing the Mini, so it might incur a huge deficit during its introductory stage. For example, anticipating competition in the future, the marketing manager might decide to price the Mini at a low penetration level in order to capture a dominant market share that future competitors would be hard-pressed to overcome. In this dominant position, profits could result from large economies of scale and the possibility of future price increases.

In considering a penetration pricing strategy, the marketing manager also considered conditions under which such a strategy is most likely to succeed. Usually required is a large, expandable, highly price-sensitive target market, and the possibility of economies of scale, with per-unit production and distribution costs decreasing with sales increases. Additionally, the lower price should effectively discourage competition.

TO SKIM OR PENETRATE?

At the other extreme, the marketing manager also considered a market skimming pricing strategy for the Mini, with prices pegged high to attract the relatively small target market more attracted to product quality, uniqueness, and status than to price. For example, marketing research strongly indicated that such a market existed among national accounts salesmen for large, affluent corporations, who would use the Mini to gain a competitive advantage in preparing estimates and proposals. Then, after sales to the primary target market began to fall off, the Mini's price would be lowered to attract members of the next target market down the line, and so on. A skimming price is appropriate if it doesn't attract excessive competition, if a high price helps support a quality image, and if there are a sufficient number of market members willing to pay the price. Additionally, a skimming price is usually mandated in situations where company policy dictates a positive return on product investment and sales.

The marketing manager's decision to employ a high, skimming price strategy during the Mini's introductory stage was motivated by three considerations. First, she was concerned that Merton would not be able to cope with the huge projected demand for the Mini sold at a low penetration price (say, $700). Second, she felt the slower sales pace characterizing a skimming strategy would provide time to work out any bugs in the new product, which could prove embarrassing under a mass-marketing penetration strategy.

The main reason, however, had to do with implicit pressures from Merton senior management for the Mini to pay back its investment in a reasonable period of time. These managers were generally oriented toward pricing objectives and policies of Merton's industrial products division, where all new product introductions had to generate at least 10 percent first year return on investment. Although they had promised the marketing manager a free hand in managing Consumer Division marketing programs, the notion of deliberately taking huge short-term losses was simply too alien to them.

YOU SHOULD REMEMBER

Pricing strategies and tactics, guided by pricing policies, aim to achieve pricing objectives pertaining to sales, profits, product image, or company stability. A cost-based pricing strategy adds a predetermined profit to computed costs to determine prices; a demand-based strategy bases prices largely on consumer or distributor needs or perceptions; a competition-based strategy prices products in response to competitive initiatives. While individual strategies might stress cost, customer, or competitive considerations, each typically includes all these considerations. Pricing strategies change over product life cycles, and with different economic climates, including monopoly, oligopoly, monopolistic competition, and pure competition. Most pricing strategies derive from an important decision to price the product above the market—a skimming strategy— or below the market—a penetration strategy. For a penetration strategy to work, economies of scale should be possible, competition should be discouraged, and a large, price sensitive market should be available. For a skimming strategy to work, a market should be available to buy the product, excess competition shouldn't be attracted, and a quality image should be maintained.

COST-BASED STRATEGIES: MARKUPS, RETURN ON SALES AND INVESTMENT

The decision to take advantage of the Mini's monopoly status led to a cost-based "return on investment" strategy, which combined and extended elements of three cost-based pricing strategies employed in Merton's Industrial Products Division: *cost-plus* pricing, *markup* pricing and *breakeven* pricing.

Cost-plus pricing, the simplest method of cost-based pricing, merely adds a predetermined profit to costs. This strategy is largely used by monopolies, such as power and light utilities, and products sufficiently unique or prestigious to be viewed as monopolies. For example, in determining the cost of its unique electronic measurement devices used in certain industries, Merton first estimated the number of units to be produced, then added total variable and total fixed costs to total desired profit. Price is then obtained by dividing this amount by the units to be produced, or:

$$\text{Price} = \frac{TFC + TVC + \text{Projected Profit}}{\text{Units Produced}}$$

To illustrate, if 100 timers are produced, and Merton desires a profit of $50,000, the price of each timer, given the following total fixed and total variable costs, would be:

$$\frac{\$250000 + \$1,000,000 + \$50,000}{100} = \$13,000$$

In addition to assuming that price does not affect demand, the cost-plus pricing strategy also assumes that fixed costs can be properly allocated to the product; common costs, or costs shared by a number of products (such as heating or lighting the factory) are not considered to be a problem.

Markup pricing, a variation of cost-plus pricing, is a relatively simple pricing method for wholesalers and retailers, who often carry thousands of products and couldn't possibly analyze demand and competitive factors for each. A simple formula for determining markup pegs the final price of the product equal to the purchase cost of the company divided by 1 minus the desired markup percentage. For example, assuming a retailer purchases a Merton modem for $60, and desires a markup of 40 percent:

$$\$60/1 - .40 = \$100$$

The sellers price would be $100.

Size of a distributor's markup depends on a variety of factors, including industry practices, manufacturer's suggested list price, inventory turnover desired, and effort required to compete successfully. Typically, distributors using markup pricing take consumer demand into account by dropping products that don't sell at the desired markup.

Breakeven-point pricing considers both costs and market demand to identify the point at which the firm begins to get its money back on a product. In essence, this breakeven point is the point at which total revenues—units sold times price per unit—equals total fixed and variable costs.

The breakeven point can be computed in terms of units or sales dollars:

$$\text{Breakeven point (units)} \frac{\text{Total fixed costs}}{\text{Price} - \text{Variable costs (per unit)}}$$

$$\text{Breakeven point (sales dollars)} = 1 - \frac{\dfrac{\text{Total fixed costs}}{\text{Variable costs (per unit)}}}{\text{Price}}$$

For example, assume the marketing manager for Merton's industrial division is considering selling, for $15, a product with $1,000,000 of fixed costs assigned to its production, and $7 in variable costs associated to each unit sold. In units, the breakeven point would be 125,000 ($1,000,000/ 15 − 7); in dollars, $1,875,000 ($1,000,000/1 − (7/15)). Both of these figures are indicated on the breakeven curve in Figure 17-1.

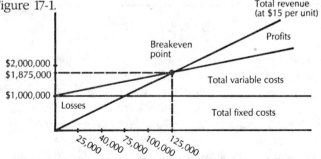

Figure 17–1. Breakeven analysis with selling price of $15 per unit.

Breakeven analyses, while useful as a rough indicator of the relationship between costs, revenues and prices, is subject to a number of limitations when used as the sole measure of these relationships. For example, it assumes fixed costs can be precisely assigned to specific products—when many shared costs can't be—and that variable costs can be clearly identified, when many semivariable costs can't be. Also, many breakeven analyses assume that total cost lines continue to rise linearly when they are much more likely to assume erratic configurations due to things like experience curves and sudden rises in costs as capacity is reached and new facilities are required.

Return on Investment (ROI) pricing, also called target return pricing, measures total investment in a product—which, in the case of a new product like the Mini, includes sizeable up-front costs in addition to current fixed and variable costs— and then sets a price that earns a predetermined profit return on this money. Target pricing is practiced mainly by capital-intensive firms, such as aircraft manufacturers, and public utilities. The method for setting prices under ROI is:

$$Price = AVC + \frac{TFC}{PV} + \frac{(ROI)\,(I)}{PV}$$

where AVC = average variable cost, TFC = total fixed cost, PV = planned volume, and I = investment.

For example, during the Mini's introductory stage, prodded by Merton senior management and the knowledge that she could generally price the Mini at will, the marketing manager decided to price the Mini at a level that would produce a 10 percent profit return on investment. Thus:

$$\$1620 = \$600 + \$5{,}000{,}000/\,5000 = .10(\$1{,}000{,}000)/5000$$

Since its demand curve indicated that 5000 Minis would be sold to its accountant target market at the $1620 price, this became the Mini's introductory price.

Like other forms of cost oriented pricing, an ROI pricing strategy assumes that planned sales volume will actually be achieved at the derived price. This assumption worked well for the United States automobile industry until the 1970s, when a recession and increased foreign competition frequently made it impossible to arbitrarily raise prices to achieve ROI profit goals.

YOU SHOULD REMEMBER

Cost-based pricing strategies are most effectively employed in situations where customer and competitive responses are not dominant factors, such as when a monopoly or large public utility sets prices. The simplest cost-based strategy, cost-plus pricing, adds a desired profit to computed costs to determine price, as does markup pricing, a version of cost-plus pricing used by distributors. Breakeven point pricing considers both costs and demand factors in arriving at price points where total revenues equal total fixed and variable costs, beyond which profits grow. ROI, or target return pricing, employs cost-plus and breakeven techniques to identify a price that will earn a desired profit on invested dollars. All cost-based approaches have similar weaknesses, especially when misapplied in situations where consumer demand and competition are key considerations.

PRICE-QUALITY STRATEGIES RECOGNIZE CONSUMER PERCEPTIONS

Unlike the cost-oriented pricing strategy employed by the Mini during its monopolistic introductory stage, the Merton modem, an imitative product, employed a pricing strategy much more oriented to buyer perceptions and competitive responses. In this sense, its pricing strategy foreshadowed consumer and competitor-oriented pricing strategies to be employed by the Mini during later product life cycle stages.

In light of its imitative status, the marketing manager conceived her problem in pricing the modem as one of finding a niche for the product in terms of price-quality features where it would be most favorably perceived by Merton's ultimate consumers and distributors. As shown in Figure 17-2, a number of price-quality combinations were possible.

| | | PRICE | | |
		High	Medium	Low
	High	Premium	Penetration	Superb value
QUALITY	Medium	Overcharging	Average value	Good value
	Low	Ripoff	Poor value	Cheap value

Figure 17–2. Price quality pricing strategies.

Although, over the life cycles of both the modem and the Mini, a number of these price-quality strategies would be employed, the marketing manager decided that, initially, the modem would employ a penetration pricing strategy. A number of competitors had already adopted a high premium strategy for their modems, which were generally perceived as overpriced. With a penetration strategy, the modem would be effectively positioned against these products on price, while maintaining the high product-quality image that would characterize all products in Merton's Consumer Products line.

OLIGOPOLISTIC STRATEGIES: COPY CATS AND KINKED DEMAND

Thanks largely to its high skimming price strategy, which attracted a few large competitors with the financial and technological wherewithal to break through the Mini's patent screen and produce Mini versions of their own, the Mini entered the second, growth stage of its life cycle somewhat sooner than anticipated. During the early phases of this growth stage, the competitive climate was analagous to an oligopolistic climate, in which a few large sellers are highly sensitive to each other's marketing and pricing strategies. This sensitivity is typically reflected in the "kinked" demand curve, whereby all competitors price products at the same point—say, at point "A" in Figure 17-3.

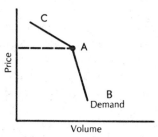

Figure 17–3. Oligopolistic kinked demand curve.

The rationale for this copy-cat pricing strategy is that if one competitor lowers its price to point B, all the competitors will follow, thus largely cancelling out the competitive advantage of the lowered price, with demand barely increasing. On the other hand, if one firm increases its price to point C, none of the other competitors will follow, and this firm will rapidly lose sales to its lower-priced competitors.

Note two characteristics of this oligopolistic pricing strategy. First, unlike monopolistic, cost-based strategies, it must also account for buyer and competitor behavior. Thus, although Merton used breakeven and ROI analyses to arrive at a kink price point, this point was now determined more by how buyers and competitors would respond to this price than by predetermined profit goals.

Second, unlike previous cost-based strategies, this oligopolistic strategy no longer aims to optimize profits, but simply to satisfy what all competitors agree, at least implicitly, are "reasonable" profit goals. In the Mini situation, this meant dropping the price from $1620 to $1400, which still produced a generous profit.

YOU SHOULD REMEMBER

Price-quality pricing strategies, based on the strong tendency of people to associate quality with price, range from a high quality/high price "premium" strategy to a low quality–low price "cheap value" strategy. Oligopoly pricing strategies, in which a few large firms compete for market share, also focus on consumer perceptions, setting satisfactory prices at a kink point from which the firms are reluctant to depart. If one firm lowers its price, the others will follow suit, and market share won't grow appreciably. If one firm raises its price, the others won't follow suit, and sales volume will decline appreciably.

MONOPOLISTIC COMPETITION: BUYER-BASED STRATEGIES

The next (maturity) stage of the Mini's product life cycle was analagous to a monopolistic competition economic climate, with many sellers, all now privy to the Mini's technology, transacting with buyers over a wide range of prices. Each of these prices, in turn, was based largely on how (and how successfully) each firm had managed to differentiate its product from competitive products. In this climate, Merton's marketing manager became much more focused on finding the combination of marketing mix elements, including price, that would most profitably differentiate the Mini from its many competitors in terms of *buyer* perceptions.

Emerging from this focus on differentiating the Mini was a major pricing strategy change initiated during the Mini's "growth" life cycle stage, and continuing into the early phases of the maturity stage. Specifically, the marketing manager adopted a buyer-based penetration pricing strategy that priced the Mini below competitive levels (at $1000) in order to entrench its strong leadership position. Largely through an effective promotion strategy aimed at both distributors and ultimate consumers, Merton managed this dramatic price reduction without losing its quality image. (Later in this chapter, we will discuss considerations involved in successfully negotiating price changes.) The dramatically increased sales volume, and economies of scale, resulting from this much lower price actually generated higher profits than were achieved during earlier life cycle stages.

DEMAND-ORIENTED PRICING STRATEGIES DISCRIMINATE, PROMOTE, AND ADJUST

When Merton made the transition from a skimming to a penetration pricing strategy, it also implemented a series of demand-based *price discrimination* and *promotional* pricing strategies directed toward ultimate consumers, and *price adjustment* strategies directed toward Merton's wholesaler and retailer intermediate customers. These strategies were designed to enhance the effectiveness of the Mini's penetration strategy by creating potent incentives for consumers to purchase the Mini, and for a mass network of distributors to carry the Mini. Creating these incentives for consumers is called a "pull" strategy, designed to pull the product through channels; when created for distributors, it's called a "push" strategy, designed to push the product through channels.

PRICE DISCRIMINATION: DIFFERENT PRICES FOR DIFFERENT SEGMENTS

Discriminatory pricing is defined as the legally sanctioned practice of selling a product at two or more prices that do not reflect a proportional difference in costs. Conditions favorable to discrimination, all prevalent in the Mini's monopolistic competitive climate, include (1) a segmentable market, with different segments (accountants, engineers, college faculty, etc.) showing different intensities of demand; (2) the inability of one segment to undersell the product to members of a segment paying a higher price; (3) cost required to police price discrimination should not exceed the extra revenues produced by discriminating; (4) price discrimination should not breed ill-will; and (5) discrimination should not violate the legal prescriptions summarized in Chapter 16.

FORMS OF PRICE DISCRIMINATION

A familiar form of price discrimination is *place* discrimination, in which, for example, a customer pays more for a seat on the 50-yard line than for a seat in the end zone, although the cost of installing and maintaining each seat is the same.

Other forms of discriminatory pricing, all implemented by Merton, included *customer*, *time*, and *product* discrimination. Following are examples of each:

- *Customer form* discrimination was employed when Merton charged college professors, who used the Minis for instructional purposes, less than the price charged members of their "accountants" target market.

- *Time form* discrimination was employed by certain of Merton's distributors, who leased Minis to small businesses. During tax preparation season, when demand for the Minis and customized software was unusually high, rental charges were considerably higher than at other periods, when prices were reduced to smooth out the demand pattern. This example also illustrates *product form* discrimination: when Merton leased its specially programmed tax preparation Minis, it charged more than for its "all purpose" models, although the actual cost of making and marketing each model was essentially the same.

FORMS OF PROMOTIONAL PRICING

Merton's promotional pricing strategy, involving both the Mini and the modem, involved pricing these products below list price, or even below cost, in order to achieve larger sales or profit goals. For example, it was not unusual for Merton's distributors to sharply discount the price of the Mini during special events, such as prior to tax preparation season when lease prices were raised, but a Mini tax package, consisting of the Mini, a modem, and a tax software program, was sharply discounted. The sizeable increase in sales of both the Mini and the modem at this attractive price easily compensated for smaller profits per unit.

Merton also made use of *loss leader* pricing when, during a special Presidents' Day promotion, it allowed distributors (in states where this practice was legal) to price the modem well below the cost to produce it. Again, additional sales of other products purchased by customers attracted to this price easily compensated for lost profits.

At the peak of its maturity stage, as competition among many Mini manufacturers became intense and differences among the Minis themselves became more difficult to perceive, Merton also made use of cash rebates as an additional incentive. This incentive had the advantage of allowing Merton to retain its original retail price and its blue chip image.

YOU SHOULD REMEMBER

During competitive climates of monopolistic competition, when products are in competitive or maturity stages of life cycles, many firms compete over a wide range of prices, and a number of demand-based pricing strategies characterize sellers' attempts to differentiate their offerings to make them more competitive. One such strategy—price discrimination—works in situations where product markets comprise segments with different demand intensities, and the discrimination won't cost too much to police, or breed ill-will, or be considered illegal. In such situations, price discrimination can favor customers, locations, time periods, or forms of the product. Another demand-based pricing strategy—promotional pricing—prices products below list or cost to differentiate offerings and attract customers. Examples include special events pricing, loss leader pricing, and rebates.

PRICE MODIFICATION STRATEGIES MEET DISTRIBUTOR'S NEEDS

Merton's early success in the marketplace—particularly the enthusiastic response among members of Merton's target markets to the innovative Mini—soon translated into equally powerful demand among retailers and wholesalers to carry Merton product lines. Before this demand among intermediary customers developed, however, Merton, with no track record to attract distributors, employed the following price adjustment strategies to reduce risk and improve income of distributors willing to stock and market the Mini.

- *Functional discounts*, also called trade discounts, are offered by manufacturers to trade channel members in return for performing distribution functions discussed in Chapter 14, including buying, stocking, selling, market research, and credit extension. As an incentive for full-line electronics products distributors to carry the Mini line, for example, Merton offered them a discount 5 percent larger than the average offered by competitors.

- *Quantity discounts* are offered to distributors who purchase merchandise in larger than normal quantities. Again, Merton offered distributors higher discounts than the competitive average to compensate them for additional costs from carrying excessive inventory.

- *Cash discounts* are price deductions offered to distributors as an incentive to pay bills on time. For example, a discount of 2/10, net 20, means that payment is due within 20 days, but the buyer can deduct 2 percent from the bill if it is paid within 10 days. Merton's terms were more generous than the average offered by competitors: 3/10, net 30.

- *Allowances* are reductions from the list price covering periodic or unanticipated contingencies such as a special promotion, or the failure of the product to sell. Recognizing early distributor perceptions that the Mini might not sell, Merton offered unusually generous return allowances to its distributors: a full refund on their purchase price, less 10 percent to cover shipping and handling charges. Promotional allowances were also extremely generous, with Merton contributing two dollars for every dollar contributed by a distributor.

In addition to this generous schedule of discounts and allowances, Merton also offered generous geographic pricing incentives to its distributors to help them compete more effectively. In devising a geographic pricing strategy, the marketing manager considered the following options:

- Under an *FOB origin* pricing strategy, merchandise shipped to distributors would be placed *free on board* a carrier, following which title and responsibility would pass on to the distributor, who would pay the freight from that point on. An advantage of this approach is its basic fairness; each distributor pays its fair share dictated by its distance from the manufacturer. However, the marketing manager perceived a sizeable disadvantage that eliminated this approach from consideration—excessively high shipping costs paid by distant distributors would put them at a competitive disadvantage vis a vis distributors paying lower freight costs.

- Under a *uniform delivered pricing strategy* (UDP), Merton would charge the same freight rate to all its distributors regardless of their location. This rate would be sufficiently high to cover Merton's shipping costs, but sufficiently low to allow individual dealers to compete effectively on price. It is inherently unfair in that freight costs are unrelated to the actual charges. For example, it might *actually* cost $20 for Merton to ship a Mini to a California distributor, and only $5 to ship the same computer to a distributor in Georgia, but under UDP, both would pay the same freight.

- Under *zone pricing*, features of both FOB and UDP are combined into a strategy that features two or more zones in each of which distributors all pay the same freight. For example, all distributors west of the Mississippi might pay a freight rate higher than that paid by distributors east of the Mississippi, but not as high as they would pay under FOB pricing. Since this approach is an amalgam of both FOB and UDP, its pros and cons are also an amalgam of these strategies: it's not as fair as FOB, but fairer than UDP· it allows distributors to keep prices at competitive levels, but for distant distributors not as effectively as with UDP.

- *Basing point pricing* is a variant on zone pricing, which takes into account the location of the firm's most lucrative markets and places a "basing point" at the center of each area, which becomes a low rate zone. For example, Merton's two largest market areas were in the New York and Chicago metropolitan areas, so each city became a basing point for low freight rates, which increased appreciably in areas of lesser potential. Even though the Minis are actually shipped from Atlanta, the assumption would be made, for freight charge purposes, that they were shipped from the basing point city.

- Under *freight absorption pricing*, the last freight option considered by the marketing manager, Merton would absorb all, or most, of the freight cost. This strategy is typically employed as a strong incentive for distributors to take on the product line. However, it can represent a sizeable profit drain to the seller.

Considering the pros and cons of these geographic pricing options in terms of Mini marketing goals—and also noting that Merton had already decided on a policy of extremely generous discounts and allowances to attract prospective distributors—the marketing manager decided on a basing point pricing strategy whereby distributors in Merton's five highest potential trading areas would pay a relatively low freight rate, which would increase in areas of lesser potential.

COMPETITION-BASED PRICING DURING PURE COMPETITION STAGE

During the decline stage of the Mini's product life cycle, analagous to a pure competition economic climate, differences among Mini models became practically impossible to perceive, and it became extremely difficult for firms to differentiate products, and base prices on these perceived differences. In this state of pure competition, the dominant pricing strategy employed by Merton and its remaining competitors was one of going-rate pricing. Similar to the kinked demand pricing strategy employed during the oligopolistic stage, this strategy had each firm base its price on the market price charged by competitors, as the best way to achieve a fair return and preserve industry harmony. To price above this market price would be foolish, because customers could get a product of equal value at a lower price; to charge below would also be foolish, because the firm wouldn't sell any more of the product than if the higher price were charged.

Another competition-based strategy employed by Merton during this decline stage, *expected profit pricing*, was used in acquiring the few large sales still available in this highly homogeneous product market. Table 17-1 shows how this approach worked in a sealed bid Merton presented to a government agency for an order of 1000 Minis.

Table 17-1. Highest expected value determines selected bid

Company Bid	Company Profit	Estimated Probability of Success	Expected Profit
$ 600,000	$ 20,000	.70	$14,000
800,000	220,000	.30	66,000
1,000,000	420,000	.05	21,000
1,200,000	620,000	.01	6,200

At the time this bid was made, Merton had managed to reduce its costs for making and marketing a Mini to $580. Thus, if it were to charge $600 for each Mini, for a total bid price of $600,000, it would make $20 profit on each Mini sold, for a total profit of $20,000. At this low bid price, collective management wisdom and past experience indicated that Merton had a 70 percent chance of getting the order, so the *expected profit* from this $600,000 bid was $14,000 (.70 × 20,000). Other expected values of bids of $800, $1000, and $1200 per Mini, following the same approach, indicated that a bid of $800,000, with a 30 percent chance of succeeding, had the highest figure—$66,000—so that was the bid Merton made.

YOU SHOULD REMEMBER

Demand-based pricing strategies can also be directed to the needs of wholesalers and retailers. Thus, a series of discounts and allowances can provide dealer incentives to effectively perform functions associated with marketing the product (functional discount), buy larger quantities of the product (quantity discount), pay bills on time (cash discount), and perform supplementary services in marketing products (allowances). Geographic pricing incentives also meet dealer needs, ranging from FOB pricing, where the dealer covers all freight charges, through UDP, zone, and basing point pricing, where freight costs are shared by dealers and the manufacturer, to freight absorption pricing, where the manufacturer assumes total freight costs. During the final stage of the PLC, analagous to a pure competition environment, competition-based pricing tends to prevail, with all competitors pricing products at the market level (going rate pricing), or using expected value pricing techniques of pricing products in relation to expected competitive prices.

PRODUCT MIX PRICING STRATEGIES: PRICE LINES, OPTIONS, CAPTIVES

Unless a product is introduced as a discrete entity in itself, pricing considerations and concerns are usually dictated by perceptions of products as components of larger product mixes and product lines. The Merton Mini, for example, was actually a line of Minis, with different price ranges and target markets; this line, in turn, was part of a mix of consumer electronics products comprising computer software, hardware, peripherals, and accessories. In this broader context, three strategies were employed by the marketing manager at various stages of the Mini's life cycle to help achieve pricing objectives: price lining, optional pricing, and captive pricing.

PRICE LINING: RANGES DEFINE QUALITY

When Merton introduced its engineer's Mini to its line of Mini PCs, many of the analyses required to peg a price for this product had already been made in pricing other PCs in the line: thus, the marketing manager already knew what profit margins the product should generate, and what kind of product image it should reflect.

Pricing this new Mini in this product line context, the marketing manager's primary concern focused on cost differences between this Mini and others in the line, prices competing firms were charging for their engineer's Minis, and customer evaluations of the Mini (generally, not as enthusiastic as perceptions of members of other Mini target markets).

Also guiding her pricing decision were considerations pertaining to establishing prices within the line of engineer's Minis, which included a number of PC models with different features and quality levels. She realized, for example, that price points must be spaced far enough apart so customers would perceive quality differences among models, or else customers will perceive no difference among the models and pay the lower price. She also realized that prices should be spaced further apart at higher levels, where consumer demand becomes more inelastic. Thus, the deluxe model at the top of the engineer's Mini line was priced at $2000—$400 more than the next lower-priced Mini, which was only priced $300 above the lowest-priced Mini.

From the viewpoint of Merton and its distributors, price lining offered a number of benefits. An assortment of products could be offered to attract many market segments, and members of these segments could be encouraged to trade up, thus increasing sales and profits. Also, a broad product line, with models throughout the price range, is an effective deterrent on competitors.

OPTIONAL PRICING: STANDARDS VS. OPTIONS

Under an *optional pricing strategy*, companies face the problem of which products to include as options, and which as standards, with their major products. For example, an auto manufacturer can offer a stripped-down model at a very attractive price, while a competitor, charging a higher price for essentially the same product, offers these options as standard equipment. Merton's marketing manager decided it was more consistent with Consumer Division marketing objectives to avoid a stripped-down image, so a number of accessories (including the modem) that competitors offered as options were standard equipment with Mini models, and agressively promoted as such.

CAPTIVE PRICING: HIGHER AFTERPRICES

Under a *captive pricing strategy*, firms produce products that must be used with the main product and that influence the price of both products and overall profitability. A camera manufacturer, for example, might set a low price for cameras, and a higher-than-market price for the film that must be used with the camera, thus making up with film profits what is lost on camera profits. This strategy proved highly effective for Merton when, during the competitive stage of the Mini's life cycle, it drastically lowered the price on its Mini; concurrently, the price on software customized to various Mini models began to rise, thus cushioning the profit drop.

PRICE CHANGE STRATEGIES: WHEN AND HOW TO DROP OR RAISE

Whether perceived as a discrete entity, or as a component of larger product mixes or lines, a product will sooner or later have to have its price changed; for example, lowered to meet competitive challenges, or raised to reflect favorable supply/demand conditions in the marketplace.

Cutting prices: Typical reasons for cutting a price were all in effect during the late maturity and decline stages of products in the Mini line; falling market share had produced excess capacity and the need to generate sales to fill this excess. Another key reason for cutting prices was illustrated by the drastic price cut in the Mini during its competitive life-cycle stage—a drive to achieve a position of market leadership, with the economies of scale associated with this position.

Raising prices: As noted in Chapter 16, a relatively small price increase can lever dramatic profit increases, assuming demand doesn't decrease appreciably as a consequence of this increase.

Although profitable price increases are almost always more difficult to implement than price decreases, they can often be justified for the following reasons:

- *Unexpectedly high demand for the product* justifies increasing a price revealed as too low.

- *Cost inflation* forces all manufacturers in a field to raise prices more or less simultaneously.

- *Unbundling of services* often provides a justification for increasing the price of individual services. For example, the tax division of a large accounting firm might unbundle financial planning services, which can be value-priced in terms of customer perceptions of the value of the service, from routine tax compliance activities, which are billed at a lower hourly rate.

- *Discounts*, allowances, rebates, and other price adjustment arrangements can permit increases in the product's price. This is precisely what the marketing manager did when the remarkable demand for early Minis forced distributors to handle the line, and these incentives were no longer needed.

- *Use of escalator clauses*, with built-in contractual assurances that an agreed-upon profit will be realized, often permits price increases in negotiating government contracts.

ANTICIPATING REACTIONS TO PRICE CHANGES

Regardless of whether a product price is raised or lowered, there is bound to be some response to this change from customers and competitors. Since some of these responses can reflect favorably, and others unfavorably, on the proposed change, an important part of the price planning process typically involves anticipating these responses and taking measures to insure that they are favorable. For example, when Merton raised the price of its Mini during its introductory stage, the marketing manager sent out a promotional message that this increase was evidence that the Mini was an excellent value, and that, as such, it might soon be unobtainable even at the new, higher price. Downplayed was the notion that the increase was related to seller greed.

Similarly, when Merton lowered the price of the Mini during competitive and maturity stages, a promotional message went out to counteract possible perceptions that the product was obsolete and about to be replaced by a later version, or that the price would come down even more if customers just waited it out.

YOU SHOULD REMEMBER

Price lining can enhance sales and profits by helping sellers segment markets, attract market members, and trade up to more expensive models. It can also help attract distributors and discourage competitors. Key considerations are that price points can be spaced so differences can be perceived, and be further apart for products at the top end of the line. Optional pricing addresses the problem of whether to include accessories as standard items with the main product, or as options at an extra charge. Either way, the strategy can be effectively promoted. Captive pricing sets lower prices for the main product in the assurance that the purchaser will have to buy a higher-priced product related to this product, such as film relates to cameras. When a decision is made to either raise or lower prices, it is usually good price planning strategy to anticipate buyer and competitor responses to this change, and try to assure, via promotion, that a favorable interpretation emerges.

KNOW THE CONCEPTS
DO YOU KNOW THE BASICS?

1. In terms of conditions favoring either a penetration or a skimming price strategy, discuss the strategy most likely to be employed by (1) a preeminent brain surgeon and (2) McDonald's, in introducing its new line of salads.

2. Assume you have rented an office, hired a receptionist-secretary, purchased necessary office furniture, and set yourself up in business as a financial advisor. During your first year, you anticipate total fixed costs for professional amenities will total $36,000. You also estimate that you will put in 150 billable hours a month, during which you would like to earn a salary of $20 per hour. Beyond this rate, you would like to make a profit of $5 an hour. Using the cost-plus formula, determine the fee you will charge your clients.

3. If a retailer purchases a can of soup for 24 cents and sells it for 36 cents, what is the percentage markup on the selling price? Using the markup formula, determine the price the retailer would charge for each can of soup, assuming a desired markup of 40 percent.

4. Assume, as the owner of a large automotive service station, you have just hired a tire specialist who will be responsible for all work pertaining to customer tires (changing, rotating, balancing, selling, recommending, etc.). You have purchased $10,000 worth of specialized equipment for this specialist to use in his work, and have agreed to pay him $25 an hour, charging customers $35 an hour for his services. Using the breakeven formula, determine the number of hours it will take to break even on your investment in this specialist.

5. What are the two major criticisms of cost-plus pricing, and how are these criticisms illustrated in the examples given in (2) and (4), above?

6. Identify the price-quality strategy implicit in the following product-market situations:

   • The Mercedes Benz automotive company never mentions price in its commercials

   • Old Original Bookbinder's restaurant in Philadelphia gets a "Not Worth It" review in the Rice-Wolf *Where to Eat in America* book: "Despite top quality seafood at top prices, you're likely to feel like an intruder..."

   • *Where to Eat in America* also gives this review to the breakfast served at Tony's Spaghetti House in New Orleans: "...the best biscuits in the city, big platters of sausage and ham at dirt-cheap prices."

7. Explain how foreign competition in the luxury automobile market segment changed the situation for domestic automobile manufacturers from that depicted in diagram A to that depicted in diagram B.

A   B

8. What kinds of price discrimination are illustrated by the following product-market situations?

• Motel chains offer discounts to senior citizens.

• The excursion rate on the Lackawanna Railroad, between the hours of 9:30 AM and 4:30 PM, is considerably less than the rush hour rate.

• Orchestra section theater seats cost twice as much as seats in the balcony.

9. In terms of conditions that favor price discrimination, why would it be difficult to implement such a policy for a Bruce Springsteen concert?

10. Describe situations in which a local department store makes use of (1) loss leader pricing, (2) special events pricing, and (3) rebates.

11. Put yourself in the position of an automobile dealer, during the early 80s, when automobile manufacturers resorted to aggressive rebate programs to sell more cars. From your perspective, what are the potential risks and benefits of such programs?

12. Describe how a large wholesaler like McKesson and Robbins might use discounts and allowances to enhance revenues and profits of its retailers.

13. Given the following data, which bid should a company make?

company bid	company profit	estimated probability of success
$5000	$1000	.80
10,000	2200	.40
20,000	3500	.20

TERMS FOR STUDY

allowances
basing-point pricing
cash discounts
cheap value strategy
competition-based strategies
customer-basis discrimination
discriminatory pricing
expected-profit pricing
FOB origin
freight-absorption pricing
functional discounts
going-rate pricing
kink point
loss leader
overcharge strategy
penetration strategy

place discrimination
product-based pricing strategies
product form discrimination
promotional pricing
quantity discounts
rebates
ripoff strategies
ROI pricing
sealed-bid pricing
skimming strategy
special-event pricing
superb-value strategy
target-market pricing
time-basis discrimination
uniform-delivered pricing
zone pricing

ANSWERS
KNOW THE BASICS

1. For the preeminent brain surgeon, conditions favor a skimming strategy: there is little chance that a high price will create excessive competition, since the brain surgeon's skills are unique. Also, there is a huge market, comprising, potentially, anyone with a heart, able to afford the surgeon's services (through insurance plans, community donations, etc.). Additionally, a high price will reinforce the aura of preeminence so important to the confidence of the doctor's patients, and help the hospital for which he works generate a desired profit return. McDonald's, on the other hand, would employ a penetration pricing strategy: it achieves great economies of scale through the high volume brought on by low prices, thanks to its production line food preparation methods; if it increases its price, it will attract strong competition from all the Wendy's and Burger King fast food restaurants which also use penetration pricing. Also, its market is large and highly price-sensitive.

2. $\dfrac{\$36,000 \text{ (fixed cost)} + \$36,000 \text{ (variable costs)} + \$9000 \text{ (projected profit)}}{1800 \text{ hours } (12 \times 150 \text{ per month})} = \$45$

3. (a) $24/36 = 33.3\%$; (b) purchase cost/1 − markup percentage
   $24/1 − .40 = 24/.60 = 40$ cents

4. Breakeven point (units) = Total fixed costs/Price — variable costs (per unit)

$$\frac{\$10,000}{\$35 - \$25} = 1000 \text{ hours}$$

5. The two major criticisms of cost-plus pricing pertain to situations in which this approach is misapplied; specifically, situations where (1) demand declines with higher prices, and/or (2) costs are difficult or impossible to assign to specific products. In situation 4, above, both of these situations probably exist: in a service business where customers can have tire work done in literally dozens of stations within a short radius, there would almost surely be a relationship between price charged and demand; also, it would seem a difficult task to determine, precisely, how such common costs as lighting and heating the service station could be precisely assigned to the work of the tire man. Situation 2, above, however, isn't quite so clear cut. Conceiveably, the financial advisor is perceived by her clients as a unique source of valuable advice, for which price would not be a dominant concern. Also, since only the advisor's billable hours are incurring these costs, they are easier to accurately assign.

6. The Mercedes Benz: High quality/high price: Premium
Original Bookbinder's: Medium quality/high price: Overcharging
Tony's Spaghetti House: High quality/low price: Superb value

7. Before offshore competition became a major factor in the domestic automobile industry, the domestic industry could be viewed as an oligopoly, with few firms—basically, the "Big Three" of Ford, Chrysler, and General Motors—holding prices at a tacitly agreed-upon kink point. (General Motors, achieving huge economies of scale through its market leadership position, held its automobile prices at unrealistically high levels in order not to undercut its competition and risk becoming a monopoly.) However, aggressive competition—primarily from German and Japanese competitors—transformed this oligopolistic environment into one of monopolistic competition, where kink points are replaced by demand curves, and successful firms manage to push their curves to the right as customer perceptions are based on nonprice features.

8. Motel chain: customer discrimination
Excursion rate: time discrimination
Theater seats: place discrimination

9. Of the four forms of discrimination, the most likely form practiced at a Bruce Springsteen concert would be *place* discrimination, with tickets close to the bandstand costing considerably more than bleacher seat tickets; time discrimination probably wouldn't be practiced, since the concert would only be given at one time in each city visited; customer discrimination probably wouldn't be practiced (except, perhaps, for a few attendees designated by Springsteen), since most attendees would be from the

same market segment; for example, there wouldn't be that many senior citizens or children attending the concert. Also, product discrimination probably wouldn't apply, since Bruce Springsteen doesn't come in different models, for which different prices could be asked.

However, the ticket scalping problem could make even place discrimination difficult, to the extent that it tends to violate 3 conditions required for effective price discrimination, i.e., one group shouldn't be encouraged to sell lower priced tickets to another group, but, during the day of the concert, bleacher seat ticket holders could get grandstand prices; also, it shouldn't cost excessively to police price discrimination, and it probably would in this situation; finally, discrimination shouldn't create ill-will, which large-scale scalping does.

10. Some examples from newspaper advertising of use of loss leader, special events, and rebate pricing by a local department store: (1) Nova Scotia salmon is priced below to store's cost to encourage people to make purchases in its gourmet food store; (2) a Presidents' Day sale offers discounted prices on such popular products as videocassette recorders and food processors; (3) In addition to discounted prices during the Presidents' Day sale, the food processor also offered a rebate on its price.

11. Possible benefits of rebates include additional sales emerging from the incentive represented by the cash refund, and the fact that the image of the product probably won't be cheapened as would be the case if the price were discounted. Possible disadvantages: other competitors will follow suit, and offer equal or larger discounts, thus also discounting the rebate incentive; also, rebates might actually deter sales if prospective customers decide to wait for these competitive rebates.

12. A large wholesaler like McKesson & Robbins would help improve the profitability of its retailer customers through a series of discounts and allowances to improve sales and reduce costs. For example, promotional allowances would help retailers finance sales programs to improve sales, while retailer costs would be reduced through functional discounts for performing such functional activities as stocking and delivering merchandise; cash discounts for paying bills on time; and quantity discounts for buying and stocking merchandise in larger, more economical quantities.

13. The company should put in a bid of $10,000 which produces the largest expected profit ($2200 $\times$ .40 = $880).

18 PROMOTION: INDIRECT

KEY TERMS

advertising any paid, nonpersonal presentation and promotion in the mass media of ideas, goods, or services by an identified sponsor

promotion the communication of information by a seller to influence attitudes and behavior of potential buyers

public relations communication with noncustomer publics including employees, organized labor, suppliers, stockholders, financial and other institutions, and all levels of government

publicity any nonpaid, nonpersonal news-oriented presentation of a product, service, or business unit in the mass media

sales promotion marketing activities (other than personal selling, advertising, and publicity) that stimulate consumer purchasing and dealer effectiveness in the short-term

---

WHY PROMOTION IS NEEDED

The world does *not* "beat a path to the door" of the maker of a better mousetrap. Even though the product or service possesses superior quality, is offered at a price that is right, and is distributed to make it easily available, there is yet another requirement that must be met before people can become customers. They need to be informed that the product or service exists, and persuaded that it presents a better solution to a problem that they perceive they have.

Because the public is exposed to hundreds of such messages each day they "tune them out" by selective exposure and selective perception. Successful marketers have to break through the jumble of "to whom it may concern" notices just to be seen or heard. Then, the message must strike a responsive chord or it will not be recalled and acted upon. This achievement of being noticed favorably has to be accomplished on a regular basis because people do not take immediate action and have to be reminded again and again.

What are the best means to get a message through to potential customers? How can their attention be attracted, and how can it be held long enough to convince them that with all the products available, a particular offer is the best solution to their problem? How can they be helped to remember who made the offer when they are ready to buy? These last two chapters discuss how the fourth component in the marketing mix, *promotion*, works to accomplish this critical communication task.

We shall see that promotional efforts must be carefully planned and coordinated since each promotion tool is best for a particular job and promotional activities interact with the other components of the marketing mix. The Islandshares Group case, introduced in Chapter 1, will be used for illustration.

The Islandshares Group

Before the young couple purchased the time-share from the Islandshares Group introduced in Chapter 1, they had been exposed to advertisements and travel pieces in their Sunday newspaper but did not read them because they were furnishing their new apartment.

The following year, they noticed an advertisement offering a free information kit titled "Summer Activities at Hilton Head Island, South Carolina" and wrote for it.

PROMOTION IS A MIX

Promotion is the communication of information by the seller to influence attitudes and behavior of the buyer. The main tools of Indirect Promotion are *advertising*, *publicity*, and *sales promotion*. In addition, *public relations, packaging*, and *word-of-mouth* also affect attitude change. Direct Promotion, which influences buyer behavior—purchase or commitment—is discussed in Chapter 19, which covers personal selling.

Just as the marketing mix is a variable blend of product-service, pricing, place-distribution, and promotion, the components of the promotion mix may be combined in an infinite number of proportions.

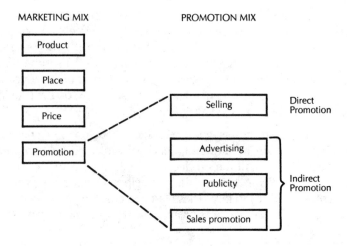

Figure 18–1. Relationship of the Promotion Mix to the Marketing Mix.

THE RELATIONSHIP OF PROMOTION TO OTHER MARKETING MIX COMPONENTS

In order to illustrate its composition more clearly, models of the marketing mix typically show each of its components—product, price, distribution, and promotion—neatly separated by lines or boxes. In practice, these functions are mingled, resulting in dynamic interaction among them. For example, if a product is targeted toward a market segment that appreciates and demands top quality, the higher costs associated with its manufacture will require a high price. Promotion must communicate to the target segment that the price reflects value because of the benefits deriving from the product's superior features. Distribution will typically be limited to select outlets where patrons expect to pay higher prices for the best merchandise, and to receive warranties and full service.

In contrast, promotion for products offered through volume-oriented outlets will emphasize discounted prices but feature a narrow selection of only the most popular models. These are usually products that have been presold by national advertising. As a camera department clerk in a chain store noted, "People don't care about model numbers. They come in and ask for 'the camera James Garner shows on TV '"

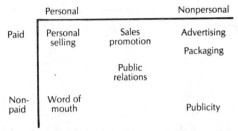

	Personal		Nonpersonal
Paid	Personal selling	Sales promotion	Advertising
			Packaging
		Public relations	
Non-paid	Word of mouth		Publicity

Figure 18–2. Promotion Mix Components.

PROMOTION MIX CHARACTERISTICS

Figure 18-2 illustrates how components of the Promotion Mix range from those involving a high degree of interpersonal contact, such as personal selling, to those where there is no personal contact, such as advertising. Sales promotion activities can overlap several areas to include, for example, members of the sales force handing out advertising literature and demonstrating the product at a trade show.

Public Relations, "organizational body language," is placed in the center of the model because it involves every activity, from personal to nonpersonal and paid as well as nonpaid, that can affect an organization's image in the minds of the publics mentioned in Chapter 3. Influences include employee appearance and attitudes toward customers, news items about company endeavors such as sponsoring a neighborhood athletic team, the appearance of company buildings and lawns (Johnson & Johnson's "Plants Can Be Beautiful" philosophy), and statements and actions during corporate crises.

Because it is not paid for, publicity cannot be controlled and is a two-edged sword that can cut both ways. Discussing publicity at a seminar in New York, one public relations specialist quipped that he spends half of his time trying to get clients' names to appear in the media, and the other half of the time trying to keep the names out! Later in the chapter we shall meet some of the tools that can help obtain more positive coverage.

YOU SHOULD REMEMBER

Contrary to popular legend, a superior product does not "sell itself." Every component of the marketing mix—the product/service, the price, place (distribution), and promotion—makes a unique, vital contribution to final sales success. The Promotion element is itself a mix, consisting of indirect tools—advertising, publicity, and sales promotion, and a direct component—personal selling. The objectives of promotion are to inform, persuade, and remind. The various functions of the promotion mix are merged into the marketing mix blend.

THE COMMUNICATION PROCESS

From ancient times, people have tried to understand what is involved in human communication—the floating of an idea from one mind to another. Aristotle described the process as having three parts: a speaker, a message, and a listener. However, the communication process is extremely complex. In the centuries since Aristotle, dozens of other definitions and models of communication have been advanced, including very mathematical ones dealing with the transfer of data bits from one computer to another.

Webster's *New Collegiate Dictionary* defines communication as "a process by which information is exchanged between individuals through a common system of symbols, signs, or behavior." Instructional or informational communication stresses learning whereas persuasion stresses yielding.

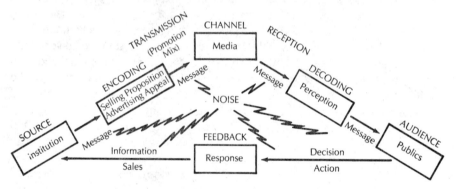

Figure 18–3. The marketing communications process.

Figure 18-3 incorporates the main concepts that are common among recent communications models and illustrates the stages through which a message passes as it flows from the sender, or *source*, to the receiver, or *audience*.

Before we can send a letter to a friend, our mental images have to be converted into a form that will be understood by our friend and that can be transmitted, so we write them down, or *encode* them. If we telephone our friend, the encoding will be in the form of spoken words—oral sounds. An amateur radio operator might literally encode the message into Morse code. The Islandshares Group combined printed copy with color illustrations to create an image that would be transmissable through print.

The next stage, *transmission* through a *channel*, requires that we affix postage and mail our letter, or pick up the telephone and dial into the telephone system. (The radio ham would switch her transmitter on and use a telegraph key to tap out the message.) Islandshares placed its copy in travel magazines, Sunday supplements, and in brochures mailed to a list of names.

At the other end of the channel, our friend *receives* and opens the mail, or answers the ring and picks up the telephone. It is obvious, but extremely important to remember, that the person at the receiving end be able to *decode* the message from the form in which it is received. If the *audience* is unable to read, or speaks a different language, or if the answering radio amateur is out of practice at deciphering Morse code, little communication occurs. Encoding and decoding depend upon a *common frame of reference.*

Because communication requires effort, expense, and time, most messages are sent with the expectation of some kind of response, or *feedback.* This may merely be acknowledgment of receipt, or it may take the form of action, such as filling out an order blank and enclosing a check, or requesting information about Hilton Head Island time-shares.

Every stage of the communication process is vulnerable to interference from *noise*, which has been defined as "any factor that reduces the effectiveness of the communication process." Noise can be internal and external. Internal noise might be distracting thoughts. External noise usually occurs in physical forms such as electrical interference in a television channel or in the radio atmosphere. It could be a loud fan circulating air in a crowded auditorium. It is all of the other messages distractingly clamoring for attention, such as the many advertisements that surrounded the Islandshares Group message. (Many of the Islandshares brochures were thrown out, unopened, by recipients who regarded them as junk mail.)

YOU SHOULD REMEMBER

Communication is the process by which information is exchanged. The source is the originator of a message. The message is encoded so as to be understood by a target audience and to pass through a communication channel common to the source and the audience. Received, the message must be capable of being decoded by the audience. For communication to occur it is necessary for the encoder and decoder to have a common frame of reference. Noise is any factor which interferes with this process.

PLANNING AND DEVELOPING EFFECTIVE MARKETING COMMUNICATIONS

As Executive Secretary of the Hilton Head Realtors Association (HRA), a trade group of real estate firms on Hilton Head Island, Sandra Weiss is responsible for planning and developing a promotional campaign to assist member firms by improving their marketing effectiveness.

With the communications model in mind, she follows the steps described by a leading marketing authority, Philip Kotler:[1]

1. Identify the target audience.

2. Determine communication objectives.

3. Design the message.

4. Select communication channels.

5. Develop the total promotional budget.

6. Decide on a promotion mix.

7. Measure the results of the promotion.

8. Manage and coordinate the total communication process.

To help *identify the target audience*, the market segment with the best prospects for becoming property owners, Ms. Weiss obtained information from member realtors about present property owners. This indicated that most property was sold to vacationers who already owned a time-share—retirees and investors.

Communication objectives are the response sought from the promotion. Depending upon whether the audience is in the cognitive, affective, or behavior stage, the response, based on the Hierarchy-of-Effects model, might be Awareness, Knowledge, Liking, Preference, or Conviction, and, ultimately, Purchase. As an aid to determining which market segments offered the most attractive potential, i.e., which groups were in the Conviction stage and thus closest to making a purchase, Ms. Weiss prepared the matrix shown in Figure 18-4. Her research, based on data collected from cooperating HRA realtors, indicated that

READINESS STAGES

TARGET AUDIENCE	COGNITIVE		AFFECTIVE			BEHAVIOR
	Awareness	Knowledge	Liking	Preference	Conviction	Purchase
Vacationers						
Investers						
Retirees						

Figure 18-4. Hierarchy-of-Effects Model.

- 90% of those who responded to the advertisements in travel magazines and Sunday supplements were from the Carolinas and Georgia, the states proximate to Hilton Head Island. Their requests for the information packet placed them in the Liking stage. With some money budgeted to the right

---

1. Kotler, Philip. *Marketing Mangement: Analysis, Planning, and Control.* 5th ed. Englewood Cliffs, NJ: Prentice-Hall, Inc., 1984.

promotion tools, a portion of this group could cost-effectively be moved into the Preference and Conviction stages.

- Test mailings to more distant states, inviting potential property buyers to visit and enjoy a free meal and free round of golf, resulted in a very low percentage response, due to lack of knowledge about the Hilton Head area. These persons would have to be brought through all of the stages of the model, from Awareness to Conviction, before they were prospects, a costly and time-consuming process.

- There was a 27-percent chance of closing (selling) relatives of existing property owners. This placed them in the Conviction stage and made them the primary target audience.

- Approximately 18-percent of time-share owners "traded up" to property ownership with some persuasion.

Message Design is concerned with the content, or appeal, and the structure, format, and source of the message. The *appeal* is the reason that the audience should take the action requested—the benefit that they will derive. It is "the one best thing to say about the product"—the Unique Selling Proposition (USP). It may be rational, emotional, or moral and it is an important device in positioning the offering against competition. Message *structure* is concerned with whether the communicator should draw a conclusion or leave that to the audience, and whether to mention shortcomings along with benefits. The message *format* includes such decisions as the headline, copy, color, and illustrations to use with a print ad, or the script, sound, and camera angles with electronic media. The final consideration in message design, the *source*, considers the credibility of the spokesperson. Credibility is enhanced by expertise, trustworthiness, and likability.

There were two appeals that Ms. Weiss felt were equally strong, depending upon the target audience segment:

- a rational appeal to investors to take advantage of property value appreciation

- an emotional appeal to vacationers and retirees stressing the great beauty and breadth of activities at Hilton Head

Inasmuch as they were not mutually exclusive, and few persons are averse to financial gain, she decided to include a low-key rational appeal along with a strong emotional theme.

Communication channels can be categorized as *Personal*, involving salespersons, experts (well-known golf and tennis professionals at Hilton Head), and social contacts, and *Nonpersonal*, including media, environments (such as stores), and events (house tours, golf tournaments). Ms. Weiss successfully utilizes both, with advertising and personal selling predominant, supported by public relations and, when obtainable, publicity. The information kit mailed to the young professional couple from Georgia, and the advertisement that prompted their request for it, are examples of the nonpersonal channel communications. Personal channels are facilitated by the extensive recreational facilities (*The Golfer's Guide to Hilton Head Island and Islands Nearby* describes 22 professional-caliber courses), which provide an environment for easy social interaction with opinion leaders, and discussion of properties. HRA also provides training in selling techniques for sales associates of member realty firms.

With the communication objectives defined, and message and channel decisions made, the *total promotional budget* can be prepared. There are several approaches to budgeting:

The *affordable* method estimates how much money can be set aside for promotional expenses and earmarks it. If the estimate is accurate or conservative, it minimizes the danger of overspending. However, this tactic does not lend itself to the aggressive promotion traditional in real estate marketing.

Computing the promotional budget as a *percentage-of-sales* precludes overspending because every promotional dollar has already paid for itself out of the sales it helped generate. Merely having to multiply the previous year's sales by a predetermined percentage simplifies decision-making. Unfortunately, sales does not cause promotion—it is the other way around. In a period of declining sales, when promotional effort should be increased to boost sagging revenues, the money available is capped off at progressively lower levels. This is analogous to a pilot taking off and, when hit by a downdraft and losing altitude, reducing the plane's throttle instead of increasing climb power.

A common method of budgeting for promotion is to estimate what competitors are spending, on the average, and then match it. The thinking goes, "All of our competitors can't be wrong, and by averaging we will be in the middle of the range anyway. We won't be encouraging a promotion war and cutting into our profits by overspending, yet we will be competitive." This *competitive parity* approach assumes that competitors are knowledgeable about promotion budgets when, in fact, they may be setting theirs by following each other. As Thomas Carlyle once said: "I do not believe in the wisdom of collective ignorance."

Because of the shortcomings of the preceding techniques, Ms. Weiss utilizes the *objective-and-task* method for establishing her promotional budget. Using a management-by-objectives approach, she obtains a consensus among member firms regarding achievable sales goals in the vacationer, retiree, and investor market segments. The grand total of all member firms is then set as the quantified objective to be achieved by the promotion mix.

Since HRA has been successful in attracting and selling prospects, Ms. Weiss decided to continue the existing *promotion mix*. Expressed in percentage of budget, this is: advertising–35%, personal selling–40%, and sales promotion–25% (including preparation of press kits for publicity). If historical data on previous campaigns were not available, she would have HRA's advertising agency run pretests of the promotional material using a sample of the target audience. During the year, to the extent feasible, Ms. Weiss monitors the progress of the promotions in each target market, and at the end of the season, *measures the results of the promotion*. She feels that the best promotion mix evolves over time, with modifications and corrections suggested by the accumulating yearly data.

Managing and coordinating the total marketing communication process, the last (and continuing) step in developing effective marketing communications, involves the implementation of the promotion mix tools. Advertising, sales promotion, and publicity will be examined next.

Table 18-1. Major Indirect Promotion Tools.

	DEFINITION	SCOPE	CHARACTERISTICS
ADVERTISING	Paid, non-personal presentation of ideas, goods, or services by an identified sponsor.	Short- to long-term Influences attitude changes. Covers large geographic area.	Public Pervasive Expressive Impersonal
PUBLICITY	Mention of organization, product, or person in print or electronic media.	Short-term May be positive or negative.	Non-paid Non-personal
SALES PROMOTION	Incentive offering to middlemen or to consumers to stimulate sales.	Short-term One-time Links and enhances other prom. tools	Informative Premiums Inviting

---

YOU SHOULD REMEMBER

Promotional Communications strategy starts with selection of the target market. Once the market segment is identified, communication objectives can be determined. These objectives are based on that segment's stage of readiness, and are designed to move segment members toward purchase.

At this point, the entire promotion mix is being assembled, and the *total* promotional budget to support it. Only after this top-level planning has been concluded can specific advertising, sales promotion, and personal selling decisions be made.

ADVERTISING

It will be recalled that advertising is *paid, nonpersonal* communication by an *identified sponsor* through *media*. Its objectives are threefold:

- *to inform* about new products, uses, changes, the advertiser, services available, and any other facts that need to be known by the market.

- *to persuade* the audience to purchase, change brands, perceive differently, request more information. The Hilton Head Realtors Association seeks to inform potential purchasers of Islandshares Group time shares or property of the availability of these offerings. Because it would be prohibitively expensive and inefficient to purchase space to provide the details wanted by interested persons, even in the three-state geographic area from which 90-percent of the customers are drawn, the advertisements persuade the audience to send for an information kit. Persons who respond have pre-qualified themselves by taking the trouble to order the kit and are a select group on the threshold of the affective stage. It is cost-effective to send them a packet crammed with information.

- *to remind* of a product's existence, of the need for a product, of where it is available.

MESSAGE DECISIONS

Message design—focusing on one memorable benefit—done in the overall promotional planning stage, now serves as the guide for generating the advertising message. Suggested criteria for message evaluation are *desirability* (something positive or interesting should be said about the product), *exclusiveness* (the product should be distinguished or set apart from competing products), and *believability* (the message itself should be credible or provable).

There are many resorts catering to vacationers and retirees. All offer a fine climate, beautiful environment, and recreational facilities. In the mind of the prospect, minor differences blur and one location is confused with others. It has been suggested that the average person can only accurately recall up to three items in a given category, due to the bewildering array of categories of things with which we are faced today. In order to cope with this complexity, people rank things—setting them on steps of imaginary ladders in the mind. If your product or location is not at the top of the ladder—positioned as number one—it is in danger of not being recalled. Attempting to unseat an image is an exercise in futility because people resist attempts to change their thinking. Creating a new category where your product will be number one is the equivalent of trying to cram another ladder in the overcrowded mindspace and is opposed. One successful approach to the problem has been to utilize the entrenched competitor as a reference—to position the new product in relation to the better-known, as in the classic "We're number two so we try harder" or "We're the Hawaii of the Caribbean."[2]

MESSAGE EXECUTION

—the style, tone, selection of words, and format of the appeal

Ms. Weiss decided on a Slice-of-life *style*, showing people enjoying the recreational facilities at Hilton Head. Other possibilities considered were Lifestyle and Mood or image. Other types of products may use such styles as Fantasy, Musical, Personality symbol, Testimonial, Scientific evidence, or Technical expertise. The tone of the message is upbeat with "The East Coast's Own Island in the Sun" slogan.

MEDIA DECISIONS

Media decisions are based on cost-effective delivery of the desired number of exposures to the target audience. Considerations are:

- *Reach*: the number of persons or households exposed at least once per specified time period to a media schedule.

- *Frequency*: the number of times within the time period that an average person is exposed to the message.

- *Impact*: the synergistic effect from having the exposure in the "right" medium for the subject matter (Hilton Head ads in a travel magazine as opposed to a hobby publication).

MEDIA TYPES

Major media types are print, including newspapers and magazines, electronic, including television, and AM and FM radio, direct mail, and outdoor. The advertising agency employed by HRA provided Ms. Weiss with rates and data and recommended the newspaper Sunday supplement with selected travel magazines, outdoor signage on the mainland, and direct mail. Criteria included *cost per thousand* persons reached by the newspaper and magazines, modified by *audience quality*, *audience attention probability*, and *editorial quality* (prestige and credibility of the vehicle).

---

2. Ries, Al, and Jack Trout. *Positioning: The Battle for Your Mind.* Rev ed. New York: Warner Books, 1986.

MEDIA TIMING

The last decision concerned the scheduling of the advertisements.

Macroscheduling is concerned with *seasonal patterns* and *monthly carryover* (the rate at which the effect of the past advertising diminishes over time).

Microscheduling deals with obtaining the maximum impact during shorter periods of time, commonly a month. Options include *concentrating* the advertising during a short period, perhaps a week, versus running the same amount at a lower level *continuously* or *intermittently*. A further variation can be obtained by modulating the level, either rising, falling, or alternating.

YOU SHOULD REMEMBER

The objectives of advertising are to *inform, persuade,* or *remind.* Advertising decisions involve two areas: *message* and *media.* Message decisions include message generation: what to say—the one best thing to say—and how to say it. Media decisions are concerned with the selection of media types (television, radio, newspapers, magazines, direct mail, and outdoor) and the cost-effectiveness of delivery, and are based upon the reach, frequency, and impact of media vehicles (specific radio and television stations, and individual newspapers, and magazines). Media *timing* is the scheduling and patterning of advertising messages in a continuous campaign.

SALES PROMOTION

Objectives–Some of the main objectives of sales promotion are:

- *Consumer-users.* encourage a higher level of usage, and attract users of competing brands.

- *Consumer-nonuser*: encourage trial.

- *Retailers*: encourage carrying of higher inventory levels and stocking of related items; build brand loyalty and offset competitors' promotions.

- *Sales Force.* assist in introduction of new products and models, and encourage more prospecting.

Tools–Samples, coupons, premiums, point-of-purchase displays, trade promotions, contests, sweepstakes, games, and presence at conventions and trade shows.

In order to move vacationers, investors, and retirees into the behavior phase and successfully sell a time-share or piece of property, it is necessary to have the sales person meet prospects face-to-face to make a sales presentation. The tools of sales promotion were employed by Ms. Weiss to accomplish this.

In the information package mailed in response to the advertisement-generated request were a copy of *Island Events*, a slick, four-color magazine with a directory of dining, recreation, shopping, and entertainment facilities, and a listing of real estate firms, an explanation of time-share advantages, and the *Golfer's Guide*. On the inside front cover of *Island Events* was a full-page, four-color advertisement with photograph of a $40 dinner and headlined "We're Giving Away Free Seafood Dinners." A telephone number was provided so that interested parties, as a necessary prerequisite to the dinner, could call to arrange a tour of the sponsoring beach and country club. Part of the tour would be the sales presentation.

Relatives of property owners on Hilton Head were reached by having a contest to see which resident could bring in the largest number of relatives and friends *who ended up purchasing property*. The winner received a Hawaiian vacation with family. Everyone who generated at least one sale received a free $40 seafood dinner.

Program Decisions–Ms. Weiss had to decide on the size of the incentive ($40 dinners and Hawaiian trip), conditions for participation (take the tour and listen to the sales presentation; bring interested prospects to listen to the sales presentation), the duration, timing, and budget. Other considerations were lead-time needed for the contest, and evaluation of the final results.

PUBLIC RELATIONS AND PUBLICITY

Objectives–To obtain favorable publicity (and counter negative publicity), and to protect the corporate image by handling rumors and adverse publicity.

Tools–Press relations, product publicity, internal corporate communications (house organs), external corporate communications (Annual Report, information brochures), and government relations (lobbying).

Ms. Weiss tried to maintain excellent rapport with the local media. Passes were arranged for reporters to attend the Heritage Classic golf tournament at which many famous golfers turned up on tour. When a celebrity purchased property at one of the plantations, this would be written up and supplied to editors. Since publicity is free, there is no control over how the article will be written up, if it appears at all. Editors are usually besieged with agents trying to place mention for their clients and may tell the agent, "Don't be greedy. You were in last month. Give someone else a chance." To improve chances of appearing in print, Ms. Weiss supplied information releases in the same format as that used at the newspaper. This simplified the job for copy editors, who didn't need to rewrite, but many exercised their prerogative and restated and edited the articles anyway.

Criteria for Publicity–The major requirement is that the piece have a "news peg" and be credible (and supported with facts). Some of the Hilton Head Island events that were written up included celebration of the thirtieth anniversary of the first plantation development, art exhibits, beauty contests, tennis and golf competitions, and sponsorship by the HRA of a dance to raise funds for southern farmers whose farms suffered from a heavy drought one summer.

YOU SHOULD REMEMBER

Sales promotion is employed with channel members (mostly retailers) and the sales force as well as with consumers. It fills a need for short-term, offpeak sales stimulation, and noncontinuous enhancement of other promotion mix components (mainly advertising and personal selling). Its tools include samples, coupons, cents-off price-packs, premiums, point-of-purchase displays, demonstrations, trade promotions, conventions and trade shows, contests, sweepstakes, and games.

The object of *public relations* is to obtain favorable publicity and to handle company crises and rumors so as to prevent negative publicity. Its main tools are press relations, product publicity, and corporate communications. *Publicity* must be newsworthy and believable and include created events such as anniversary celebrations, exhibits, contests, and sponsorships.

KNOW THE CONCEPTS
DO YOU KNOW THE BASICS?

1. Research indicates that while most mousetraps are set by men, it is women who dispose of the dead mice. More mousetraps might be sold if the task were less unpleasant. You have developed a better mousetrap: the "Rodent Roundup" is enclosed in a plastic container and the entire device is disposable. What elements of the marketing mix will you employ to cause the world to "beat a path to your door"?

2. Using the Model of the Marketing Communications Process, track through each of the stages the message by a microcomputer manufacturer who is introducing a new model.

3. What advertising, publicity, and sales promotion tools might be combined to market a new health food additive?

4. Since 1977 professionals (e g. physicians, lawyers, dentists, chiropractors) have begun to promote their services. Outline a promotion plan for a veterinarian

TERMS FOR STUDY

advertising
audience
communication channel
cost-per-thousand
decode
direct promotion
encode
feedback
frequency
impact
indirect promotion
message content
message execution

message structure
noise
positioning
press kit
promotion mix
public relations
publicity
reach
sales promotion
source
transmission
Unique Selling Proposition

ANSWERS
KNOW THE BASICS

1 *All* of the elements. The famous "Build a better mousetrap   " statement, attributed to Robert Burns, implies that the "Product 'P' " is the only necessary component of the marketing mix. It overlooks the necessity to price the mousetrap so that the customer perceives value for the cost It fails to consider distribution, limiting its market to the area from within which a customer can cost-effectively travel to purchase it. And, it does not provide for the promotional communications which would inform potential customers how the new trap solves their problem, and where it can be purchased.

This case has a real-life counterpart. A mousetrap manufacturer designed an innovative, throwaway mousetrap like the one described. The newfangled traps remained stacked on store shelves and were withdrawn from the market because consumers didn't know what they were. The product quality was excellent, the price was competitive, and the traps were being distributed through the normal channels, but there had been no promotion.

2. With the customer-user in mind, and based on survey research, the computer manufacturer should:

Translate the new product's features into customer-perceived benefits (supplied with 640K RAM = enough memory to support popular spreadsheet programs; high resolution monochrome monitor = less eyestrain; fully compatible with the leading microcomputer = will run all available software)

Encode the most important or unique benefit into the advertising appeal—Unique Selling Proposition ("The FULL-MEMORY computer that lets you do serious work at home.")

Transmit this message through selected media representing the communications channel (Microcomputer publications).

When the message is received it must be decoded. Therefore, along with the jargon of the computer buff, the advertiser should provide a translation, in everyday English, to help broaden the market for the new computer to include serious computer novices. Its content will be perceived by each member of the audience in terms of that member's unique life experience, attitudes, and wants/needs.

Throughout the process, noise can be expected to pervade but its negative effects can be minimized by careful, unambiguous wording of the message, and repetition (redundancy).

The success of the communication can be estimated from the amount of feedback—the level of desired response (dealer inquiries, user inquiries, and, indirectly, sales).

3. The market for health food and related products (vitamins and minerals, organically grown fruits, vegetables, herbs, and spices, and "natural" food items and body care products) is substantial and growing. Add to the following list. Use your imagination.

Advertising

Ads in health magazines
Commercials on radio programs about healthcare
Mailing to nutritionists on leased mailing lists
Mailing to health publication subscriber lists

Sales Promotion

Samples or trial size in counter display
Booth at healthcare exhibitions

Publicity

Press kit to newspapers and radio stations

4. The veterinarian should first determine the target audience—which clients' patients is he or she going to work primarily with: large animals (horses, cattle), small animals (dogs, cats, and other pets), or not specialize?

Advertising—Yellow pages, local newspapers, sign in front of or over the animal hospital.

Sales Promotion—If he or she is just starting the practice there can be a Grand Opening with free gifts (pet brushes, nutritious food samples, lit-

ANSWERS **413**

erature about animal health care, and decals with the clinic telephone number for emergencies.) In an established small animal practice a "rabies clinic" can be advertised. The veterinarian should selectively join some local clubs and service organizations, and be a speaker on timely subjects relating to members' pets. Author a book or pamphlet on animal health care. *Publicity*—The veterinarian's talks and seminars on animal health care are newsworthy items. The veterinarian should volunteer to be listed as a resource on animal medicine by newspapers and radio stations. When reporters call to get background information on stories they are writing, the veterinarian will be cited as an expert.

19

PROMOTION: DIRECT MAKING THE SALE

KEY TERMS

creative selling getting orders by overcoming objections and asking for a purchase decision (closing)

lead the name and address of a possible customer, or "suspect"

qualified lead an individual or organization that is "ready, willing, and able" to buy, and about which are known the logical and emotional reasons why; a *prospect*

referred lead a lead provided by a source who has given permission to use his or her name in connection with the reference

sales management executive planning, direction, coordination, and supervision of personnel engaged in the process of selling

---

IMPORTANCE OF SELLING

This chapter on direct promotion is positioned at the end of the book because the purpose of everything previously discussed is to lead to the sale. *Selling is the only direct profit-producing activity.* It has to pay for the performance of all of the other business functions, each of which generates costs and expenses. Sales must also cover overhead costs such as rent or depreciation, interest expense, and insurance. If the salesforce is not successful, then one of management's next tasks may well be to file for protection from creditors!

Some readers may feel that these introductory remarks overstate the importance of selling because organizations do have other sources of income, such as leaseholds, ventures, interest from investments, and royalties from patents. This is true, but these are usually ancillary to the main purpose of the business, and to establish each of these arrangements some decision-maker had to be persuaded to act—it was selling that implemented the deals.

In the previous chapter, using the Hierarchy-of-Effects model, we saw how a subset of marketing communications, indirect promotion—advertising, sales promotion, public relations, and publicity—attempts to move the target audience toward Conviction. In the case example, the Executive Secretary of the Hilton Head Realtors Association (HRA) developed a promotion plan for helping members sell more properties. Aimed at target audiences identified as being in the Liking and Preference phases of the Model, the plan prescribed advertising a free information package about time-share and property investments available on Hilton Head Island. Members of the target audience who answered the ad were sent descriptive brochures and invited to enjoy a free seafood dinner at one of the finest restaurants on the East Coast. To take advantage of the invitation, all that was necessary was to make a reservation for a free tour of the Island and listen to an informative presentation outlining the opportunities available. In a separate promotion, the "Help a Friend Become a Neighbor" contest, the winner was to be the property owner who provided the most names of people who purchased property during the three month period of the contest.

Now we shall examine how direct promotion—personal selling—capitalizes on these supporting functions of indirect promotion to effect an exchange. In terms of the Hierarchy-of-Effects model we shall discuss how friendly persuasion acts to move members of the target audience from the liking and preference to the conviction phase, and then into the behavior stage, a purchase. With the selling process understood, we shall then turn our attention to how this vital function can be facilitated by knowledgeable management. For examples we shall observe the sales follow-up of the HRA promotion by the Islandshares Group, introduced in Chapter 1.

THE SALES JOB

There are basically three types of jobs in the sales field:

- **Order Getters** are engaged in *creative* selling—creative because by going out and getting orders, they are *creating customers* and they have to be creative to accomplish it. "Friendly *persuaders*," who are taught that "the sale doesn't begin until the prospect says 'No'," are the profit producers mentioned in the first paragraph. It is this brand of selling on which we shall focus.

- **Order Takers** are responders. Merchandise is bought from them rather than sold by them. Examples of order takers are retail clerks, delivery route persons, and Inside Sales/Customer Service personnel who receive telephoned orders.

• **Supporting Salespersons** are specialists who work with order getters and supply technical assistance, freeing the order getters to call on more customers and make more sales. Packaging engineers, applications experts, installers, and trainers are some of the subtitles in this category.

CREATIVE SELLING

A master salesman once said, "There are only two types of salespeople: the quick and the dead." He was referring to the fact that there is no room for mediocrity in selling (from here on, when we mention "selling" or "sales," we will be referring to creative selling). With the use of the computer, there is daily reporting by territory of individual accomplishment compared to quota, associated costs matched with budget, sales volume by product, and whatever other information in whatever form is desired.

The entire organization watches the sales "scoreboard" to follow its "team" as it strives against the competition. If a player's performance is substandard, that salesperson will be pulled out of the game, not only because the company is not receiving value for its investment but *if customers are not being properly sold, the company will lose the entire territory to competition.* On the other hand, for the fast-track person, sales offers an opportunity to have achievement recognized. During economic downturns, wise companies increase their selling effort to maintain income, providing steady opportunities for creative sales people with a proven track record.

YOU SHOULD REMEMBER

Creative selling, persuading companies and individuals to purchase the product or service offering, is the mainstay of every business. The individual who is successful in sales is like a star athlete and is in demand during all economic conditions.

The Islandshares Group

Harry Byrne, Marketing Manager of Islandshares Group, a member firm of Hilton Head Realtors Association, appreciated the large number of appointments generated by Ms. Weiss' successful promotion strategy. However, because each sales representative can effectively work with only so many couples in a normal day, it is important that the people met are seriously considering purchase. There is no time to waste on "lookers" or "freeloaders" who accept the invitation to take the tour and listen to the presentation just to get a free dinner.

Because the visitors know it is going to be a sales presentation, they are wary and defensive. They arrive with a high degree of sales resistance, having considered all of the objections they can raise. No one likes to be "sold" anything, even if it is something they might consider owning. They will want to "think it over" and depart.

Mr. Byrne's sales associates must be able to overcome the objections and obtain a commitment to buy a piece of property at the time of the presentation.

THE CREATIVE SALES PROCESS

Selling has been called the highest paid hard work and the lowest paid easy work that exists. While this statement refers to the amount of preparation and effort put forth by a representative, there is another dimension. If the representative uses and believes in the product, he or she will radiate sincere, contagious enthusiasm, and selling will be a matter of educating and helping others to solve their problems by sharing the salesperson's solution. On the other hand, if a salesperson does not feel respect for an employer, and believes that by making a sale, he or she is "putting one over" on the customer, the money gained is not worth the sleepless nights, and that salesperson should change positions. (And the company had better reexamine itself and its offerings!)

Islandshares Group sales associates are proud of the product that they offer. The luxury condominiums and villas with breathtaking views of the sea or the sound, and within easy walking distance of professional recreational facilities, are an attractive investment. When a sale is made, the purchaser, Islandshares, and the sales associate that produced it, should all feel satisfaction in terms of their own objectives.

The Model of the Creative Sales Process (Figure 19-1) will be used as a focus for the material that follows. The Objectives and Strategies sections are discussed under Sales Management.

PROSPECTING

THE IMPORTANCE OF LEADS

It has been estimated that a business loses up to twenty percent of its customers annually. This attrition can be the result of competitors' activities, changes in material requirements, changes in purchasing policies, relocation, business failure, merger with or acquisition by a firm with prior purchasing affiliations, retirement, death, breakup of partnerships, or litigation. This underlying negative

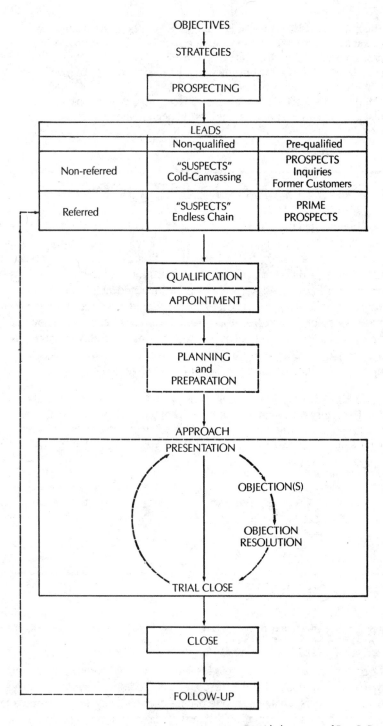

Provided courtesy of Roy C. Brown, 1985

Figure 19-1. The Creative Sales Process

movement is similar to walking up a down escalator. The lost sales volume must be regained just to "stay even" but since growth and increased market share are usually among company objectives, it can be seen that new leads have to be found continually. In fields such as insurance, or in the case of Islandshares real estate, each sale eliminates a Conviction- or Behavior-stage prospect, at least for the near future. If the pool of prospects is not replenished, there will be fewer to call on, and since only a fraction of sales contacts result in a sale, future sales volume will surely drop. Prospecting—searching for leads—eliminates the problem of salespeople with "no one to call."

OBTAINING LEADS

Cold canvassing is sometimes done if the salesperson is already in the vicinity calling on prospects and can make some additional contacts without losing too much time. A technical representative selling supplies to factories would "shoot smokestacks" if there were some plants located near or enroute to his customers. During slack periods, salespeople can make cold calls to telephone book listings. However, to let all sales depend upon such a hit-or-miss approach would be most inefficient.

A better organized, analytical approach is suggested by Patty[1]:

1. Analyze the product line or service in terms of benefits offered.

2. List the kinds of business organizations or individuals who would value the benefit(s).

3. List sources of leads, such as directories, association membership lists, and mailing lists (contact the Business Research Librarian at any library).

4. From the sources, specific leads (company and individual, with title, address, telephone number, and other pertinent information that is available) are developed.

Other sources of leads include requests for information in response to advertisements, such as returned Reader Preference ("bingo") cards, and the requests for the Hilton Head Island information packet

Whether or not a sale is made, at the conclusion of a sales call, the salesperson should help the prospect think of others who might be interested in the product. (The prospect who is not interested in buying is often glad to provide some names and a reference to encourage the salesperson to move on.) These referred but nonqualified leads are, in turn, sources for more leads. Each of these persons when called on is a potential buyer and can provide several more leads. This "endless chain" technique is useful because of the sales truism: "The more calls made, the more sales made."

---

1. C. Robert Patty, *Managing Salespeople.* 2nd ed. Reston, VA: Reston Publishing Company, Inc., 1982.

Although purchase of insurance or real estate removes the prospect as a potential customer for the same product or service, these customers, if satisfied with their purchase, are the best prospects for *other* products in the line, such as other kinds of insurance or investment properties. Also, satisfied customers are interested in upgrading at the end of what sales trainer Tom Hopkins calls their "itch cycle."[2] By reviewing sales records and telephoning some current owners, it can be ascertained how long, on the average, customers have a product before they are ready to add to it or trade it in on something bigger or better. For example, the person who purchases a home computer, having mastered the basics, wants more sophisticated software and additional memory, then a hard disk, turbo chip, math coprocessor, higher resolution monitor, a better printer, and a modem. Then, after the system has been upgraded, that person is ready for a new model computer.

> Harry Byrne makes sure that his sales associates maintain contact with customers to whom they have sold a time-share. He knows from his extensive experience and feel for his profession that in three to five years many of these people will be prime prospects for villas, or condominiums.

QUALIFYING

There is a qualitative as well as quantitative dimension to prospecting. *Qualification* involves finding out whether a lead:

1. wants or has a *need* for the product.

2. is *able* to buy (can obtain the necessary cash or credit).

3. has the *authority* to buy (is the decision-maker).

4. is *accessible* to the salesperson.

5. is *eligible* (meets the seller's requirements to purchase—for example, is a legitimate wholesaler, or can pass a life insurance physical examination).

With a *qualified lead,* the salesperson has the logical and emotional reasons why the prospect should purchase and can preplan the presentation.

If someone known to the prospect agrees to let the salesperson mention his name as a reference, the lead is said to be a *referred lead.* If the lead is both qualified and referred, the chances of making a sale are much, much greater.

A telephone call should be made to the prospect to verify and update the information. If there is no *condition*, an appointment can be made at the conclusion of the call. A condition, in contrast to an objection, is a reason why a

---

2. Tom Hopkins, *How to Master the Art of Selling Anything* [Audio Cassettes]. Scottsdale, AZ: Tom Hopkins Champions Unlimited, 1979.

person or organization cannot be a prospect at this time. There may be a credit problem, or they may just have purchased a competing product, or they no longer need the product because they have changed their production process. It is this kind of information that should be obtained during qualification so that the time, money, and effort invested in a sales call are not wasted.

> Mr. Byrne's Islandshares sales group qualifies prospects by having them fill out a short information card while waiting to eat the free $40 seafood dinner. Everyone complies because the cards are entered in a drawing to win reimbursement of all expenses, approximately $400, for the entire weekend. (It is also mentioned that these expenses will be deducted from the down payment on the purchase of a piece of property.)
>
> Information requested includes name, home address, telephone number, age, children's names, employment status, value of present home, whether owned or rented, amount of mortgage, value and location of second home, other investments, favorite recreations and hobbies, and category of family income.

YOU SHOULD REMEMBER

To enjoy success in creative selling, one should believe in the company and product. To have people to sell, it is necessary to prospect for leads. A lead received from a person who has given permission to use his or her name as a reference is a referred lead. Each lead is then qualified as to need, ability, authority, and eligibility to buy. A lead that passes this screening process is known as a qualified lead. A lead that is both referred and qualified offers the highest opportunity for making a sale.

PLANNING AND PREPARATION

The professional will preplan every important presentation in writing, bringing the future into the present. The greeting and the impression to be made on the approach are visualized. Benefits to stress to this particular prospect, based on the qualifying information at hand, will be listed and ranked from most important to least important. The benefit used to obtain the appointment will be enlarged and supplemented with others to be used to overcome anticipated objections, and one perhaps held in reserve to clinch the close. The appropriate, image-creating adjectives and adverbs will be chosen, instead of groping for them during the presentation. Since the salesperson will want to control the interviews by asking questions and get the *prospect* to state the product's advantages and to answer his own questions, the phrasing of these questions will also be written.

A useful device is a scenario of action sequences with projected dialogue. While the actual events will, of course, depart from the script, a "dry run" helps uncover all kinds of loose ends and missing information. General Dwight Eisenhower used to say, "In an emergency a plan is useless, but the *planning* is indispensable."

THE APPROACH

The approach, or initial contact, should aim at reducing the prospect's tension, and encourage the prospect to like and trust the salesperson, and begin to feel excitement about the product or service. The salesperson's general appearance, dress, and physical movements should be calculated to create a favorable first impression. The greeting should be sincere, natural, and accompanied by a smile and eye contact. Handshaking preferably should be initiated by the prospect. By being alert to the prospect's body language, the handshake can appear to be spontaneous.

> Islandshares sales associates, because they are usually dealing with a couple, are prepared to shake hands with the husband at the slightest encouragement but with the wife only if she extends her hand first. Because of the involuntary nature of the meeting, the salespeople try to eliminate any impression of overzealousness.
>
> The approach leads smoothly into the presentation. Cordial questions about what the couple have liked best so far reduce their tension and supply the sales associate with Hilton Head features to stress as benefits as the presentation proceeds.

THE PRESENTATION

"Success is finding the people to sell, and selling the people you found."

Presentations (never "pitches"!) can be categorized as

1. *structured* or formula, sometimes referred to as "canned" presentations. Based on the stimulus-response theory, which asserts that when subjected to certain stimuli, the prospect will respond with Pavlovian predictability. Used by inexperienced part-time salespeople, perhaps selling cookware door-to-door, and effective for some types of insurance, this approach is easily derailed by an unpredictable customer response.

2. *sequential*, or key action, based on the AIDA model. The salesperson, by observing whether the prospect is in the attention, interest, desire, or action

stage, knows when to introduce the next idea calculated to move the prospect to the next stage. While this technique provides logical, step-by-step tactics for selling complicated products or services, it assumes that all prospects share the same thought sequence; but, as you recall from the Consumer Behavior material, this is not always the case.

3. *need-satisfaction.* Based on the theory that all purchasing is need-based or problem-solving, salespersons employing this strategy (1) determine the prospect's perceived problem, (2) obtain the prospect's confirmation of the problem, and (3) offer a solution to the problem. The only drawback to this presentation is the cost, time, and effort needed for intensive sales training and for the presentation itself.

4. *problem-solution.* Combines the sequential approach to problem solving with the *need-satisfaction* technique to provide a cooperative, customer-oriented presentation that creates solid customer relations. As might be expected, the negative aspects are the same as with the related *need-satisfaction* approach. Because of the associated costs, the need-satisfaction and problem-solution presentations are mainly used in industrial selling.

5. *Hybrid*, a combination of techniques modified to fit the needs of a particular product-market situation. Mr. Byrnes' Islandshares sales associates used parts of the *sequential* and parts of the *need satisfaction* approaches in a presentation tailored to their unique situation.

TECHNIQUES APPLICABLE TO ALL OF THESE PRESENTATIONS

• There is always the possibility that the prospect is secretly delighted to see a salesperson because he or she is ready to order. However, if the salesperson is not sensitive to this state and becomes involved in a lengthy presentation, he may unknowingly "buy back" the product because the prospect has had time to wonder about the features and whether a better price might not be available from competition. Every sales representative should keep "ABC" in mind from the outset—Always Be Closing.

• The salesperson should maintain control by asking questions. Having to think of answers keeps the prospect involved, and by the nature of the answers the representative can determine what the prospect is thinking.

• The sales demonstration has been described as 'show and tell." The "show" refers to the demonstration, which may be a hands-on use of the product by the prospect (trial driving a car, sitting in the furniture, playing the piano), a working model, visual aids, or computer-animated graphics.

• After an interruption or on a revisit, the representative should restate the agreed-upon benefits to bring the prospect back up to the same mental and emotional stage where he or she was when the interruption occurred.

YOU SHOULD REMEMBER

A salesperson should plan every presentation, preferably in writing, visualizing the scenario and anticipating the dialogue. The approach, or initial contact, should strive for a positive first impression of the salesperson by the prospect. Presentations range in structuring from the formula, or canned, to the problem-solution approach, with hybrid combinations tailored to particular product-market variables. With the exception of the canned approach, the presentation should encourage customer dialogue as an indication of agreement or disagreement.

The Islandshares Group

Islandshares Group prospects' objectives are categorized as vacation, retirement, and investment. The one that is dominant depends upon individual goals, which are influenced by the phase of the family life cycle the prospect is in. Since this information is obtained from the cards filled out for the Free Weekend Drawing, sales associates are able to plan the presentation for each upcoming appointment.

After a brief further qualification during which the prospect's preference for Ocean or Sound view, and two- or three-bedroom size is elicited, the sales associate can show the available properties that are closest to the prospect's needs.

OBJECTIONS

The sales professional welcomes objections because they can be regarded as disguised requests for more information, they indicate that the prospect is listening, and they reveal what is in his or her mind. When the information, perhaps proof of an assertion, has been supplied, a *trial close* can be attempted. If it succeeds, the salesperson then moves into the close. If it is rejected, then the salesperson resumes the presentation. *Conditions*, real reasons why an organization or individual cannot purchase now, should have been discovered during qualification.

If no objections are voiced, the salesperson should ask involvement questions requiring assent. ("This feature of the model would certainly seem to solve your problem, *don't you agree?*") If the agreement is not forthcoming, then the salesperson can probe to find out why, and further explain the feature or find other features on which there *is* assent. Since a sale is a series of agreements, when no objections remain, the close should be merely one more "Yes." Each objection overcome is a step up the ladder leading to the sale.

HANDLING OBJECTIONS

The proper way to handle an objection is to:

1. *hear the prospect out.* Although the representative has heard the objection hundreds of times, the prospect hasn't voiced it before and deserves the courtesy of polite attention. By being a sympathetic listener the salesperson learns what the prospect knows (which may *not* be what the salesperson anticipated!) and is therefore at an advantage because the prospect does not know what information the salesperson possesses. In addition, by allowing the prospect to discharge his pent-up feelings, the salesperson will receive a better ear because the prospect won't be tuning out the salesperson's comments in order to recall what *he* wants to say!

2. *repeat the objection,* letting the prospect know that the objection was understood.

3. *question it,* to encourage the prospect to amplify it, giving more information that can be used to

4. *answer it.* When it has been answered, obtain acknowledgment from the prospect by a comment like "I guess that solves that, *doesn't it?*" and wait for agreement before proceeding.

Some objections may be common with certain products. These can be anticipated by the salesperson during the presentation to disarm the prospect. "You may be thinking that with all of these features and an ocean view, this villa costs more than some others. You would be correct, but let's see how the difference is really not that much ..."

YOU SHOULD REMEMBER

A condition is a concrete reason a person or organization cannot be a customer at the present time. An objection is a disguised request for more information.

To illustrate some techniques in presentation, overcoming objections, and trial closing, we return to the Islandshares case.

The young professional couple introduced in Chapter 1 had responded to one of Ms. Weiss' earlier promotions and had purchased a time-share that gives them the first week in May on Hilton Head Island every year. Now they wish that they could spend more time there and could be there for the

Heritage Golf Classic in April. Since the couple, John and Heather Thompson, are started in their careers and have their townhouse decorated, they are considering purchase of a condominium for vacations and as an investment. Along with the visitors who responded to Ms. Weiss' current promotion, the Thompsons have an appointment with Islandshares Group.

Myra Hall, one of Mr. Byrnes' sales associates, greeted them and ascertained that they both enjoy golf. Since Ms. Hall also is a "golfer for fun, until I break 80" there was friendly recollection of courses all three had played on. Now, more as friends who shared a common interest they began to talk about other things they all liked. Myra guided the conversation to desirable features of real estate and, to help John and Heather decide what they wanted to look at, showed some slide transparencies of available properties, watching their body language as well as listening to their comments.

They selected one of the villas to visit, and the Thompsons liked the ocean view but thought that the $160,000 price was too much. Myra verified that the price was the only thing standing in the way of purchase and asked "How much too much?" They said they had hoped to find something for around $125,000 at most. Since Myra knew she would be showing this property, she had coffee, toast, and cookies in the kitchen. They all sat at the kitchen table, and Myra worked up some figures on a Cost Analysis sheet while the couple admired the view and sensed what it would be like to have such a vista with all of their meals.

Myra handed John her pocket calculator "to check my figures," which showed that with a down payment of $16,000—part of which could come from trading in their $4000 time-share—monthly costs (including principal and interest), condo fee, property taxes, and utilities would come to $1673 per month. However, if they limited their own use of the place to no more than two weeks per year and rented it for the rest of the time, they would have the rental income and be eligible for additional tax deductions. With the tax savings, in their income bracket, they could actually be ahead $246 per month, and have a hedge against inflation, all with leveraged principal of only $16,000.

Heather, the accountant, hesitated. "This presumes we can rent the premises for at least 20 weeks, but suppose we can't? Also, it seems that with prices so high inflation has to level off somewhere. Perhaps we should wait until next year..."

Myra replied, "That's good thinking and we should all be glad accountants are taught to be conservative, don't you agree?" When all had nodded, she added, "But properties on Hilton Head have been averaging over 12% annual appreciation, and those who last year decided to wait are kicking themselves. I can see that you two enjoy this view from the kitchen and I would hate to see you disappointed because this is unique. I have six more appointments today and I know that this will be gone by this afternoon."

The couple looked at each other silently. "We just can't decide what to do."

"As an accountant, Heather, you can appreciate what Ben Franklin used to do in such a situation," said Myra, gently laying a blank sheet of paper on the table, between the Thompsons. "When old Ben was faced with an important decision, he wanted to be sure that he made the right choice. He would take a sheet of paper, draw a line down the center, like this, and another across the top, like this, to make a 'balance sheet.' He would label the first column "For" and the other "Against" and then list the reasons favoring and against purchase under the appropriate headings. Often the decision was made for him by the weight of evidence." While she was talking, Myra was drawing the lines and labeling the columns. "Why don't we try it?" she asked, and as she reiterated each benefit she waited for the couple to agree and then listed it under "For."

"Let's see, we have appreciation—at over 12% per year... leveraged principal of only $16,000... rental income... a hedge against inflation... and, last but not least, the privilege of seeing sunrises over the Atlantic!" She laid down the pen and asked, "Who wants to list the reasons against?" After some hesitation, Heather picked up the pen and wrote "Unsure economy" and everyone agreed. "And we're not sure we can rent it for at least 20 weeks."

John interposed. "Actually, we want to be able to spend more than two weeks here, anyway."

Heather replied, "But to satisfy IRS we can't."

With a conspiratorial smile, Myra said softly, "Of course, the IRS allows you to be here between renters for maintenance."

The couple looked at each other in silence. As the seconds ticked away, tension mounted. Suddenly Myra smiled and said, "My dear grandmother always used to say, 'Silence is assent.' Was she right?" The couple broke into a relieved laugh, picked up the pen, and signed the purchase agreement.

THE CLOSE

The close is the goal of the presentation, the purpose of the sales training, and the reason for all the indirect promotion efforts that set it up. It is the reward, the payoff, the bottom line. It could even be said that it is the basis for the organization's mission. Certainly it provides the financial support for that mission.

When a quality product or service is sold, all parties to the transaction gain. It builds business for the company that sold it. It rewards the representative monetarily. It provides a solution to a problem that the buyer has.

Considering this importance, it is surprising how many salespersons fail to move for the close—to *ask for the decision*. The reason most often advanced is the salesperson's *fear of rejection*. More likely, it is insufficient training and drilling in closing techniques. The prospect has more objections than the salesperson has closes!

In the Islandshares case example we saw the *Ben Franklin Balance Sheet Close*. Some other popular closes are the:

• *Order Blank Close*—During the presentation, the salesperson fills out an order blank. If stopped by the prospect, he or she replies, "I like to organize my thoughts and put everything in the proper perspective. I write the facts on the order form so I don't forget anything." At the conclusion of the presentation, if the prospect doesn't object further and has indicated which model, color, and quantity he would buy "if he were going to buy," the representative turns the order form around and asks the prospect to "initial a trial order."

• *Puppy Dog Close*—(the close that sold many of the early, high-priced television sets.) The prospect is given the product to "try for a week" at the end of which time it has become indispensable and, already in use, is purchased.

A common resistance to a close is "I want to think it over." This is usually just a delaying tactic to give the prospect an opportunity to shop for a lower price. Given this opportunity, some other salesperson somewhere will cash in on the work of the first, because the prospect has already bought the concept! Therefore the representative must try to close. The response (with the questions asked in rapid fire sequence so the prospect doesn't get an opening to reply, "I want to think *everything* over") is "Why certainly. I agree that such a decision deserves every consideration. But just to clarify my thinking, *what is it you want to think over?* Is it the integrity of my company? My personal integrity? Benefit A that we agreed upon? Benefit B that we agreed upon?" Of course the prospect answers "No" to each of these and struggles to think of something to think over. After listing each benefit agreed upon, in effect providing a benefit summary, and having the prospect admit that it isn't what is going to be thought over, the salesperson asks if it is the money and the prospect eagerly agrees. By getting the prospect to say how much too much the price is, the salesperson can add up the savings associated with purchasing the product, subtract the losses from not using it, divide the cost over the expected payback period, and show how its use will multiply efficiency, customer satisfaction, or any other pertinent benefit.

There are other types of selling in which the close may be based on other considerations, such as negotiation or bargaining, such a sale in which an organization's annual requirements are being anticipated and ordered. Because of the large size of the order, the buyer demands concessions such as storage of a certain level of supply, available for callout within twenty-four hours, warehousing to be paid for by seller. The salesperson selling the contract attempts to hold back some of these extras as bargaining points or to protect profit margins.

FOLLOW UP

Follow-up refers to recontact of a customer. It may be a telephone call to check if material was delivered, or to provide promised additional information. Whatever the reason, it is an indication to the customer that the salesperson cares and did not forget If the product or service is expensive or regularly used, then follow-up after the sale is of utmost importance. Follow-up can benefit the salesperson in several ways:

• *Reinforcement of sale*. If there is a complaint, timely follow-up may be able to resolve it and prevent cancellation of the order and return of the merchandise.

• *Referred leads*. We have seen the value of referred leads. Those received from a satisfied customer are the best because they are given with enthusiasm.

• *Repeat business*. Really successful sales professionals cultivate customers like a farm crop, following up sales with inquiries about how the product is performing. This keeps them in touch so that when a new model is out and that customer's itch cycle is nearing, another sale is assured.

• *Add-on business*. The representative who keeps in touch will have the best opportunity of selling accessories to upgrade the item purchased and to recommend when the item should be replaced.

YOU SHOULD REMEMBER

The close, getting the order, is the basis for all marketing activity. A close can be tried after successfully overcoming an objection. The successful salesperson will know more closes than the prospect knows stalls and objections.

Follow-up should be regarded as a companion to the close, especially in cases where the product or service is costly. Excluding minor purchases at retail, follow-up is indicated where the customer may be seen again. Benefits derived from follow-up are referred leads, rapport with customers, and an advantageous position from which to upgrade the customer or sell a new model when the customer is ready.

SALES MANAGEMENT
THE NATURE OF SALES MANAGEMENT

Sales Management refers to management of sales personnel, not management of sales. Like all managers, the Sales Manager delegates responsibility and commensurate authority to others to multiply his or her effectiveness. However, there are some basic differences between supervising a field sales force and managing an internal department. One of these concerns the dynamic nature and external focus of sales management. It is the difference between office-based and field-mobile, between a game plan for our team and persuading independent business-people. Someone once described it: "If management is like a game of golf, then selling is like a game of tennis."

One requirement of the creative selling job, as we have seen, is to satisfy the customer. Thus, the sales manager's people are additionally working for a second boss. There is the geographic dispersion of the field force, precluding much face-to-face communication and complicating the process of communication and supervision.

Harry Byrne, Sales Manager for Islandshares Group, pondered these differences as he updated his own job description. A topnotch sales professional as well as an efficient manager and dynamic leader, Mr. Byrne had been promoted to Vice-President, Corporate Marketing, and was preparing to search for a new Sales Manager. The job description would be a useful guide in determining the "fit" between the individual and the organization. It would not be easy to locate such a person, however, because of the broad range of responsibilities involved. The responsibilities of the Sales Manager include *planning, budgeting, forecasting, designing the sales force,* and *managing the sales force.*

PLANNING
ETHICAL AND LEGAL CONSIDERATIONS

Through the years, Mr. Byrne had found one word that seemed to provide the best test for whether or not an action had been or would be ethical—the word was "fairness." If a manager is trying to be fair, his or her people will support that manager's decisions, even though some may be unpopular ones. However, if subordinates even suspect that a manager is showing favoritism, or taking credit for their work, or blaming them for problems that are not of their making, there will be no respect. On the contrary, an "every man for himself" attitude will replace any *espirit de corps* that ever existed. Regarding legal aspects, salespeople are company agents and as such have to be kept informed about regulations covering their products/service, or industry, as well as the law of contracts.

DEFINITION OF GOALS

Sales Department goals should derive from the corporate mission, and should not conflict with those of other departments.

DEFINITION OF OBJECTIVES

Sales force objectives include developing new business, selling, and protecting the territory against inroads from competition. The company-representative relationship should be built on a framework of mutually agreed-upon objectives. These objectives guide the formulation of sales strategies.

When Mr. Byrne interviews applicants for a position as sales associate, their personal goals and philosophies are matched with those of the organization. Islandshares Group wants to increase its market share by fifteen percent within the next two years, and expects its sales people to accomplish this by communicating and selling. The typical sales associate wants financial security and an opportunity to grow professionally. These objectives are satisfied by Mr. Byrne's incentive and training programs.

CONTINGENCY PLANNING

Salespeople come and go. They retire, resign, become incapacitated, die. The dynamic, unpredictable, uncontrollable influences such as the economic environment, of which marketing is a subset, and the legal and regulatory environment cause property values to fluctuate with inflation, recession, stagflation, and changing tax laws. Since most business executives would agree with Harold Geneen that they don't like surprises, the planning framework should incorporate several premises, including a worst-case scenario.

BUDGETING

Like all department heads, the sales manager must develop a budget. For the sales department, this includes costs of administration, training, and expenses associated with selling, such as travel, meals, lodging, entertainment, vehicles, communications, sales meetings, shows and exhibits, and memberships.

FORECASTING

The whole organization looks to the sales manager's input to the forecast of what and how much can be expected to be sold. In a manufacturing operation, capacity, raw materials, components, labor, and space requirements are derived from the forecast. If it is too optimistic, the company has to bear the high cost of excessive inventories and the bad publicity from laying off surplus labor. And, as Professor

Vertrees used to say, "You can't lay off a machine." On the other hand, if the forecast is low, the manufacturing group doesn't have the productive capacity to fill all of the orders received. In this case, not only these orders but many customers are lost, along with the money invested to get them to order and all of the future business they represent. The situation is not unlike trying to control the flow of water into a badly leaking container so that the container will always be brim full but not overflowing. And it is the Sales Manager's responsibility, through the sales forecast, to predict the rate of inflow—demand.

The forecast is approached from two converging directions. The Breakdown or Top Down estimate is based on projections of the national economy and its effect on market potential—the total amount that could be sold by all suppliers in the industry if every customer bought. From this the company's maximum share of the market, which could be realized only by budgeting for maximum sales-generating activity (called the sales potential) is estimated. Finally, the probable actual sales of the product are stated as the sales forecast.

In the meantime, using the Build-up or Bottom Up technique, all field sales-persons are contacting the customers in their territory, obtaining their estimates of purchases to be made during the forecast period. These territory forecasts are combined by district or regional sales management and sent to the Sales Manager, who aggregates them into a national sales forecast. Now the figures from the Breakdown and Buildup approaches are compared and the final sales forecast is made.

YOU SHOULD REMEMBER

The Sales Manager's responsibilities include planning, budgeting, forecasting, and designing and managing the sales force.

Typical sales force objectives are developing new business, selling, and protecting present business.

One of the most important words in human relations is *fairness*.

SALES FORCE DESIGN
SALES FORCE OBJECTIVES

The objectives developed during the planning stage—prospecting, communicating, selling, servicing, and information gathering—are operationalized by determining what proportion of time is to be devoted to each.

At Islandshares Group, the promotion implemented by Ms. Weiss generates prospects, and since these are members of clearly defined groups (vacationers, retirees, and investors), most of the information had been gathered and was merely updated. There was little servicing to do, other than keeping in touch with buyers to help them increase their investment when they were ready. Therefore, Mr. Byrne's salespeople were able to concentrate on effective communicating and selling.

SALES FORCE STRATEGY

Derived from the sales objectives, the sales force strategy involves deployment of sales people and considers whether to use free-lance sales professionals called Manufacturers' Representatives, or reps. These latter work on straight commission and may be used to cover territories where there are few customers and too little sales potential to support a full-time company salesperson. Historically, reps were used by small start-up companies until the reps literally sold themselves out of a job by developing the market until sales were good enough for the company to hire its own sales force. Since a rep may represent a dozen or more principals, with each receiving but a fraction of the rep's selling time, the rep did not miss the account that much. In the meanwhile the new company's sales force, by devoting full time to selling only the company product, was building sales faster than the rep. It is interesting to note that present economic conditions have reversed this process and companies that have had their own sales force for years are turning to reps. The reason is the high cost of the sales-related expenses mentioned earlier under "Budgeting." By using reps on straight commission, selling costs fluctuate with sales volume and the profit percentage remains constant.

Mr. Byrne and his sales force hold periodic strategy sessions at which they review the advantages to vacationers, retirees, and investors, of owning a piece of Islandshares property. At these informal get togethers they also air new objections that they have heard, and discuss ways of overcoming each one. Through the years these meetings have covered nearly every objection, and by arming the sales associates with predetermined responses, they have proved to be tremendous confidence and morale builders. Sales associates, instead of fearing or resenting objections, anticipate them and welcome the opportunity to hone the techniques they have learned.

SALES FORCE STRUCTURE

The sales force structure may be based on geography (territorial), product, customer type, or a combination of these. For example, Mr. Byrne could assign members of his sales force to *territories*—areas from which prospects came (Georgia, South Carolina, Northeastern states, . . .) or he could have specialists by *product* (time-shares, condominiums, and villas).

The sales force could be structured by *customer types* (vacationers, retirees, and investors). At the present, a combination structure is employed, with every sales associate cross-trained to understand all of the product offerings. However, older members tend to deal with retirees, and sales associates whose college majors were finance, accounting, or economics deal with larger, serious investors.

COMPENSATION

Compensation should fairly reflect the sales objectives. If the emphasis is on service, and the management desires to maintain strong control, straight salary is usually paid. If sales volume is most important, and profit margins are critical, straight commission is a popular arrangement, because expenses are "prepaid" by sales.

It was mentioned that Manufacturers' Representatives are used because sales and commissions fluctuate together, maintaining a constant profit percentage. Since the percentage, usually around 15%, is paid "off the top," it is as if the rep owns a piece of the business. If sales are good, the salesperson on straight commission can earn more than the company president. Most professional salespeople with a good product or service offering prefer commission for this reason. Islandshares sales associates are on straight commission with draw, which means that the company lends them money when they need it and this is repaid from commissions.

Combination plans can be structured to achieve a desired balance of the advantages of each of the compensation plans and are quite popular. The package can be further modified by offering a bonus based on a predetermined performance level over a defined period of time. A problem with bonuses is that they are too often regarded as a benefit and if the performance expectations (such as total annual sales) are not realized and the bonus is not paid, it can hurt morale and affect performance.

YOU SHOULD REMEMBER

A sales force may be structured geographically (into territories), by product type, customer types, or a combination of these.

Straight salary provides management with the strongest control and is used where servicing of the account is important.

Straight commission gives management the least control, but since expenses fluctuate with sales, the profit percentage is constant.

SALES FORCE MANAGEMENT
RECRUITING AND SELECTING

If there are five jobs that need to be filled right away and there are only seven applicants, the person hiring has little choice. The objective of recruiting is to have a pool of applicants large enough to contain a sufficient number of persons with standards that meet the selection criteria, thus offering the recruiter the opportunity of critical selection. Because they bring to the job formal training in marketing, accounting, computers, the sciences, and other disciplines, college graduates are often recruited for sales training.

But recruiting costs money and takes time. Many sales jobs are filled through the Hidden Job Market—they are never advertised because the Sales Manager called some business acquaintances and asked where some good people might be found. There is always a certain amount of flux and good people changing jobs and if the opportunity is made sufficiently attractive, the job can be filled and is never advertised. Contacts and networking are the best approach to tap the Hidden Job Market.

Hiring people whose objectives mesh with the organization's can reduce turnover, the single greatest personnel cost in industry today. Whenever an employee exits the company, the investment in orientation and training is lost along with the future potential. When a salesperson leaves, a territory temporarily receives inadequate coverage and this not only reduces revenue due to lost orders but jeopardizes customer relations. If competition moves in, not only are orders lost, but customers are lost, and a customer is worth not only the investment in indirect and direct promotion but all of the future business that will not be received. Selection of salespeople is done after the recruit's personal history, aptitude, and intelligence test results have satisfied predetermined criteria. It is based on interviews with sales executives who have the unique experience to judge an applicant's potential contribution. It is important to be realistic and honest with recruits regarding promotion path and potential earnings. A rosy picture painted to attract an outstanding candidate sows the seed of disappointment and early departure.

TRAINING AND DEVELOPING

By increasing the employee's productivity and resultant earnings, training and development increase job satisfaction and reduce employee turnover. Training consists of:

- *company orientation*, important because the person will be representing the company; also, the representative needs to know whom to call for a customer with a technical problem, an inquiry about a credit line, or information from a specialist.

• *product knowledge*; the salesperson is the expert on the product, whether showing a Hilton Head condominium or telling a physician about a newly synthesized alkaloid. He or she must be thoroughly versed in product features and their derivative benefits.

• *selling techniques*, discussed in the first part of this chapter.

• *nonselling activities* such as servicing, forecasting, sampling, handling complaints, and helping customers understand company credit and billing policies.

• *market knowledge*, including potentials, trends, competitive activity. Some of this will be learned in the field. The salesperson, as eyes and ears of the company, will be reporting market conditions via Daily Call Reports. Not the least of this knowledge is getting to know the customer's problems and point-of-view.

Development is a continuous process of reviewing basics (for, as various sales trainers have said, "People aren't smart enough to remember all they know") and introducing the sales force to new products and models. This latter is important because something new gives the representative an excuse to recontact every customer and sell those who always want the latest features. Even those who are satisfied with their present model may be curious enough to give the representative an opportunity to show and tell (the word "new" is such a powerful selling tool it is controlled by law—to be called new, a product must satisfy government-defined material changes and can then only be advertised as new for a limited amount of time).

Mr. Byrnes' sales associates are trained in sales techniques with emphasis on overcoming objections and closing. In addition, practice sessions are held in real estate arithmetic. Hand calculators are used with clients but sales associates get a feel for the numbers by working on spreadsheets in a microcomputer. By playing "what if" with inflation values, down payment amounts, and other variables, they see the effect on, for example, payments and equity.

DIRECTING AND CONTROLLING

Directing and controlling a far-flung group of ambitious, independent, creative, customer-oriented, hard-driving producers is a challenge. One of the reasons many persons enter sales is to be their "own boss," within limits. Unfortunately, the number of individuals who have the ability to set priorities and manage their time efficiently could be much larger. Since the advantage of personal selling over forms of indirect promotion is physical presence and the ability to overcome objections and close, a salesperson works most effectively when with the client.

But, under normal conditions, the typical salesperson has time to make only six calls per day. Since Friday afternoon isn't too productive because of some customers leaving early to beat weekend traffic, many representatives do their paperwork on Friday, leaving four days per week to make calls. Subtract three weeks for vacation, and subtract seven holidays, time spent at development and sales meetings, storm days, and personal business, and we can see that it is essential for the salesperson to make maximum use of what time is available.

Prioritizing customers into key accounts, medium, and small accounts by applying the 80/20 rule—80% of the business comes from 20% of the customers—helps to make more efficient use of time. Establishing call norms for these customer targets, and specifying that a minimum of, say, 20% new business should be added each year, guides the representative in territory planning and gives the Sales Manager a yardstick with which to measure performance.

MOTIVATION

It is particularly important in sales to counteract demotivating forces such as demanding customers, aggressive competition, fear of failure and insecurity, or, at the other extreme, a windfall such as very high commission income, or reduced ambition because the mortgage has been paid off. However, motivation cannot be stimulated from the outside—it is an inner drive. Moreover, every individual marches to a different drummer. There are no universal motivators—ideally, each salesperson should have his or her own motivation mix, based on individualized career paths. The components of that mix can be categorized as direct and indirect incentives.

Direct incentives include

- creating an *organizational environment* in which participation and communication are encouraged.

- setting *quotas* that are achievable by the majority of the sales force *with a moderate amount of extra effort.* (It's better to have a sales force of enthusiastic winners than disappointed losers. Furthermore, since their sales are too low to be able to achieve quota this period, some of the losers may decide to let orders from customers who are not in a rush, accumulate until the next period, creating peaks and valleys in scheduling.)

- recognition, awards, and other *nonmonetary* incentives.

Indirect incentives such as

- contests, have to be carefully planned so that they do not result in an effect opposite to that planned. For example, a contest to generate business during an off-peak period might be based on total volume of orders written during that period. If rules are not clear, or if there are insufficient controls, some salespeople might explain to key accounts that they need orders to win a contest and get the customer to anticipate future requirements and place the orders early, with the understanding that shipment and billing will be delayed. This results in an insufficient volume of business during the regular season and creates peaks and valleys instead of smoothing them.

EVALUATING

The Sales Manager's evaluation of the sales force will typically consist of both informal and formal approaches.

Informal assessment may be based on reports, a work plan or territory marketing plan, and field trips with the representative to visit key accounts.

Formal reviews are characterized as comparison with other salespersons as to productivity and cost control and current performance compared to past performance.

YOU SHOULD REMEMBER

Employee turnover is the greatest personnel-related cost in industry. Training and development help reduce turnover by increasing employee productivity and earnings.

The kinds of knowledge needed by a salesperson are a company orientation, product knowledge, selling techniques, nonselling activities, and market knowledge.

KNOW THE CONCEPTS
DO YOU KNOW THE BASICS?

1. You are just starting a job selling photographic supplies and accessories to retailers. Describe how you would prospect for leads.
2. Design a reporting system that will provide you with a record of customer status (activity and when last purchased) and product sales.
3. What preparation should be done prior to contacting a lead, Mr. Prospect?
4. Building on your answer to Question 3, write a brief dialogue for a telephone qualification of Mr. P. for a financial service.
5. Write a scenario for your initial sales call on Mr. P.
6. Assume that you are a district sales manager with a field force of seven sales people. How can you be sure that you are being fair?

TERMS FOR STUDY

Always Be Closing
approach
Ben Franklin Balance Sheet Close
canned presentation
closing
cold canvassing
compensation
condition
creative selling
direct incentives
direct promotion
endless chain technique
follow-up
hybrid presentation
itch cycle
lead
need-satisfaction presentation
nonmonetary incentive
objection

Order Blank close
order getter
order taker
planning scenario
problem-solution presentation
prospecting
Puppy Dog close
qualified lead
referred lead
sales forecasting
sales management
sales quota
sales training
sequential presentation
straight commission
straight salary
structured presentation
suspects
trial close

ANSWERS
KNOW THE BASICS

1. In a local library, look through the Yellow Pages of telephone books that cover your territory and jot down the names, addresses, and telephone numbers of each photography store. Note names of proprietors, store specialties, and branches if given. Don't overlook photo departments in larger stores, and commercial photographers.

   Try to obtain a list of members of any association or of stores that buy as a group.

   As you travel through your territory, be on the lookout for new stores that might not have been listed in the telephone directories. Ask your customers about competition.

2. The simplest system would be a 3 × 5 card file, or a loose leaf ledger. Use one card or page for each customer. Note the date of each sales call and what was purchased. Keep a running sub-total.

   On a separate spreadsheet, preferably a multicolumnar accounting worksheet, head a separate column for each product you sell with the name of the item and its unit price. As sales are made, write the customer name at the left and the items purchased in the proper columns. Weekly, subtotal the columns and "cross-foot" the rows. This will provide you with sales by customer and sales by product.

More sophisticated systems are available from business supply houses, or your vendor may have a system that they prefer you use.

An excellent investment, as your sales grow, would be a microcomputer and printer. The foregoing information can then be recorded on one of the electronic spreadsheet programs and printed out as needed.

3. If it is a referred lead, make sure you have the name of the referrer correct, and that you have obtained as much information from the referrer as you can. Determine what additional information you need to qualify the prospect and list the questions to be answered to obtain it. Based on what you know about the prospect, think about his or her problem(s) and how your product or service can help. Plan what you are going to say when you telephone, remembering that the purpose of the call is to get an appointment to see qualified prospects. Work on the phrasing of the first few sentences to create a favorable first impression and lead into your qualification questions. *Anticipate and write down the various replies that could be made to each question* and what you will say in return. Add to this list with each telephone call and revise your replies until you have the wording that works best. As you continue to make calls your experience and feel for the situation will result in an improving "batting average" of appointments, which will increase your confidence and enthusiasm. Never forget that you must answer the unasked question, "Why should I take the time to listen to this stranger?"

4. You have obtained the lead from a membership list of a professional association, which suggests that the person is in a middle- to upper-tax bracket and probably a good prospect for the brokerage firm you represent. However, this does not mean that he or she is "ready, willing, or able" to buy your service.

"Good morning, Mr. Prospect. My name is _____ and I represent _____. Do you do any investing?"

No, never.

"Thank you. Have a good day."

Not right now.

Are you "parked on the side" like so many people now?

Do you plan to get back into the market? When? (for follow-up).

Yes—Fine, may I send you my card? (Get address)

A little.

Would you mind telling me what areas you are interested in?

(Determine amount and if sufficient to warrant a call, close for an appointment.)

This process can be expanded, adding the various possible responses and the assortment of best replies to each.

5. Have a checklist of materials to take, including order forms, samples, brochures, audio-visuals, spare pen, business cards, etc.

Since customer will want to know how soon they can have it if they order, review shipping lead times and delivery information.

Coordinate what you will wear based on weather, temperature, formality of call.

Determine greeting—formal versus informal (what was the tone of the telephone conversation?)

What are your objectives on this call? What product benefit are you going to stress, based on their problem as mentioned over the phone? If you are going to determine these answers from the preliminary conversation, list the questions that will pinpoint what they perceive their immediate problem to be. This is much more effective than trying to present all of the features of your product.

What objections do you anticipate, and how will you overcome them? What additional, related benefits will you mention to help you close?

6. Always keep in mind, "If I can't do it for everyone, I shouldn't do it for anyone." Decisions establish precedents. Permitting one of your people to take an extra week without pay because he is going on vacation in Europe means that when the next person requests a departure from company vacation policy you will either have to grant it or will have to answer the question "You did it for _____, why won't you do it for me?" Obviously flexibility is needed, but be prepared to inform everyone why a decision was made *before they hear about it on the grapevine along with rumors and opinions* that will be difficult to lay to rest.

20
INTERNATIONAL MARKETING

KEY TERMS

international marketing marketing goods and services outside the firm's home country, but with an essentially domestic orientation.

multinational marketing a form of international marketing in which a firm engages in operations in many foreign countries, often using foreign manufacturing and marketing strengths to serve individual markets. Domestic operations are viewed as part of the whole.

global marketing international marketing on a worldwide scale, with personnel, sources, finances, and facilities utilized from areas of the globe that best meet the firm's needs.

This chapter begins by examining the United States role in the international marketplace, and reasons to expand this role. Then, we examine how the marketing process differs as applied in domestic and international markets. Finally, we propose an approach for assessing, entering, and growing in the international marketplace.

We will continue to refer to the Islandshare Group (IS) case for illustrative examples, assuming the following additional information about the status of this real estate development company in the early 1990s:

> Two interrelated events in the late 1980s adversely impacted Islandshare's businesses of building and marketing vacation villas and time-share condominiums: (1) tax code changes that made it much less desirable to purchase property for vacation or rental purposes (for example, mortgage interest and costs resulting from indirect "passive" management of rental properties could no longer be written off), and (2) a real estate slump that afflicted the entire Southeastern coast from the mid-1980s into the 1990s. One impact of these events: between 1985 and 1992, the average price of an IS villa declined 20 percent, from $250,000 to $200,000.

Exacerbating these problems was a general lack of desirable locations for new vacation resorts, and fierce competition from larger development firms for those that were available.

Given these circumstances, Harry Byrne, IS's marketing manager, planned a presentation to persuade IS's board of directors that the company should broaden its operations to encompass resort properties in the international marketplace. He believed this move would offer greater profit opportunities than were available in IS's U.S. market, and help capitalize on IS's name and reputation as a developer of Blue Chip vacation properties.

THE UNITED STATES ROLE IN INTERNATIONAL MARKETING

In 1990, U.S. merchandise exports of over $350 billion represented about 12 percent of total world exports, and 7 percent of overall U.S. gross domestic product (GDP). Major exports included chemicals, aircraft, machinery, food grains, scientific instruments, and services such as management consulting and insurance.

Against this export figure, the United States imported more than $450 billion of merchandise in 1990, leaving a trade deficit—the amount by which the value of imports exceeds that of exports—of $102 billion. This was the tenth consecutive year in which the United States ran a foreign trade deficit in excess of $100 billion, during which period it went from being the largest lending nation to the largest debtor nation. This massive trade deficit strengthens the competitive position of countries—such as Japan and members of the newly formed European Economic Community (EEC)—who hold much of this debt. For example, Japanese banks, which have become large and powerful primarily as a consequence of these deficits, wield great power to influence both debt structure and U.S. firms' capabilities to expand.

Reducing this trade deficit by increasing participation in international markets can also have a direct, positive influence on the U.S. economy; for instance, every billion-dollar increased in exports creates about 20,000 jobs in the domestic market.

That the United States is capable of much greater participation in international markets is documented by figures from the Commerce department showing that. Although more than 100,000 U.S. firms were engaged in some level of exporting in 1992, fewer than 300 of these firms—led by multinational giants like General Motors, Ford, Boeing, General Electric and IBM—accounted for more than 90 percent of all U.S. exports. The United States isn't even the world's largest exporter; Germany is, and other countries are catching up.

Statistics from the General Accounting Office further document the comparative lack of participation by U.S. firms in international markets: During the entire decade of the 1980s, for example, although foreign direct investment in the

United States soared 616 percent, U.S. outbound investment rose just 9.9 percent; only one in five U.S. companies in a position to export actually did so.

One reason for this dramatic imbalance in international investment derives from differences in opportunities among nations. For example, the United States, with its relative affluence, stable political climate, and strong commitment to free trade, represents a much more attractive opportunity for foreign investment than many other countries represent for us. Many developing and third world nations, with more than 75 percent of the world's population, simply don't have the capacity to absorb enough of our output to qualify as profitable markets. And even among many developed, or developing nations, there is often resistance to lowering trade barriers for U.S. exports.

Other reasons for the lack of United States participation in the global marketplace include high labor costs that often make U.S. products less competitive; the decision of U.S. firms to virtually abdicate such markets as televisions and VCRs; and increasing competition in foreign markets. Perhaps the main reason, however, derives from a complacent attitude regarding the depth and plenty of the domestic market, and a lack of understanding of opportunities available in many foreign markets, or of approaches for exploiting these opportunities.

INTERNATIONAL MARKETING: MORE RISKS, MORE REWARDS

Harry Byrne began his presentation to IS's board of directors with a brief summary of two assumptions that put his recommended plan for entering the international marketplace into perspective:

- **Marketing processes are generally similar regardless of circumstances:** Whether the firm is large, small, or medium-sized; produces a tangible product or an intangible service; and is attempting to sell its product in domestic or foreign markets, the basic process will be the same. Buyers must be found and defined; products must be conceived, priced, promoted, and distributed to reach these buyers; and "uncontrollable" factors, such as changing customer needs, the state of the economy, and competitor initiatives, must be taken into account when devising plans to bring buyers and products together.

- **International marketing is riskier, but prospectively more rewarding, than domestic marketing.** Although domestic and international marketing processes are similar, the carrying-out of these processes is usually more difficult in the global marketplace. If these difficulties can be understood and addressed, however, benefits of entering foreign markets can dramatically exceed those offered in domestic markets.

DIFFICULTIES IN ENTERING FOREIGN MARKETS

Byrne then listed some of the difficulties, as well as benefits, that could derive from entering foreign markets.

Competition: IS would face an unfriendly competitive climate in a number of older industrialized European countries, where tourism is a major industry, and locations for new vacation property developments are few and far between. In Japan, IS properties might be squeezed out by "Keiretsu" systems, comprising tightly interlocked manufacturers, suppliers and finance companies that effectively dominate many markets.

Sociocultural Factors: Personal beliefs, aspirations, motivations, interpersonal relations, and social structures all differ among countries, and each difference could have a profound impact on the success of an IS project. In devoutly religious Islamic countries, for example, the notion of an American style vacation experience would probably border on blasphemy.

Economic Factors: IS would want to be assured that various measures of economic viability—such as the population's standard of living and the country's stage of economic development and currency stability—were sufficient to justify the expense, effort, and risk of entering a foreign country with an expensive line of vacation products and services.

Demographics: Unfriendly demographic environments in global markets might include a lack of people in age groups, income groups, or professions who would be likely to use IS vacation amenities.

Technology: Backward infrastructure, such as would exist in some newly emerging Eastern bloc countries, along with inadequate transportation and communication networks, would make it too expensive to construct and market IS vacation amenities in these countries.

Legal/Political: Hostile attitudes by host country government toward foreign firms could kill IS's chances to profitably market its products and services. Manifestations of such attitudes could include confiscatory taxes and tariffs; quotas that limit the amount of imports that will be accepted; embargoes that won't accept any amounts; and "local content" regulations requiring use of host country products, personnel, funds, and facilities.

YOU SHOULD REMEMBER

The dramatic difference between the relatively small increase in U.S. investment in foreign markets and heavy foreign investment in U.S. markets derives largely from the more favorable "free trade" environment in the United States, and a lack of understanding of approaches for penetrating international markets. Marketing programs for achieving foreign market penetration are generally the same as for penetrating domestic markets, beginning with an identification of target markets and environmental threats and opportunities, and culminating in plans and programs designed to bring together these markets and product/place/price/promotion marketing mixes. In international markets, however, applying the process is, typically, considerably more risky than in domestic markets, due largely to differences and difficulties in competitive, sociocultural, economic, demographic, technological, and legal/political environments.

BENEFITS OF ENTERING FOREIGN MARKETS

Continuing his presentation before the IS board, Byrne then listed benefits of entering the international marketplace that, in his considered opinion—and assuming an intelligent marketing planning effort—would more than offset the implicit risks:

- **Increase profits.** Byrne cited a number of instances of U.S. firms whose overseas strategies had produced profits well in excess of domestic markets. For example, whereas American automobile firms suffered huge profit losses in the domestic market in the late 1980s, their European operations remain profitable.

- **Exploit comparative advantage:** One reason why companies—and countries—frequently make more profits in foreign than in domestic markets has to do with the notion of comparative advantage, meaning they can exchange goods and services in which they have a relative advantage (e.g., better resources, specialization, mechanization or climate) for those in which they are at a relative disadvantage. For example, IS has a relative advantage over companies in many foreign countries in its ability to build and manage resort properties, in exchange for which these countries can provide scenic, historic locations not available in the United States for locating these properties.

- **Leverage strengths:** As more markets in foreign host countries are entered and developed, a number of "leverage" benefits—in addition to comparative advantage leverage—accrue to companies to enhance efficiency and profitability. For example, were IS to achieve multinational status, with resort properties in many countries, it could apply strategies, systems, sources of materials or funds, or promotional ideas that prove successful in one country's market to markets in other countries. Indeed, Byrne recalled that the original "time-share" concept of buying and trading vacation weeks had originated in Europe.

- **Keep up with (or escape) competition:** A number of larger real estate development firms with which IS competed in the U.S. market were already achieving leveraged benefits of an international marketing strategy, which also gave the leverage to put IS at a competitive disadvantage in the domestic marketplace. For example, it was easier for them to accumulate capital from worldwide sources, and test new concepts in vacation property marketing in foreign countries. In other foreign countries, not as fully penetrated by these competitors, IS resorts could achieve a similar dominant competitive position as well as strengthening its position in the U.S. marketplace.

- **Achieve tax advantages**: Many countries entice businesses by offering incentives in the form of reduced property, import, and income taxes for an initial time period. Multinational firms may also adjust revenue reports, or operations, so the largest profits are recorded in countries with the lowest tax rates. These tax strategies permit many U.S. firms to earn more than one-half of their after-tax profits from overseas operations.

- **Prolong product life**: Often, exporting provides an opportunity to market products and services that are no longer competitive in home markets; for example, Hollywood has found a booming market for vintage U.S. "B" motion pictures in Asia.

OFFSHORE PLANS: INTERNATIONAL TO GLOBAL

Continuing his presentation, Byrne stressed that problems and benefits implicit in entering foreign markets would be taken into account in planning IS's global marketing strategy. He also noted that these plans contemplated a generally cautious, staged entry into the global marketplace.

Initially, IS would achieve international status by entering one or two "host country" target markets. Host country facilities would initially be used to market U.S. vacation products, later to be supported by home country personnel, supply sources, finances, and facilities.

Then, learning from a hopefully successful experience, multinational status would be achieved as additional foreign countries were entered, with greater use made of host country personnel, supply sources, finances, and facilities to construct and market IS vacation properties. This is what the Japanese, for example, did in transplanting automobile manufacturing capabilities to the United States after years of just marketing their automobiles here.

Conceivably, over time, IS could achieve global status, with worldwide marketing capabilities and personnel, sources, finances, and facilities utilized from any area of the globe that best met the firm's needs. For example, lower interest rates and a stable currency might suggest the United States as the best source of funds; wage rates, worker skills, and scenic values might suggest Ireland as a good locale for developing resort properties, and so on.

YOU SHOULD REMEMBER

Benefits of foreign market entry include increased profits deriving from less competition; comparative advantage; more favorable tax policies; extended product life; and leveraging strengths discovered in specific countries. In achieving global status in international markets, a firm will typically achieve international status by entering one or two host country markets, then multinational status as additional host countries are entered and greater use made of host country personnel, supply sources, finances, and facilities. Global status provides opportunities to leverage worldwide personnel, production, finance, and marketing strengths.

HOW GLOBAL AND DOMESTIC MARKETS DIFFER

The next phase of Byrne's presentation to the IS board focused on differences between domestic and international markets that made it more difficult to implement the following five stages of the marketing process: (1) identifying prospective customer groups and defining their needs; (2) analyzing and understanding "uncontrollable" environmental forces that can help or hinder a marketing plan; (3) devising product/place/price/promotion marketing mixes that relate to needs of prospective customers; (4) designing marketing plans that bring together customer groups and marketing mixes, and (5) carrying out and monitoring these plans.

The first three stages of the marketing process—defining target market groups, assessing environmental threats and opportunities, and building attractive marketing mixes—are basic prerequisites for selling products in domestic or foreign markets. IS, for example, wouldn't consider building a resort complex on speculative information; before recommending such a venture, IS's marketing manager would research the market to generate demographic data pertaining to the size, age, and average income level of this population; psychographic characteristics of the prospective market, including needs relating the vacation resorts, attitudes toward existing resorts, and perceptions of IS's proposed offering. He would also want information on behavioral characteristics of the market, such as when members take vacations, how long these vacations last, and what kinds of resorts they visit.

Combined and analyzed, this information helps to identify and define and target markets and determine if the potential of these markets justifies the effort and expense of a marketing campaign.

For IS, this information will also provide marketing mix ideas for designing the resort property, pricing it, positioning it favorably in terms of customer needs and attitudes, and developing a promotional campaign that communicates this position to prospective customers.

In the domestic market, this information is relatively easy to come by. Literally thousands of organizations—including commercial research houses like Simmons, Nielsen, and Arbitron; public organizations on all levels of government, such as the census of Population and the Statistical Abstract of the United States; magazines, books and monographs—continuously collect and distribute a wide range of statistics and descriptive materials about the U.S. market in general and groups of consumers in particular. If the marketing manager isn't satisfied with information from these sources—much of it free— he can initiate his own research studies in a domestic market that, in spite of regional and cultural differences, is generally homogenous, and offers few constraints to the development of research data.

In many global markets this wellspring of information about domestic markets and submarkets is often little more than a trickle, and must be developed in the face of such constraints as differences in language, culture, political freedom, and communication technology; people are frequently reluctant to talk to outsiders. Furthermore, instead of analyzing the single, relatively homogeneous U.S. marketplace, the researcher in international markets must analyze a number of national markets, many with low profit potential that permits only a modest research expenditure.

TAILORING MARKETING MIXES TO MARKET NEEDS

Even assuming sufficiently valid information is generated to project accurate profiles of target market needs and environmental threats and opportunities, the problem of devising attractive marketing mixes can pose challenging problems in the international market not typically faced in domestic markets.

Many of these problems relate to individual elements of the marketing mix. Thus, citing the construction of a single IS vacation villa in a foreign country, Byrne noted the following mix problems:

- **Product:** In the domestic market, a relatively small number of villa designs would meet most target market needs; in foreign markets, a variety of design strategies could result from different environments. With a *straight extension* strategy, IS would build and market the same villa models as in the United States; with a *product adaptation* strategy, U.S. models would be modified to meet local needs; with a *backward invention* strategy, IS would make and market simpler, less sophisticated villa models; with a *forward invention* strategy, IS would design more sophisticated models to match increased sophistication in such resort areas as the Riviera. Again, understanding market needs would be the key.

- **Place:** Planning for the place, or distribution component of the marketing mix, would require information about distribution systems—retailers, wholesalers, and jobbers—that would make available the materials and suppliers needed to build IS villas, as well as transportation for bringing prospective owners to the villas. He noted that most third world and many ex-Soviet bloc countries, lacking "place" facilities, might not qualify for entry.

- **Price:** A diversity of questions would have to be answered in setting prices for IS villas in foreign countries. For example, could IS set a standard price in all foreign markets? Probably not, if local customs, taxes, and tariffs forced "outsiders" to price properties at higher levels, or average income levels mandated lower prices. Alternately, higher income levels, and lack of competitors, in foreign countries might permit much higher than standard prices. And in what currency should prices for IS villas be quoted? If prices are set in terms of U.S. currency, with the risk of foreign currency devaluation passed on to buyers, pricing control will be maintained, but prospective customers might be confused and turned off. Also, the foreign government might insist that transactions be quoted in its currency. And what about terms of sale, such as middlemen discounts, refund policies, and transfer of ownership? In many recently freed-up Communist bloc countries, for example, such considerations are only vaguely defined.

Other problems encompassed all the elements of the marketing mix. For example, if IS plans to enter diverse foreign markets—sometimes within a single culturally diverse country—the initial question arises: which of these markets offer the potential to justify the expense of creating, and implementing, an entire mix? Management might decide to cut back on one component of the mix—promotion, perhaps—in one market in order to invest more heavily in mix components in a market with greater potential.

Another, related issue not generally faced in homogenous domestic markets pertains to the extent to which marketing mix elements will be tailored to the nature and needs of each foreign marketplace. Using a *standardized* approach, a firm's marketing mix would be the same for all its markets; that is, the same products would be sold, with the same promotional appeals, prices, and distribution strategies.

A *nonstandardized* approach assumes that each market is different, and requires a unique marketing mix. Then the decision becomes how much, and in what ways, each marketing mix element should vary from the standard to meet the needs of each foreign marketplace. This approach is considerably more expensive than the "standardized" approach of using a single marketing mix to cover all markets.

YOU SHOULD REMEMBER

Implementing the stages of the marketing process—particularly the first two stages of defining customer needs and analyzing environmental threats and opportunities—is difficult in foreign markets because of the general paucity of research data, and the political, sociocultural, demographic, and competitive diversity among nations. Implementing the third stage of the process—devising marketing mixes attractive to identified target markets—also poses challenges not generally encountered in domestic markets. For example, is a much less expensive standardized approach—in which all foreign markets receive essentially the same product/place/price/promotion mix—feasible, or is a nonstandardized approach mandated? The answer depends on different needs among nations in such areas as product design, pricing levels, and distribution networks.

MARKETING PLANNING IN GLOBAL MARKETS

The final two steps in the marketing process—devising and implementing a marketing plan for bringing together markets and marketing mix components—also pose problems in international markets not generally encountered in domestic markets.

In the relatively homogenous domestic market, all the elements of a marketing plan—the firm's mission, objectives, situation analysis, target market, marketing mix elements, monitoring devices—usually are based on reliable research data not as readily available in international markets. Also, whereas in domestic markets, objectives will change somewhat from territory to territory, as will emphasis on different elements of the marketing mix and perceptions of target market needs and environmental "uncontrollables," the change is nowhere as dramatic as in quixotic, diverse international markets. In dissimilar foreign markets, even the firm's mission can change, with each change adding to the plan's complexity and risk.

Actually, implementing the marketing plan involves risks that the strategies and tactics for bringing together target markets and marketing mixes won't be appropriate to the nature and needs of specific target markets, or that implementation won't be appropriate to the strategies and tactics. These systems, covered in chapters 4, 5, and 6, include a marketing information system for generating information needed to devise and implement marketing plans; a control system, needed to monitor and, if necessary, modify marketing plans; and an organizational system needed to hold together and harmonize the interacting elements of the marketing program

STRATEGIES FOR ENTERING INTERNATIONAL MARKETS

To minimize risks implicit in all stages of a marketing process geared to entering the international marketplace, Byrne proposed, first, a careful, comprehensive research approach for identifying worthwhile foreign market segments, then a cautious staged approach with entry strategies appropriate to each stage.

To identify and define offshore countries for initial entry, Byrne proposed an approach that would match profiles of prospective foreign target markets with those established U.S. target markets for IS vacation properties. These profiles focused on economic, demographic, and technological criteria, and were based on Craig and Keegan's "Indicators of Market Potential." (Fig. 20-1)

Byrne noted that application of these profile criteria indicated that only three large markets—Japan, Europe, and the United States—could support IS marketing programs. With only 15 percent of the world's population, these markets accounted for 73 percent of the world's wealth, as measured by Gross National Product (Fig. 20-2)

Countries comprising these three markets, categorized as *industrial economies*, are major exporters of goods and investment funds, which they trade among themselves or for raw materials and finished goods. Generally rejected

1. Demographic characteristics
   Size of population
   Rate of population growth
   Degree of urbanization
   Population density
   Age structure and composition
      of the population

2. Geographic characteristics
   Physical size of a country
   Topographical characteristics
   Climate conditions

3. Economic factors
   GNP per capita
   Income distribution
   Rate of growth of GNP
   Ratio of investment to GNP

4. Technological factors
   Level of technological skill
   Existing production technology
   Existing consumption technology
   Education levels

5. Socio-cultural factors
   Dominant values
   Life style patterns
   Ethnic groups
   Linguistic fragmentation

6. National goals and plans
   Industry priorities
   Infrastructure investment plans

Source: Susan P. Douglas, C. Samual Craig, and Warren Keegan. "Approaches to Assessing International Marketing Oppportunities for Small and Medium-Sized Business." *Columbia Journal of World Business.* Fall 1982. pp. 26–32.

Figure 20–1. Indicators of market potential:
Criteria for selecting host country focus on level of development.

	United States	Soviet Union	Japan	European Community	China
Population (in millions)	243.8	284.0	122.0	323.6	1,074.0
GNP (in billions of 1987 U.S. dollars*)	$4,436.1	$2,375.0	$1,607.7	$3,782.0	$293.5
Per capita GNP (1987 U.S. dollars†)	$18,200	$8,360	$13,180	$11,690	$270
GNP Growth Rate 1981–85 (annual average) 1987	3.0% 2.9%	1.8% 0.5%	3.9% 4.2%	1.5% 2.9%	9.2% 9.4%
Inflation (change in consumer prices)	3.7%	−0.9%	0.1%	3.1%	9.2%
Total Labor Force (in millions)	121.6	154.8	60.3	143.0	512.8
Agricultural	3.4	33.9	4.6	11.9	313.1
Nonagricultural	118.2	120.9	55.7	131.1	199.7
Unemployment rate	6.1%	N.A.	2.8%	11.0%	N.A.
Foreign Trade Exports (in billions of U.S. dollars)	$250.4	$107.7	$213.2	$953.5††	$44.9
Imports (in billions of U.S. dollars)	$424.1	$96.0	$150.8	$955.1**	$40.2
Balance (in billions of U.S. dollars)	−$173.7	$11.7	$80.4	−$1.6	$4.7
Energy Consumption (in billions of barrels of oil equivalent per capita)	55.6	37.3	22.7	24.4	4.8
Military Active armed forces	2,163,200	5,096,000	245,000	2,483,400	3,200,000
Ready reserves	1,637,900	6,217,000	46,000	4,565,800	1,200,000
Defense expenditures Share of GNP	6.5%	15–25%	1.6%	3.3%	4–5%

Source: Taken from Karen Elliott House, "The 90s and Beyond: For All Its Difficulties, the U.S. Stands to Retain Its Global Leadership," *Wall Street Journal*, January 23, 1989, p. A10.

Figure 20–2. Triad of key markets: Most global wealth is concentrated in three industrialized market aggregates.

for consideration were *subsistence economies,* whose people mostly engage in agriculture and consume, or barter, most of their output, *raw material exporting economies,* whose income is derived from exporting one or more natural resources, and *industrializing economies,* where manufacturing accounts for between 10 and 20 percent of output.

Once the most desirable foreign markets have been identified and defined, Byrne stated that initial entry strategies would reflect the need to minimize risk and cost. There are generally three such entry strategies—*exporting, joint ventures,* and *direct ownership.* Typically, a firm will begin with an exporting strategy during the first, international stage of a long-term entry strategy, and move to the others during multinational and global stages. As shown in Figure 20-3, commitment, risk, resource needs, and degree of control all increase with joint venture and direct ownership strategies; flexibility, or the ability to change or terminate an entry strategy, is highest with joint ventures, lowest with direct ownership.

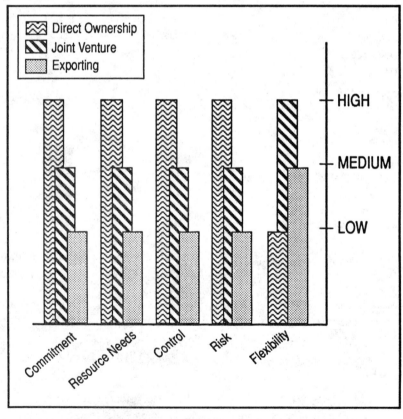

Figure 20–3. Alternative strategies for global marketing:
Criteria for organizing for global entry show that risk and cost
increase from exporting to direct ownership strategies.

In considering IS's entry into the international marketplace, Byrne envisioned the flowing pros and cons of each entry strategy:

- **Exporting:** Using this strategy, IS would purchase properties abroad and market them to foreign customers, either directly—through IS's sales force located in either the United States or host country—or indirectly, through host country developers. This low-risk, low-cost approach works best when customers are concentrated and easy to locate. A big drawback: lack of control over host country distributors, who may not be sufficiently knowledgeable to market IS resort properties.

- **Joint ventures:** This strategy, the marketing manager noted, assumed a number of formats, all of which had in common a partnership arrangement between IS and a host country company to combine some aspect of construction or marketing in order to share expertise, costs, and/or connections. Potential advantages of joint ventures include lower costs, and more favorable trading terms, before foreign ownership is established. (Some countries require joint ownership with a local company as an entry condition.)
  Potential disadvantages to IS include losing patents and potential profits to host country owner, if IS isn't wise enough to maintain a controlling interest in the jointly-held company, complete control could be lost. Also, there is the possibility that a host country co-owner could become a future competitor. Joint ownership formats considered by the marketing manager included (1) *licensing,* under which, for a fee or royalty, a host country company would be assigned the right to use the IS name, production, and or marketing expertise; (2) *contract manufacturing* under which contracts would be negotiated for host country companies to construct resort properties that IS would market, with IS keeping control of any patented processes; (3) *management contracting,* under which IS would only contract to provide management expertise to a host country export development; (4) *joint ownership,* whereby IS would join with foreign investors to create a local business in which they would share joint ownership and control of resort properties.

- **Direct Ownership Arrangements:** Under these arrangements, IS would fully implement and control international operations, with ownership of production, marketing, and other facilities.

ORGANIZING FOR INTERNATIONAL MARKETING

Byrne concluded his presentation with a discussion of organizational changes planned for IS to develop and implement marketing plans for the international market. As with the plans themselves, organizational structures would change as markets and marketing mixes changed.

Initially, an export department would be set up at IS with primary responsibility for purchasing and marketing desirable foreign resort properties. Then, as foreign sales and profits grew, the export department would grow, apace, into an international department, as additional marketing services were added, including training personnel to staff foreign offices, and working with IS's U.S. advertising agency to develop comprehensive promotion programs for foreign markets. In substance, the international division would be responsible for coordinating construction, marketing, research, finance, and personnel among domestic and foreign operations.

YOU SHOULD REMEMBER

In the international marketplace, a relatively small number of industrial economies are likely to have disproportionately large percentages of desirable economic, technological, and demographic attributes not generally found in subsistence, raw material exporting, and industrializing economies. Forms of entry into foreign markets differ in degree of control, risk, and resource commitment, with more of each typically required as firms move from exporting, through joint ventures, to direct ownership arrangements.

Key organizational structure decisions focus on the stage of development of specific foreign markets, ranging from a simple export office to a highly sophisticated international department responsible for coordinating a full range of production and marketing activities.

KNOW THE CONCEPTS
DO YOU KNOW THE BASICS?

The assignments below ask you to apply chapter concepts to explain the success of these two U.S. companies in the Western European marketplace, as well as prospective problems and opportunities each would face in the Eastern European marketplace:

Dell Computer Company, which began European operations in 1987, had sales of $240 million in 1992, or 30 percent of total Dell sales, and 2 percent of all personal computer (PC) sales in the European market. (During the same period, IBM's European PC sales dropped from 21 to 17 percent.) Central to Dell's success was a direct mail discount campaign that observers said wouldn't work; Europeans never purchased big ticket items like PCs through the mail, and tended to equate discounted prices with shoddy merchandise. Dell management disagreed. Research showed that PC prices in Europe, set by firms like Groupe Bull's Zenith Data Systems and Olivetti, were about twice that charged in the United States, and that European dealer networks were sluggish and expensive. Dell began its campaign with an intense "education program" featuring a series of ads in computer magazines, and direct mailings throughout Britain and the continent, stressing Dell's reputation for high quality, fast service, and lowest price. Future plans: institute a single price throughout its Western European market, with a guarantee of 5-day delivery and 2-day service.

Bandag, Inc., an Iowa-based tire retreading business, faced two major problems when it undertook to increase sales in its European market: (1) competition would get fiercer when the firm's last payment ran out in 1992, and (2) the firm's network of European distributors, following local custom, charged high prices and didn't focus on aggressive selling. Bandag's solution: replace the existing distribution network with franchises used in the U.S. market, each priced at $150,000 and featuring Mercedes "rolling workshops" that went to customer jobs. Result: Bandag's share of the Western European retread market increased 20 percent by 1991, tying it for the first place with France's Michelin. Future plans: capitalize on falling trade barriers when the European Economic Community integrates, and expand into the cost-conscious, newly emerging Eastern European market (retreads sell for half the price of new tires).

1. In terms of cultural, economic, technological, and political legal environmental aspects, discuss benefits for Dell in entering the European marketplace.

2. Discuss Bandag's growth in the Western European marketplace in terms of a favorable environmental climate.

3. Discuss how Dell and Bandag capitalized on perceived weaknesses in the Western European competitive climate to effectively modify marketing mix elements.

4. Bandag plans to expand into the "cost-conscious, newly emerging" Eastern European market, where it anticipates cost savings it offers will be especially popular. Discuss how economic, technological, and legal/political aspects of the Eastern European environment might adversely influence a decision by Dell to enter this marketplace.

5. Line up the situation described in column A below, with the appropriate entry strategy in column B.

Column A	Column B
Dell sets up a subsidiary operation in England to manufacture its PCs.	exporting
For a fee, Bandag permits a retreading operation inHungary to use its name and patents.	joint ownership
Dell provides managerial expertise in helping a Russian electronics manufacturer develop PC components to Dell specifications.	licensing
Bandag and its franchisees both have a financial stake in the "rolling workshop" distribution and servicing operation.	management contracting
Using its own equipment and personnel, and locals, Bandag sets up a retreading operation in Albania to test the market potential.	direct ownership

6. Line up the term from column B below, that best defines the product mix strategy described in column A:

Column A	Column B
Promotion for Bandag's new tire retreading operation in Hungary stresses cost savings instead of fast, efficient service.	straight extension
Dell develops a more sophisticated, specialized version of its PC to handle software applications in its French marketplace.	nonstandard promotion
Dell plans a single discounted price throughout its Western European marketplace.	forward invention
Dell's PCs, and associated software, are the same in England as in the United States.	standardized pricing

TERMS FOR STUDY

backward invention
comparative advantage
domestic marketing
European Economic Community
forward invention
free trade
global companies
imports
international companies
international marketing
joint ventures

Keiretso systems
leverage benefits
licensing agreements
management contracting
multinational companies
nonstandardized approach
product adaptation
standardized approach
straight extension
trade barriers
trade deficit

ANSWERS
KNOW THE BASICS

1. Cultural language, lifestyles, and goals in the Western European marketplace are all consistent with a computerized economy:

Economic: The standard of living for Western Europe, as measured by
comparing item prices with per capita income, is obviously sufficiently
high to afford the higher prices (as compared to the U.S. market) that they
are willing to pay for personal computers. Additionally, the stage of
economic development is sufficiently advanced to require the use of
computers, and European currency rarely fluctuates excessively to discourage imports of computers from the United States. (For example, if the
value of the German mark were to fall to the point where twice as many
marks were required to purchase a single dollar, an American computer
would also cost twice as much, and the market could disappear).

Technological development: Human resources, including a highly trained
cadre of computer technicians and technologists, were in place in Western
Europe to ensure that U.S. computers could be used and maintained.
Other resources, including sophisticated computerized networks and
availability of electric and electronic power sources, were also in place to
ensure a "user friendly" reception for Dell PCs.

Political/Legal: Among the factors favorable to Dell's entry into the
Western European marketplace: few tariffs or trade quotas applied to
imports from the United States which reciprocate "most favored nation"
policies of the United States toward Western European countries (these
policies mandate that every nation covered obtains the best import/export
contract terms available to any single nation): stable governments, which
help ensure consistent, predictable policies toward exporters like Dell;
little internal instability of the kind that might discourage market entry.

2. Bandag's technological advantage in the Western European market,
resulting from its patent-protected tire-retreading process, also produced a
competitive advantage. The pending unification of common market
countries, as well as the market economies developing in freedup Soviet
bloc countries, represented a political element favoring the growth of
Bandag's market, enhanced by the continent's anticipated economic
growth.

3. In the case of both Dell and Bandag, inefficient, expensive distribution
systems and high prices in the European market created excellent profit
opportunities. To exploit these opportunities, Bandag, a service, focused
on the "place" and "price" elements of the marketing mix: "place" by
relying on motivated franchisees with fast service capabilities, and "price"
by emphasizing cost savings in retreading vs. purchasing tires. An effective
promotion campaign communicated this place/price messge.

In Dell's case, as in Bandag's, primary emphasis was on place, price, and promotion in leveraging strengths from its domestic marketplace to achieve sales and profit growth not available in the U.S. market—notably, a productive, persuasive direct marketing campaign that allowed Dell to circumvent traditional European distribution channels in spelling out price/quality benefits of Dell personal computers.

4. All the factors that favored Dell's entry into the Western European marketplace should be critically examined before arriving at any decisions regarding the feasibility of entering the Eastern European marketplace. Although some countries, such as East Germany, might qualify on the basic of economic, cultural, political/legal, and technological criteria, most probably would not. For example:

Economic: The standard of living of populations in many Eastern European countries would not be sufficiently high to afford a Dell personal computer, even at its discounted price; additionally, the stability of the currency might prove to be a real problem, as witnessed by the continued loss of value of the Russian ruble against the American dollar, to the point where even a product like the Big Mac costs, in rubles, a day's income. And is the stage of economic development of the Eastern European country sufficiently advanced to create a market and justify a marketing effort?

Technological: In the context of Dell's entering the Eastern European marketplace, technological sophistication would imply people who needed and could operate and maintain personal computers; electric and electronic facilities, accessories and supply sources; and logistical and communication technologies capable of supporting programs to market the PC. The likelihood of all three being in place in most Eastern European countries would be slim indeed.

Political/Legal: Many newly freed-up Eastern bloc countries—the Baltic States, Czechoslovakia, Yugoslavia, among others—tend to develop divisive, unstable governments that produce inconsistent and incoherent policies and practices that are inhospitable to foreign investment. Excessive tariffs, taxes, harsh local content laws, even government takeovers are ever-present possibilities.

5. Line up the situation described in column A, below, with the appropriate entry strategy in column B.

Column A	Column B
Dell sets up a subsidiary operation in England to manufacture its PCs.	exporting
For a fee, Bandag permits a retreading operation in Hungary to use its name and patents.	joint ownership
Dell provides managerial expertise in helping a Russian electronics manufacturer develop PC components to Dell specificiations.	licensing
Bandag and its franchisees both have a financial stake in the "rolling workshop" distribution and serving operation.	management contracting
Using its own equipment and personnel, and locals, Bandag sets up a retreading operation in Albania to test the market potential.	direct ownership

6. Line up the term from column B, below, that best defines the product mix strategy described in column A:

Column A	Column B
Promotion for Bandag's new tire retreading operation in Hungary stresses cost savings instead of fast, efficient service.	straight extension
Dell develops a more sophisticated, specialized version of its PC to handle software applications in its French marketplace.	nonstandard promotion
Dell plans a single discounted price throughout its Western European marketplace.	forward invention
Dell's PCs, and associated software, are the same in England as in the United States.	standardized pricing

INDEX

More selected BARRON'S titles:

BARRON'S ACCOUNTING HANDBOOK, 2nd EDITION,
Joel G. Siegel and Jae K. Shim
Provides accounting rules, guidelines, formulas and techniques etc. to help students
and business professionals work out accounting problems.
Hardcover: $29.95, Canada $38.95/ ISBN 6449-6, 880 pages

REAL ESTATE HANDBOOK, 3rd EDITION,
Jack P. Freidman and Jack C. Harris
A dictionary/reference for everyone in real estate. Defines over 1500 legal, financial, and
architectural terms. Hardcover, $29.95, Canada $39.95/ ISBN 6330-9, 810 pages

HOW TO PREPARE FOR THE REAL ESTATE LICENSING EXAMINATIONS SALESPERSON AND BROKER, 5th EDITION,
Bruce Lindeman and Jack P. Freidman
Reviews current exam topics and features updated model exams and supplemental exams,
all with explained answers. Paperback, $12.95, Canada $16.95/ ISBN 2994-1, 340 pages

BARRON'S FINANCE AND INVESTMENT HANDBOOK, 4th EDITION,
John Downes and Jordan Goodman
This hard-working handbook of essential information defines more than 3000 key terms,
and explores 30 basic investment opportunities. The investment information is thoroughly
up-to-date. Hardcover $35.00, Canada $45.50/ ISBN 6465-8, approx. 1200 pages

FINANCIAL TABLES FOR MONEY MANAGEMENT
Stephen S. Solomon, Dr. Clifford Marshall, Martin Pepper, Jack P. Freidman and Jack C. Harris
Pocket-sized handbooks of interest and investment rate tables used easily by average
investors and mortgage holders. Paperback

Real Estate Loans, 2nd Ed., $6.95, Canada $8.95/ISBN 1618-1, 336 pages
Mortgage Payments, 2nd Ed., $5.95, Canada $7.95/ISBN 1386-7, 304 pages
Bonds, 2nd Ed., $5.95, Canada $7.50/ISBN 4995-0, 256 pages
Canadian Mortgage Payments, 2nd Ed., Canada $8.95/ISBN 1617-3, 336 pages
Adjustable Rate Mortgages, 2nd Ed., $6.95, Canada $8.50/ISBN 1529-0, 288 pages

Barron's Educational Series, Inc.
250 Wireless Blvd., Hauppauge, NY 11788
In Canada: Georgetown Book Warehouse
34 Armstrong Ave., Georgetown, Ontario L7G 4R9   (#11) R6/95

More selected BARRON'S titles:

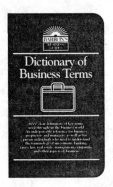